Olga Alekseevna Novikova

Russia and England from 1876 to 1880

A protest and an appeal

Olga Alekseevna Novikova

Russia and England from 1876 to 1880
A protest and an appeal

ISBN/EAN: 9783337299200

Printed in Europe, USA, Canada, Australia, Japan

Cover: Foto ©ninafisch / pixelio.de

More available books at **www.hansebooks.com**

RUSSIA AND ENGLAND

FROM

1876 TO 1880

A PROTEST AND AN APPEAL

BY

O. K.

AUTHOR OF 'IS RUSSIA WRONG?'

WITH A PREFACE

BY

JAMES ANTHONY FROUDE, M.A.

SECOND EDITION
REVISED AND ENLARGED

LONDON
LONGMANS, GREEN, AND CO.
1880

To the Memory of

NICOLAS KIRÉEFF

THE FIRST RUSSIAN VOLUNTEER KILLED IN SERVIA

JULY $\frac{6}{18}$, 1876

This Book is Dedicated

PREFACE.

LITTLE more than two years ago, when a war with Russia seemed probable and even imminent, a book was published in London explaining the view of the Russians themselves on the cause of their quarrel with Turkey. The writer, a Russian lady, described herself only under the initials O. K.: and as under these circumstances an introduction of some kind was thought desirable, at the request of the authoress I wrote a few words of preface to this book. I was the more willing to do it, because as far back as the Crimean War I was one of the few Englishmen who considered that for us to quarrel with Russia in defence of the Ottoman Empire was impolitic and useless, and that so far from simplifying the problems which were coming upon us, not in Turkey only, but throughout Asia, it would enormously increase them. When the Emperor Nicholas spoke of the Turk as the sick man, for whose approaching end he invited us to assist him in making preparation, it appeared to me that he was speaking the truth, and that to refuse to acknowledge it would prove as futile in the long run as the denial of any other fact of nature. Fact, as always happens, had asserted itself. The sick man's state could no longer be questioned by the most obstinate incredulity. But the provisions which the Emperor Nicholas desired had not been made. The European conflict which he foresaw would follow from the absence of it, was on the point of breaking out; and small as the prospect of peace appeared when the Russians were advancing upon Constantinople, I was glad to be able to assist, in however slight a degree, the courageous lady who was pleading the cause of the Slavs before the English public.

The danger is no longer immediate. The Russian army and the English fleet were almost within the range of each other's guns: a mistaken telegram or the indiscretion of a commander on either side might have precipitated a collision, and all Asia, and perhaps Europe also, would at this moment have been in conflagration.

The moderation of Russia prevented so frightful a calamity. The Treaty of San Stefano was modified, and the English Cabinet, if it won no victory in war, was able to boast, with or without reason, of a diplomatic triumph. Continental statesmen could no longer speak of the effacement of England as a

European Power. England had shown that she had the will and strength to interfere where she chose and when she chose. But the question remains whether our interference answered a useful purpose, or whether in effect we had proved more than a boy proves who shows that he cannot be prevented from laying a bar across a railway, and converting a useful express train into a pile of splinters and dead bodies.

Happily the common sense of Europe and the large minority of right-minded Englishmen had forbidden a repetition of the follies which accompanied the Crimean war. No cant could be listened to at Berlin about the integrity and independence of the Ottoman Empire. No English Prime Minister could affect to believe in Turkish progress, except as progress to destruction. A war might still have risen from the disappointment of the English Cabinet at the turn which events had taken, had not Russia surrendered something that she had won. But the purpose for which she had interposed in Turkey was substantially accomplished. No more Bashi Bazouks and Circassian hyenas will massacre Christian men in Bulgaria and dishonour Christian women.

In Europe the power of the Ottoman is gone to a shadow. In Asia, in spite of our protests, we have been ourselves obliged to undertake that it shall be no longer abused as it has been. For the time there is a respite, and we can breathe again. But the death-rattle is in the Ottoman's throat. The end is close upon us. In a few years at most, a dozen questions as hard as the Bulgarian will be pressing for a settlement. So far as Europe is concerned, the Eastern policy of the Cabinet has not been a success. Sir Henry Layard would not pretend that the Russian and Turkish war had terminated as he hoped that it would terminate. The English people themselves, in their own consciences, know that it has not. Their warlike propensity had been roused. They hoped to have fought Russia nearer home, and, to allay their disappointment, a demonstration against Russia, which turned into a war, has been got up in Afghanistan. This adventure also has not been wholly prosperous, and it promises ill for the future. What is to be the end of this determined animosity against the Russians, and what are we to gain by it? What harm can Russia do us, unless we go out of our way to attack her? She cannot invade us at home: no sane person, not Sir Henry Rawlinson himself, imagines that she can invade us in India. We are not wild enough to covet the barren steppes which form her costly, unfruitful, uninviting Asiatic Empire. Is it necessary to our self-esteem that we must have some imaginary enemy whom we must always be defying and quarrelling with? and that we select Russia, because of all the Great Powers she is the one which we think can least materially hurt us? A thoughtful consideration of our relative positions will suggest a different conclusion.

Russia and England are not likely to come into collision in Europe. The Great Powers who might themselves be involved will forbid it for their own sakes. In Asia we stand side by side as the representatives of Western civilisation, and on the attitude which we assume to one another the future condition of that enormous Continent may be said to depend. It is for us and for us alone to decide whether we are to be allies or enemies. If we can act in concert, if we can dismiss our jealousies, take each other's hands and be friends, the position of each of us will grow stronger, and along with it our power of doing good. Civilisation will advance on an even course, bringing with it industry and good government, and the Asiatic races will have reason to bless us, as the bearers among them of peace and prosperity. If, on the other hand, the spirit is to be permanent which has guided our Eastern policy for the last four years and has been so generally prevalent in England, then these wretched myriads of people (amounting—if we include the Chinese, who will not long escape—to half the human race) will be simply torn in pieces as a carcase between us, till they learn to hate, and justly hate, the very name of the civilisation which will have brought misery so infinite upon them.

Which of these two courses is to be chosen, depends upon England. Russia has long sought an English alliance. She has sacrificed her interests, she has sacrificed her pride; she has stooped, perhaps, below her rank as a Great Power in suing for it. We still hold off, and are cold and suspicious. Is it because Russia is aggressive? we are more aggressive. Is Russia without a Constitutional Government and therefore not to be trusted? We govern two hundred million subjects in India, to whom we do not dream of giving a Constitution. Is it because Russia does not observe her engagements? That may be our opinion; but ask a Russian, or, for that matter, any foreign statesman, whether we more accurately observe ours. Nations can never be friends while each insists on the other's faults and is blind to its own:—

> Qui ne tuberibus propriis offendat amicum
> Postulat, ignoscat verrucis illius.

If we act otherwise, it can only be because we have no wish to be friends with Russia. And why should we not be friends with her? Is it because we Islanders are so independent, that we will brook neither rival nor companion on any road which we choose to follow, and that being established in Asia we must have Asia to ourselves? Such a feeling no doubt is to be found in large masses of Englishmen. I cannot pay our Premier or his colleagues so bad a compliment as to suspect them of sharing it. They know well that if we were inflated with so vain an ambition, this great Empire of ours would burst like an air bubble. It is hard to credit, either, that the English Tory party really believes that Russian autocracy is dangerous to rational liberty. The love of the Tory party for liberty has not hitherto been of so violent a kind. My own early years were spent among Tories, and Russia I heard spoken of among them as the main support that was left of sound principles of government. Docile as they are under the educating hand of their chief, the country gentlemen of England cannot have fallen into their present attitude towards Russia on political conviction. I interpret their action as no more than a passing illustration of the working of Government by party. Having obtained power they wish to keep it. They have seen an opportunity of making themselves popular by large talk about English dignity, and by appeals to the national susceptibility. The interests of Europe, the interests of Asia, have been simply used as cards and counters in a game, where the stake played for is the majority at the next election.

Alas, the real stake in this reckless adventure is the future position of England itself. The world will understand and partly tolerate a selfish policy if it is really a national policy. The world will scarcely be satisfied to find its interests trifled with, that Tory or Liberal may rule in Downing Street. It is to be hoped therefore that English people, who prefer their country to the factions which divide it, will endeavour for themselves to examine the questions supposed to be at issue between ourselves and Russia with more care than they have hitherto bestowed on them. We can understand nothing till we have looked at both sides of it. Thus, it is with no common pleasure that I commend to my countrymen the new volume with which this Russian lady again presents us. For her own sake I could have wished that some weightier person than myself should have written a preface for her, if preface was needed, but it is as well perhaps that her book should appeal to our attention on its own merits, rather than through the authority of some powerful name.

The writer, known to us hitherto only as O. K., fills out her initials for herself, and tells us that she is one of a family whose noblest representatives have devoted themselves for the Slavonian cause. She alludes to her eldest brother, General Kiréeff, now on the Staff of the Grand Duke Constantine, and a most active member of the Slavonian Committee. The story of the second which resembles a legend of some mythic Roman patriot or mediæval Crusader, the reader will find told, as no other English writer could tell it, by Mr. Kinglake. Under the influence of the same passionate patriotism which sent her brother to his death, the sister has laboured year after year in England, believing that, however misled, we are a generous people at heart, and that, if we really knew the objects at which Russia was aiming, we should cease to suspect or thwart them. Her self-imposed task has been so hard that only enthusiasm could have carried her through it. We, in our present humour, believing that the world is governed wholly by selfish interests, have forgotten that there were times in our own history, and those the times best worth remembering, when interest was nothing to us, and some cause which we considered holy was everything. Among those of us who have heard of this lady many have regarded her as a secret instrument of the Russian Court, and persons who have held such an opinion about her are unlikely to change it, however absurd it may be, for any words of mine. By those who can still appreciate noble and generous motives, the Kiréeffs will be recognised as belonging to the exceptional race of mortals who form the forlorn hopes of mankind, who are perhaps too quixotic, but to whom history makes amends by consecrating their memories.

The object of this book is to exhibit our own conduct to us, during the past four years, as it appears to Russian eyes. If we disclaim the portrait we shall still gain something by looking at it, and some few of us may be led to reflect, that if Russia is mistaken in her judgment of England, we may be ourselves as much mistaken in our judgment of Russia. As to execution and workmanship, no foreigner who has attempted to write in the English language has ever, to my knowledge, shown more effective command of it. O. K. plays with our most complicated idioms, and turns and twists and points her sarcasms with a skill which many an accomplished English authoress might despair of imitating. She seems to have read every book that has been written, and every notable speech which has been uttered, on the Eastern question, for the last half century. Far from bearing us ill will, she desires nothing so much as a hearty alliance between her country and ours. She protests justly against the eagerness with which every wild story to Russia's disadvantage obtains credit among us, and against the wilful embittering of relations which ought to be friendly and cordial.

She tells us that Russia has spared no effort, short of the sacrifice of honour and duty, to humour our prejudices or consider our interests. If it is all in vain, if we persist in meeting the advances of Russia with ill will, in misrepresenting her policy, and in crossing and denouncing it when it is identical with the policy which we pursue for ourselves under analogous circumstances, she warns us that we may desire Russia's friendship hereafter and may not find it. There will grow up in her people a corresponding feeling of settled resentment, and in the end a determined antagonism.

We are now at the parting of the ways: it is for us to choose what the future is to be; and in choosing let us bear this in mind, that there runs through the affairs of men a slow-moving but sure and steady tide of justice, which even steam-driven ironclads will find in the end that they cannot overcome. When the drama, which is to be acted, is on so vast a scale, it is not the will of one nation which will be able to prevail, still less the will of one party in that nation. Therefore those who most wish to see England continue great and strong and honoured as it has been honoured in the past, must embrace in their thoughts some wider object than immediate seeming advantage or partisan success, if they would have their country in the place which they desire for it when the curtain falls upon the play which is now opening.

With these few words I recommend this excellent book to the attention of my countrymen.

J. A. Froude.

CONTENTS.

PART I.

THE RUSSIAN PEOPLE AND THE WAR.

CHAPTER	PAGE
I. INTRODUCTORY	3
II. THE TWO RUSSIAS: MOSCOW AND ST. PETERSBURG	8
III. SECRET SOCIETIES AND THE WAR.—MR. AKSAKOFF'S SPEECH ON THE SERVIAN WAR	18
IV. CROSS AND CRESCENT	40
V. BEFORE THE FALL OF PLEVNA.—MR. AKSAKOFF'S ADDRESS ON RUSSIAN DISASTERS	45
VI. THE BULGARIANS AND THEIR LIBERATORS	61
VII. AFTER PLEVNA	70
VIII. ENGLISH NEUTRALITY	77
IX. ON THE EVE OF THE CONGRESS	88
X. AFTER THE CONGRESS.—MR. AKSAKOFF'S SPEECH ON RUSSIAN CONCESSIONS	95
XI. DIVIDED BULGARIA	111

PART II.

THE FUTURE OF THE EASTERN QUESTION.

CHAPTER	PAGE
I. Lord Salisbury as Herald Angel	123
II. The Anglo-Turkish Convention	134
III. The Heirs of 'the Sick Man'	142
IV. 'The Last Word of the Eastern Question'	160

PART III.

MISUNDERSTANDINGS AND PREJUDICES.

I. Some English Prejudices	181
II. Poland and Circassia	196
III. Siberia	209
IV. Russian Autocracy	223
V. Constitutionalism in Russia	239
VI. The Attempt on the Emperor	252

PART IV.

THE ANGLO-RUSSIAN ALLIANCE.

I. Friends or Foes?	263
II. England's 'Traditional Policy'	272
III. Russia and English Parties	277

CHAPTER	PAGE
IV. RUSSIA'S FOREIGN POLICY.—A REPLY TO MR. GLADSTONE.—LETTER FROM M. EMILE DE LAVELEYE	290
V. RUSSIAN AGGRESSION	321
VI. RUSSIA AND THE AFGHAN WAR	332
VII. RUSSIANS IN CENTRAL ASIA	346
VIII. TRADITIONAL POLICY OF RUSSIA	352
IX. SOME LAST WORDS	367
APPENDIX	371
INDEX	379

PORTRAIT . . . . . . *To face Title.*

MAPS.

BULGARIA : ETHNOLOGICAL AND POLITICAL.

THE THREE BULGARIAS; CONSTANTINOPLE, SAN STEFANO, AND BERLIN.

} *To face p.* 120

PART I.

THE RUSSIAN PEOPLE AND THE WAR.

1. INTRODUCTORY.
2. THE TWO RUSSIAS: MOSCOW AND ST. PETERSBURG.
3. SECRET SOCIETIES AND THE WAR.—MR. AKSAKOFF'S SPEECH ON THE SERVIAN WAR.
4. CROSS AND CRESCENT.
5. BEFORE THE FALL OF PLEVNA.—MR. AKSAKOFF'S ADDRESS ON RUSSIAN DISASTERS.
6. THE BULGARIANS AND THEIR LIBERATORS.
7. AFTER PLEVNA.
8. ENGLISH NEUTRALITY.
9. ON THE EVE OF THE CONGRESS.
10. AFTER THE CONGRESS.—MR. AKSAKOFF'S SPEECH ON RUSSIAN CONCESSIONS.
11. DIVIDED BULGARIA.

CHAPTER I.

INTRODUCTORY.

CONSTANTINOPLE may be the last word of the Eastern Question, but it is certainly not the first.

For a good understanding between England and Russia the first thing needful is to clear up the misunderstanding about the origin of the recent war in the East. If it were true, as our enemies assert, that the Russian Government deliberately planned the war, in order to pursue a policy of plunder, so far from attempting to justify its action in the English press, as a patriotic Russian, I should sympathise with those who denounced a Government guilty of so grave an international crime.

But the assertion is a baseless calumny. Even if there were, as has been so frequently asserted, understandings between the three Emperors as to the rearrangement of territory in the East on the natural break-up of the Ottoman Empire, of which I know nothing, that is a very different thing from a determination to make war in order to partition 'Turkey.' It would merely be a statesmanlike *concert préalable* in view of a probable contingency, such, as I am free to confess, I would very much desire to see established among the Powers to-day.

Between such an understanding, entered into in order to minimise the disastrous consequences which would in any case follow the collapse of the Ottoman Empire, and a determination to go to war to bring about that collapse, there is a wide gulf fixed.

Russian diplomacy, as your Blue Books prove, laboured assiduously to prevent the overthrow of the Turkish Power. The attitude of the Russian Government was thus clearly and accurately defined by Prince Gortschakoff to Count Schouvaloff, in a despatch from Ems, $\frac{2}{14}$ June, 1876 :—

'From the commencement of the troubles in the East our august Master's sole aim has been to check their spread and to prevent a general conflagration in Turkey. We, like Mr. Disraeli, have no belief in the indefinite duration of the abnormal state of things we see in the Ottoman Empire. But, as yet, nothing is prepared to replace it, and were it suddenly to fall, there would be a risk of catastrophes, both in the East and in Europe (et sa chute subite risquerait d'ébranler l'Orient et l'Europe). Thus it is desirable to maintain the political *status quo* by a general improvement in the lot of the Christian populations, which appeared, and still appears, an indispensable condition of the existence of the Ottoman Empire. . . . . The success of the diplomatic action in which we were associated depended on the unanimity of the Cabinets. In default of this unanimity, which alone could restrain the passions raging in the East, an explosion was foreseen, and we have not had long to wait for it. At the present moment, as was the case eight months ago, we see no reason for desiring a decisive crisis in the East, because matters are not sufficiently ripe for settlement. We are ready to welcome any idea which the London Cabinet may communicate to us for securing the pacification of the East. We sincerely desire a good understanding with them.'[1]

A week later, Count Schouvaloff explained to the Earl of Derby the views of the Russian Government as to the pacification of the East. 'With regard to the remedies to be applied to the present state of affairs,' writes Lord Derby to Lord Augustus Loftus, ' Prince Gortschakoff agrees with me that these are the best which offer the most practical solution. For this reason the Russian Government incline to the plan of vassal and tributary autonomous States. Such an arrangement would not alter the political and territorial *status quo* of Turkey, while it would lighten the burdens which now exhaust the financial resources of the Porte.'[2]

The only difference between the policies of England and Russia was, that England ignored, while Russia recognised, the fact that a 'genuine improvement of the condition of the Christian populations' was really indispensable for the maintenance of the *status quo*.

The internal and political *status quo* of the Ottoman Empire was incompatible with the maintenance

[1] *Blue Book*, Turkey, 3 (1876), p. 283. [2] *Ibid.*, 3 (1876), p. 313.

of the territorial *status quo* in the East. Russia was ready to sacrifice the former to preserve the latter. England insisted on maintaining both, and as a consequence both were destroyed.

A cordial co-operation on the part of the English Cabinet with the other Powers would have enabled the Russian Government to have restrained the forces, national, religious, and humanitarian, which, by the pro-Turkish policy of Lord Beaconsfield, were let loose on the Ottoman Empire.

The ' passionate desire for peace ' which Lord Salisbury truly declared was the predominating feeling of our Emperor, was paralysed by the acquiescence of European diplomacy in the obstinate refusal of the Turks to make any amelioration of the condition of their Christian subjects. The Emperor told the English Ambassador that, ' if Europe was willing to receive these repeated rebuffs from the Porte, he could no longer consider it as consistent either with the honour, the dignity or the interests of Russia. He was anxious not to separate from the European concert; but the present state of things was intolerable and could not be allowed to continue, and unless Europe was prepared to act with firmness and energy, he should be compelled to act alone.'[1]

Europe refused, and Russia acted. With the hesitation and reserve of Russian diplomacy, due, no doubt, largely to the intense desire of the Emperor for peace and the knowledge of the Government that they were quite unprepared for war—the Russian

[1] *Blue Book*, Turkey, 1 (1877), p. 643.

people had no sympathy. While in your eyes the Russian Government was eagerly pressing for the destruction of the Turks, the Russian nation was indignant at the restraint placed by its diplomacy upon the fulfilment of our national duty.

To enable the English reader to look at the war from the Russian point of view, and to realise the feelings of the Russian people, I reproduce in these pages some letters, most of which I addressed to the *Northern Echo* in 1877 and 1878, together with two or three speeches of Mr. Aksakoff, the President of the Moscow Slavonic Committee, making material additions and alterations, in order to bring the narrative down to the present time.

CHAPTER II.

THE TWO RUSSIAS — MOSCOW AND ST. PETERSBURG.[1]

' So the people who made the war are already repenting of their folly ! ' sneers a cynical politician, as he lays down the *Times* of last Wednesday, after perusing a letter from its St. Petersburg correspondent with the above heading. ' Indeed ! ' I exclaim, with unfeigned surprise, ' that is strange news. Who says so ? What is your authority ? '

' The St. Petersburg correspondent of the *Times*,' rejoins the cynic, ' who, as the *Pall Mall Gazette* says, is known as the writer of a famous book on Russia, which appeared some months ago—in other words, all but naming Mr. R. Mackenzie Wallace.'

' And Mr. Wallace says the people who made the war are repenting of what they did,' I continue. ' Where does he say so ? I don't see any such statement in his letter.'

[1] The *Times* of Nov. 14, 1877, published a letter from its correspondent in St. Petersburg, describing a minority in the Russian capital as wearied of the war and anxious to make peace, regardless of the fate of the Southern Slavs. The *Pall Mall Gazette*, noticing his remarks under the suggestive heading ' Reported return of reason in Russia,' exulted in the hope that the Russians were about to abandon their heroic enterprise. This delusion can be removed most effectually by the simple statement of facts, too often ignored in England.

'Do you not?' he asks in amazement. 'What can be plainer than his account of the regret with which the war, its objects, and its sacrifices are spoken of in St. Petersburg by men "who consider themselves good patriots?" Here, for instance, he speaks of the statesman or official dignitary, the representative of the St. Petersburg Liberal press, and the commercial man, all of whose sentiments are faithfully reproduced. What more would you have as a proof that those who made the war are repenting in sackcloth and ashes of their Quixotic undertaking?'

I could not help smiling. 'And so that is the evidence upon which you and Mr. Wallace build your theories of "peace possibilities in Russia!" These people—they did not make the war! Not they, indeed! It was not these "patriots" to whose voices our Emperor gave ear!'

And so dismissing my Turkophile acquaintance, let me in a few sentences correct the false impression which that letter in the *Times* has produced, as the high character and deserved reputation of its author may mislead many.

The English people were told last year, and truly told, that there are two Russias. There is official Russia, and national Russia. There is, in a word, the Russia of St. Petersburg, and the Russia of Moscow.[1] Now, the *Times* correspondent lives in St. Petersburg,

[1] An English lady residing in Moscow from 1876 to 1878, described with simple fidelity the enthusiasm prevailing in the ancient capital of Russia, in a series of letters to the *Daily News* and to the *Northern Echo*, which Messrs. Remington & Co. republished in a volume—*Sketches of Russian Life and Customs*, by Selwyn Eyre.

and he transmits faithfully enough to England his impressions of public opinion in St. Petersburg. The only danger is that his readers may mistake St. Petersburg for Russia. But St. Petersburg, thank God! is not Russia, any more than the West-end of London is England. The whole course of European history, for the last two years, would be utterly incomprehensible on the contrary hypothesis. It was because foreigners took their impression of Russia from St. Petersburg that they blundered so grossly about the course which events would take in the East, and they will blunder not less grossly if, disregarding the lessons of the past, they once more entertain the hollow fallacy that the national opinion of Russia can be ascertained in the *salons* of St. Petersburg or by interviewing official personages on the banks of the Neva.

There are good men and true in St. Petersburg, as there are good men and true even in the clubs of Pall Mall; but the typical St. Petersburger, of whom Mr. Wallace writes, is as destitute of faith and of enthusiasm as the West-ender. But just as you say London is Turkophile, although many Londoners are anti-Turks, so we say St. Petersburg is anti-Slav. But then it must not be forgotten that St. Petersburg is not Russia. Peter the Great styled it 'a window out of which Russia could look upon the Western world;' but it is not a window by which the Western world can look in upon Russia. No, St. Petersburg is not Russian! It is cosmopolitan. It is not vitalised with the fierce warm current of Russia's life-blood. It stands apart. It undoubtedly exercises a great influence in ordinary times, but at great crises it is powerless. St. Petersburg did its best to avert the war. It sneered at our Servian volunteers—nay, if it had had its way it would have arrested them as malefactors. Those who went first to Servia on their heroic mission were compelled to smuggle themselves as it were out of the country for fear of the interference of officialdom supreme at St. Petersburg. St. Petersburg would, if it could, have suppressed our Slav Committees, and it did its best to induce our generous Emperor to violate that knightly word which he pledged at Moscow, amid the unbounded enthusiasm of all his subjects, to take up the cause of the Slavs, 'although he had to take it up alone.' In the midst of the great uprising of the nation occasioned by the Bulgarian atrocities and the Servian war, St. Petersburg was comparatively unmoved—a mere dead cold cinder in the midst of the glowing warmth of our national revival. All the diplomatic negotiations which preceded the war are inexplicable unless this is borne in mind. My countrymen, rising in the sacred wrath kindled by the inexpiable wrongs inflicted upon their kinsmen, pressed sternly, steadily onward to redress these wrongs, to terminate for ever the *status quo*, which rendered them chronic, inevitable. Official Russia, unable to arrest the movement entirely, nevertheless attempted, and attempted in vain, to divert it by diplomatic contrivances. We had one device after another invented in rapid succession to avoid the war by which alone our brethren could be freed. It is humiliating to recall the tortuous windings of Russian diplomacy, the inexhaustible expedients by which the Petersburg party endeavoured to balk the fulfilment of the national aspirations.[1]

The last of these was the Protocol! By that famous document official Russia consented, for the sake of the European concert and the peace of the Continent, to postpone indefinitely all action on behalf of the Southern Slavs, receiving in return for this sacrifice of her mission a promise that the Great Powers would watch the Turks, and after a period of time, not particularly specified, when it had once more, for the thousandth time, been demonstrated to the satisfaction even of the diplomatic mind that Turkish domination is utterly incapable of reform, improvement, or other amelioration than its total destruction, the Powers promised—oh, great concession!—to consider what should then be done to save our tortured brethren from the Ottoman horde. This was the patent St. Petersburg device for disappointing the hopes of the Russian people, and eagerly these officials, representatives of the Liberal press, and commercial men, who are now prating of peace to the *Times* correspondent, hoped

[1] In the Memoirs of Baron Stockmar occur some observations about diplomacy and diplomatists which are often too true:—'Diplomatists are for the most part a frivolous, superficial and rather ignorant set of people, whose first object is to lull matters to sleep for a few years, and to patch up things for a time. The distant future troubles them but little. They console themselves with such maxims as "Alors comme alors," "sufficient unto the day is the evil thereof." With statesmen of this kind it is sorry work discussing the conditions of a new political creation to be carried out under difficult circumstances. They have no real conception what work of this kind means. To those who point out the difficulties, they reply, "It will all come right in time," or they attempt to throw dust in the eyes by vague promises.'—*Baron Stockmar's Memoirs*, vol. i. p. 121.

that it would stave off what they are deriding now as the 'Quixotic enterprise' of the War of Liberation. In Moscow, however—that great heart of the Russian Empire—the suspense occasioned by the negotiations about the Protocol was one longdrawn-out agony. Those who lived in the very heart of the national movement can never forget the terrible forebodings of those dismal days. We all moved under the pressure of a great dread. Was it to end thus? Were all our sacrifices to be sacrificed? was the blood of our martyrs spilt in vain? Was Holy Russia Holy Russia no more, but a mere appanage to cosmopolitan St. Petersburg? When the news came that the English Cabinet was insisting upon alterations, we breathed more freely. 'Demobilisation!' we cried. 'No, it is not demobilisation; it is demoralisation! The Emperor is too noble, too good a Russian; he will never consent to that!' But, then, again the news came that even that was to be accepted; and the sky grew very dark overhead, and we went about as if in the chamber of death, speaking in low accents and oppressed by a terrible fear of that national dishonour which we Russians, strange as it may appear to some people, dread even more than death! At last, to our great relief, the cloud lifted, the darkness disappeared, for the Turks rejected the Protocol; and the declaration of war was as grateful to us as the bright burst of sunlight in the east after a long, dark, stormy night.

And here may I venture, as a Russian, to say that, in securing by his provisoes the rejection of the Protocol by the Turks, Lord Derby has at least done one good thing at the English Foreign Office. He may not have intended it, but, as a matter of fact, he was our most efficient ally. But for him St. Petersburg might have triumphed. Russia might have been disgraced, and the Turks might have received a new lease of power. The Slav world has reason to thank him for having secured the victory of our cause by rendering it impossible for Russia to refrain from drawing the sword in the cause of the Southern Slavs.

Even St. Petersburg could not shrink from the contest after that last deadly blow was administered by the Turks to the schemes of the diplomatists. The war began. It is going on, and it will go on until the end is accomplished. No babble of St. Petersburg will now be able to bring that war to a dishonourable close; and no peace can be honourable that does not secure the object of the war. St. Petersburg is even worse than usual just now. Its best elements are in Bulgaria and Roumania. The Emperor is there, and the sight of the fiendish atrocities perpetrated by the Turks upon our patient soldiers can only confirm his resolution to persevere 'until the end.' And behind him there stands, arrayed as one man, the whole Russian nation, ready to endure any sacrifices rather than leave the Turk to re-establish his desolating sovereignty over our brethren.

Is it so strange to Englishmen that there should be two Russias? Are there not two Englands? The England that is true to English love for liberty, and the England that sees in liberty itself only a text for a sneer? There is the England of St. James's Hall and the England of the Guildhall. An England with a soul and a heart, and an England which has only a pocket. In other words, there is the England of Mr. Gladstone and the England of Lord Beaconsfield. We Russians, too, have our sordid cynics, but they are in a minority. They may sneer, but they cannot rule; and, with that distinction, let me conclude by saying that these St. Petersburg *Tchinovniks*, whose views Mr. Wallace reproduces, are now what they have always been, the Beaconsfields of Russia!

The above letter was written in the middle of November, 1877.

Rightly to understand the genuine spontaneity of the national Slavonic movement which forced our Government into a war at a time when they were notoriously unprepared for such an enterprise, it was necessary to have resided in Russia when the news of the rising of the Christians in the Balkans stirred the national heart to its depths. Whatever doubts might prevail outside Russia, no one, be he ever so prejudiced, who witnessed the explosion of national and religious enthusiasm which shook Russia from her centre to her circumference, could deny the reality and spontaneity of the all-prevailing sentiment, the fervour of which our officials in vain endeavoured to abate. Even the English Ambassador was impressed by the unprecedented spectacle of a torrent of enthusiasm, sweeping away an entire people. Writing to the Earl of Derby, from St. Petersburg, on August 16, 1876, he says :—

The enthusiasm for the cause of the Servians and Christian Slavs is daily increasing here. The feeling is universal, and it pervades all classes from the Crown to the peasant. The sympathy of the masses has been roused by the atrocities which have been committed in Bulgaria, and bears a religious and not a political character.

Public collections are being made for the sick and wounded. Officers with the 'Red Cross,' and ladies of the Court and of society go from house to house requesting subscriptions. At the railway stations, on the steam-boats, even in the carriages of the tramways, the 'Red Cross' is present everywhere, with a sealed box for donations. Every stimulant, even to the use of the name of the Empress, is resorted to, with a view to animate feelings of compassion for the suffering Christians and to swell the funds for providing ambulances for the sick and wounded.

I am informed that such is the excitement in favour of the Christians that workmen are leaving to join the Servian army. Within the last fortnight seventy-five officers of the Guards have announced their intention to accept service in the Servian army, and it is reported that 120 officers at Moscow and in Southern Russia are on the point of leaving to join the Servian ranks.

I have also received private information that 20,000 Cossacks are going to Servia in disguise to join the Servian army.

The number is probably greatly exaggerated, but the fact of a considerable number of Cossacks having volunteered for service in aid of the Christians is undoubtedly true.

The religious feeling of the Russian nation is deeply roused in favour of their Christian Slav brethren, while the impassioned tone of the press is daily exciting the popular feeling.

From the foregoing symptoms it might be feared that

should any fresh atrocities occur to influence the public mind, neither the Emperor nor Prince Gortschakoff would be able to resist the unanimous appeal of the nation for intervention to protect and save their co-religionists.[1]

Lord Augustus Loftus inclosed an extract from a letter published in the *Moscow Gazette*, from a 'Retired Cossack,' who writes from the capital of the Cossacks of the Don. The writer, describing the state of excitement in which he found the Cossacks, says:—

Even women, old men and children speak of nothing but the Slavonic war; the warlike spirit of the Cossacks is on fire, and from small to great they all await permission to fall on the Turks like a whirlwind. At many of the settlements the Cossacks are getting their arms ready, with a full conviction that in a few days the order will be given to fall on the enemies of the Holy Faith, and of their Slav brethren. There is at the same time a general murmuring against diplomacy for its dilatoriness in coming to the rescue. Deputies have arrived from many of the Cossack settlements to represent to the Ataman that the Cossacks are no longer able to stand the extermination of the Christians.[2]

There is abundance of similar testimonies in your Blue Book.

Those who are not satisfied with official testimonies, will find unofficial confirmation of the reality of the popular movement in the pages of Mr. D. Mackenzie Wallace's 'Russia,'[3] a work which is certainly not characterised by too great a partiality towards us.

[1] Turkey, 1 (1877), No. 55, pp. 44–5.
[2] *Ibid.*, Inclosure in No. 55, pp. 45–6.   [3] Vol. ii. p. 453.

CHAPTER III.

SECRET SOCIETIES AND THE WAR.[1]

LORD SALISBURY recently advised the victims of the baseless scare of a Russian invasion of India to buy large-sized maps and learn how insuperable are the obstacles which nature has placed between the land of the Tzar and the dominions of the Empress. Would it be too presumptuous in a Russian to express a wish that Englishmen would pay a little attention to the history of their own country in the days of the great Elizabeth, before attempting to pronounce an opinion upon the action of the Russian people in this war?[2] Perhaps the discovery that only three centuries ago the heroism and enthusiasm of the English Protestants anticipated in Holland and France the course taken last year by the newly-awakened enthusiasm of the Russian people in Bulgaria and Servia would moderate the vehemence of their censure, even if it did not secure for my countrymen the sympathy which Englishmen used to feel for those who are

---

[1] This letter was written at the beginning of November, 1877.

[2] Lord Salisbury, in 1879, speaking at Hatfield, said Lord Beaconsfield's Government had pursued a truly Elizabethan policy: a statement which probably was meant to be interpreted by the rule of contrary.

willing to sacrifice all, even life itself, in the cause of Liberty and Right.

Without sympathy understanding is impossible. Prejudice closes the door against all explanation. But no one who had entered into the spirit of the times when Sir Philip Sydney went forth to fight in the Low Countries, and Francis Drake swept the Spanish Main, could possibly have made so many grotesque blunders as those which are to be found in most articles professing to describe Pan-Slavists and the Slav Committees. It is not very difficult to understand the source of their inspiration. Instead of ascertaining the objects of the Slavophils from their own lips, they repeat all the stupid calumnies wherewith our enemies have vainly attempted to prejudice our Emperor against the Slav cause. That is not fair. If a Russian writer were to describe the operations of the Eastern Question Association and Mr. Gladstone from the slanders of the English Turkophiles, he would not err more from the truth than do those English writers who caricature the Slav Committees by repeating the calumnies of some of our official enemies.

'The Slav Committees,' it is said, 'have brought about this war,'—an accusation of which I am proud, for the only alternative to war was a selfish abandonment of our Southern brethren to the merciless vengeance of the Turks.[1] But when they say that we

---

[1] 'It is when those Public Societies, which are called Governments, fail in their duty and abdicate their proper functions, that Secret Societies find their opportunities of action.'—Duke of Argyll, *The Eastern Question*, vol. i. p. 273.

brought it about in order 'to crush in Russia the present form of Government—the absolute rule of the Tzar,' they state that which is not only untrue, but what is known to be an absurdity by every Slavophile in Russia. The statement is even more absurd than the assertion made by Lord Beaconsfield that the Servian war was made by the Secret Societies. The Slavonic Committees are not secret, and they are certainly not composed of Revolutionists. It used to be the reproach of the Slav party that it was in all things too Conservative. Now we are told that we are Radicals, who hate the present form of the Russian State. Both reproaches can hardly be true. As a matter of fact, both are false. Some writers charge Mr. Aksakoff with being, as President of the Moscow Committee, the head-centre of revolutionary Russia. As one of Mr. Aksakoff's numerous friends, I may be permitted to say that there never was a more monstrous assertion. Mr. Aksakoff, although no courtier, is devotedly loyal. His wife was our Empress's lady-in-waiting, and governess to the Duchess of Edinburgh; and he himself, although abused in the Turkophile papers as a Russian Mazzini, is one of the last men in the world to undertake a crusade against the Tzardom. Simple, honest, enthusiastic, Mr. Aksakoff is no conspirator; he is simply the leading spokesman of the Russian Slavs, by whom he was elected to the post of President of the Moscow Slavonic Committee with only one dissentient voice. Much surprise was expressed that there should be even one vote against his appointment. But that surprise was succeeded by a smile when it was announced that the solitary dissentient was Mr. Aksakoff himself. So far from aiming at the destruction of the Russian State, they aim at the much less ambitious and more useful task of emancipating their Southern brethren from Turkish oppression. There is no mystery about the operations of our Committees. There work is prosaic in the extreme. Brought into existence long ago by the operation of the same benevolent spirit which leads English people to send tracts to Fiji cannibals, these Committees laboured unnoticed and unseen until the close of 1875. At that time occurred the great revolt of the Southern Slavs against their Turkish despots; and it is the peculiar glory of the Slavonic Committees that they were able to give rapid effect to the enthusiasm kindled in Russia by the story of the sufferings of our brethren, and, by sustaining the struggle for emancipation, were able to keep the condition of the Slavs before the Powers, until at last the Russian Government stepped in to free them from bondage. All Russia—Emperor, Government and all—became but one vast Slavonic Committee for the liberation of the Southern Slavs; and we have far less reason for wishing to destroy a State which has so nobly undertaken the heroic task of liberating our brethren than Englishmen have for desiring to upset their Parliamentary system which has enabled a Lord Beaconsfield to balk the generous aspirations expressed by the nation during the autumn of 1876.

It is entirely false that to our Slav Committees belongs the honour of having originated the insurrection of the Herzegovina. After it began it attracted our attention, and we would have assisted it if we could, but, unfortunately, the Russian people were not aroused, and there were next to no funds at our disposal to assist the heroic insurgents whose desperate resolve to achieve liberty or death on their native hills first compelled the Powers to face what Europe calls the Eastern Question, but what we call the Emancipation of the Slavs. The utmost that we could do in the first year of the insurrection was to collect some 10,000*l.* for the relief of the refugees in the Herzegovina, Montenegro, and Ragusa. English sympathisers, notably Mr. Freeman, also collected contributions for the same cause. General Tchernayeff proposed in September to take fifty non-commissioned officers to Montenegro, with arms for five hundred men ; but he could not carry out his scheme because we had no funds. I state this as a matter of fact, which I regret.

Proof of this melancholy fact can be had, I regret to say, in only too great abundance, but it will be sufficient here to refer the sceptical to the most interesting account of the rising in the Herzegovina by Mr. W. J. Stillman, who was correspondent of the *Times* in that region during the insurrection, in which he will find ample confirmation of my confession that our Russian Committees could not claim the honour of having encouraged the Herzegovinese at the first to strike that blow for freedom which led to the ruin of the Ottoman Empire. Russian influence at first was an influence of constraint. It was not until December

1875, that the Slavonic sympathies of the Russians were felt in the Herzegovina.[1]

It is the duty of free Slavs to assist their enslaved brethren to throw off the yoke of bondage. Our war may be condemned, but the heroism of our volunteers is appreciated even by those who support the Turks. Can Englishmen wonder that we Russians, brethren in race and in religion to the Rayahs of Northern Turkey, should endeavour to assist them as the English of Elizabeth's reign endeavoured to assist the Protestants of Holland and of France? But the fact that we would glory in assisting our enslaved brethren to throw off the yoke of the Turk should entitle us to be believed when we sorrowfully admit that, as a matter of fact, we have no claim to the credit of having fomented the insurrection which every one now can see was a death-blow to the domination of the Ottoman. It was not till after the insurrection had made considerable progress—not, in fact, until the atrocities in Bulgaria and the Servian war—that Russia awoke and assumed the liberating mission which, after great and terrible sacrifices, promises at last to be crowned with complete success.

It is a mistake to say, that our Russian volunteers in Servia were paid. It is also false that 9,000 Russians went to Servia. We could only find the travelling expenses of 4,000; none of whom received any other pay, but all of whom were eagerly ready to die for the cause. One-third of them perished as martyrs, but their blood has not been shed in vain.

[1] See *Herzegovina and the late Uprising*, p. 101.

Their death sealed the doom of the Turks. The Emperor has undertaken the championship of the Slavonic cause, and the war will only end when the liberation of the Southern Slavs is complete. So far from desiring the war to destroy the Tzardom, we were never so proud of Russia as we are to-day; never were we so unanimously and enthusiastically united in support of our heroic Emperor, who, after liberating twenty-three millions of serfs at home, is now crowning his reign with glory by emancipating the Southern Slavs.

In the foregoing letter I have referred to Mr. Aksakoff. It is better that he should speak for himself. Here is a condensed translation of the speech which he delivered, on November 6, 1876, before the Moscow Slavonic Committee, which I published in English in the same month. I may preface it with one sentence from Mr. Wallace's 'Russia,' endorsing it heartily. 'As to the authenticity of the testimony, I may add, that I have known Mr. Aksakoff, and have never in any country met a more honest and truthful man.'[1] Mr. Aksakoff said :—

It may be thought that the hour has at last arrived for Russia to resign into the hands of the State this great and important work, which during so many months the people have carried on with incredible exertion, without any help or co-operation from the Government. I do not speak here of the help afforded to the sick and the wounded, the famished and the destitute Bulgarians and Servians of different denominations. I do not speak of the

[1] Vol. ii. p. 452.

help in the shape of money and clothes, but the help of the nation's blood, the toilsome work of deliverance—in one word, the active share the Russian people took in the Servian war for Slavonic independence. The armistice lately signed by the Porte does not insure with certainty the conclusion of such a peace as would satisfy the lawful claims of our brethren, the honour of our people, and repay the bloody sacrifices made by Russia. The temporary cessation of the war cannot be a reason for relaxing the exertions which have signalised the last few months of our public life. This is not the moment to send in our resignation. The time has not yet come for our Society to lay aside the heavy burden of this uncommon, unforeseen and unexpected activity.

I have said 'uncommon, unforeseen and unexpected,' because what has been done lately in Russia is indeed unparalleled, not only in the history of Russia, but in that of any other nation. The Society, or rather the people, without the help of the Government (which is unconditionally true to its diplomatic obligations), and without the help of any official organisation, carry on a war in the person of some thousands of her sons (I say *sons*, not *hirelings*), at their own expense, in a country which, though bound to ours by strong ties of relationship, is little known to the masses, and has been up till now rarely spoken of. And this is done neither for the sake of gain, nor in view of selfishly practical or material interests, but for interests apparently foreign and abstract. The war is carried on, not stealthily or secretly, but openly, in sight of all, with full conviction of the lawfulness, right and holiness of the cause. This plain and spontaneous movement cannot be understood by Western Europe, where most public movements appear to be the result of a prepared conspiracy, and can only take place under the direction and through the medium of regularly organised secret societies. It is therefore not to be wondered at that some persons like Lord Beaconsfield, and not he alone, but even some Russians, ignorant of their own country, and mostly of the highest rank, find secret societies even in

Russia, so that all the 'shame,' or, as we think, all the honour, of the Russian popular interference in the Servian war is to be ascribed to the Slavonic Committee.

One cannot read without a smile such strange ideas of the power of our Society. You, gentlemen, know better than any how little our Society deserves the honour attributed to it. Such is the nature of this popular movement that it could never have been invented by the Committee, nor could it have shrunk into the narrow moulds which the Society could have formed for it. In reality it has far overstepped its borders, and has nearly crushed by its force our modest organisation. At present it is not the concern of the Slavonic Committee, but of the whole of Russia; and it is the greatest honour of our Society to become the simple instrument of the popular idea and the popular will—an instrument, to our regret, very feeble and insufficient.

That there was no premeditation in the action of the Committee can be best seen in the fact that the Society was not prepared for the immense activity which fell to its lot. Our Committee of management, composed only of three or four persons without any regular office, continued for a long time to work in its usual way, though with great difficulty. In July they engaged a paid secretary, and, thereafter yielding by degrees to necessity, they enlarged the number of officials, and accepted at the same time the zealous and efficient co-operation spontaneously offered by many members of the Slavonic Committee, and of nearly the whole staff of the Mutual Credit Society, of which I have the honour to be the President. If this frank acknowledgment of ours can draw upon us the reproach of want of foresight, it can on the other hand serve as a most eloquent answer to the calumnies of foreign newspapers. The English Premier, I suppose, would be very much astonished if he verified his notions of our Committee by an examination of our ledgers and accounts. But even the reproach of shortsightedness would be unjust. The popular movement has surprised not only the whole of Europe, but also Russian society (that is, the educated reflecting part of Russia), precisely because it was *popular*, not in the rhetorical, but in the plain literal meaning of the word. For scores of years the preaching of the so-called Slavophils resounded, and was, it seemed, as the voice 'of one crying in the wilderness.'

Twenty-two years ago the Crimean war broke out also as a result of the Eastern, or, more strictly speaking, the Slavonic, Question, and evoked a powerful expression of patriotism. It did not, however, awaken the historical self-consciousness in those classes of the people in which are the roots of the Russian power, both spiritual and external. Unseen by us and invisible is the secret process of the popular ripening and the working of the popular organism.

We could certainly assume that with the abolition of serfdom, and of many legal class distinctions, together with the spread of elementary education, the intellectual view of the people must expand and their mind acquire greater freedom of action. But the events which have occurred have surpassed the most sanguine expectations. I confess frankly that every new appearance of popular sympathy came upon me as a delightful surprise, until at last it was manifested in its full power and truth. Not less astonished was I by the gradual change in the thoughts and expressions of our so-called intelligent circles and in our press. All the literary parties and factions intermingled, and found themselves, to their mutual surprise, in agreement and unity on this question. The opponents of yesterday found themselves friends, as if they had broken their stilts, come down to the ground, thrown off the disguise of harlequins, and shown themselves—what they are in truth—Russians, and nothing else.

There was, in all this, enough to surprise any one who remembered the past of our social life. It was cleared up not at once, but gradually, by the current of events.

When the rising in the Herzegovina began, rather more than a year ago, and the Slavonic Committee of Moscow, as well as the St. Petersburg branch, published the appeals of the

Servian and Montenegrin Metropolitans, and these appeals from the ecclesiastical personages were made known (only made known and nothing else), the donations assumed unheard-of dimensions.

The limits of the Orthodox world began to widen before the eyes of the people; new vistas of fraternity were opened up to them; but all was still in confusion. Not less confused were the ideas of the higher classes. When General Tchernayeff arrived in Moscow in September last year, and proposed to take with him to Montenegro fifty non-commissioned officers, and arms for 500 persons, his plan could not be put into execution because the Committee had no funds, and private persons did not show any readiness to supply them.

The subsequent activity of the Committee was for some time, in appearance and reality, of a charitable nature. The volunteers who started for the Herzegovina were all South Slavonians, Servians and Bulgarians living in Russia. The only exceptions were two Russian officers, who had expressly come to Moscow, after having been refused assistance in St. Petersburg.

When on the Slavonic horizon appeared the dawn of a new, and in the political sense a more important, struggle— the struggle between the Servian Principalities and the Porte for the freedom of the Slavonic territories tributary to the Turks—and when at the end of last March General Tchernayeff announced to the Committee his intention of going to Servia, the Committee could but perceive the great significance of such an event as the appearance of Tchernayeff at the head of the Servian army. But neither the Committee nor Tchernayeff could then foresee what would happen to the Russian people. It was clear to the Committee that the act of self-sacrifice on the part of Tchernayeff could not but raise among the Slavonians the honour of the Russian name, greatly compromised by diplomacy, and could not fail at the same time to raise the moral level of Russian society by increasing its self-respect. It was necessary to remove some pecuniary difficulties which prevented the departure of Tchernayeff. A sum of 6,000 roubles was needed, and the Committee did not hesitate to advance it.

Soon after Tchernayeff's arrival in Servia began the Turkish atrocities in Bulgaria.[1] No special efforts were required to awaken Russian sympathy and compassion. For the Russians there is no enemy more popular than the Turk. Donations of money and effects flowed in in torrents.

The Servian war began. With breathless anxiety Russia followed the uneven struggle of the little Orthodox country —smaller than the province of Tamboff—with the vast army, gathered together from Asiatic hordes dispersed over three quarters of the globe. But when the Servian army suffered the first defeat; when on the soil of the awakened popular feeling fell, so to speak, the first drop of Russian blood; when the first deed of love was completed; when the first pure victim was sacrificed for the faith, and on behalf of the brethren of Russia, in the person of one of her own sons, then the conscience of all Russia shuddered.

As from the first, so afterwards, the Muscovite Slavonic Committee offered no invitations nor allurements to secure volunteers. One after another came, retired officers requesting advice and directions how to go to Servia, and enter the ranks of the army under the command of Tchernayeff. The news of the death of Kireeff, the first Russian who fell in this war, at once stimulated hundreds to become volunteers, —an event which repeated itself when the news was received of other deaths among the Russian volunteers. Death did not frighten, but, as it were, attracted, them. At the beginning of the movement the volunteers were men who had belonged to the army, and chiefly from among the nobles. I remember the feeling of real emotion which I experienced when the first sergeant came, requesting me to send him to Servia—so new was to me the existence of such a feeling in the ranks of the people. This feeling soon grew in intensity when not only old soldiers, but even peasants,

[1] May, 1876.

came to me with the same request. And how humbly did they persevere in their petition, as if begging alms! With tears they begged me, on their knees, to send them to the field of battle. Such petitions of the peasants were mostly granted, and you should have seen their joy at the announcement of the decision! However, those scenes became so frequent, and business increased to such an extent, that it was quite impossible to watch the expression of popular feeling, or to inquire into particulars from the volunteers as to their motives. 'I have resolved to die for my faith.' 'My heart burns.' 'I want to help our brethren.' 'Our people are being killed.' Such were the brief answers which were given with quiet sincerity. I repeat there was not, and could not be, any mercenary motive on the part of the volunteers. I, at least, conscientiously warned every one of the hard lot awaiting him, and, indeed, even at first sight, no particular advantage could appear. Each one received only fifty roubles, out of which thirty-five went to pay the fare through Roumania, and the rest was for food and other expenses. The movement assumed at last such dimensions that we had to establish a special section for the reception of the volunteers and the examination of their requests and depositions.

All parts of Russia were desirous of having branches of the Slavonic Committee. From every town propositions were sent to us, but, to our regret, we were unable to satisfy their urgent demands. The permission to establish fresh sections did not depend upon us, but upon the Minister of the Interior. Fortunately there is a society in Odessa called the Benevolent Society of Cyril and Methodius, which rendered great services to the general cause. Fortunately also, in some of our provincial towns, there were governors who took a part in the popular feeling, and who allowed the inhabitants to organise small societies for the reception of donations. These latter became afterwards centres for local activity. But when a movement embraces tens of millions of people, scattered over an extent equal to nearly a quarter of the globe, it is impossible to arrange and regulate the expression of feeling, and particularly without the requisite publicity. Those who imagine that it is easy to subordinate such a movement to any Committee or organisation, do not know the nature of popular movements, especially in Russia. The donations became special, according to the wish of the donor. Many towns, villages, and private persons, without communicating with the Committees, wrote direct to Tchernayeff, Prince Milan, Princess Nathalie, Prince Nicholas of Montenegro, or the Metropolitan Michael. They even sent deputations, volunteers, money, and clothes, minutely explaining the purpose for which each article was intended, expressing at the same time their sympathies and hopes. All this irregularity was quite natural, for the thing itself was most unusual and unprecedented.

Yes, gentlemen, there was no precedent, no experience, either in Russian society in general, or in our Committee in particular. The Committee had not only to distribute help in money, but also to take the duties of superintendence, inspection, providing medicine, arms, provisions, and, one might even add, duties of the general staff. There is not the least doubt that such an unaccustomed work, organised so suddenly, was fraught with many mistakes, and sometimes, notwithstanding all our efforts, did not obtain the desired results. But one must also bear in mind that there was a total absence of any sort of organisation in Servia herself. Be this as it may, the Slavonic Committee worked hard and conscientiously. I come now to the question of the accounts. We cannot give, however, at present very detailed or precise ones, for from various places we have as yet not received them ourselves.

I foresee that the amount of our receipts will greatly disappoint the public. We have heard and read daily that Russia has sent to the Slavs millions of money; and the stern question arises, 'What became of these millions?' The rumours set afloat about these millions have as much truth as those concerning the numbers of volunteers, of whom it is said we sent 20,000, when in fact only a fifth part of that number—perhaps less—were sent. The truth is, at Moscow and St. Petersburg we received a little more than a million and half of roubles. It must be borne in mind that we had to give help to the Herzegovina, Montenegro, Bosnia, Bulgaria, and Servia. During the last months, many small Committees were formed over the whole of Russia, and sent out their donations independently of us. But these sums were comparatively small. Nearly all Western Russia dispensed with the co-operation of our Slavonic Committee. Some societies and commercial establishments—as, for instance, the St. Petersburg Municipal Credit Co., which had remitted to Tchernayeff 100,000 roubles, and had given also the same amount to the St. Petersburg Committee—likewise sent out help themselves. It is therefore still impossible to state the precise amount of the donations; but it may be said that, including the money spent by the chief Society for the tending of the sick and wounded soldiers, the total sum would be scarcely more than three millions of roubles. The value of the articles given may amount to half a million more.

The sum is enormous, and yet it is small—that is to say, in comparison with the requirements; for upwards of three millions of our Orthodox brethren of the Balkan Peninsula are in want of the most important and essential things—food, clothing, and shelter. It is small compared to the size of Russia, with her 80,000,000 of inhabitants and her power—small in comparison with the scores of millions reported. It is enormous, if you consider the source from which it came, our social condition, and the impediments which came in the way—enormous, because two-thirds of the donations were given by our poor peasants, much oppressed by want; and every copper coin they gave will weigh undoubtedly heavier in the scale of history than hundreds of ducats. One may remark, in general, that the amount of the donations decreased according to the exalted position of the donor in the social scale. There were a few exceptions to this rule, and we must also consider the bad harvests of the last years. It is an undoubted fact, however, that the eminently wealthy took no share in the movement, probably from a lack of sympathy. Finally, the sum is enormous, considering the novelty of the matter, the inability of working together, the difficulty of intercourse between the different parts of Russia, and the impossibility of using freely the help of the press.

I shall not stop now to explain the particulars of our receipts, though they are of great interest. But because they are so full of interest they demand a minute exposition; and our honourable Secretary, who is also a professor of history, is now engaged on that work. The letters, which came with the donations, are now assorted; and many of them, being the simple expressions of the popular feeling, bear witness to the truth of the present historical movement.

Mr. Aksakoff then gave a detailed statement of expenditure, of which the following are the leading features :—' Herzegovina, Bosnia, and Montenegro, 185,000 roubles; General Tchernayeff and his staff —none of the volunteers were paid by the Servian Government—79,000 roubles; General Novosseloff and the Russian volunteers on the Ibar, 21,000 roubles; sick and wounded in Servia, 31,000 roubles; army and telegraph, 9,000 roubles; movable churches and volunteers' clothes, 10,000 roubles; and 159,000 roubles were still on hand.'

Mr. Aksakoff continued :—

The expenses, as you perceive, are not so great after all, considering the importance of the matter and the multitude of urgent wants. We have still to face unavoidable expenses imposed upon us by the national conscience; we have to provide for the Russian volunteers who are still in Servia, for the wounded, and for the families of those who have fallen, and we must give to the surviving volunteers the means for returning home. We now have taken measures to form a regular system of paying salary to the volunteers in the service of Servia (which we had not done before), and this will be continued as long as we have the means of doing so.

The Russian people will not abandon the work which it has begun; of that we may be sure.

One cannot but remark that in the last few days, under the influence of the newspaper correspondence, the public sympathy for the Servians has cooled. Whatever may have been the faults of some Servians towards some Russians, on the whole *we* are to blame—not the Servians. Yes, we, as a community, as Russia. The Servians cannot be expected to know, and cannot understand, that the help offered to them is merely the result of private efforts. Nor can they understand the peculiar conditions in which we are placed. They write, print, and talk about the help from Russia, 'the millions of Russia.' Under the name of Russia, the Servians and all Trans-Danubian Slavonians do not understand a certain class of society, but the Russian Empire in its entirety. In a word, they are not accustomed to distinguish in Russia between the people and the Government; and, trusting to Russia, they began a struggle above their strength.

The results of this mistaken belief are known to everybody. Towns in flames, hundreds of villages destroyed, the occupation of the third part of their land by the Turks, exhaustion of means, and general ruin. Are we to punish them for their ruin? We must also not forget that the Servians of the Principality have fought not only for their country, but for the deliverance of all the Slavonians who are suffering and dying under the yoke of the Turk, and whose fate is just as near to the heart of the Russian people. *We are in debt to the Servians!* But we shall not long remain so. The Russian people will not allow the Russian name to be disgraced; and the blessed hour so much hoped for by all is near, when this work, which belongs properly to the State, will pass into the hands of our strong organised Government. Being led and aided by the popular force, the Government will take into its powerful hands the defence of the Slavs. So let it be!

The reference which Mr. Aksakoff makes to the death of my brother will be better understood by reading the following extract from the brilliant pages of Mr. Kinglake, the historian of the Crimean War, who writes as follows, in the Preface to the sixth edition of his great work:—

The Russians are a warm-hearted, enthusiastic people, with an element of poetry in them, which derives perhaps from the memory of subjection undergone in old times and the days of Tartar yoke, for if Shelley speaks truly—

> Most wretched men
> Are cradled into poetry by wrong,
> They learn in sorrow what they teach in song.

. . . . They can be honestly and beyond measure vehement in favour of an idealised cause which demands their active sympathy. That the voice of the nation, when eagerly expressing these feelings, is commonly genuine and spontaneous, there seems no reason to doubt. Far from having been inspired by the rulers, an outburst of the fraternising enthusiasm, which tends towards State quarrels and war, is often unwelcome at first in the precincts of the Government offices.

After referring to the Servian War and to the presence of a few Russian volunteers in the Servian camp, Mr. Kinglake says:—

This armed emigration at first was upon a small scale, and the Servian cause stood in peril of suffering a not distant collapse, when the incident I am going to mention began to exert its strange sway over the course of events.

The young Colonel Nicholai Kireeff was a noble, whose

birth and possessions connected him with the districts affected by Moscow's fiery aspirations; and being by nature a man of an enthusiastic disposition, he had accustomed himself to the idea of self-sacrifice. Upon the outbreak of Prince Milan's insurrection, he went off to Servia with the design of acting simply under the banner of the Red Cross, and had already entered upon his humane task, when he found himself called upon by General Tchernayeff to accept the command of what we may call a brigade—a force of some five thousand infantry, consisting of volunteers and militiamen, supported, it seems, by five guns; and before long, he not only had to take his brigade into action, but to use it as the means of assailing an entrenched position at Rokowitz. Kireeff very well understood that the irregular force entrusted to him was far from being one that could be commanded in the hour of battle by taking a look with a field-glass and uttering a few words to an aide-de-camp; so he determined to carry forward his men by the simple and primitive expedient of personally advancing in front of them. He was a man of great stature, with extraordinary beauty of features; and, whether owing to the midsummer heat, or from any wild, martyr-like impulse, he chose, as he had done from the first, to be clothed altogether in white. Whilst advancing in front of his troops against the Turkish battery, he was struck—first by a shot passing through his left arm, then presently by another one which struck him in the neck, and then again by yet another one which shattered his right hand and forced him to drop his sword; but, despite all these wounds, he was still continuing his resolute advance, when a fourth shot passed through his lungs, and brought him, at length, to the ground, yet did not prevent him from uttering—although with great effort—the cry of 'Forward! Forward!' A fifth shot, however, fired low, passed through the fallen chief's heart and quenched his gallant spirit. The brigade he had commanded fell back, and his body—vainly asked for soon afterwards by General Tchernayeff—remained in the hands of the Turks.

These are the bare facts upon which a huge superstructure was speedily raised. It may be that the grandeur of the young Colonel's form and stature, and the sight of the blood, showing vividly on his white attire, added something extraneous and weird to the sentiment which might well be inspired by witnessing his personal heroism. But, be that as it may, the actual result was that accounts of the incident—accounts growing every day more and more marvellous—flew so swiftly from city to city, from village to village, that before seven days had passed, the smouldering fire of Russian enthusiasm leapt up into a dangerous flame. Under countless green domes, big and small, priests chanting the 'Requiem' for a young hero's soul, and setting forth the glory of dying in defence of 'syn-orthodox' brethren, drew warlike responses from men who cried aloud that they, too, would go where the young Kireeff had gone; and so many of them hastened to keep their word, that before long a flood of volunteers from many parts of Russia was pouring fast into Belgrade. To sustain the once kindled enthusiasm apt means were taken. The simple photograph, representing the young Kireeff's noble features, soon expanded to large-sized portraits; and Fable then springing forward in the path of Truth, but transcending it with the swiftness of our modern appliances, there was constituted, in a strangely short time, one of those stirring legends which used to be the growth of long years—a legend half-warlike, half-superstitious, which exalted its really tall hero to the dimensions of a giant, and showed him piling up hecatombs by a mighty slaughter of Turks.[1]

The mine—the charged mine of enthusiasm upon which this kindling spark fell—was the same in many respects that

[1] The able correspondents of our English newspapers lately acting in Servia took care to mention the exploit and death of Colonel Kireeff with more or less of detail, and the information they furnished is for the most part consistent with the scrutinised accounts on which I found the above narrative. The corps in which the Colonel formerly served was that of the Cavalry of the Guards, but he had quitted the army long before the beginning of this year.

we saw giving warlike impulsion to the Russia of 1853; but then now was added the wrath, the just wrath at the thought of Bulgaria—which Russia shared with our people. . . . .

Thus the phantom of Kireeff, with the blood on his snowy-white clothing, gave an impulse which was scarce less romantic, and proved even perhaps more powerful than the sentiment for the Holy Shrines.

Mr. Kinglake concludes by declaring that 'the impulse which has been stirring the Russian people was for the most part a genuine, honest enthusiasm.'[1]

Before concluding this chapter, permit me to quote the following testimony to the national character of our war, which, if viewed as a speculation, was mad enough, no doubt, but which in reality was one of the most heroic wars ever fought. The writer, the learned Dr. J. J. Overbeck, whose intimate acquaintance with Russia and the Russians entitles him to speak with authority, says:[2]—

It was not a political war, planned by statesmen; it was a *national war*, *a holy war*, and the first victim in it was Nicholas de Kireeff, a splendid pattern of a Christian soldier, whose name will for ever shine in the annals of history.

As we were personally acquainted with Colonel Nicholas de Kireeff, we cannot refrain from adding that his heroic death was only the legitimate crowning of an heroic life—a life of self-sacrifice for the benefit of his suffering brethren. Nicholas Kireeff was an upright and zealous Orthodox; and he did not only *believe*, but *acted* accordingly. If ever practical Christianity shone forth from the life of a man, we find

---

[1] The year 1853 and the year 1876. A Preface to the sixth edition of the *Invasion of the Crimea*, vol. i. pp. vi–xv. See also Wallace's *Russia*, vol. ii. p. 453. Salisbury's *Two Months with General Tchernayeff in Servia*, pp. 104–7.

[2] *Orthodox Catholic Review*, vol. vii. p. 10. Trübner & Co.

it here. Never the poor applied in vain to him. Never the hungry passed his door unfed. His last roubles he shared with two poor Bulgarians. Such virtues could not fail conquering even his enemies. Russia, able to produce such a man, shows her own healthy and vigorous life, and may be sure of its final victory in the present momentous struggle.[1]

[1] I cannot dismiss this subject without a passing reference to the influence which Mr. Gladstone's pamphlet is supposed to have had in leading Russians to volunteer for service in Servia. The movement, as Mr. Aksakoff states, assumed national importance at the end of July, after my brother's death. On page 16 I quote a despatch, the date of which is worth noting, for it shows that on August 16 the British Ambassador reported the state of feeling in Russia to be such that volunteering was going on everywhere. It was not till September 6 that Mr. Gladstone published his pamphlet, and it was not translated into Russian until the close of the month. To ascribe the departure of Russian volunteers to Servia as being due to Mr. Gladstone's pamphlet is chronologically as absurd as, to a Russian, it is grotesquely ridiculous. The speech delivered by Sir William Harcourt in Parliament, August 11, and that of the Duke of Argyll at Glasgow were also translated into Russian. Unaccustomed as Russians are to hear impartial generous utterances in favour of the Eastern Christians from English sources, they were happy to point out these noble exceptions. But to imagine, as the Hon. R. Bourke appears to have done, 'ever since October, 1876,' that Russians needed to be taught their duty by an Englishman, and that the numbers of volunteers with General Tchernayeff were affected by Mr. Gladstone's pamphlet, is one of the most curious illustrations of insular British delusions which ever excited the laughter of astonished Russians. We did not need English advices as to our duty towards the oppressed brethren, nor did Mr. Gladstone ever advise our intervention. On the contrary, he strongly deprecated it. He wrote: 'Every circumstance of the most obvious prudence dictates to Russia for the present epoch what is called the waiting game. Her policy is, to preserve or to restore tranquillity for the present, and to take the chances of the future.' The whole pamphlet was a plea for concerted, as opposed to isolated, action in the East.

CHAPTER IV.

CROSS AND CRESCENT.

WHY do the Russians hate the Turks?

Because they know them.

An all-sufficient answer. Our knowledge was not bought without bitter tears. The Tartar wrote his character across our Russia in letters of flame. You English people are not touched with a feeling of the sufferings of the rayahs, because you have not been in all points afflicted as they: Russians have. In centuries of anguish they have learned the lesson of sympathy with those who are crushed beneath an Asiatic yoke. We feel for them because we suffered with them. As they are—so we were. They are not only our brethren in race and religion, they are also our brothers in misfortune, united to us in 'the sacred communion of sorrow.'

Many of my English friends know but little about the causes of hereditary hatred of the Russian for the Turk. I venture, therefore, to state briefly the facts which my countrymen can never forget.

It is not more than six hundred years since first the Russian people fell under the curse of Tartar domination. Before that time the Russians were as free, as prosperous, and as progressive as their neighbours. Serfdom was unknown. The knout, Mr. Tennyson's abomination, was not introduced until two hundred and fifty years after the Tartar conquest. There were Republics in Russia as in Italy, and the Grand Prince had no more power than other sovereigns. But in the middle of the thirteenth century Russia, lying nearest to Asia, experienced a Tartar invasion. An accident of geographical position subjected her to a visitation, from the consequences of which she has freed herself by superhuman struggles.

It was in 1224 that the Tartars first established themselves as conquerors in South-Eastern Russia. It was not till the close of the sixteenth century that we finally rid ourselves of these troublesome intruders. The Tartar domination, however, did not last much more than two hundred years. It was in 1252 that St. Alexander Nevsky received the title of Grand-Duke from the Tartars. It was not till 1476 that we ceased to pay tribute to our conquerors. But long after Ivan III. had broken the power of the Mongol horde the Tartars spread desolation and death through Russia. As late as 1571, when England, under Elizabeth, had just given birth to a Shakespeare, Moscow was burnt to the ground by a wandering host of Asiatics. It is easy to write the words, 'invaded by the Tartars;' but who can realise the fact? Western Europe, which felt afar off the scorching of the storm of fire which swept over Russia, throbbed with horror. Kind-hearted

St. Louis of France prayed 'that the Tartars might be banished to the Tartarus from whence they had come, lest they might depopulate the earth!' All the monsters who to you are mere names were to us horrible realities. The Khans, the Begs, of whose pyramids of skulls the world still hears with dread, rioted in rapine throughout the whole of Russia. Five generations of Russians lived and died under the same degrading yoke as that which has crushed the manhood out of the Bulgarians.

For centuries every strolling Tartar was as absolute master of the life, the property, and the honour of the Russians as the Zaptieh is of the lives of the Southern Slavs. To you English people atrocities are things to read of and imagine. To us Russians they are a repetition of horrors with which we have been familiar from childhood. Moscow has twice suffered the fate of Batak, and nearly every city in Russia has suffered the horrors inflicted upon Yeni-Zagra.

For at least three centuries our national history is little more than a record of the struggle of our race for liberty to live. Our national heroes are the warriors who did battle with the Asiatic intruder, and to this hour in our churches the images of St. Michael of Twer being put to death by the Tartars for refusing to become a renegade stir the patriotism and excite the imagination of the youthful Russian. The path of liberty was steep and thorny. Again and again our efforts were baffled. A town revolted, and it was consumed. Bands of armed peasants who resisted the Tartars were from time to time massacred to a man. But the Russian nation did not despair. As your own Byron sang—Byron, who gave his life to the cause for which thousands of my countrymen are giving theirs to-day—

> Freedom's battle, once begun,
> Bequeathed by bleeding sire to son,
> Though baffled oft, is ever won.

Gradually Russia shook off the yoke of her oppressors. Her advance resembled that of Servia and Roumania. After having enjoyed administrative autonomy, she secured her position as a tributary State, and then, at last, waxing strong with freedom, she burst the chains with which she had been so long bound.

Russia was free from the Asiatic oppressor, but the evil results of his domination remained. Mr. Gladstone, in one of his grandest speeches on the Eastern Question, explained the comparatively low intellectual condition of the Southern Slavs, by referring to the sandy barrier which, while producing nothing valuable itself, nevertheless keeps the destroying wave from encroaching upon the fertile land. What the Southern Slavs did for Southern, Russia did for Northern Europe. Upon us the Asiatic wave spent its force. We were overwhelmed. But we saved Europe from the Mongol horde.

While we saved, we suffered; we emerged from the flood of barbarism ourselves partially barbarous. Our progress had been arrested for centuries. All our national energies had been diverted into the struggle against our conquerors. What had once been flourishing towns were blackened ruins.

Liberty itself disappeared for a time. To fight the Tartar all power was centred in the hand of one ruler. Serfdom was amongst the legacies of Tartar domination. While the rest of the world had advanced, Russia had even been forced back.

It was a terrible visitation, but it left behind it at least one benefit. But for the tortures of these sad centuries, the Russian people might have been as indifferent as the French and the English to the cries of those who are still under the power of the Pashas. But for the sympathy of the Russian people, Chefket Pasha and Achmet Aga might have ruled for ever in Bosnia and Bulgaria. The Tartars prevented that. They taught the Russian people what the rule of the Asiatic is,—a dreadful lesson, creating that hatred of the Turk which will ultimately secure his ejection from Europe.

The death-warrant of the Ottoman Empire was signed by Timour the Tartar.

CHAPTER V.

BEFORE THE FALL OF PLEVNA.[1]

RUSSIAN papers mention a great personage who, on overhearing some discussion about the possible conclusion of peace, observed significantly that the time was too serious for jokes. Whoever the personage may be, we may bless him for his remark. Yet English people discuss the possibilities of peace without any consciousness that their talk cannot be regarded as serious. There is evidently an insurmountable difficulty on the part of Englishmen to understand the way in which we regard this war in Russia. Were it not so, we should hear less of the hopes so freely expressed and so thoughtlessly cheered that foreign advice might guide Russia in bringing our war to a close. In England you have evidently forgotten all about the object of the war in the eagerness with which you have followed its details. The death-struggle in Bulgaria and Armenia is to you what a gladiatorial combat was to the pampered populace of ancient Rome. You sit as spectators round the arena, cheering now the Turk and now the Russian, as if these brave men were being butchered

[1] This letter was written a few weeks before the fall of Plevna.

solely to afford you an exciting spectacle. Tired at last, you cry, 'Enough, enough! clear the ring, and pass on to some other sport.' But had you not ignored the nature of the fight, you would never ask to do that. It is not a mere gladiators' war. It is not a duel between two Powers about some punctilio of offended honour, which might be satisfied—as Mr. Freeman so well says—by the killing of a decent number of people. Were it either of these things, there would be some reason for the tragedy to close, for it would have been a crime from the first. But the war in which my countrymen are dying by thousands, so far from being a crime was an imperative duty, for it was the only means for attaining an end the righteousness of which all Europe has admitted. It was the only way for Russia of being consistent.

We did not make war for the sake of war. We sorrowfully but resolutely accepted that terrible alternative because we had no other choice, since ill-advised Turkey would not listen to the voice of justice. To us it would be a crime if, after having begun the work, we were to draw back without having accomplished the object which alone justified so terrible an undertaking. Hence all this talk of mediation, intervention, conferences, and of peace proposals sounds to us as mere mockery. There can be no peace until we have attained our end, and that we cannot do until we have completely freed the Christian Slavs. The war to us is a cruel reality, instead of merely a theatrical spectacle. We bear the blows the mere sight of which unnerves you. It is our hearths that are darkened by the shadow of death. Yet in all Russia you will hear no cry for peace until we have secured our end. I grieve to say Russia has its Beaconsfields. But as I said before, they are in a minority, and they become what they ought to be—thoroughly Russian, when asked to die for their country. Amongst the heroes whose deaths Russia deplores were people who—thanks to foreign influences, thanks to an idle, unoccupied life—became estranged from national interests; but their hearts throbbed afresh on hearing cries for help in accents of agony, and on seeing with their own eyes the appalling miseries of their brethren. The war brings out to daylight the best, the noblest elements of my country. Our armies are appreciated by the whole world. Colonel Brackenbury's eloquent tribute to the Russian character, published by the *Times*,[1] carries with it a strong conviction of its absolute accuracy. As a Russian I read it with deep emotions of gratitude. There is another side of the question, which, although seldom mentioned by the press, deserves the highest praise—I mean the part played in the war by the Russian women. From the highest to the lowest rank, regardless of any social differences, they devote themselves entirely to the relief of the sick and wounded, both on the field of battle and at home. In fact, the Red Cross Society includes in its ranks the whole womanhood of Russia. This spirit of self-

[1] December 1, 1877.

sacrifice and devotion is shown even by those who, before the testing moment, appeared to be utterly lost in worldly, frivolous pursuits.

Yes, this grand war has given a new impulse to Russian life, a deeper feeling of higher missions in this world. Someone said that life was nothing but an examination one had to pass in order to die nobly, and to prove that we did not make a bad use of the greatest privilege given to mortals—that of moral liberty. My countrymen and countrywomen are passing their examination splendidly; and the Slavs—the cause of this new heroism of the whole of Russia—have claims upon our gratitude as much as upon our sympathies! If it had not been for Servia and the Russian volunteers, the Slavonic world might have waited for its deliverance many, many years more.

In vain we try to pierce the impervious veil which conceals the future, but we know that our Tzar is the very incarnation of his country, and that having often shown a remarkable kind-heartedness, he has also given striking proofs of his firm will in great, decisive moments. The fate of the Christian Slavs is in noble and generous hands. The result of the war no Russian can for one moment doubt. Come what may, the Slavs will be freed. All 'possible terms of peace,' that do not include the ejection of the Zaptieh and the Pasha, bag and baggage, from the Balkans are manifestly impossible. Deluded and obstinate as the Turk is, he will not go out until he is beaten *à plates coutures*.

After the barbarian is swept away the task of reorganising the government of these lands will be much simplified. It will not be impossible to maintain sufficient order in the province whilst its inhabitants are gradually acquiring, like the Serbs and Roumans, the habit of self-government. As to Constantinople, even if the fortune of war should compel us to enter that city, we should enter it as the Germans entered Paris, to celebrate a triumph, not to make an annexation. Our Emperor's word upon this was solemn and conclusive.

The refusal to believe such an assurance from such a man implies an incapacity to understand the very existence of good faith. Certain suspicions reflect discredit only upon those who entertain them. The nobler England is above such unworthy distrust.

Roumania stretches as a barrier between us and the soil of Turkey, which we are supposed to covet, and Roumania will not suffer for her alliance with Russia.[1]

We have no warmer allies than the foremost statesmen and scholars of England. Only two or three days ago Sir George Cox, the eminent historian of Greece, urged his countrymen to present an address to the Tzar, ' assuring him that in the great work of freeing Europe wholly and for ever from the defilement of Turkish rule we heartily wish him and

---

[1] Roumania gained both independence and the Dobroudja, a large territory and three seaports. Do not be so innocent as to suppose that Roumania in her heart of hearts is actually displeased with the exchange. We know something about that.

all his people "God speed," and that we wait impatiently for the day when the Russian Emperor shall proclaim the freedom of the Christian subjects of the Sultan in the city of Constantine. There only can the work be consummated; and there, by establishing European law, and then withdrawing from the land which he shall have set free, he will have won for himself an undying glory, and, what is of infinitely greater moment, he will have done his duty in the sight of God and man.'

Well, it is a difficult question! The *Guardian*, I see, advises us to annex Armenia. Mr. Forster and Mr. Bryce declared that for the Armenians Russian annexation would be a great change for the better. They received our troops as deliverers, and thousands accompanied them on their retreat into Russian territory. We cannot surrender these poor creatures into the hands of the Turks. What must we do, then? If we retire, the Turk will return, and the last state of Armenia will be worse than the first. Russia is wealthy enough in territory, but what are we to do about the Armenians? This difficulty is not felt by Russians alone, but is shared by Englishmen who have studied the question. One of those whose name stands high in the literary world, remarked, the other day :—

'You have captured Kars thrice this century. Why should you give it up? The Germans did not give up Metz. They did not desire any conquest, they aimed at no aggrandisement; but they kept Metz as a safeguard against another war. Suppose you keep Kars, who has any right to complain? Not the Turks, for the victor has a right to the spoils. As for the other Powers, if they had helped you in your battle, they might have claimed to be heard, but not now.'

Then there is Batoum. It is close on our frontier. It is notorious that it is solely due to a misspelling in an old treaty that it is not already ours. Why should we not rectify the clerical mistake of the transcriber? Batoum is the natural port of Russian Armenia. Its harbour is most frequented by Russian ships. It was certainly not worth while going to war for Batoum or Kars, and the Turkish fleet into the bargain. But now that we have had to go to war, is it not a moral duty to make the Turks pay as dearly as possible for the sacrifices which they have cost us? If we could punish the Turks without annexing any territory, I would not annex either Kars or Batoum; but if that is the only way in which they can be punished, and the Armenians protected, my scruples against annexation may disappear.

There were many of us in Russia when war was declared who believed that the whole of the campaign would be simply a military promenade. Many said, 'We will occupy Constantinople in June or July, and, after dictating in that capital our terms of peace, we will return home with the happy consciousness that we have arranged everything to our satisfaction!' But now we are in November; we have lost 71,000 men killed and wounded; we are spending millions and millions for the war, and we are not yet in occupation of Constantinople. The difficulty and costliness of the enterprise render it impossible for Russia to secure any adequate compensation for her sacrifices. We may get some kind of an indemnity—using the word to signify a war fine—and it is well to distinguish between a war fine and compensation. We have made great sacrifices, and we may yet have to make still greater should Lord Beaconsfield succeed in arraying England against us; but the liberation of the Slavs is now certain. Between the *status quo ante bellum* and the present lie too many precious graves for it ever to be restored. Our military promenade has transformed itself into a gigantic burial procession; but when its end is attained our regret for the brave who have fallen in the fight will be rendered less poignant by the joy with which we shall hail the resurrection of the Southern Slavs.

About the time I was writing the above letter, the same subject was treated in a speech of characteristic fervour and eloquence by Mr. Aksakoff in an Address to the Moscow Slavonic Committee. Here is a slightly condensed translation of that speech:—

The last time I conversed with you we hailed the declaration of war as the approach of a great and difficult historical day. Russia is now at work. We have entered on the busiest harvest time. There is need of labour—hard, obstinate, gigantic labour, corresponding to the gigantic task which we have undertaken. The end of it is not yet in sight, and not soon will the labourers be able to rest. As President of the Slavonic Society, I ought to describe to you the general position of the Slavonic world. But all its attention is fixed on the seat of war, and it lives on the news received daily from the Caucasus and the Danube. On those two points are centred all its most essential and most vital interests. The question of its existence is being decided there, where flows in torrents our Russian blood. Of what else can we speak or think about at this moment? The time has not yet come for calculating results, for the war, with all its accidents and vicissitudes, is still raging fiercely. Let us confess openly and boldly that we have had little opportunity of being spoilt by military success. But it was not on fortune that Russia placed her hopes. Our consolation and our joy are as yet not in the results of the war, but in the wonderful bravery of our soldiers. Never before did their bravery appear with such a sacred halo. Above all that heap of contradictory rumours, scandal, intrigues, calumnies, and accusations produced by the war, rises in unquestionable greatness only the bright image of the Russian soldier—good-natured, simple, and impregnably strong in his religious faith and resignation. He has conquered all the passionate partiality and prejudices of hostile spectators, and now the European world respectfully recognises his military firmness and his humane, genuine goodness of heart. Already half a hundred thousand of these heroes have been put *hors de combat*. And what has been obtained by their superhuman efforts and their precious blood? It is not for us, and perhaps it is not yet the proper time, to judge of the art, the knowledge, the ability, and the talents of the military commanders. We can speak only of what is felt and experienced at present by all Russia. Seeing such an expenditure of efforts and blood, and at the same time such relatively insignificant results, Russia is at a loss to understand the fact. Like one of the old fabled heroes, suddenly paralysed by a wicked enchanter, she is astonished and involuntarily inquires why she is thus powerless. Light! light! as much light as possible—that is what she now requires. In light are health, force, power, and the possibility of recovery. But the light is sparingly granted to us, and comes to us chiefly from foreign distant lands. With morbid eagerness Russia peers into the darkness, and sees, as it were through a mist, only the sad vision of innumerable heroic sacrifices. With morbid eagerness she listens, and hears from the organs of the authorities nothing but the frightful numbers of the killed and wounded and fragmentary, confused intelligence. Is it not strange and disgraceful that all Russians, from the highest to the lowest ranks, are condemned to find the best accounts of the great struggle in the letters of foreign correspondents? That high honour has fallen chiefly to the lot of two English correspondents, Forbes and MacGahan. Their independent, impartial voice has inspired confidence, more than the timid evidence of Russia, carefully filtered by the Censure. We have to thank them for the sympathy which they have shown to our cause, for their pious respect to our soldiers, for their praises of our officers' bravery, and, above all, for the calm, bitter truths they have spoken. That truth, in the translations of Russian newspapers, has spread over all Russia, for there is now scarcely a village in which newspapers are not read.

Yes, the people have been unable to understand, and perplexity has, like a heavy cloud, spread over the land; but only perplexity, not depression. On all that boundless expanse amid the millions of the popular masses, is heard no word of complaint or murmur. No one asks, With what aim, on what account, or for what purpose, do we carry on war? The people are simply unable to understand why it is carried on thus, and not otherwise; why the most heroic war in the world has hitherto given no victories. Not for a single moment has a doubt crept into the popular mind as to the holiness of the enterprise. Never has there been the least hesitation about finishing what has been begun. The people will bear the burden to the end, will bring out on their broad shoulders the dignity of Russia untarnished, and the fulfilment of her historical mission—redeeming with their blood the sins which have prevented victory. These sins, however, lie not at the door of the common people—not on 'the younger brothers,' as people in our class haughtily and patronisingly call them—but on us, the 'elder brothers,' who have committed the deadly sin, which is the root of all our social evils—the sin of forsaking Russian nationality. Never has the difference between the people and the educated classes come out so clearly as in the present war. At a moment when our enemies rejoice, when our soldiers are generously sacrificing themselves in thousands, when those who remain alive have been made stronger and firmer on the anvil of adversity, and anxiously expect from Russia words of encouragement and approval, what voices, rising louder and louder, do they hear? The voices of those who lament and predict for Russia almost thorough defeat. 'Look, look!' say these prophets of evil in a wailing tone, trying in vain to hide their malicious delight and parodying the part of lovers of the people, 'We were right! We tried by every means to oppose that mad, useless war, forced upon Russia by the impudent boldness of the Slavonic Committee, by the raving of the penny-a-liner, and by other fanatics, who unfortunately were not repressed. What have we to do with Slavs, Bulgarians, and Servians? We are, first of all, Russians, and ought to think only of the interests of Russia. What business have we to emancipate and educate others when we have misfortunes enough of our own? All this we said again and again; but we were not listened to; our advice was rejected, and what has been gained?'

So speak the political wiseacres. It may seem idle to pay attention to their expression of cheap wisdom and self-satisfied light-headedness, but, unfortunately, that intellectual and moral emptiness to which every one who forsakes his nationality is condemned, has been invested with a certain significance and has exercised wide-reaching influence. Apart from accidental failures, who but these people are the chief causes of our disasters, of our misfortunes, and of that multitude of sacrifices which they bewail? On whom, if not on them, must fall the responsibility for superfluous bloodshed? Was it not they who strengthened the enemy by holding

back the blow which might have been dealt at the proper
moment, thereby giving him time to prepare? They talk
about a war without cause—a war forced upon them.
Having eyes they see not, and having ears they hear not.
Like foreigners, they cannot understand the natural simplicity of the popular motives and the historical significance of
the struggle. They ought, by their education and social
position, to be the highest organ of the popular consciousness, but in reality they are utterly unacquainted with these
elements of the national spirit which exist in the masses and
create historical life. It may, perhaps, be objected that the
masses know nothing about historical missions and ideals.
In a certain sense this is true. If we ask individual peasants
or a group of peasants what the historical mission of Russia
is, we find, of course, that they know nothing about it. We
ought, however, to remember that neither individuals nor
groups of individuals fully represent a people. A people is
a peculiar, entire organism, ruled by its internal historical
laws, and possessing power of development, memory, aspirations, missions, and aims, all of which can be reflected
only very imperfectly by individuals. The processes of this
organic national life can be perceived and understood only
by a few who have raised themselves by thought and education above the ordinary level. The Russian common people
have little historical knowledge and no abstract conceptions
about the mission of Russia in the Slavonic world; but they
have historical instinct, and they clearly perceive one thing,
that the war was caused neither by the caprice of an autocratic Tzar nor by unintelligible political consideration.
Free from all ambition and all desire of military glory, they
accepted the war as a moral duty imposed by Providence—a
war for the faith, for Orthodox Christians of the same race
as themselves, tortured by the wicked enemies of Christianity.
We had illustrations of this in the Servian war of last year.
Some village communes, desirous of taking part in the great
Christian work, equipped volunteers, and these volunteers,
when we asked them why they wished to go to Servia, replied

simply and sincerely that they wished to suffer and die for the faith. To our 'Conservatives' all this seemed foolishness. They mocked, ridiculed, condemned, calumniated those who were animated with such religious feelings, and succeeded in making the Government doubt the sincerity and genuineness of the popular movement. They even represented the movement as revolutionary, and the consequence of this has been that the ablest Russian actors in the Servian struggle (Tchernayeff and his staff) have not been allowed to take part in the present war. That struggle was the prologue to the great drama which is now being played out, and yet those who are now fighting for the emancipation of the Bulgarians seem to disown the crusade undertaken last year for another branch of the Slav family.

That which the masses have recognised as a moral, absolute duty is at the same time the historical mission of Russia as the head and representative of the orthodox Slavonic world, not yet fully created, but capable of being created, and awaiting its concrete historical form. All the importance of Russia in the great world lies in her peculiar religious and national characteristics combined with external material force—in her Orthodoxy and Slavonism, which distinguish her from Western Europe. She cannot attain her full development without securing the triumph of those spiritual elements in their ancient homes and re-establishing equality of rights for races closely allied to her by blood and spirit. Without the emancipation of the orthodox East from the Turkish yoke, and from the material and moral encroachments of the West, Russia must remain for ever mutilated and maimed. For her the war was a necessity, an act of self-defence, or rather the natural continuation of her historical organic development. Blessed is the country whose political missions coincide with the fulfilment of a high moral duty! The triumph of Russia is the triumph of peace, liberty, and fraternal equality. In this respect her position is very different from that of certain 'Christian' and 'civilised' Powers, whose very existence reposes on the humiliation, enslavement, and demoralisation of foreign races, and, consequently, contains the germ of condemnation and ruin. For the interests of Great Britain, for instance, it is necessary that the population of the Balkan Peninsula should be kept in misery and perpetual minority, that the Turks should rule over the Christians, and that the Bible should be trampled on by the Koran. Turkish atrocities, slaughter of Bulgarians, and wholesale massacres of women and children, all that is permitted by England in order to deprive Russia of her triumph, and is for England a matter of patriotism! So it is likewise for Austro-Hungary, whose existence is founded on injustice to the Slavs. But all this has remained unintelligible to our Conservatives. When the Tzar, who stands and acts before the face of history and is responsible for the destinies of Russia, recognised the necessity of the long-expected struggle, they put in motion all the influences in their power to prevent the declaration of hostilities. Poor unfortunates! They dreamt of stopping the march of history. In that they did not, of course, succeed; but they did succeed in obstructing, diverting, and distorting it. Turkey, unprepared for the struggle, blessed them and made preparations. And what did we do? Who threw into confusion, weakened and kept back the preparations which we had to make? Who strengthened the hands and raised the courage of our enemies? Who undermined from the very beginning the external force and energy of Russia?

Diplomacy, the true reflection of that absence of individuality and nationality, began its work, advantageous for our enemies and disadvantageous for us. Europe, believing the assertions that Russia was unprepared and not disposed for war, subjected us to the torture of gradual humiliating diplomatic concessions. Whose dominant opinions obscured the plain indications of history and prevented Russia from making the preparations necessary for the fulfilment of her mission? Our so-called Conservatives. Thanks to them, the Russian soldier went forth to fight laden with heavy weights which prevented all free exercise of his strength. For the sake of European peace the war was condemned to localisation. The interests of Europe! That is one of those empty phrases in which Europe herself does not believe, but which serve as a bait to catch Russian simplicity and Russian pretensions to Europeanism. Since the natural development, perhaps the very existence, of Russia is inconsistent with European interests, ought we not to contract or even entirely efface ourselves for the tranquillity of the West? But what did the localisation mean? It meant the freeing of Turkey from all trouble with regard to Servia, Bosnia, Greece, Epirus, Thessaly, Egypt, and the directing of all its forces against the Russian army in Bulgaria, the practical result of all which was Plevna, thousands of killed and wounded, the prospect of a winter campaign, and perhaps, after all, a European war.

But this is not all. The Turks know well that for them it is a question of 'to be or not to be,' and therefore for them the war is a war of race and religion. In the Russian popular consciousness it is likewise a war for the faith; but our Conservatives have done all in their power to deprive it of its true significance and to repress all manifestations of the Russian popular spirit by forbidding the use of such words as 'Orthodoxy' and 'Slavdom.' There lies the chief cause of our defeats. The Conservatives, who have abandoned your nationality, are like ships without ballast—light-headed, not serious people. Your inevitable portion in life is light-headedness, superficiality, ignorance, and misconception of the vital wants and interests of the country. Though you are filled with patriotism and knightly honour, and go fearlessly into the fight, meeting death bravely on the field of battle, your conceptions are narrow, your patriotism merely external and political. You care not for the essential elements of Russian nationality. Ready to lay down your life in the struggle with Europe for the outward dignity and independence of the Empire, you at the same time slavishly prostrate yourselves in spirit before European civilisation and the moral authority of the West. Dying at Shipka or Plevna, you sow with your blood the seeds of a new Slavonic, Orthodox world, the very name of which was distasteful to you during your lifetime. O, you who know how to die, but do not know how to live as Russians, will you ever awake and remember who you are?

But enough! We are all of us, in our own way, guilty and responsible for the present state of affairs. Let us put away mutual recrimination, and, bearing each other's burdens, let us take upon ourselves, all together, the sin and the punishment and repentance. A new day is dawning. As the rising sun chases away the terrors of the night, so now the light beaming from the hills of Armenia and the heights of Plevna has shown us our errors and our shortcomings. If we profit by the lesson taught by much blood, the heroic sacrifices will not have been in vain. There must be no hesitation, as there is no choice. We must conquer. Russia cannot retreat or stop, though all Europe should place itself as a wall in our path. Retreat would be treachery towards the suffering Slavs, treason to our historical mission, and the beginning of political death. Let us accept new burdens and make new sacrifices. The nation has an unbounded confidence in the watchfulness and justice of the Tzar. Its historical path has been and is still surrounded and obstructed by many obstacles and many trials; but with the help of God it has overcome them in the past, is overcoming them in the present, and will overcome them in the future!

CHAPTER VI.

THE BULGARIANS AND THEIR LIBERATORS.[1]

'LIGHT, more light!' murmured Goethe on his death-bed. We Russians are in more urgent need of light in order to live. Mr. Aksakoff last month said, 'Light! light! as much light as possible—that is what Russia now requires. In light are health, force, power, and the possibility of recovery.' That light, he said, comes to us chiefly from abroad, and we owe most of it to two English correspondents—Mr. MacGahan and Mr. Forbes. In the name of the whole of the Russian people, which even in its remotest villages has read and re-read their letters, Mr. Aksakoff thanked these Englishmen, not only for their sympathy, but still more for 'the calm, bitter truths' which they had spoken.

Since Mr. Aksakoff spoke Mr. Forbes has published an article in the *Nineteenth Century*.[2] He praises my

---

[1] This letter was written in reply to an article by Mr. A. Forbes (a correspondent of the *Daily News*) in the *Nineteenth Century* of November, 1877, on 'Russians, Turks, and Bulgarians at the Seat of War.'

[2] Mr. Archibald Forbes, in an article in the *Nineteenth Century*, of January, 1880, on 'War Correspondents and the Authorities,' says, that 'during the past six months, war correspondents have been altogether prohibited from accompanying a British army in the field,' which he seems to think is hardly an advance upon the custom of the 'barbarous Muscovite,' who, 'in the recent war admitted all comers decently vouched

countrymen, and I thank him for doing them justice.[1]
for on very simple stipulations.' Mr. Forbes remarks: 'The Russians are wise in their generation. At Plevna, in July, 1877, they sustained a terrible reverse. It fell to the present writer to record that event in its sadness alike and its unavailing heroism. The record neither spared blame nor stinted praise. Its author did his work in the full conviction that his candour would cost him his permission to witness the succeeding episodes of the campaign. But the Russian military authorities, recognising the solid virtue of truthfulness, accepted his narrative of the battle, and authorised its publication in their home newspapers, with their imprimatur on it as an accurate record of a miserable failure relieved by gallant courage.'

[1] Mr. Forbes's testimony to the character of the Russian soldier may perhaps be forgotten. I therefore reproduce it here. He says:

'The Russian private is the finest material for a soldier that the world affords. He is an extraordinary marcher, he never grumbles, he is sincerely pious according to his narrow lights; and this, with his whole-hearted devotion to the Czar and his constitutional courage, combines to make him willing, prompt, and brave in battle. He is a delightful comrade, his good humour is inexhaustible, he is humane, he has a certain genuine and unobtrusive magnanimity, and never decries an enemy. As for Russian "atrocities," 'on soul and conscience,' exclaims Mr. Forbes, with solemn emphasis, 'I believe the allegations of atrocities to be utterly false. Constantly accompanying the Cossacks in reconnaissances, I never noticed even any disposition to cruelty; Cossack lances and Russian sabres wrought no barbarity on defenceless men, women, and children. The Russian of my experience is instinctively a humane man, with a strong innate sense of the manliness of fair play.'

In confirmation of this testimony of Mr. Forbes, is the evidence of an eye-witness whose experience during and subsequent to the war was much more extensive. He dates from Bucharest, February 2, and his letter appeared in the *Times* on February 5, 1880:—

'I have seen so many references in English journals of recent date to the Mussulmans having been driven from Bulgaria that it appears to be necessary once more to repeat the denial which the facts of the case demand. The truth is, that the Mussulmans were not driven from Bulgaria, and *I defy any one to mention one solitary village from which the Mussulman population was expelled during the late war.* In all cases in which the Turkish peasants ran away at the approach of the Russian forces their exodus was the result of their own fears or of the counsels of their Turkish superiors. During the campaign I made the most minute enquiries on this subject of the Turks themselves who remained inside the Russian lines, and *never found a single case* in which a Mussulman was interfered with in any way whatever. I saw many Turks bringing

He criticises their administration, and I thank him still more for his candour in assisting us to remedy our shortcomings. He severely condemns some of our military commanders, and, if true, these things cannot be too plainly exposed. We are not infallible, we Russians, as is the Holy Father, whose infallibility, however, has not prevented him from sympathising with the infidels against whom his no less infallible predecessors preached crusades. Like other nations, we make mistakes, and no one can do us better service than by pointing them out. Mr. Forbes might have spared us a few sneers, but these we can overlook. As a Russian, I do not complain.

But as a Slav I protest against the way in which he abuses the Bulgarians. I am indignant at these

in supplies for the Russians, and they always told me that they were paid for their material. Since the war I have visited the country occupied by the Russians, and in the various villages in which the Mussulmans remained in their homes they invariably assured me that they had not only been unmolested, but had sold all their produce to the Russians for higher prices than they had received in former years. Even in Turkish villages lying on both sides of a *chaussée* where thousands upon thousands of soldiers had passed I was assured that they had lost nothing. It is, however, true that, with very few exceptions, the houses of Turks who fled before the advanced guards of the Russians have been destroyed. All abandoned property was seized by Bulgarians or soldiers, generally by the former, and the bands of Mussulman fugitives, while on the road in flight, were in a great many cases most cruelly and brutally treated by the Bulgarians whom they encountered *en route*. Every Turk with whom I have conversed since the war cordially cursed the Kaimakam or Pasha who advised them to flee from the Russian advance; and when the former residents of ruined villages, deserted by their owners, returned after the conclusion of peace, and found their fellow Mussulmans in adjoining hamlets, who had remained inside the Russian lines, with flocks, herds, and houses unmolested, and with more hard silver in their pockets than they had ever had before, their own hapless condition, contrasted with the prosperity of their neighbours, fully justified the opprobrious epithets bestowed upon their former Kaimakams.'

virulent attacks upon the feeble and those who have no helper. Better—far better—that he should denounce us and spare them. We are strong, but they, the weak, the wretched, the oppressed—is it manly to heap insults upon such as these? They cannot reply. They cannot resent his abuse, no matter how undeserved. And it is undeserved! Mr. Forbes has never been for a single day in Bulgaria under Turkish rule. He has only seen Bulgarians after the Pasha, the Zaptieh, the Tcherkess, and the Bashi-Bazouk had fled 'bag and baggage' before our liberating army. How is he to know what they suffered? Mr. MacGahan, who visited Bulgaria when the Turk was in possession, gives a very different account of the happiness of the Bulgarian. Mr. Forbes has never been across the Balkans. He has never been near the scene of the atrocities. But he admits that the Turks are 'persistent, indomitable barbarians.' He says they 'wield the axe and the chopper of ruthless savages,' that they mutilate the dead and torture the wounded. The Bulgarians are at the mercy of these men. Unless they become renegades,—and the Greeks and other Europeans who serve Turkish interests and persecute the Christians are the very worst kind of renegades,—their complaints and testimonies are not accepted by the Turkish tribunals. Power which elsewhere is believed to be too vast to be entrusted to the most civilised of men, in Bulgaria is exercised by the Ottoman barbarians, and from their will there is no appeal.

In Russia we sometimes indignantly say that the

heart of England is eaten up with love of gold. Surely that cannot be true. Still, what is Mr. Forbes's argument, so eagerly repeated by Turkophiles? Is it not based upon a belief that money is everything? The Bulgarian, unlike 'Devonshire Giles,' has more than nine shillings a week. The fact, in the first place, is not general, but, if it were, does it prove that therefore he needs no liberation? His wives and daughters are at the mercy of the Zaptieh. But is woman's honour really nothing compared with 'nine shillings a week'?

Russians are pretty good judges of courage. Well, there is not one Russian, who fought side by side with the Bulgarians, who does not praise their courage and their simple, determined way of meeting death. Mr. Forbes himself, in his description of the Shipka battles, showed that he shared Russian views upon this matter. A certain way of sacrificing life is a very charming argument in favour of the moral character of the nation.

The result of Turkish oppression on the character of the Bulgarians is not favourable. But even that, in Mr. Forbes's eyes, tells in favour of the Turks, as the Bulgarians are so degraded they are not worth saving. If four centuries of Turkish misrule have brutalised these poor Bulgarians, is it not time that it ceased? Permit me to extract some words of Earl Russell's I find in a pamphlet, given to me by Messrs. Zancoff and Balabanoff, the Bulgarian delegates. He wrote: 'It would indeed be a hopeless case for mankind if despotism were thus allowed to take advantage of its own wrong, and to bring the evidence of its own crimes as the title-deeds of its right. It would be, indeed, a strange perversion of justice if absolute Governments might say, " Look how ignorant, base, false, and cruel people have become under our sway: therefore we have a right to retain them in eternal subjection, in everlasting slavery." ' Yet this 'strange perversion of justice' is employed in order to damage the cause of the Southern Slavs.[1]

[1] Mr. MacGahan, who knew the Bulgarians much better than any other correspondent of the English press, and certainly than Mr. Forbes, wrote of them in the *Daily News*, October 30, 1877 :—' They are a quiet, peaceable, hard-working, thrifty people, more adapted to civilisation and to civilised life than perhaps any other of the Slav races. They are a miserable, wretched, downtrodden race, now gagged, bound hand and foot, with nobody to plead their cause. The attacks that have been made on them, the slanders, accusations, and lies that have been heaped up against them, are disgraceful, shameful, and unworthy anybody who has the least regard for justice and fair play.' Sir Henry Havelock's testimony as to the Bulgarian character contradicts that of Mr. Forbes, and confirms that of Mr. MacGahan. On his return from Bulgaria, Sir Henry Havelock told his constituents he did not think the Bulgarians deserving of the abuse they had received. ' He had lived in their villages and they were undoubtedly a timid people, and in some respects a selfish people. These were vices inherent in a people trodden down for the last four hundred years. On the other hand, he would say that he believed the Bulgarians were improvable, and that they were patriotic and truthful. The sight that struck a stranger was that in the Bulgarian village there was first of all a fine church, and that too where people seemed to have a difficulty in making both ends meet. The next thing they saw was a magnificent schoolhouse. Among the Bulgarians there was a universal love of learning and of improving themselves when opportunity occurred. There were many hundreds of them who had been educated in the American Colleges in Constantinople, or in the Colleges of Roumania. These were educated, refined men, speaking four or five languages, as attached to liberty as we ourselves, and quite as capable of making use of it. Russia has found it necessary to raise a Bulgarian legion, which consisted of Bulgarians, who were sent into action for the first time at Eski-Zagra. That legion numbered 1,800 Bulgarians, and though fortune was against the Russians, out of the 1,800 men, 800 remained wounded or killed upon the field. He thought the people who could act in this

The Russian administration, according to Mr. Forbes, is so very corrupt that a French correspondent has employed himself in collecting and authenticating cases of peculation with a view to its future publication. If that French correspondent does his work thoroughly he will be entitled to the gratitude of the Russian people. There are corrupt contractors I suppose in Roumania, as there have always been in all wars, and perhaps always will be, and we are more interested in their detection and punishment even than Mr. Forbes. But it is a mistake to attach so exaggerated importance to such stories. Gambetta's contractors sold the new levies paper-soled boots. Great fortunes were made by dishonest purveyors to the army of the Potomac; and the English army in the Crimea was not too well served at the commencement of the war. Is there no bribing in England—not even among the detective police?[1] Are 'tips' and 'commissions' known only in Russia? But this is beside the question. If Mr. Forbes will substantiate his accusations, we will thank him for revealing the weak places in our armour. The charge that Russian officers are willing to betray their country for a bribe is too serious to be made in such vague terms. It ought either to be supported with details, dates, and names, or it ought not to be made at all. Vagueness in a case like this is simply cruel to

way during a first essay in war were not unworthy of efforts to improve them.'

[1] In November 1877, when this letter was written, the English papers were full of reports of the trial and conviction of London detectives on charges of corruption.

the whole Russian army. At present it cannot be investigated; but, as an act of simple justice, Mr. Forbes should so far overcome his 'melancholy' as to enable the Russian nation to punish these traitors.

One word more about our officers. I am not a military authority, and do not meddle with these things. Englishmen, of course, who never have any little difficulties between the Horse Guards and the War Office, and who select their Commander-in-Chief, not because he is a Royal Highness, but solely because he is the greatest military genius in the land, cannot understand the existence of such a thing as favouritism in the army. But it is not necessary to resort to such an argument to explain the absence of those generals named by Mr. Forbes from the seat of war. Todleben, for instance, who, according to Mr. Forbes, was only sent for as a last resource, was engaged at the beginning of the campaign in putting the Baltic ports in a position to resist the anticipated attack of the English fleet. Kaufmann remained in Turkestan because he of all men was best fitted for the arduous and responsible work of governing Central Asia. Only foreigners consider Turkestan a sinecure or a Paradise. As for the 'neglected retirement' of Prince Bariatinsky, it is the usual accusation that the Bariatinskys are in too great favour at Court. Both charges cannot be true, and one may be left to answer the other. Count Kotzebue is in command in Warsaw, nor is the position one to be despised. As for the lion-hearted Tchernayeff, to whom I am heartily glad to see Mr. Forbes pays a well-merited word of praise, we regret as much as any one that he was not permitted to take a prominent part in the campaign. But can Englishmen not suspect the reason why the General who fought against Turkey when Russia was at peace, is not appointed at once to high command now that Russia is at war? No one fought in Servia without first resigning his commission in the Russian army, and diplomatic susceptibilities might be offended if the Russian Government were so completely to condone the part played by Tchernayeff in the Servian War.[1]

In conclusion, let me say that Mr. Forbes, as unfortunately so many of our critics, generalises too hastily from imperfect *data*. He jumps to erroneous conclusions, and prefers his own theories to the well-attested evidence of trustworthy eye-witnesses. Mr. Aksakoff thanked him for stating 'calm and bitter truths.' The statements in his last article may be 'bitter,' but they certainly are not 'calm,' and many of them as little deserve the name of 'truths.'

[1] See *ante*, Aksakoff's Speech on Russian Reverses, p. 57.

CHAPTER VII.

AFTER PLEVNA.

PLEVNA fell in December, 1877. Before the New Year our armies were across the Balkans driving before them the defeated and disorganised hosts of the Turks. But by the very triumphs of our troops the interest of the Russian people was directed from the seat of war in the Balkans to the diplomatic campaign in the capitals of Europe, and especially in London. Those who had noted with eagerness the professions of English sympathy with the Slavs in 1876 and 1877 looked forward with some anxiety to see whether at the critical moment these professions would be justified by deeds. The others, who had bestowed but little attention on the preceding phases of the diplomatic conflict, heard with indignation that it was possible the fruits of their victories might be snatched from them by the intervention of foreign Powers. Hence it happened that the attention of Russians was concentrated upon England just at the time when England was most hostile, not merely to Russia, but to the cause of liberty in the East. Those who expected the least were not the most disappointed, and those who had always declared that England was insincere in her professions of sympathy for the

Bulgarians found only too many proofs in the policy of the English Government to support their views. Russia, her hand upon her sword, listened impatiently for some clear declaration of England's policy, either of peace or war, but it only heard across the Continent a confused chorus of blustering voices singing 'Rule Britannia' and the Jingo Song.[1] During that period of prolonged anxiety, some faint idea of the feelings of the Russian people may be gathered from the following extracts from letters written from Moscow between January and April 1878, giving at foot their dates.[2]

We live in a state of feverish excitement. Expecting the worst, we are compelled to take precautions. Already for spring are ordered great military preparations. More sacrifices, more lives, more treasure! Well, so be it, if it must be so. We will not, dare not, shrink from obeying the voice of duty; but my heart sinks within me when I think that our two nations may very shortly be at war. Is it England's will that the Slavs should not be free? Or only Lord Beaconsfield's? We are watching with wonder to see whether your Parliament will vote the money for the war. We have respected every British interest which the English Government specified. We have made concessions which as a Russian I think you have had no right to demand, and such as you never would have made to Russia.

It is impossible for us to listen to those who would re-establish the Turkish Government in Bulgaria, which it cost so many precious lives to overthrow. Is it so unreasonable? Put yourself in our place. If all England was one vast ambulance, if there was not a town or village which had not

---

[1] In England, as in Russia, after the fall of Plevna, equal uncertainty prevailed as to the probable course of England's policy.—*Vide* Appendix, Mr. Froude's preface to *Is Russia wrong?*

[2] January $\frac{26}{14}$, 1878.

its wounded to watch and its dead to lament, perhaps even your Queen might be as determined as our Emperor not to sacrifice the sacrifices of his people by consenting to a shameful peace which left unremoved the causes of the war. Not for that did our brave soldiers perform these deeds of prowess, in spite of all the horrible difficulties and obstacles of a Balkan winter, which have no parallel in history.

* * * * * *

The indignation here is very great.[1] We are almost as disappointed with our Government for its want of energy as we are indignant with yours for its insults and menaces.

Out of deference to British susceptibilities, out of regard to the imaginary interests of your Government—which from the first has been hostile to the cause for which we have shed rivers of our blood—we consented not to enter Constantinople, if England abstained from acts of hostility. And how were we rewarded for our concessions? No sooner is our heroic army brought to a halt within sight of the distant domes of Constantinople, out of deference to the pledges given to your Ministers, than we are startled with the news that the English fleet is ordered to the Bosphorus!

Our promise not to enter Constantinople was strictly conditional upon England preserving a strictly neutral attitude. As we were grateful to your Cabinet for securing the rejection of the Protocol, which enabled us to liberate our brethren in Bulgaria, so were we not less grateful to your Ministers for opening to us the gates of Constantinople.[2] But we were disappointed. Our statesmen, it seems, had not even yet exhausted their concessions. If our Government had listened to the unanimous voice of the Russian people, instead of sending useless warnings, they would have taken the only step, at once rational and dignified, by occupying Constantinople without further loss of time. They

---

[1] February $\frac{22}{10}$, 1878.

[2] This is also the opinion of the Duke of Argyll: 'It cannot be denied that it was precisely such a step as Russia would have desired if she had wished for an excuse to occupy Constantinople.'—*Eastern Question*, vol. ii. p. 93.

have not done that; and in Moscow, as elsewhere in Russia, there are everywhere heard the most vehement expressions of disappointment and of indignation.

* * * * * *

Straightforward manly fighting against us would have created far less irritation here than the malice with which the English Government has persisted in its provocations all through this trying time.[1] We can respect an honest enemy. We are irritated by the intentional insults of a professed neutral. On every side military preparations are being pushed forward with great rapidity. Millions upon millions are being spent in order that we may be ready if Lord Beaconsfield persists in humiliating us first and declaring war afterwards. It is a terrible prospect. Everywhere the horizon is dark. We have, however, only ourselves to blame. If it is a sin for a woman to please everybody, it is still worse for a Government to have that weakness. For every concession we have been rewarded by an insult. If the voice of the Russian nation had been heard there would have been but short work made with these repeated deferences to Lord Beaconsfield. We should have done our duty without hampering ourselves with unnecessary engagements to respect limits which the English Government violates itself the moment it suits it. It was the English, and not the Russians, who forced the Dardanelles, the Treaty of Paris notwithstanding.

The exact terms of peace from San Stefano are published here, and do not by any means give unmixed satisfaction. Everybody is delighted with the extension of Montenegro. Bulgaria is not badly off; but it would be infinitely better if no European interference were allowed next year. Bosnia and the Herzegovina have been sacrificed—to please Austria. Our troops are deeply humiliated by not being permitted to march through Constantinople. The Bulgarian fortresses are to be demolished—to please Europe. Adrianople remains Turkish—to please England and the Sultan. Bessarabia

[1] March 21/9, 1878.

will only be taken from Roumania in exchange for the Dobrudscha. The bargain is not a bad one for Roumania. The narrow strip of Bessarabia belonged to Russia before Roumania even existed. It was in 1856 given up to Turkey, not even to Moldavia. In 1792, by the Treaty of Jassy, Russia exacted from Turkey the right to protect Moldavia, and twenty years afterwards she brought from the Hospodar of Moldavia the district of Mourouri, which is now called Bessarabia. Its value to us arises chiefly because it was torn away from us after the Crimean War. On the whole, while the Slavs are freed, England has spoiled our work. But, as I have said, it is our own fault, for why should we have permitted her to influence our deeds?

* * * * * *

Russia was abused in England for attacking the independence of the Sultan, and was accused of a desire to change the law of the Straits. What do we see to-day?[1] England forces the Dardanelles. Her ironclads anchor in Turkish waters. The Sultan's protest is ignored by his best friends. The much-vaunted independence of the Turk is categorically denied. By her own acts England abolishes the Paris Treaty. In international law the forcing of the Dardanelles is as much an invasion of Turkey as our passage of the Danube. England in this follows our example, with a difference. She waits till her ally is helpless to invade her waters, and she acts solely for her own interest.

We welcome your adhesion to the cause which our sacrifices have rendered it safe for you to adopt. But in your enthusiastic zeal you overdo it. Our heroic volunteers rallied to the aid of the Slavs in the Servian War, and died in the cause to which they had devoted their lives. You abused them for a glaring violation of neutrality, which could only have been committed by so lawless a nation as Russia. One year later, when we went to liberate Bulgaria, England solemnly proclaimed her neutrality and forbade any Englishman helping the belligerents. With regard to helping us,

[1] March $\frac{28}{16}$, 1878.

nothing could exceed the respect paid to that proclamation. But on the other side it was different. The Turks had volunteers in plenty from England—Her Majesty's proclamation notwithstanding. You sent an admiral to command the Turkish ironclads and a general fresh from penance to command a Turkish army. There were others also, but again there was a difference. Our volunteers sacrificed everything—home, family, friends, country, life itself—in order to free their brethren, and one-third fell on Servian soil. Your volunteers, less idealistic and more practical, sold their services for gold, and all of them seem to have succeeded pretty well in preserving their precious skin.

English Turkophiles objected to our arming before the Constantinople Conference—as a 'menace to Europe.' But whilst the Berlin Congress was talked of, was England completely forgetful of guns and loaded revolvers? Is the six millions vote not an imitation of a partial Russian mobilisation?

* * * * * *

Lord Salisbury's Circular fills everyone with indignation.[1] 'British interests' no longer availing to pick a quarrel with Russia, your Government must now reward the respect we showed for the interests you mentioned, by making Turkish power a British interest! Of course, if you insist upon restoring the jurisdiction of the Sultan, there can be no other issue than war. But unless your Government means to force us to fight, why demand what we cannot concede?

We know too well what war is to think of a new war with a light heart. Moscow is silent and sad, although sustained by the consciousness of having achieved a great success in a heroic cause. Few households but mourn for some one who has perished in the fight. Russia is not rich—better be poor than be suffocated with wealth. I would that Russia took nothing for herself—nothing at all. But we cannot sacrifice our honour, forget our sacred duty, and abandon our brethren in Bulgaria to the vengeance of the

[1] April 12 / March 31, 1878.

Turks. Is that not what Lord Salisbury wants? To tear up our Treaty, and to leave these millions of Slavs, who depend entirely upon us for freedom and protection, to the tender mercies of their oppressors?[1]

Turkophiles say 'Europe will protect Bulgaria.' Europe is a mythological lady who does nothing but stupid mischief when she interferes with the Slavs. Much to our regret, Bosnia and the Herzegovina were left to the protection of Europe—and has Europe protected them? There are still outrages, atrocities, refugees—all is unchanged. So it would be in Bulgaria if Russia ceased to guard the liberties which she has won.

You indulge in strange illusions when you say Bulgaria will be Russian if it is not Turkish. Is Greece Russian—Greece that owed her independence chiefly to us? Is Roumania Russian—Roumania whose liberties we defended in so many wars? The point is worth insisting on. We Russians have very clear views on this matter, and no illusions.

We are not particularly satisfied with the San Stefano Treaty. It might have been much better. Montenegro and Bulgaria are not ill treated; but the Herzegovina, Bosnia, Servia, Epirus, Thessaly, Albania—we would have made them all really happy if we could only have consulted the Liberals of England and the Slavs of Austria, and not the English and Austrian Cabinets. With Lord Beaconsfield and the Magyars to please, our work has been spoiled.

As for the Greek provinces, that is England's fault. If poor King George had dared to disobey Lord Beaconsfield, Epirus and Thessaly would belong to him now. But Russians are anxious to give every support possible to Greece. Poor Greece, she trembles with fear because England can destroy her at a moment's notice! but still we hope she may receive her provinces.

---

[1] Fortunately, a few weeks later, Lord Salisbury judiciously modified his views, and concluded the secret agreement with Count Schouvaloff, in which practically he abandoned the position taken up in his Circular.

CHAPTER VIII.

ENGLISH NEUTRALITY.

'THE determination of the Government is for neutrality. But for what neutrality? The House will give me leave to say for an honest and real neutrality. Any other would be unworthy of the nation. The choice is between neutrality and war. If we mean war, let us openly choose it, but if we mean neutrality, let it not be neutrality under the mask of non-interference with one party whilst a secret support is given to the other. If you ask me what are the lines, rules, and limits of a just neutrality, I will tell you them in one word. There is a golden maxim which applies as well to politics as to morals—" Do unto others as you would that others should do unto you." But to England I say, " Do unto others what you have made others do unto you." ' [1]

So spoke Mr. Canning in 1823 concerning the policy of England in relation to the French Expedition to Spain, and if Mr. Canning had been in Lord Beaconsfield's place when the Eastern question was reopened in 1876, the relations between England and Russia would have been very different from

[1] *Memoirs of Canning*, pp. 485-6.

what, unfortunately, they are to-day. For Mr. Canning would have pursued 'a policy worthy of England,' whereas Lord Beaconsfield has persistently acted upon that unworthy policy which Mr. Canning denounced more than half a century ago. How often the best voices in England use almost the same words and express the same counsels as those which Russia has been uttering all through the troubles in the East. When the European concert was destroyed by England's refusal to coerce the Turks on behalf of the Bulgarians, as Mr. Canning coerced the Turks on behalf of the Greeks, all that Russia asked for—and surely it was not too much to ask—was that England would not pursue a policy which Mr. Canning branded as ' unworthy of the nation.' Unfortunately this boon, small as it was, was denied to us, and the pretended neutrality of the English Government during the war excited the bitterest feelings in Russia, which were still more inflamed by its active intervention at the Congress for the re-enslavement of Southern Bulgaria.

It is better not to reopen the old sores. They are, however, far from healed, but festering; and it may not be useless simply to express the universal feeling excited in Russia by your sham neutrality.

No one can object to that phrase 'sham neutrality,' for English neutrality during the war was exactly defined by Mr. Canning as that which is neither honest, nor real, nor just—' Neutrality with the mask of non-interference with one party, whilst a covert support is given to the other.' It is always difficult to put oneself in another's place ; but if Mr Canning's principle is a just one, perhaps you could do that if you imagined Russia playing the part in Afghanistan that England played in our war with Turkey.

The parallel, I admit, is not diplomatically exact. Afghanistan is 'beyond the sphere of Russian interests.' Turkey, on the other hand, is a matter of concern to all the Powers. But these distinctions are little thought of on the battle-field. Their place is in the Cabinet, not in the camp; and although politicians would be more scandalised by Russian neutrality *à l'Anglaise* in Afghanistan, the popular heart is more keenly touched by such covert interference as took place in 1877 in Constantinople than by anything we could do at Cabul.

Russia's war in Bulgaria to Russians was a religious, humanitarian, unselfish struggle, to liberate kinsfolk from cruel oppression—an object in which England professed to be deeply interested.

England's war in Afghanistan is a war confessedly of prestige, of conquest, of rivalry between England and Russia. If Russia had interfered covertly to thwart it, however guilty she might be of violating diplomatic compacts, she would not be interfering to frustrate an object which she ostentatiously professed to have at heart.

How, then, would you like us to do to you in Afghanistan as you did to us in Turkey? Suppose as a 'delicate mark of attention' we had sent the bitterest and most unscrupulous Anglophobe we could find in all Russia to represent us at Cabul, whose notorious conviction was that the preservation of the Afghan kingdom was indispensable to Russian interests, and permitted him to assure the Ameer that the Emperor 'felt true sympathy for him, and the liveliest concern in his happiness and welfare.' Suppose, further, that the whole time of that Anglophobe Ambassador was taken up in intriguing against the progress of the British armies, telegraphing to St. Petersburg horrible legends of British atrocities, and consulting with the Ameer how best to secure the defeat of the English invaders and the intervention of Russia.

Would you regard that as an honest and just neutrality?

It is no new thing in diplomacy for your Ambassador at Constantinople to pursue a much more pronounced pro-Turkish policy than that which is professed at Downing Street. Let me recall one striking instance of this which occurred a little more than a hundred years ago. It furnishes a curious precedent for the conduct of Sir Austin Layard; but I regret to say the British Cabinet has not followed the good example of the Cabinet of Lord North.

In 1772 England was represented at Constantinople by Mr. Murray, who shared your present Ambassador's notions about the terrible danger of 'Russian aggression,' and encouraged the Turks to continue their war against Russia in the presumed interests of Great Britain and of Poland. His conduct brought upon him the grave reproof of the Earl of

Rochford, whose despatch of July 24, 1772, shows that English statesmen in those days had a keener sense of the duties of neutrality than appears to prevail in the Beaconsfield Cabinet. Lord Rochford wrote :—

'His Majesty and his Ministers could not but consider as an extraordinary misapprehension of your duty the advice you have, on your own speculation, upon the intended dismemberment of Poland, taken upon you to give to the Porte, tending directly to retard the conclusion of that pacification which it has been his Majesty's constant wish to accelerate as much as possible. His Majesty,' Lord Rochford continued, "was disposed to overlook the offence; but if it should be made a ground of complaint against you by the Court of St. Petersburg, as is too probable, it will be difficult to find a vindication of so unfriendly a conduct in his Ambassador.' Referring to the partition of Poland, Mr. Murray was informed: 'The commercial Powers have not thought it of such present importance as to make a direct opposition to it or enter into action (as your Excellency supposes necessary) to prevent it. The King is still less inclined to try the indirect method of encouraging the continuance of a Turkish war, which, exclusive of the evils it carries with it of interruption of commerce and devastation, could by no means answer the end in a manner desirable to Great Britain. For if carried on successfully by Russia the Porte must be more and more unable to interfere in regard to the independence of Poland, and, if unsuccessfully, it must greatly weaken an Empire, which, although there has not been lately shown on their part that openness and confidence in his Majesty which he justly deserves, he cannot but look upon, nevertheless, as a natural ally of his Crown, and with which he is likely sooner or later to be closely connected.'[1]

This, however, by the way. The appointment of Sir Austin Layard, unfortunately, was only the beginning of the mischief. Suppose the Persians sent a contingent to assist the Afghans, and Russia were to forbid you to land a single soldier on the Persian coast, or show a single gunboat on the Persian Gulf, and then add to these prohibitions a veto upon, first, the annexations, and then even the occupation of the city of Cabul. For Persia, read Egypt, and for Cabul, Constantinople, and you have exactly two conditions of your neutrality in the recent war.

These conditions were at least open and straightforward. But suppose the most effective force under the Afghan standard was commanded by a Russian officer in receipt of regular pay from the Russian Exchequer until the war actually broke out, and that this force, led by this ex-Russian General, were to make raids upon the Indian plains, bombarding Indian cities with Russian guns, would England tolerate that singular manifestation of Russian 'neutrality?'

Wherein lies the difference between such service by a Russian General and the operations of the Turkish Fleet under Admiral Hobart? The first shell fired on the Danube into the Russian ranks was fired

[1] Mahon's *History of England*, vol. v. App. p. 37-38.

by the English Admiral from an English gun, as he swept on an English-built gunboat down the river to the sea, amid the enthusiastic applause of the English press

In the American War the Government of the Union was indignant at English neutrality, but no Englishman commanded the fleets or armies of the Confederates. It was held to be an offence merely to build the ships and supply the weapons for the South. As Lowell sang :—

> You wonder why we're hot, John?
> Your mark wuz on the guns,
> The neutral guns, thet shot, John,
> Our brothers an' our sons.

Russia would have been well content if England's assistance to the Turks had been limited to the supply of munitions of war to the Turks, although Russia has not even supplied a rifle to the Afghans, who, indeed, were armed by the English Government in hopes of their becoming our enemies. I think this latter fact will not be denied even by the 'veracious' Lord Salisbury.

How would England have enjoyed the news that the Ameer had appointed a distinguished Russian cavalry officer to the post of General of Brigade in order to 'raise and discipline' a non-existent gendarmerie in Afghanistan? Would you have heard with composure that, with the sanction and approval of the Russian Government, he had been joined by the following officers on half-pay—two colonels, three majors, seven captains, and an adjutant[1]—most of

[1] *Blue Book*—Turkey, I. (1878), 461.

whom, in flagrant defiance of the proclamation of neutrality, took an active part in resisting the British arms at Cabul?

I hardly think that if the Afghans at the battle of Charasiab had been commanded by a Russian officer the English Government would have manifested the same composure which was displayed at St. Petersburg when ex-Colonel Baker covered the retreat of Sulieman Pasha from the Balkans.

And here, to anticipate objections, allow me to say that I am not going to defend the intervention of General Tchernayeff in Servia from the point of view of International Law. It was condemned at the time by our own Government, and can only be justified by referring to considerations of race, religion, and humanity, which only occasionally combine in sufficient force to justify such enterprises, and such ties, so far as I know, do not exist between the English and the Turks. But General Tchernayeff in Servia should rather be compared to Sir Philip Sydney in Holland, of whom you may well be proud, than to Hobart Pacha in the Black Sea.

England in her advance did her best to detach the hill tribes from Afghanistan, if not to turn their arms against the Ameer.

If Russia had brought all her influence to bear in a contrary direction, and supported her representatives by an army corps in the passes of the Hindoo Koosh, I fear we should have had some little difficulty in persuading English people that we were really observing neutrality, although we should be doing no more than you did in Greece.

Even after the war was over, you subsidised the Lazes at Batoum, who were resisting our arms.[1] This, I suppose, will not be denied. But it is not generally known to what an extent the English Government was committed by its officials to the support of the Turkish cause. I append in a footnote[2] a curious manifesto signed by your Consuls Blunt and Merlin, which was addressed to the Hellenes, who had taken arms against the Turks in May, 1878. It is somewhat strange 'neutrality' which, even after peace was made with the Turks, permits your Consuls to describe Russia to the Greeks as 'the great and common enemy of yourselves and Europe.'

Two unofficial Englishmen had a good deal to do in promoting the Rhodope insurrection; and Sir Austin Layard exerted himself to the utmost to excite oppo-

[1] Duke of Argyll, *The Eastern Question*, vol. ii. p. 137.

[2] *To the Greeks in Insurrection.*

Esteemed Hellenic chiefs and men.—We are sent by the Government of our august Queen, the Sovereign of Great Britain, as mediators between yourselves, insurgents, and your fellow-countrymen the Mussulmans. Both of you are men carrying on a struggle which menaces the ruin of both peoples—for the great and common enemy of yourselves and Europe has overrun with his armies Turkey in Europe and Asia, so that having abolished Mussulman sovereignty, it threatens to change to Slavs, both Mussulmans and Christians, to which, we believe, both peoples are opposed.

Be united then, and after the enemy shall have been driven from your country, Europe, taking into consideration your just complaints, will accord to each what is right; and thus, we are convinced, you will live together as brothers. In the name then of the Government of our august Sovereign we counsel you to lay down your arms.

       Signed BLUNT,
             MERLIN.

sition to the Treaty of San Stefano, just as Mr. Butler Johnstone, professing to speak in the name of Lord Beaconsfield, is said to have eagerly advised the Turks to resist the pressure of the Constantinople Conference, while Lord Salisbury used quite a different language.

I forbear to allude to the speeches wherein your Prime Minister encouraged openly the resistance of the Turks, for, perhaps, it is the Turks who have most reason to complain.

Can you wonder that a neutrality *à l'Anglaise* is regarded as very little better than war *à la Russe*?

'We were neutral,' reply some Englishmen; 'but we were bound to show a friendly neutrality to the Turks;' and, therefore, I suppose, a hostile neutrality to Russia. 'Neutrality and friendly!' once exclaimed Kossuth, 'a steel hoop made of words.' *Contradictio in adjecto*! But English statesmen have themselves exposed the hollowness of the pretext. Earl Granville, in his despatch to Count Bernsdorff of September 15, 1870, wrote: 'It seems hardly to admit of doubt that neutrality, when it once departs from strict impartiality, runs the risk of altering its essence, and that the moment a neutral allows his impartiality to be biassed by predilection for one of two belligerents, he ceases to be a neutral. The idea, therefore, of benevolent neutrality can mean little less than the extinction of neutrality.' Again, on October 21, Lord Granville wrote; 'Good offices may be benevolent, but neutrality, like arbitration, cannot be so.' When Mr. Canning and Lord Granville,

English Foreign Ministers in 1823 and 1870, agree in condemning such a 'neutrality' practised by England in the late war, need you be surprised if the conduct of the English Government during the recent war has not contributed to the realisation of that cordial friendship between England and Russia which is so desirable for both?

CHAPTER IX.

ON THE EVE OF THE CONGRESS.[1]

REALLY, it is quite bewildering! Transformation scenes succeed each other so rapidly that one begins to lose consciousness of one's own identity! It is but six months ago that I was in England. Englishmen then, although a little indignant at the sufferings of their interesting *protégé*, the Turk, still retained their self-possession. Even those who hated us poor Russians—describing us, as Mr. Carlyle said, as if we were 'evil spirits'—at least paid us the compliment of believing that we were not mere children. Before we took Plevna there were many who attributed all sorts of daring designs to my countrymen. They were accused of meditating the annexation of Constantinople, the invasion of India, the capture of Egypt, the subjugation of the world, and some other enterprises equally easy. 'Russia is ruthless, reckless; her ambition and audacity have no bounds,' cried some very penetrating politicians. I ventured sometimes to protest, and, of course, protested in

[1] This letter was written from Moscow, on June 7, 1878, on the Eve of the Congress, when the fact that the Schouvaloff-Salisbury Memorandum had annulled the Salisbury Circular, was as yet only known to the three Governments who were privy to its negotiation, and to Mr. Marvin—the indiscreet copyist of the English Foreign Office.

vain. One likes to be feared, but one is bound in honour to calm people whose fear takes the shape of a kind of moral paralysis. But the more frankly I spoke, the less were my words accepted. 'Russia,' I was told, 'might veil her designs while she was still in the midst of the battle; but the moment she is victorious, she'll throw off the mask, and will reveal the natural aggressiveness of a military despotism,' and so on.

Well, Russia has been victorious. Moltke, the great German military genius, never admitted for one moment that our troops could pass the Balkans in winter time. The Russians did, however, undertake that impossible thing, and have succeeded. They are now, and for many, many weeks past have been, at the gates of Constantinople. The whole of the world is now informed of the San Stefano Treaty. Far from fulfilling the fears of my English friends, Russia has displayed a magnanimity which is even culpable. The prostrate barbarian is not only allowed to live, but even to tyrannise still over a great many Christians. In that Preliminary Treaty Russia is wrong, and I am jealous of the good which united Europe may do in improving it[1] whilst Russia had the power to strike the great blow herself. We lost more than one hundred thousand Russians, and *what* Russians? the best, most self-sacrificing and gallant men we had—in order to stop half-way, and leave everything unfinished.

---

[1] Jealousy, alas! quite unfounded, for as the result proved, United Europe did anything but improve it.

People tell me here, 'Oh! but you see we are on good terms yet with England; we could not forget her wishes.' Of course, if our first object in life is to please Lord Beaconsfield we are right in being wrong. But I don't see that in the least, and not for the life of me shall I ever take your Premier as the best representative of the real England. I know many of your countrymen, as generous and as chivalrous as some of our departed Russian friends; and I think it unjust not to insist upon this point, even if Lord Beaconsfield should choose the Congress as a new arena for his threats and insults, and even if war between Russia and England should be the result of the coming 'friendly' meeting.

The curious fact, however, to which I should like to allude, is that now—since we have 'the key of Constantinople in our pocket'—we are all at once described as so weak that we dare not defend even the humble half-measure called 'The Stefano Treaty' against one Power. Russia, yet unsuccessful, was a terror to Europe. Russia, victorious, turns out to be a nonentity to be sneered at! This, indeed, is a startling transformation. The 'Colossus' turns out to be a wretched weakling, trembling at the sight of a drawn sword!

It did not need the jingling of Six Millions Vote of Confidence, 'warranted not to be spent,' to convince us that England was rich. In fact, we thought she was so rich that she would not have needed to have gone a borrowing to raise so small a sum. Anyone can borrow, even poor, dear Austria!

The other warlike demonstrations that followed frighten, perhaps, some old English ladies, but here they raise only a good-natured smile. The handful of your Reserves—about one army corps—give us a very pacific view of your warlike threats. Surely you do not think that 40,000 of reserves can terrify a military empire that counts its soldiers not by tens, but by hundreds of thousands? We have at this present moment more Turkish prisoners of war in Russia than all your reserves.

But what amuses us and fills me with doubts whether the England which I know and love so well has not disappeared altogether, is the delusion that Russians are to be frightened into compliance with Lord Beaconsfield's dictates by the sudden apparition of your Indian soldiers. Chinese rather like sham demonstrations of this sort, and employ pasteboard dragons, and shields painted with horrible demons, to frighten European soldiers. Why should Lord Beaconsfield imitate the Chinese?

England—and we Russians know it very well—is the greatest naval Power in the world. But it is not given to one nation to be supreme in both elements. To attempt it, is to provoke failure. You can bring, not one, but several handfuls of Orientals to threaten us, but you'll obtain the very opposite result to that which you desire. You should always keep in mind that Russians are not cut off from all access to official information published by your Indian Office, and we also understand why certain measures are taken when Parliament is prorogued.

Why should we be afraid of your Indian soldiers? Turkey had more soldiers to oppose to our armies than England can put in the field, but that did not save her from defeat. Your Premier forgets that, although Russia has made but small annexations in Asia compared with England, yet we govern enough territory there to understand the conditions of Empire in the East. Asiatic dominion impairs, instead of increasing, the power of intervention in Europe.[1] You send 6,000 Sepoys to Malta. Well and good. But, in order to be able to get these 6,000 Asiatics, you have to maintain nearly 60,000 English troops in India.

Since the Crimean War India has become a greater drain than ever upon your resources in men. Have you not had to keep 15,000 more English soldiers in India since the Mutiny than when you fought us at Sebastopol? And these 15,000 Englishmen, were they not worth many 6,000 sepoys?

Your Indian Viceroy, I see, has been taking measures of precaution in India, which somehow strangely conflict with the impression that India is glowing with enthusiastic fervour to send her sons to fight the battles of England. The taxes are being increased, the armies of your tributary princes are complained of as too large, and the native press is to be put under the censure.

Lord Napier's celebrated Minute on your Indian Army is too categorical in its exposition of the military dangers of the English position in India to be

---

[1] Afghanistan, to wit.

effaced by bringing 6,000 sepoys to Malta. According to the Indian Commander-in-Chief, the natives of India do not seem particularly devoted to their Empress. Were not the sepoys the greatest danger to English rule during the Mutiny?

But why should these unworthy demonstrations be continued? Surely no serious Englishman can believe that Russia will yield to England that which she believes to be unjust, because Lord Beaconsfield has added to the forces of the Empress 40,000 reserves and 6,000 sepoys? We knew before these 'spirited demonstrations' that England was rich, and we also knew the precise limits of your military resources.

Why do you forget our history? Napoleon took Moscow, but he did not conquer Russia; nor did England, with all her allies, succeed in doing more than capture Sebastopol. Vulgar insults and ridiculous threats do a great deal of harm—but not in the sense some people imagine.

I say 'England,' not Lord Beaconsfield, for it seems as if Englishmen, bold enough to be guided by some other consideration than a fear of embarrassing the Cabinet, form a very weak minority for the present, and our diplomatists are right in having only your Cabinet in view when they write and speak about England. But a party may be weak in a certain sense, and nevertheless worthy of the admiration of all who can yet admire that which stands on a high moral level. Mr. Bright and his few friends did not succeed in preventing the Crimean

War. Mr. Gladstone, Lord Derby, Lord Carnarvon, Mr. Chamberlain, Mr. Fawcett, Mr. Courtney, and some few others will not prevent its repetition if Lord Beaconsfield insists upon his own objects; but the following generations will not forget their protests, even if at present they should be made in vain.

CHAPTER X.

AFTER THE CONGRESS.[1]

ENGLISH papers are still filled with accounts of Lord Beaconsfield's triumphs; his reception at the Guildhall on the same night that a majority of 143 in the House of Commons accorded him full Parliamentary approval for all his doings. It is all very charming for Lord Beaconsfield, no doubt; but was it not a little cruel to bring him in the last scene of the comedy to Guildhall? Is it not associated in history with his terrible threat, 'to fight three campaigns in defence of the integrity and independence of the Ottoman Empire?' Were there no echoes of his former speeches lingering about the gorgeous roof to mock the speaker whose voice has been so often uplifted there in defence of a policy which is violated by almost every clause of the Treaty which he was applauded for signing? Pardon my frankness if I say that the English seem, indeed, to have short memories, and are capable of rapid conversions; but it puzzles me to explain the triumph accorded to Lord Beaconsfield by men who, some months ago, were abusing Mr. Glad-

---

[1] The following letter was written on August 25, 1878, after the 'triumphant' return of the British Plenipotentiaries from Berlin.

stone for recommending far less sweeping changes than those which Lord Beaconsfield has sanctioned. Are they only making believe now, or were they making believe then?

Lord Beaconsfield, according to some of his adherents, seems to be infallible. Now such, I need hardly say, is not the view in Russia. We have his utterance *ex cathedrâ* to prove that Turkey is strengthened by losing half her territory. If any one else had ventured to argue in that way last year who would have listened to him? But then, of course, every one has not the gift of making people believe that black is white merely by saying so. Henceforth it strikes me that we have now two Popes. I thought one was already more than enough; yet it seems that the Pope at Downing Street makes quite as exhaustive demands upon the faith of the Faithful as the Holy Father at the Vatican.

If we had entered upon the war simply to annihilate Lord Beaconsfield's policy, the Berlin Treaty would be a great and complete success. But, in drawing the sword, we did not even think of Lord Beaconsfield, except as a possible foe. Our object was a nobler and a higher one; and, therefore, although Lord Beaconsfield at Berlin gave up entirely his former policy and became one of the partitioners of the Ottoman Empire, he nevertheless, according to our views, did a great mischief, which rankles in the heart of every true Russian. There is hardly a demand that our diplomats have made for Russia that your Premier has not granted kindly enough. But the proposals which extended the area of freedom and emancipated the Slavs—these he has curtailed with the willing assent of interested and designing intriguers, who see in the dissatisfaction of those betrayed peoples the effectual instruments for achieving in the future their aggressive designs.[1]

England has conspired with Austria to deprive the Slavs of the liberty which we promised them, and to betray them into the hands of those from whom our brothers died to free them for ever.

Had Bulgaria been entirely free, Russia would have had no reason for interfering again. The weaker Bulgaria is, the more she depends upon us, and the more absolutely she is in our power.[2]

It is a terrible game! It involves the betrayal of a sacred trust, of a solemn pledge. But the reckless enthusiasm, the sympathies of the Russian people, have not been extinguished at Berlin. We keenly feel the shame of having surrendered the interests of those who had no other protector. England, through her representatives, was their persecutor, and we unfortunately played at Berlin a part condemned for

---

[1] 'We baulked and defeated Russia in what she sought on behalf of oppressed and suffering humanity; in what concerned our own pride and power we suffered, not only suffered, but effectually helped her to get her way.'—Mr. Gladstone, 'The Friends and Foes of Russia,' *Nineteenth Century*, January 1879, p. 179.

[2] On this point the Earl of Derby's words are very clear. 'A large Bulgaria reaching to the sea would be necessarily much more independent of Russian influence. It would contain a mixed population not exclusively Slav, and by mere contact with the sea would be more open to your influence. But the small State is also entirely inaccessible to you, and the influence exercised over it will be exclusively Russian, and if you want to put pressure on the people there is not a point where you can do it.' Speech in House of Lords on Berlin Treaty, July 18, 1878.

nearly two thousand years—that of a 'practical' Pilate.

The indignation throughout the whole of Russia on hearing of the first exaggerated reports of the abandonment of the cause of the Southern Slavs at the Congress was very intense. This feeling found what now appears perhaps even too vehement an expression in the speech of Mr. Aksakoff, although at that time, I must admit, he only expressed the universal opinion at Moscow. Addressing the Moscow Slavonic Committee on July 4, 1878, he said:—

Gentlemen,—A funeral oration inaugurated our two last meetings. Four months ago we attended the funeral of a man, illustrious by his intelligence, who freely gave his life to serve a sacred cause—the liberation of the oppressed Slavs. We were then deploring the premature death of the civil administrator of Bulgaria—Prince Tcherkassky, whose fame will ever be remembered in connection with one of the most notable deeds in the history of modern Christianity. At that time, in truth, the whole of Bulgaria had begun to enjoy a new life, and there remained not one single enslaved Christian in the wide expanse of territory on which was dispersed the Bulgarian people, from the Danube to the Maritza. We now meet once more, and are we not again met together to attend a funeral—not, indeed, of one man, but of many, many thousands, the populations, not of towns merely, but of whole countries—to attend the burial, as it were, of all hopes of liberating Bulgarians and of securing the independence of the Servians?[1] Are we not now burying the cause which all the Russians have at heart—the legacies, the traditions of our ancestors, our own aspirations, the

[1] In so far as Servia was concerned these exaggerated rumours were fortunately as false as Mr. Aksakoff declared them to be; the independence of Servia, secured at San Stefano, was not annulled, but ratified by the Congress.

national renown, the honour, the conscience of the Russian people? No! no! I repeat the word No! Were all the victories and sacrifices of the war, the untold burdens cheerfully borne by the mass of the Russian people, no more than a fable, a legend, the outpouring of an overheated brain? Who knows? But if all this has actually taken place, can it be true, that there is any truth in the reports which reach us on every side of shameful concessions at the Congress—tidings placed before the Russian nation (and never contradicted by the Russian Government) causing it now to redden with shame, now exciting the pangs of conscience, and then overwhelming her with a heavy load of uncertainty? And what revelations are here made public? Lies! Even if letters and telegrams should exhibit Russia in such a monstrous light, that very monstrousness would be the best voucher that this is not truth, but falsehood. Not that we doubt the truth of what refers to the plotting between Great Britain and Austria, and the pretensions put forward by these Powers, hectored by the German Chancellor. In no wise. The injustice, the insolence of the West towards Russia, and in general towards Eastern Europe, has no limit, and is now, as always, immeasurable. This axiom in our history, together with all historical warnings, are forgotten by Russian diplomatists and by those who pull the strings at St. Petersburg. Only too probable, alas! appears to us what is told of the conduct of our representatives at the Congress when we remember 'the services' for which Russia had to thank her national diplomacy during the last two years. But by whatever 'generous concessions' our diplomatists may have gratified the enemies of Russia at the cost of our national honour, can it be that Russia, in the person of her august and revered representative, has pronounced the last word? Nay, we will not believe this generosity, which renders useless that shedding of torrents of Russian blood and makes light of the national honour, can possibly meet with the approval of our supreme ruler. We refuse to believe it, and shall persist in refusing to do so till it appears under the authorisation of an official announcement on the part of the Government. To do so sooner would be no less a crime than that of abusing the dignity of the ruling power which sways the destinies of this great nation! And in truth, is it possible that such a mountain of absurdities, that heart-rending folly which characterises the decisions of the Congress, that long list of insults levelled against Russia, could ever become a *fait accompli*? Judge for yourselves. What caused this war to break out? What prompted Russia to engage in it? A general massacre of populations which inhabit Southern Bulgaria. What problem, then, was this war intended to solve? To deliver the Bulgarian peoples from the Turkish yoke. Never was such an universal interest, an interest so keenly excited by any war. Never did any war originate such sacrifices prompted by sublime charity, and deserve in the full meaning conveyed by these words the name of a national war.

By the Treaty of San Stefano, to which was appended the signature of the Emperor of Russia and that of the Sultan himself, the whole of Bulgaria, on this side and on the farther side of the Balkans, was raised to the rank of a Principality; and arrangements were made to summon a national assembly. At length, O long-afflicted land, for a moment you believed yourself free; a bright future which seemed to be dawning filled you with exultation; resuscitated, you now breathed freely, when lo, as would now appear, with the sanction of that self-same generous liberator of Russia, Bulgaria is sawn asunder alive, and the best, the richest portion of her territory, that beyond the Balkans, finds itself anew under the Turkish yoke! And the Russian hosts, those very armies which shed their life-blood to secure the independence of Southern Bulgaria, have assigned to them the duty of rivetting upon them once more the chains of the vanquished monster, to surrender in person to Turkish brutality the Christian women and children who hailed the Russians as friends and deliverers! In St. Petersburg, according to the papers, there are those who dare to insult our Bulgarian brethren for distrusting Russian promises; but let us ask whether, after so shamefully breaking our word, are we worthy of the confidence and of the affection of this people? Alas! poor Russian soldiers! You will shrink now from looking in the face your 'younger brothers.' And how is it that you, too, thanks to the Russian diplomacy, have now fastened upon you the odious stigma which attaches to the word 'traitor'? What, then, has happened? Is it that we have met with some terrible disaster, worse than what occurred on the fatal day of Sedan—for this even did not move France to make peace or deter her from continuing a struggle which lasted five months longer? No disaster has occurred, no battle, no defeat. Beaconsfield stamped his foot, Austria held up a threatening finger, Russian diplomats were terrified, and all was surrendered. What makes this the more difficult to believe is that Russia, however others may deceive themselves about the lot of the inhabitants of Southern Bulgaria, knows full well that the hope of reform, grounded on the appointment of a Christian governor and divers improvements is illusory.[1] History furnishes the Russian Government with too many proofs to

[1] Alas! so far as the larger portion of Southern Bulgaria was concerned, the Congress did not even provide for the appointment of a Christian Governor, but redelivered to the direct authority of the Porte, without taking any guarantee for reform, one third of the Bulgarian land which Russia had freed. I cannot understand how it is that Englishmen —even Liberal Englishmen—should so strangely ignore the fact that 'Eastern Roumelia,' so far from being co-extensive with Southern Bulgaria, does not include one half the Bulgarian lands south of the Balkan. In 1876, Mr. Gladstone wrote:—'If it be allowable that the Executive power of Turkey should renew at this great crisis, by permission or authority of Europe, the charter of its existence in Bulgaria, then there is not on record, since the beginning of political economy, a protest that man has lodged against intolerable misgovernment, or a stroke he has dealt at loathsome tyranny, that ought not henceforward to be branded as a crime.' In 1878, the Turkish charter of absolute authority in South Western Bulgaria, annulled by Russia at San Stefano, was deliberately restored by Europe at Berlin, but against this outrage has even Mr. Gladstone so much as uttered a single protest?

the contrary; and, at the Conference at Constantinople, did it not moreover forcibly demonstrate the insufficiency of such guarantees? England did not permit the discussion of such reforms in the wide sense of administrative autonomy, and authorised it solely with a view of facilitating with some show of decency the withdrawal by Russia of her claims. Not only was it in opposition to British interests to relieve the Southern Bulgarians, but she used every effort to efface from Southern Bulgaria every vestige of nationality, and even the name itself. If, after the not very dignified withdrawal of the Imperial Commissary of Philippopolis to Tirnova; if, after the retrograde movement of the Russian armies across the Balkans, Turkish barbarities should recommence; if blood be shed anew; if once more Turkish outrages on Christian women recommence, and we hear again of such things, Russia, her blood boiling with indignation and smarting with many wounds—would she not rise to a man and fall on the Turk, sending off to her diplomatists a good budget of maledictions? Fall on them! But in what way? Is it not to guard against such generous Russian fervour that all Beaconsfield's measures of precaution have been taken, and taken, it would seem, in concert with Russian diplomatists? The English Minister, with all the candour of one who knows the forces he has at his back, has he not said openly that his object is to protect Turkey against victorious Russia, be the Christians martyred as they may?—in a word, that the Congress is nothing more nor less than an undisguised conspiracy against the Russian people? A conspiracy plotted with the concurrence even of the Russian representatives themselves. Experience having shown that the Balkans, viewed hitherto as an insurmountable natural obstacle, could not prevent the advance of our armies, the Congress has issued orders for the construction of a line of forts (of course with the aid of English engineers and English money) along the whole extent of the Balkan range, which, manned by Turkish garrisons, will render the Balkans virtually impregnable.

Was it for this, then, that our brave troops toiled so indefatigably, and died so heroically, in escalading the Balkans in the height of winter? Without a deep blush of shame, without heartfelt grief, can the Russian henceforth pronounce the words Shipka, Carlova, Bayazid, and all those names of places rendered illustrious by the valour, thickly strewn with the graves of our heroes, given over now to be dishonoured by the Turk? Our soldiers, on their return home, will not thank those diplomatists who wrested from the Congress the fruits of this campaign. And some would have us believe that all this has received the sanction of our supreme ruler. Never! Our diplomacy seeks to console itself by the thought that the Congress has permitted the Danubian portion of Bulgaria to be elevated to the rank of a Principality. Oh, touching simplicity! Have we reason to believe that England and Austria will take no measures necessary to secure their interests here—measures which will effectually paralyse all the importance of the Principality, and bring it under their influence in all matters political and economic? Details are relegated to special commissions in the Embassies at Constantinople, and in these details England and Austria will entangle the Bulgaro-Danubian Principality, and will enclose her in an iron band, out of which she will find no further means of escape! Words fail when we correctly characterise this betrayal, this perfidy, done in the face of historical tradition and of the duty and sacred mission assigned to Russia. To abide by all this is no more or less than to formally abdicate one's post as the chief representative of all the Slav races and of all the orthodox East; it means to lose, not merely our influence and to sacrifice our interests, but to forfeit the esteem of these races, our natural allies—the only allies we really have in Europe. The liberty, the intellectual development, the moral progress of the Slavonic nationality can only be attained by union and an *entente cordiale* with the Russian people. .... Russian diplomacy thinks otherwise! And was it then for this that the Russian nation, the only powerful and independent portion of the Slavonic race, has shed its precious blood, offered as a holocaust hundreds of thousands of her sons, has reduced herself temporarily almost to beggary, and in very deed won the thorny crown of martyrdom, only to make her victories themselves the means of securing her humiliation and depriving her of her proud position among Slavonic peoples, of enlarging the possessions and increasing the power of their enemies, and of submitting the orthodox Slavs to the authority of German and Catholic adverse elements? Martyr in a vain cause, despised conqueror, admire the work of thy hands!

When, during the Constantinople Conference, we discussed—our cheeks burning—the buffets received there, what shall we say now of these solemn insults of daily recurrence? And the Russian diplomatists, if the journals are to be credited, after each blow content themselves with attesting the same, and for Russia only ask in return a voucher of disinterested motives. Yes, very disinterested indeed, and the voucher is forthcoming. Words fail one, the mind is chilled and bewildered by the extravagant conduct on the part of the Russian diplomatists by this terrible display of servile folly. The bitterest enemy of Russia and of her Government could not conceive of anything more prejudicial to her peace. See, then, our true Nihilists, for whom exists neither Russia nor Russian nationality, nor orthodoxy nor traditions, beings who resemble our Bogoluboffs, Sasulitch and Company, deprived like these of all sympathy with history, of all sentiments of ardent national enthusiasm. Judge for yourselves who then among these, whether the mere anarchists or the Government Nihilists, not less lacking faith and patriotism, who, in point of fact, are those Russia has most cause to fear, who are those most prejudicial to her moral development and her civic dignity? Is it possible that Turkey, which threatened, by audaciously resisting its authority, to make a dead letter of the Congress, should be called upon to play the part of guardian angel of

Russian honour? No; be the doings of the Congress what they may, however our national honour may be insulted, her crowned guardian, he lives, he is strong, he is also her natural avenger! If the mere reading of the papers makes our blood boil in our veins, what, then, must experience the Sovereign of Russia, who bears the weight of the responsibility which history will lay on his shoulders? Did not he himself give the appellation of a 'holy undertaking' to the war in question? Is it not he who, on his return from the Danube, proclaimed triumphantly to deputations from Moscow and other Russian towns 'that the holy undertaking should be completed?' Terrible are the horrors of war, and the heart of our Sovereign cannot lightly call on his subjects for a renewal of deaths, and a fresh shedding of blood—on his subjects ready for all sacrifices. And yet it is not by concessions which are detrimental to the national honour and conscience that one can counteract disasters. Russia wishes not for war, but less still would she desire a peace which dishonours her. Question the first you meet in any way you please: would he not prefer to fight till blood could flow no more and strength offer no further resistance if thus the Russian name could be rescued from opprobrium, and the part of a traitor should not be played in the presence of his brethren in Christ? There is no disgrace in sometimes yielding to superior forces of united enemies after long-contested and heroic battles, as we ourselves yielded in 1856, without detriment to our glory, as recently yielded France. But to give way preventively, without a battle, without firing a shot: this is not a concession, it is a desertion. But who, then, in Europe would have quite decided on war? Not England, indeed, who has only her Indian monsters on land, for even in a naval warfare she would suffer more than we should. Not Austria, indeed, whose whole body is no more than a heel of Achilles, who, as well she may, fears more than anything else a war with Russia, for the raising of the Austrian question depends on the will of Russia alone! . . . Invincible, invulnerable is the Russian Czar, from the moment when, with a firm belief in the mission of his people, putting aside thoughts about the interests of Western Europe—interests hostile to our own—he will lift up, as say our ancient chronicles, 'with dignity, severity, and honour,' the standard of Russia, which is also the standard of the Slavs and of all Eastern Christians. The nation is agitated, irritated, troubled each day by the proceedings of the Congress at Berlin, and awaits, as manna from on high, the final decision of its ruler. It waits and hopes. Her hope will not prove vain, for the words of the Tzar will be fulfilled: 'The holy undertaking shall be accomplished.' The duty of faithful subjects is to hope and believe, but the same duty forbids us to keep silence. In these days of turpitude and iniquity, which raise up a wall of separation between Tzar and country, between the wishes of the Sovereign and those of his people, is it possible that an answer should ever reach us from high quarters in these authoritative words—'Silence, honest tongues! let us now listen to no words but those which give utterance to flattery and lying!'

Such were the glowing and fervent words of the fearless Aksakoff; which, I repeat, faithfully expressed the feelings of us all in Moscow, at the time when we were daily receiving the exaggerated reports of the extent to which the Treaty of San Stefano was spoiled in Congress.[1]

But while we did not suffer, he, although but the exponent of our opinions, was less fortunate. He was exiled, not, I am happy to say, so far away as to Siberia, as was reported in the English press, but nevertheless to a place even more inaccessible. He

[1] Russians are not alone in believing that the Berlin Congress did nothing but mischief. The Duke of Argyll says—'The Congress, and the English Plenipotentiaries especially, did nothing but sanction what they could not prevent, and to limit to the utmost those liberties which from very shame they could not altogether refuse.'—*Eastern Question*, vol. ii. p. 205.

was ordered to leave Moscow and go to his country residence, a place which the President of the Slavonic Committee did not possess. I need hardly add, that his friends did not lose time in supplying the deficiency, and he spent a couple of months at a country place four or five hours distant from Moscow. Mr. Aksakoff returned to find that his place in the bank, in which he was one of the chief directors, had never been filled up, and was open for him at once. His colleagues had shared between themselves his work, but his salary remained untouched. Mr. Aksakoff thanked them for the money, and immediately used it for the maintenance of the Slav orphans.

Shortly after Mr. Aksakoff's departure from Moscow, we were agreeably surprised by the appearance, in the official Government's *Messenger*, of a very remarkable declaration of Russia's attitude in relation to the Treaty of Berlin, which expressed, of course in very calm and dignified moderation, the same dissatisfaction with the Berlin 'settlement' which prevailed generally throughout Russia. The significance of this declaration was somewhat strangely overlooked in many circles. The following is an extract from the concluding passages of the article:—

As for Russia, she recovers possession in Europe of a territory temporarily severed from her rule after the Crimean war, and which again places her in contact with the Danube. In Asia she acquires territories, strategic positions, and a port which will serve her as elements of security and prosperity. Assuredly these results are far from realising what Russia had a right to expect after the sacrifices of a victorious war. They are far even from answering to the interests of the East and of Europe, which would have been the gainers from seeing a *more complete and more regular solution issue from this crisis. The work has many weak points.* One of those most to be regretted is the arbitrary settlement of boundaries by geographical and political considerations without regard to nationalities. The Imperial Cabinet had proposed a more rational and equitable plan, which would have left all the Eastern races free to develope themselves each in its natural limits. This it was *with regret* obliged to abandon. But everything depends on the way in which the decisions of the Congress will be carried out. It cannot be too often repeated that the difficulties of the Eastern Question lie, not in Turkey, but in Europe. Whatever the complications it presents, they cannot be in excess of the forces at the disposal of the civilised Powers. If they unite in the common idea of strengthening the germs created by the Treaty of Berlin, in order to make them the starting-point of a prosperous development of the peoples of the East, the work of the Congress may be fertile both for the East and Europe. The Imperial Cabinet pushed conciliation to the furthest limits in order to effect that concert of will which is the pledge of general peace and of the welfare of the Christian East. Henceforth its task is to see that so many efforts do not remain unfruitful. Such, moreover, has been the issue of all our Eastern wars. Despite all our successes, we have not been able to complete our task. We have always had to pull up before the inextricable difficulties of this problem and before the solid mass of interests and passions it excites. But each of our wars has been an additional step towards the final goal, and thus has been traced the sanguinary but glorious furrow which our traditions have left in history, and which must lead up to the accomplishment of our national mission—the deliverance of the Christian East. However incomplete it may be, the work of the Berlin Congress marks a fresh step in that path —an important though painfully secured step. It only remains to consolidate and develope it. This will be the task of the future. The Treaty of 1856, that monument of political passions which had led to an unjust war and an unjust peace, that document which forced on Russia a position which a great nation could not tolerate, which for twenty-two years had tied her hands and Europe's, secured impunity to the Turkish Government, and produced permanent disorders, the causes of the late war—the Treaty of 1856, violated by everybody, renounced even by its authors, no longer exists. The victorious arms of Russia have torn it up. The Berlin Congress has expunged it from history. Russia has secured the right of watching over its work, and she will not let it be reduced to a nullity. The Ottoman Empire has contracted a new lease with Christian and civilised Europe. If it frankly enters on the path open to it by scrupulously carrying out the clauses which guarantee the autonomy of its Christian populations, a prosperous existence may be insured to it. Russia, who in her vast territory numbers millions of Mussulman subjects, and who protects their religion and security, so far from menacing it, may become its best ally. In the opposite case, it will have signed its own condemnation. If the laborious childbirth of the Eastern world is no longer but a question of time, is not yet terminated; if regrettable restrictions produced by distrust, prejudices, political rivalries, and the selfish calculations of material interests and party struggles still hamper it; if much remains to be done to finish it, much has nevertheless been done. Russia has the consciousness of having powerfully contributed to it by her generous and resolute initiative, as well as by her moderation. She has the conviction of being placed in the current of the great laws which govern history, and that, despite the momentary obstacles offered by the passions, littlenesses, and weaknesses of men, humanity nevertheless pursues its invariable march towards the goal appointed by Providence. The Berlin Congress has been a stage in this laborious path. Looking at it from this standpoint, Russia can draw from the past her confidence in the future.

The subsequent policy of the Russian Government showed that this declaration was not merely a series of empty words, but proved that though Russia, for the sake of European peace, had made concessions at Berlin, she remained faithful to the Slavonic cause in the Balkan. If the Turkish garrisons are at this moment absent from 'Eastern Roumelia,' the Bulgarians of that province know perfectly well to what Power they owe the practical abandonment of that mischievous clause which England contributed to the Treaty of Berlin.[1]

[1] The importance of this practical modification of the Berlin Treaty was forcibly stated by Sir W. Harcourt when he addressed his constituents in January 1880. He said: 'I told you last year that if there was any attempt to carry into effect the provisions of the Treaty of Berlin as to Eastern Roumelia there would be resistance and war. Her Majesty's Government and the Porte came later to the same conclusion; and when the time arrived for placing Eastern Roumelia under the direct military and political authority of the Sultan, according to the Treaty of Berlin, the attempt was judiciously abandoned. Eastern Roumelia exists in name as a Turkish province, but the authority of the Turk is extinguished within its borders. When Eastern Roumelia passed, as it has practically passed, out of the hands of the Sultan, the whole fabric of the Government plan of the Treaty of Berlin crumbled to pieces. The line of the Balkans, which was to be the bulwark of consolidated Turkey, was lost, and all the bombast of the triumphal return from Berlin may be thrown into the waste-paper basket. You will see, then, that the Treaty of Berlin, so far from realising to any extent the intentions and desire of its authors in restoring and repairing the Turkish Empire, has only advanced its destruction.'

CHAPTER XI.

DIVIDED BULGARIA.[1]

'ANOTHER insurrection in Turkey! Rising of the Bulgarians!' As I read these words I am filled with conflicting emotions. As a Russian, I blush. I foresee with dread the new torrents of blood, the new victims of a struggle for that liberty—which we promised to achieve for them. To me it is but a poor consolation to say that other countries are to blame for what Russia had to leave undone. When numerous honest voices were heard in Moscow deploring the shameful results of the Berlin Congress, they were accused of ridiculous self-devotion, of 'longing for martyrdom;' and they were told 'that after all Bulgaria had gained much, chiefly thanks to the Russians.'

Well, we now see the terrible results of our Berlin endeavours to conciliate our enemies. Had our diplomacy had more confidence in the readiness of Russians to make new sacrifices and in the support of

---

[1] This letter was written in October, 1878, on receiving the news of the first rising, after the Berlin Treaty, in South-Western Bulgaria, a struggle, which although hitherto unsuccessful, will never be abandoned until the whole of Bulgaria is united and free from the Danube to the Ægean.

the better part of England—had English Slavophiles been more courageous in their sympathies for a grand cause, which they unanimously supported only at the St. James's Conference—things would have taken another turn, and at this moment there might have actually been 'Peace with honour.'

It happened to me this summer to discuss this very question with a foreign statesman. He 'chaffed' me, to use an English colloquialism, upon the brilliant results of the Congress. Without giving way to my feelings, I honestly confessed that I should prefer losing Batoum, Kars, Bessarabia, everything, to giving up one inch of the Slav territory for the benefit of Turkish Pashas. 'You know Russian people very little indeed,' said I, 'if you think that we are pleased with the so-called Russian acquisitions. We want to stand high morally, to see our every word backed by deeds. As to the cost, as to poverty—dear me! what wretched considerations those are.' 'Oh,' said he eagerly, ' we would have willingly allowed Russia to have taken much more; but we all made a point of opposing the actual independence of Bulgaria.' It struck me that a sham independence—like everything that is sham—could be of no value.

We now see the results of our conciliatory efforts, of Russia's yielding, of England's triumphs. A new struggle is beginning in the East. Bulgaria, after all—poor, wretched, unsupported as she is—objects to be 'sawn asunder alive.' 'Like a great high priest of sacrifice,' say the Bulgarians in Philippopolis in their address to Her Majesty the Queen of

England, 'Lord Beaconsfield has sacrificed Bulgaria at Berlin on the altar of the golden calf of Great Britain.'

I know that there are Englishmen who feel deeply the harm done in the name of their country, and who blush even more than I do at the sacrifice of the Slavs. But it was not as a lone unit of the Semitic race that the Premier appeared at Berlin. He acted in the name of England, and England did not protest. England seemed generally to be silenced—to be paralysed; and the whole English nation apparently abdicated precisely when its support was most needful. Suddenly it became 'unpatriotic' to sympathise with the oppressed; it was declared 'to be playing Russia's game' to support those whom she, unfortunately, was abandoning! Oh! you do not know how keenly we —those who had only one soul and one word—suffered in observing your silence and your paralysis! We— the ridiculed Muscovites—were sneered at when we still spoke of England's love for liberty, love for justice, love for high aims and beliefs! Yes; you were not our friends 'in need.' You became frozen and wise![1]

[1] This conviction is also shared by many Liberals. Mr. Leonard Courtney, M.P., speaking to his constituents at the close of 1878, said:— 'We of the Liberal Party have not been true to our duty—have not been true to our principles. In critical moments we have fallen away. Instead of giving voice, trumpet-tongued, to what we believed and to what we held to be the truth, we have been silent.' I rejoice to be able to quote further the following generous outburst of indignation from the same speaker:—' Though Russia were ten times our enemy, I cannot think of those poor Russian peasants sent to their graves, I cannot think of their women folk loaded with affliction, I cannot think of a great nation arrested in its progress of civilisation, for the petty vanity of the Earl of Beaconsfield, without being filled with indignation against the man who has brought these evils about, and who has degraded the national spirit

Well, admire now the new rising of the Roumelians, and console yourselves by accusing some non-existent secret Russian societies of having done all the mischief. As to us, we seek for no consolation of that kind. We were blind in supposing it could be otherwise.

The famous Berlin Congress divided Bulgaria into three unequal parts: Bulgaria proper wholly free; South-eastern Bulgaria (baptized Roumelia), half free; and the large tract of country stretching westward from the Rhodope to Mount Pindus, which was handed back to the absolute dominion of the Sultan. According to the celebrated German Geographer—Kiepert—the Bulgaria of San Stefano—the Bulgaria that Russia emancipated—consisted of 65,560 square miles, with 3,980,000 inhabitants.

The Congress 'Bulgaria' consists only of 24,404 square miles, with 1,773,000 inhabitants. Eastern Roumelia, which was only half-freed, has 13,646 square miles, and 740,000 inhabitants. Thus the

---

of Englishmen. In order that he might have his way, the Bulgarians, who were emancipated, those upon whom the dayspring from on high had arisen, have been shut out from light and freedom, and have been consigned once more to Turkish tyranny. Can you conceive that in Roumelia, south of the Balkans, those Bulgarians who know that their brothers in the north are going to be free, and that they themselves in the south are to be shut out from freedom through the action, shame be it said, of an English Minister, that these populations will bear good-will towards England? Can you conceive that they, thrown back into servitude, will feel anything other than indignation at the country which, being free itself and enjoying the blessings of freedom, has, through the most miserable jealousies interfered to prevent the giving of freedom to others, or speak of Englishmen excepting as of those who would sacrifice all human progress in order to further their most petty and miserable designs?'

Bulgaria and Eastern Roumelia, whose emancipation and semi-emancipation the Congress legalised, consist only of 38,050 square miles, with 2,500,000 inhabitants, and a great area of 27,510 square miles, with a population of 1,500,000, was re-enslaved by England at the Congress without any guarantee from the Turks against a repetition of the atrocities which occasioned the war.

The Bulgaria handed back to what an English friend of mine described as 'the uncovenanted mercies of the Turks' is actually greater in extent, and almost equal in population to the Bulgaria north of the Balkans, which alone was really freed. It is in this portion of Bulgaria, given back unreservedly to the Turks, that the insurrection has broken out.[1]

Unchanged and unchangeable, the Turk will repeat that which only two years ago awoke in the civilised world an outcry of horror and indignation. What will England do now when her Moslem *protégé* in the regions restored to him by Lord Beaconsfield, lights up once more the flames of Batak and rehearses again the ghastly tragedy of 1876?[2]

---

[1] The following were the early centres of the rising:—the first and strongest, along the Struma Valley, in the Perimdagh and the Malesh Planina, extending from Djuma and Kriva down to Meliki and Doriana the second, south of Kustendil, at Kosjak, and the Devanitza Planina, down to Karatova; and the third, in the country west of the Vardar Valley, ranging from the Karadagh, near Uskub, down to Monastir and Zlorina.

[2] As I revise this, there lies before me an important letter from a distinguished Bulgarian in Philippopolis, which says:—'It is almost incredible how little attention is paid in England to the condition of unhappy Macedonia, from which, alas, we daily receive dreadful reports of Turkish atrocities on our helpless compatriots, who, as you know, compose the great majority of the population.'

The locality where the insurrection has taken place is very instructive. Although there is a great agitation in Eastern Roumelia, the insurrectionary movement exists in that part of Bulgaria which the Congress handed back to the direct rule of the Turk without any guarantees. A strange ignorance prevails on this point even in well-informed English circles. It is said 'the Bulgaria of San Stefano was too big, and what you call South-Western Bulgaria is Macedonia, and belongs not to the Slavs but to the Greeks.' In reality it is not so. The boundaries of Bulgaria in the south-west are tolerably well defined. Lord Salisbury at the Constantinople Conference drew them substantially the same as they appear in the Preliminary Treaty of San Stefano.

Can you wonder that the Bulgarians of Macedonia, for whom Europe demanded the irreducible minimum of the Conference, and Russia the complete emancipation of the San Stefano Treaty, should object to being, as before, surrendered to Turkish misrule, in order to please some few diplomatists? You know very well that a settlement of this kind must be unsettled by the most natural course of events. The intelligent leader of the Bulgarians of Philippopolis writes thus:—'We beheld with astonishment the present attitude of the English nation, which, in 1876, at the time of the massacres, gave its assistance to the suffering Bulgarians. The sympathy which is shown to us by the English press is not in harmony with the acts of the English Government, which strives continually, and by all means, to keep us in thraldom. It seeks again to thrust us under the intolerable yoke of the Turkish Government, which treated us like wild beasts for five centuries.'

Against this the Bulgarians have risen in revolt. Why should you be astonished? Have you already forgotten the fate of the Treaty of Villafranca, that miserable document which brought to a sudden and disappointing close a war, undertaken for the liberation of Italy 'from the Alps to the Adriatic?' That Treaty was annihilated in less than a year—and why? Because it ignored the national aspirations of the Italians. So will the Treaty of Berlin disappear, not by the all-powerful ' Russian intrigue,' but because it was a mockery of a whole nation, deciding its future in a merciless way, without even the semblance of consulting its interests.[1]

Was England simply playing a part in her rejoicing when Garibaldi's sword and Cavour's statecraft completed the emancipation of Italy? Was she then hypocritical. And, if not, how can she curse Bulgaria for attempting to free herself from an enemy even worse than the Austrians and the Pope? Have you then been sincere? Prove it now. The whole Slavonic world watches you with eager interest.

[1] Mr. E. A. Freeman, added to his many services to the Slavonic cause, that of writing on October 30, 1878, one of his most vigorous and spirited letters in defence of the insurgents, from which I venture to make the following extract:—'England must once more insist that the rulers of England shall at least do nothing against the cause of right and freedom. We must speak out and tell Lord Beaconsfield and Lord Salisbury that, if Macedonia can keep its freedom, either alone or by the help of Russians or any other people, we at least will not hinder it. Let all men understand that we will not be helpers in bringing Christian men under barbarian bondage. If the Treaty of Berlin binds us to do so, it binds us to do evil, and a promise to do evil is not binding.'

Whether the Russian Government likes it or not—whether once more our officials try above all to soothe Lord Beaconsfield's feelings—'Bulgaria, United and Free from the Danube to the Ægean,' will be the battle-cry of the struggle which has now commenced. Again, I ask:—Put to this new test, what will the free, humanitarian, the noble England do? Now, the Slavs want deeds, not merely words. 'Enough of compliments!' Energetic, active sympathy is now wanted.

Let us hope that the men of Macedonia may accomplish a task which has baffled Christendom.

But the Treaty of Berlin—that solemn European compact, does it bind the Bulgarians? Protocols, though written with a golden pen, do they express their wishes? Have they been signed by them? Were the poor Slavs consulted about their destinies and those of their children? Greeks were heard. Roumanians, even Persians; but Bulgarians, on whose behalf war was undertaken, were not permitted to raise their voices in the Areopagus of Europe!

Against the injustice of Diplomacy behold in South-Western Bulgaria the protest of Humanity! I quote once more, for the last time, from the Bulgarian protest addressed to your Queen, which is dated July 31, 1878:—

We raise our voice to protest loudly against the unjust decision of the Berlin Congress, and declare we can neither accept it nor bow our heads before the attempt of England to destroy us as a people. We cannot submit again to the Turkish domination. Our nationality will defend itself to the last drop of its blood, rather than fall again under Turkish rule. It will, therefore, be required that new torrents of blood be shed in our unfortunate and devastated country.

If Bulgaria is not crushed by her former oppressors, if she gains her longed-for liberty, it will happen in spite of what was done at Berlin. A parchment may be torn, but a nationality has more vitality than paper.[1]

[1] As these pages are passing through the press, I have received a copy of the latest appeal which the unfortunate Bulgarians of Macedonia have addressed to the Powers which handed them over to the vengeance of their oppressors. This appeal is moderate in tone, and reasonable in its request. It is dated January 1, 1880, is signed by 102 representatives of Bulgarian communities, and is addressed to the Ambassadors of the Powers at Constantinople. The following are its salient passages:—' The state of affairs in Macedonia becomes daily, through the fault of the local authorities, more and more intolerable. Thefts, misdemeanours, murders, abuses, and crimes of all kinds increase in a most terrifying manner. The criminals who were seized by the Christians and handed over to the authorities remain not only unpunished, but are even acquitted, and they use their freedom to continue, being armed from head to foot, their former cruelties against the unarmed Bulgarians. The authorities openly show their partiality for the Mahometans. These facts deprive us of every hope that the local authorities will redress these grievances. The public insecurity, of course, greatly endangers labour and wages; the number of those in need of their daily bread is, therefore, already very large. 'The Sublime Porte has obliged itself, by means of Article XXIII. of the Berlin Treaty, to introduce reforms into European Turkey, which should, in order to make them correspond to the wants of every province, be deliberated upon by Commissions in which the respective local elements should be prominently represented, the final settlement of the projected reforms to be made by a European Commission. The Bulgarians of Macedonia most respectfully solicit the attention of the Government represented by your Excellency for a speedy realisation of the above-mentioned Article XXIII. A benevolent intervention of the powerful Government of your Excellency can end the sufferings of the Macedonian Christians, sufferings which, it is hoped, will be redressed by the introduction of reforms.'

A vain hope! Article XXIII., like all other articles of the Berlin Treaty, depending for their execution on the Turk, remains a dead letter, and will remain such as long as the Turk remains in his place of power.

Univ

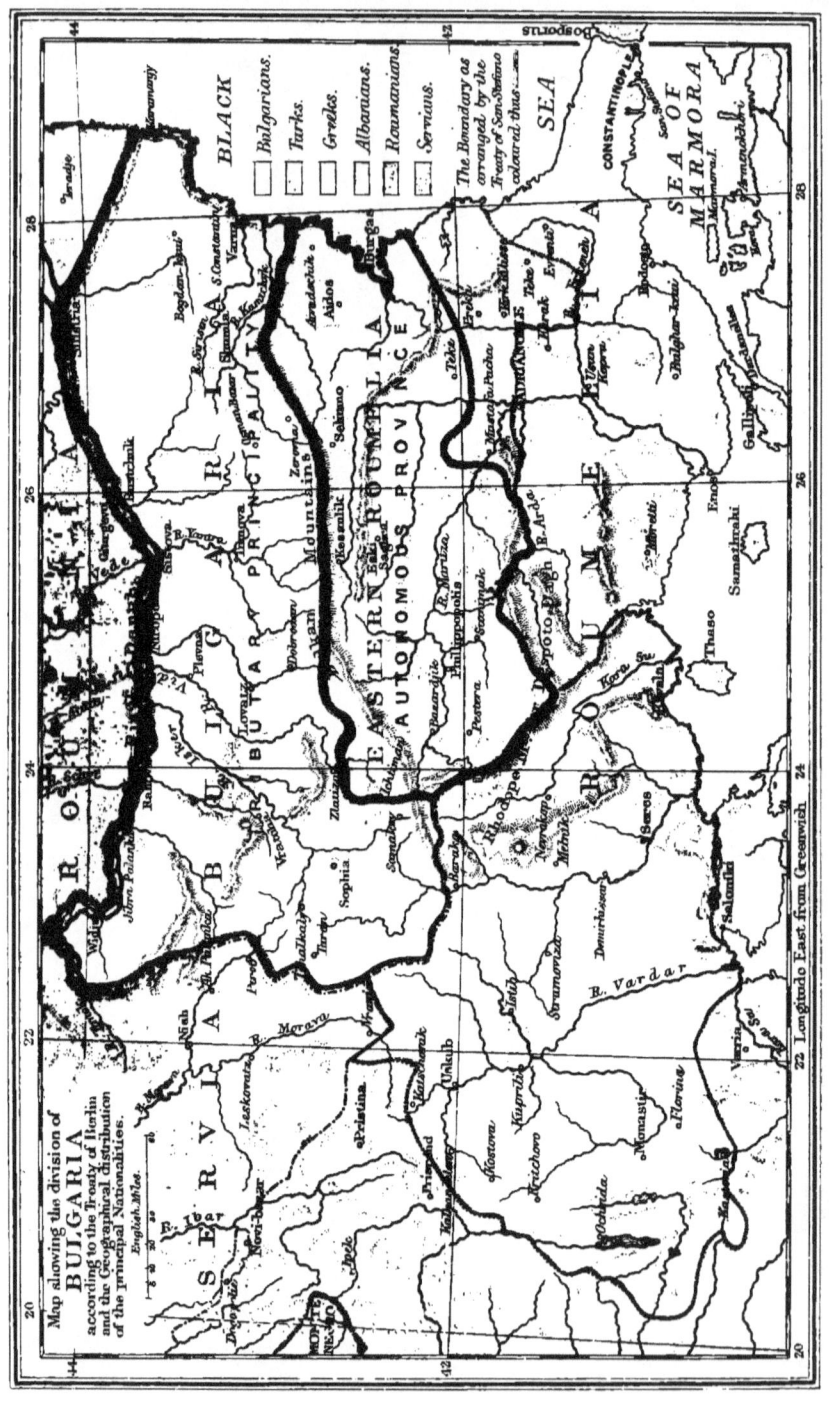

BULGARIA, ETHNOLOGICAL AND POLITICAL.

The accompanying Map gives the distribution of the different races in the Balkan Peninsula as shown by Kiepert *before the war*. During the war and since the conclusion of peace there has been a considerable change, which no mapmaker has as yet ventured to represent. There are now fewer Turks in Bulgaria and Eastern Roumelia than there were before the war, and there are fewer Bulgarians outside the limits of the free and autonomous States. It will be seen at a glance that the Bulgaria of San Stefano corresponds much more exactly with the ethnological facts than the Bulgaria of Berlin, from which the most strictly Bulgarian district in the Balkan Peninsula has been excluded. Lest any reader should question the authority of Kiepert, I will quote here the testimony of Sir George Campbell, M.P. Referring to the distribution of races in the Balkan, Sir George Campbell writes :—

'So much of the present Eastern Question depends on a due appreciation of the geographical area of the Bulgarian country, that it should be rightly understood how much they occupy the whole centre, and it may be said, body, of European Turkey.... On the South of the Balkan, almost as far as Salonica, the Bulgarian race prevails. There is a small but very clear German ethnological map by Kiepert, lately published, which gives the races very well as far as they can be roughly delineated on a small scale. I am bound to say that all my inquiries and personal observations, so far as they enable me to test Kiepert's map, go to confirm its general correctness. From collating consular and other reports, and other inquiries, I had made out the Bulgarian area to be much as Kiepert puts it before I had seen his map, and in the parts of the country which I visited, my inquiries led to the same result. ... Kiepert gives the Greeks the country up to and including Adrianople—that seems about as much as they can fairly claim. From the Danube then to near Adrianople and Salonica, and from the Black Sea (less a small Greek fringe) to the Albanian Hills, is the Bulgarian country, except so far as Turkish settlements are interspersed in greater or less degree.'

A Very Recent View of Turkey, pp. 11-13.

THE THREE BULGARIAS—CONSTANTINOPLE, SAN STEFANO, AND BERLIN.

It will be seen from the accompanying Map, which is taken from the two official maps published by the English Foreign Office, that the Bulgaria of San Stefano corresponds much more closely than the Bulgaria of Berlin with the Bulgaria of the Constantinople Conference. The only material difference between the Bulgaria of San Stefano and the Bulgaria of Constantinople is, that the former takes in a tract of distinctly Bulgarian country between the Rhodope and Salonica, which the latter left out. It is worthy of note that the third part of Bulgaria, entirely re-enslaved at the Congress of Berlin, contained before the war hardly any larger proportion of Moslems, including Albanians, Pomaks, and Circassians, as well as Turks, than either the Principality or Eastern Roumelia.

The following are Kiepert's figures :—

	Inhabitants.	Moslems.	Per cent.
The Bulgaria of San Stefano	3,986,000	1,538,000	39
Divided at Berlin :			
The Free Principality	1,773,000	681,500	38
Half-free Eastern Roumelia	746,000	265,000	35
Re-enslaved South Western Bulgaria	1,467,000	591,500	40
Total	3,986,000	1,538,000	39

The extra two per cent. of Moslems in South Western Bulgaria over the percentage in the Principality, is accounted for by the inclusion of some non-Bulgarians resident in the littoral, and by the inclusion of the tongue of land south of Adrianople; but the South Western District included in the Constantinople Conference Bulgaria, although much more Bulgarian than the Principality, was handed back to the Turks without any guarantees such as were provided for Eastern Roumelia.

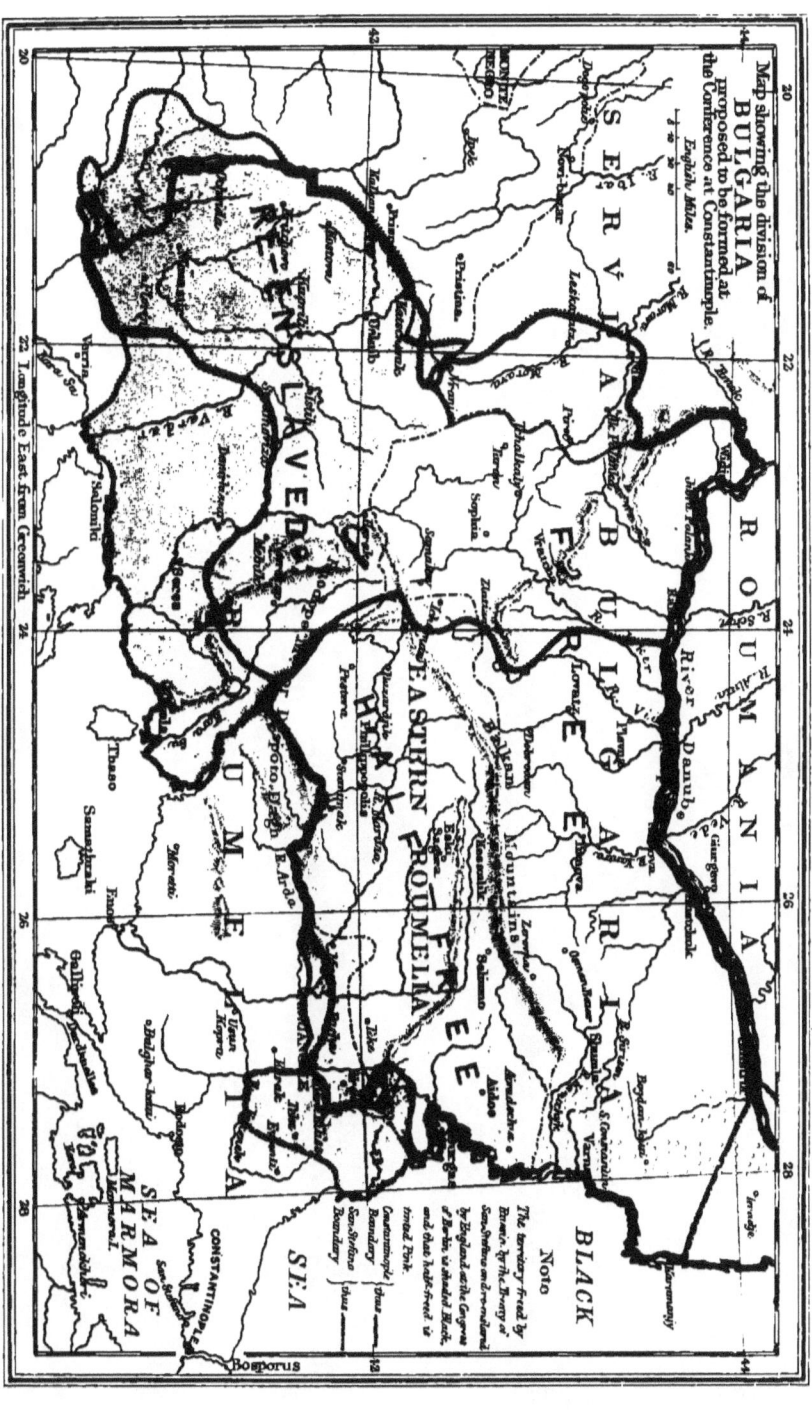

UNIV. OF
CALIFORNIA

PART II.

THE FUTURE OF THE EASTERN QUESTION.

---

1. LORD SALISBURY AS HERALD ANGEL.
2. THE ANGLO-TURKISH CONVENTION.
3. THE HEIRS OF THE SICK MAN.
4. THE LAST WORD OF THE EASTERN QUESTION.

CHAPTER I.

LORD SALISBURY AS HERALD ANGEL.[1]

WITHIN the last few years Russians have been much puzzled by the rapid changes through which one of

[1] Lord Salisbury, Secretary of State for Foreign Affairs, speaking at a Conservative Banquet in the Free Trade Hall, Manchester, October 17, 1879, used the following expressions:—' If the Turk falls, remember that Austria is now at Novi Bazar, and has advanced to the latitude of the Balkans, and that no advance of Russia beyond the Balkans or beyond the Danube can now be made unless the resistance of Austria is conquered. Austria herself is powerful. I believe that in the strength and independence of Austria lie the best hopes of European stability and peace. What has happened within the last few weeks justifies us in hoping that Austria, if attacked, would not be alone. The newspapers say—I know not whether they say rightly—that a defensive alliance has been established between Germany and Austria. I will not pronounce any opinion as to the accuracy of that information; but I will only say this to you and all who value the peace of Europe and the independence of nations—I may say without profanity—that it is " good tidings of great joy."'

'The conception of constituting Austria the gaoler of the Slav nationalities is a conception which is unworthy of practical statesmen, and altogether repugnant to Liberal principles. Russia has pursued a policy far more astute. She has won the hearts of those provinces by making herself the patron of their independence. She leaves it to Austria to assume the position of the conqueror of alien races and of a dissatisfied people. We have had " glad tidings of great joy " declared to us by an uninspired and not particularly angelic Secretary of State, but the proclamation of that evangel has not been followed by peace on earth or goodwill towards men. It is my belief that that mischievous speech has done more to embitter the passions and inflame the jealousies of nations than any words which have been spoken in our time; and principally, I believe, as a consequence of it, we are threatened every morning by the organs of the Government with a new European war.'— Sir William Harcourt, Jan. 13, 1880.

your Ministers have passed; but, accustomed as we have been to the transformations of the modern Proteus, we were hardly prepared for his sudden advent as a Herald Angel. His proclamation to the Manchester representatives of the Shepherds of Bethlehem of the 'Good tidings of great joy' has hardly been accepted in Russia as a message of peace and goodwill. It is not the facts, or assumed facts, that disturb us. It is the spirit of the speech which excites the indignation occasioned by insulting menace of wanton war. It is difficult to exaggerate the feeling aroused by. Lord Salisbury's speech in all Russian circles. It even extends to the long-suffering Ministry of Foreign Affairs. That humble paper, the semi-official *Journal de St. Pétersbourg*, seldom expresses the most legitimate sentiments save in the most timid, hesitating, over-diplomatic manner, but even that journal declares. that it could not believe that any Minister, especially the Foreign Minister of a Great Power, could have made a speech so entirely contrary to all the traditions governing Ministerial utterances concerning Powers with which they entertain friendly relations. 'The proceeding,' it remarks, ' is little suited (*peu conforme*) to the dignity of a great nation with which our country is living at peace.' That is the reserved fashion in which our semi-official organ, respecting the conventionalities of the diplomatic intercourse which Lord Salisbury so rudely violates, implies rather than expresses the universal feeling of indignant surprise which the speech excited in Russia. For the frank, outspoken expression of that feeling you must look to the *Moscow Gazette*, rather than to the French St. Petersburg paper, and the utterances of that best representative of the views of the Russian people contrast strongly with the few stammering remarks of its wellbred St. Petersburg contemporary.[1] The conviction

[1] The *Moscow Gazette* is the *Times* of Russia in one sense, but not in another. It is the first paper in the Empire, but it leads rather than follows public opinion. The *Times* changes with the times. The *Moscow Gazette* adheres to its own views. The *Times* is impersonal, anonymous. The *Moscow Gazette* is Mr. Katkoff, and Mr. Katkoff is the *Moscow Gazette*. He has his colleagues, but his individuality permeates the paper.

Few men have influenced more deeply the course of events in Russia since the Emancipation than the quondam Professor of Philosophy in the University of Moscow. A Russian of the Russians, married to Princess Shalikoff, daughter of a Russian poet, he was at one time so ardent an admirer of England and the English that his friends reproached him for his Anglo-mania. A brilliant author, a learned professor, a fearless journalist, Mr. Katkoff's chief distinction is due to the fact that he more than any man incarnated the national inspirations at three crises in Russian history.

It was in 1863 that he first attracted the attention of Russia. In that year the determination of the Poles that half of Russia should be included in the limits of the Poland to which a Constitution was about to be granted, brought them into violent collision with the Russian Government. All the Powers of Europe began to intermeddle in the matter. 'You must do this; you must not do that,' and so on. The despatches came pouring in from this Court and from that, until even little Portugal and barbarous Turkey ventured to send us their prescriptions for pacifying Poland! Russians felt profoundly humiliated, and not a little indignant. 'Were we not to be masters in our own house? Were we to be treated as if we were the vassals of the West?' These angry questionings filled every breast; and, amid the irritation occasioned by the intermeddling of the Foreign Courts, everything was forgotten but a stern resolve to vindicate the national independence. At that crisis in our history Mr. Katkoff came boldly to the front, embodied the thoughts of millions in his fiery articles, and gave voice and utterance to the patriotic enthusiasm of every Russian. When the storm had passed, and all danger of war was averted by the adoption of the independent policy which he had so vigorously advocated, the intrepid spokesman of the national sentiment occupied the highest place in the esteem of his countrymen ever attained by any journalist in Russia before or since. A public subscription was raised, and Mr. Katkoff was presented, in the name of thou-

is universal that it means mischief. 'If they did not mean war,' our people naïvely say, 'they would not provoke it. Surely serious statesmen have no time for *mauvaises plaisanteries*. If they are in earnest, let us be prepared.' The conclusion is as natural as the consequences are deplorable. But although Lord Salisbury has threatened and blustered in the past, only to be answered by a slap in the face from the Turks, it is, of course, not impossible that he may sometime or other attempt to make good his words.

Apart from the bad results it has had on my

<small>sands of sympathisers throughout the Empire, with a massive silver figure of a soldier, in the old Russian uniform, holding proudly aloft a standard, bearing 'Unity of Russia' as its inscription.

Some years later Mr. Katkoff came once more to the front. The question of classical education then excited intense interest throughout Russia; and the *Moscow Gazette* led the van of the fight, which resulted in the complete victory of the classical party. As one result of this success, 'The Lyceum of the Grand-Duke Nicholas' was founded at Moscow, in honour of the late Tzarewitch. Mr. Katkoff and Mr. Leontieff, his *alter ego*—and a very distinguished scholar—were associated at first in the superintendence of the new institution. Since the death of the latter—which was lamented throughout Russia as a national loss—Mr. Katkoff has discharged alone the duties of President.

The third great crisis in which Mr. Katkoff and the *Moscow Gazette* did good service to the Russian cause was in the Slavonic movement of last year. Mr. Katkoff has never been identified with the Slavophile party. But when the Servian war awakened the national enthusiasm, Mr. Katkoff threw himself heart and soul into the Slavonic cause. He guided, directed, and sustained more than any single man the tumultuous current of Russian opinion. The *Moscow Gazette* became once more the exponent of the national conviction, and to this hour it maintains the honourable position of the leading journal of Russia.

Mr. Katkoff publishes not only the *Moscow Gazette*, but also a monthly literary organ—the Russian *Messenger*. He is famous throughout Europe for his incisive style and his vigorous hard-hitting. The courage with which he has assailed abuses has not prevented the appointment of his daughter, Miss Barbe Katkoff,—now married to that brilliant journalist, Prince Léon Schohofskoy,—as demoiselle d'honneur to Her Majesty the Empress.</small>

countrymen, the speech rather amuses me. It is so diverting to congratulate a Foreign Minister upon the discovery of the existence of the German Empire. What a pity he did not discover it sooner! Writing two years ago on 'England's Traditional Policy,' I ventured to insist upon the obvious fact that the establishment of the German Empire had transformed the whole European situation, and for ever 'saved the Continent from the dread of absolute predominance of Russia.' As no one believes that poor, dear Austria contributes largely to the strength of the 'Alliance,' I fail to see in the new Gospel of Lord Salisbury anything more than a somewhat undignified 'Eureka'—almost as fresh as the virtues of large maps. '*Il fait de la prose sans le savoir*,' and a hero of the Berlin Congress has been somewhat tardy in perceiving the political significance of United Germany.

Not so long ago the will of our Emperor was law in the Diet of Germany. At that time the small German princes were known as the 'poor relatives of the Tzar,' and their subservience to their august patron was notorious. All this was changed, not when Prince Bismarck favoured Vienna with a call, but since the proclamation of the German Empire in 1871. Is it not known even at the English Foreign Office that Russia had some little part in that historic drama? Surely not even the 'veracious' Lord Salisbury—as Sir Wilfrid Lawson so cruelly calls him —would claim the German Empire as the product of Lord Beaconsfield's diplomacy. If Russia were so given up to an aggressive policy, it was hardly consistent to have aided so effectively the realisation of the German national idea.[1]

Some people seem to think that Germany may imitate the example of Austria, and 'astonish the world by her ingratitude.' Surely we may hope, on the contrary, that a race which, with Russia's support, has retained the realisation of its national idea, will not oppose, but even support the equally legitimate and natural aspirations of the Slavonic race to secure the freedom and independence so cruelly denied to that long-oppressed nationality.

We have no wish to pick a quarrel with Germany, nor has Germany, I believe, any intention of quarrelling with us. There may have been some slight personalities between personages, but that is all. Even this has been ridiculously exaggerated. Take, for instance, the sensational report published by the *Soleil* of an alleged interview between its correspondent and Prince Gortschakoff. Our Chancellor has a rule, to which he makes no exception, never to receive any newspaper correspondents. I heard the other day that the famous 'interview' took place in the street. The correspondent of the *Soleil*, armed with a letter of introduction from a distinguished French statesman, accosted our Chancellor, who, excusing

---

[1] Not so long ago it used to be a stock charge against us by our enemies that Russia maintained for her own selfish purposes a weak and divided Germany. A rabid writer during the Crimean war attacked Russian policy under Alexander I. specially on that ground. He said:—
'Whatever endangered, impoverished, disgraced Germany, and kept Germany down, was a stone added to the vast, but hollow, edifice of the Russian autocracy.'—*Foreign Biographies*, vol. ii. p. 137.

himself for being unable to receive him, disengaged himself from his would-be interviewer with a few civil commonplaces. Upon this the ingenious correspondent allowed his imagination to fabricate the article which created such a stir amongst the credulous. Russians—unfortunately perhaps—are so loath to correct absurd stories, so persistently invented to their discredit for sensational or for party purposes in the West, that it is unfair—to say the least—to conclude because no contradiction or explanation is given, that, therefore, every legend must be true.

The policy of Russia—nearest neighbours, fastest friends—is too deeply rooted to be easily shaken. In one respect, I am sorry to say, I resemble Lord Salisbury. I am not in the secrets of European Cabinets, and have, like that Foreign Minister, to seek my information in the reports (not always particularly trustworthy) of the newspapers. But if it be true that the Triple Alliance is at an end, I do not mourn over its decease. As Mr. Forster so truly said in his forcible speech at Bradford, alliance with one Power implies hostility to another. Now we have no hostility to France. Quite the contrary. And if we are isolated, what harm is there in that? Is isolation not generally accompanied by independence, and would it not give us a free hand at home as abroad?

It is universally assumed that Russians regard Austria-Hungary with animosity. It is not so. There can be no national hatred between Russians and Austrians, because there are no Austrians. As Prince

Gortschakoff once wittily observed: 'Austria is not a nation; she is not even a State; she is only a Government.' In the vast conglomeration of nationalities included in the dominions of Francis Joseph there is even now a majority of Slavs. Every step southward increases the preponderance of the Slavonic element. With the Slavs of Austria and Hungary—that is, with the majority of the subjects of the Hapsburgs—the Slavs of Russia can only have the liveliest feelings of sympathy and fraternity.[1]

Lord Salisbury implies that the Austrian occupation of the Bosnian Provinces was a triumphant device of English diplomacy to checkmate 'Russian aggression.' But here, as in Germany, the great 'barrier to Russian aggression' was raised by Russian hands. The proposal that Austria should *occupy* the Provinces emanated from our Government. It was suggested by Russia in the autumn of 1876,[2] then again in the autumn of 1877, and only accepted in Berlin in 1878. But in 1876 Lord Salisbury, perhaps, was too much engrossed in 'creating a pretext' for

---

[1] A feeling, I may add, that is warmly reciprocated by them, as may be seen by the following extract from a letter, addressed during the recent war by Dr. Rieger, the influential leader of the Bohemian Panslavists to the Moscow Slavonic Committee:—' How is it possible that the Bohemian people should not desire from the bottom of its heart the complete success of the Russian arms? Do not the Russians go to battle for right, freedom, religion, for humanitarianism, for the honour of the family which have been long enough insulted on the soil of Christian Europe? The glory of the Russians in that struggle is our glory, and it raises the pride of all Slavonians, and their self-consciousness that the blood of our brethren will be shed for our brethren. We cannot but rejoice when the powerful Slav, by defending the weak Slavs, has earned a right to the gratitude and love of the whole Slavonic family.'

[2] *Blue Book*, Turkey, 1 (1877), p. 405.

invading Afghanistan to notice such trifles as the fate of the Ottoman Empire.

In spite of the newspapers—the oracles of English diplomacy—I do not believe that the 'Austro-German Alliance' has the significance attached to it by certain interested politicians. But if an offensive and defensive alliance has been concluded, why do you imagine that it has any reference, much less exclusive reference, to Russia? In all the accusations levelled against Russia for the last twenty years, who has ever accused us of meditating war on Germany or Austria? But are such purposes actually unknown in other lands? The revindication of former frontiers, the redemption of unredeemed territory, these are not the watchwords of Russian policy—although, perhaps, they are not altogether unfamiliar to German and Austrian statesmen.

I have not yet heard any antiphon from across the Channel answering the song of the Herald Angel of Manchester, proclaiming as good 'tidings of great joy' the formation of an offensive and defensive alliance between Austria-Hungary and the possessors of Alsace and Lorraine. If Lord Salisbury sacrifices with a light heart the *entente cordiale pour les beaux yeux* of Prince Bismarck and Count Andrassy, he will, of course, find his hands freer in Egypt and the Mediterranean for counteracting aggressive designs on British interests.

It is strange that the Austro-German Alliance should be so heartily welcomed by an English Foreign Secretary on the understanding that it foreshadows

Austria's succession to the inheritance of the Turk, which would involve her total transformation. The thrusting of Austria eastward was originally devised to weaken England. Prince Talleyrand, who, like Lord Salisbury, held curious theories as to the use of language, was its author. In the excellent 'History of Russia' by that brilliant writer M. Rambaud,[1] so well translated into English by Mrs. Lang, Lord Salisbury will find the following passage, which is not without some little interest :—

In 1809 Talleyrand had submitted to Napoleon a project which consisted in indemnifying Austria by putting her into possession of the Roumanian Principalities and of the Slav provinces of Turkey, which would have created a permanent conflict of interests between Russia and Austria. The former, repulsed from the Danube, would have been forced to turn towards Central Asia—towards Hindostan. In this emergency she would in her turn, have found herself at perpetual war with England; and all germ of coalition against the French Empire would by this means have been extinguished.

The danger foreseen by Talleyrand is not more remote to-day; but I do not think it is greatly to be dreaded.

Russia will not permit Austria to possess herself of the Balkan Peninsula any more than you will permit France to possess Egypt—of that there is no question. It is more probable that the development of the East will result in the conversion of Austria-Hungary and the States of the Balkans into a Confederation of the Danube, which, after the German and Italian elements had sought their own, would be

[1] Rambaud's *History of Russia*, vol. ii. p. 252.

an essentially Slavonic State. It is a joke in Moscow that the 'Sick Man' at Constantinople being *in articulo mortis*, the attention of Europe will have to be turned to the 'Sick Woman' of Vienna-Pesth. But surely, after the experience of the late war, Russia will not be left, by the abdication of the European concert, to settle another Eastern question by herself.

CHAPTER II.

THE ANGLO-TURKISH CONVENTION.[1]

WHAT do Russians think of the Anglo-Turkish Convention? Frankly speaking, very little. It excited some attention at first, but now it is not regarded seriously. In spite of the emphatic speeches one hears on every side about the sacredness, the inviolability, the eternity of treaties, somehow or other it seems as if your Ministers themselves never considered that secret arrangement to be a reality. It is rather regarded as an ideal, which, like every ideal, by its very nature cannot be realised.

When it was first announced, of course, Russians, like other people, thought there must be something in it. This impression was strengthened by the extraordinary triumphs accorded to Lord Beaconsfield and his *alter ego*—Lord Salisbury. London seemed enraptured. The two conquerors were enthusiastically welcomed, even ladies being anxious to accompany their victorious procession, to testify before the eyes of the world their delight and sympathy.

Little by little, however, the scene began to change like a mirage of the desert. Indiscreet questions were

[1] Written Nov. 1878.

heard to the effect as to who was the real gainer—Turkey or England? Lord Beaconsfield or the Sultan? Was it really a case of 'diamond cutting diamond?' Some sober minds appealed to facts, and tried to sum up the real significance of these transactions. The purchase of Cyprus was ironically designated in Russia as a new '*Qui perd, gagne.*' Prudent and practical, as you ever are, you undertook besides to defend the Sultan's territory, without having ever had it definitely explained what that defence would actually involve.[1]

When you really are in earnest you do not take things so easily. In India you are invading Afghanistan with what the *Times* calls 'a great army' of 34,000 men, which actually constitutes almost one of our army corps, and all this simply in order to preserve your frontier from even the shadow of a Russian visitor—a hundred miles off at Cabul. Even the adherents of the Afghan campaign admit that the rectification of your north-western frontier will cost you many millions. The great natural rampart which divides you from the terrible Afghans is pronounced by your Premier to be haphazard, and therefore it

[1] While discussing Russian opinions on the Convention it may be well merely to mention that in December the *Nord* published the following significant sentence in a letter from St. Petersburg :—' You have been right in saying that the separate Convention between England and the Porte relative to the island of Cyprus and Asia Minor does not bind any of the other Powers. Not only this, but they are ignorant of its existence, or rather for them it does not exist. By the Treaty of Berlin, Asia Minor remains subject to the stipulations of the Treaty of Paris, and England having signed both treaties she is, with regard to the other Powers, bound only by their stipulations. The question of this separate Convention would certainly have been raised if Lord Beaconsfield's Cabinet, continuing its first attempts, had pretended to any particular rights in the internal affairs of Asia Minor.'

must be replaced at once by a scientific frontier. Yet, haphazard though it be, your Indian frontier, compared with that of Asiatic Turkey, is simply impregnable. But you do nothing to strengthen the latter, although it lies defenceless at the feet of our garrison at Kars.

The poor Turks, after their new Convention, cannot even get a little money from you to build new fortresses and equip their army. Actions always speak louder than words, and as we interpret your Convention by your conduct, Lord Beaconsfield's 'Halt,' seems to us to have no more reality than the previous 'three campaigns' with which he tried to prevent Russia doing her duty two years ago.

If you meant to fulfil your obligations, you would prepare to meet your responsibilities. But, seeing that nothing is done, we conclude that you are somewhat uncertain as to the necessity of carrying out any new policy. Are we so wrong, after all? Or do you defy every indiscreet investigation? Of course, we can only judge from our point of view, and thus we can only be 'one-sided.' But is not that the case with every poor mortal, however anxiously he pretends to be the very opposite? If we are mistaken, be patient with us, and we will pay you with your own coin. Besides, people differ so much about certain notions. Some call 'Peace and honour' what others declare to be 'War and humbug,' to mention one among many similar instances, and so granting the fallibility of our judgments, let me express them nevertheless.

Although the Anglo-Turkish Convention practically seems to us to mean nothing, theoretically, it is very highly esteemed in Russia, at least by some Russians, and these not the least influential. It is the historical justification of the Treaty of Kainardji, the tardy, but complete, admission by England of the principle adopted by Russia a hundred years ago.

There are those who speak of the Treaty of Berlin as annihilating the results of the Crimean War. In one sense they may be right, but in another they are quite wrong.

The vital principle of the Paris Treaty, the recognition of which by Europe was the great result of the Crimean War, was not annihilated, but reaffirmed and strengthened, by the Berlin Treaty. But that principle —the European concert established by the Western nations against Russia at the Paris Congress—has been annihilated by the Anglo-Turkish Convention. The work of Lord Clarendon has been undone by Lord Beaconsfield, and the Russian principles, eclipsed by the disasters at Sebastopol, have been vindicated at last by the English Government.

This is all the more gratifying to Russians, because it was the unsolicited act of our opponents. The Anglo-Turkish Convention is but the Treaty of Kainardji written large and applied to Asia, where there was much less need for it than in Europe, where our protectorate was needed for the protection of the Christian nationalities. It involves the formal repudiation of the European concert, now publicly derided by Lord Salisbury, and the adoption of the old Russian principle of direct dealing with the Porte, with exclusive privileges of interfering in the internal affairs of the Ottoman Empire. For maintaining this, Russia was denounced as the enemy of civilisation; but, now that it is affirmed by Lord Beaconsfield and Lord Salisbury, you load them with honours and decorations. To simple-minded people like ourselves it seems a curious inconsistency.[1]

The re-establishment of the principle of direct dealings with the Porte is not merely a complete vindication of Russia before the tribunal of history, it is most important with relation to the future development of events in the East. Russia loyally recognised the authority of the European concert even when England was destroying it. We carried our Preliminary Treaty of San Stefano to the European Areopagus—to be mutilated by diplomacy— only to learn that England, which had made no sacrifices but those of (what we call) honour and

[1] Speaking on November 27, 1879, in Midlothian, of the Anglo-Turkish Convention, Mr. Gladstone said:—'For who would have believed it possible that we should assert before the world the principle that Europe only could deal with the affairs of the Turkish Empire, and should ask Parliament for six millions to support us in asserting that principle, should send Ministers to Berlin, who declared that unless that principle was acted upon they would go to war with the material that Parliament had placed in their hands, and should at the same time be concluding a separate agreement with Turkey, under which those matters of European jurisdiction were coolly transferred to English jurisdiction; and the whole matter was sealed with the worthless bribe of the possession and administration of the island of Cyprus? In the case of the Anglo-Turkish Convention, we have asserted for ourselves a principle that we had denied to others—namely, the principle of overriding the European authority of the Treaty of Paris, and taking the matters which that treaty gave to Europe into our own separate jurisdiction.'—*Political Speeches*, p. 60.

truth, had made a secret treaty with the Sultan, which she refused to submit to the Berlin Congress.[1] Many people thought that measure not exactly chivalrous, but the refusal to have any judge as to her actions, the determination to follow only her own views without any coquettish desire to gratify everybody, displayed a certain defiant self-assertion with which I can sympathise.

The lesson was a painful one, but at least we have henceforth a free hand. Russia evidently has now the right to make Conventions with the Porte as well as England; and, frankly speaking, we could afford to

[1] Speaking at Glasgow in December, 1879, Mr. Gladstone said 'the Anglo-Turkish Convention was in itself a gross and manifest breach of the public law of Europe. Because, by the Treaty of Paris, the result of the Crimean war, it was solemnly enacted that everything that pertained to the integrity and independence of Turkey, and to the relations between the Sultan and his subjects, was matter, not for the cognisance of one particular Power, but for the joint cognisance of the great Powers of Europe. And what did we do in 1878? When the Russian war with Turkey came to a close, we held Russia rigidly to that principle. We insisted that the treaty she had made should be subject to the review of Europe, and that Europe should be entitled to give a final judgment on those matters which fell within the scope of the Treaty of Paris. We did that, and we even wasted six millions in warlike preparations for giving effect to that declaration. We then brought together at Berlin, or assisted to bring together at Berlin, the Powers of Europe for the purpose of exercising this supreme jurisdiction; and while they were there, while they were at work, and without the knowledge of any one among them except Turkey, we extorted from the Sultan of Turkey—I am afraid by threatening him with abandoning the advocacy of his cause before the Congress—we extorted from the Sultan of Turkey the Anglo-Turkish Convention. But the Anglo-Turkish Convention was a Convention which aimed at giving us power, in the teeth of the Treaty of Paris, to interfere between the Sultan and his subjects; and it was a Convention which virtually severed from his empire the possession of the island of Cyprus. It interfered with the integrity. It interfered with the independence. It broke the Treaty of Paris, and the Treaty of Paris was the public law of Europe.'— *Political Speeches*, p. 92.

let you have much more than Cyprus to regain the right of direct dealing with the Sultan without foreign intermeddling.

The principle of European concert is sometimes very good. Russia has maintained it at great cost to herself on more than one occasion, when England insisted on isolation, and it is not Russia who has destroyed it. But England having done so, can you be surprised if we, who have most to do with Turkey, should shed no tears on that account? Our treaties henceforth will not be 'preliminary,' which really is too humble and ridiculous, nor will they be politely submitted to the mutilation of a Congress.

I am told in England that the loss of Cyprus has neither diminished the Sultan's dominions nor has it impaired his independence. Well, I daresay there are other 'Isles of Cyprus' as yet belonging to the expiring 'Sick Man,' and other Powers will perhaps take upon themselves the philanthropic duty of 'civilising and improving them.'

Russia has at least as much to offer as England as the price of Cyprus concessions; nor is Lord Beaconsfield the only Minister who can guarantee the Turkish frontier or the Sultan's independence against aggressive encroaching Powers. But we have also other equivalents to offer, without giving troublesome guarantees—as, perhaps, you may some day discover.

If, in spite of our efforts, a jealous antagonism has to continue between us, if we are to be still rivals; we cannot sufficiently express our obligations to Lord Beaconsfield, whose only fault is that by always moving his pieces into our hands he makes the game too easy to be exciting or even interesting. Thoroughly to enjoy sport it is really necessary to have to encounter difficulties and to overcome a certain cleverness and skill. But Lord Beaconsfield positively seems to enjoy making the game dull. His touching satisfaction at our annexing Batoum without 'shedding one drop of blood;' so contrary to the indignation expressed by the whole of the Ministerial press, was quite a curious surprise.

But perhaps the most curious feature of the Anglo-Turkish Convention, is the fact that, while it conditionally guarantees Asiatic Turkey, it leaves the Sultan in unguaranteed possession of Constantinople. Neither England nor any other Power guarantees to the Turk the continued possession of Constantinople or of one yard of European soil.

CHAPTER III.

THE HEIRS OF 'THE SICK MAN.'

THE SICK MAN is very sick—sick even unto death. What do you propose to do with his inheritance? Surely that question is not now too indiscreet?

When the Emperor Nicholas made a similar inquiry, many years ago, you were shocked beyond expression. Lord Palmerston was positive that this interesting patient would soon be quite well, and 'in great force.' Russians, however, turned out to be better diagnosists. You hear the Sick Man's death-rattle. Who are to be his heirs?

A friend of mine who sits at Stamboul, with his finger on the Sick Man's pulse, writes that he does not dare to leave the city even for a few days, lest on his return he should find in place of the invalid only a corpse on the Bosphorus. The definite catastrophe is as near as it is unavoidable. The Empire, which received a new lease of life at Berlin—'thirty or forty years at least,' Lord Salisbury said—is already in dissolution. What is to be done with its remains?

That great triumph of English diplomacy—'the resuscitation of the Ottoman Empire'—is hardly so dazzling now as it was last year. The Palace is in want of mutton, the army in want of bread, the treasury in want of funds, the Cabinet in want of statesmen, the whole country in want of security —both moral and material. Everywhere within this sublime Empire nothing but insurrection. The Druses are astir, the Arabs are seething in discontent, Kurds and Armenians, plunderer and plundered, are equally hostile to the Constantinople Pashas—these common foes of human kind. Greek and Albanian are even more hostile to the Sultan than the Slav. The sword of the Turk has been wrenched from his gore-stained hand; and the East, with wicked incredulity, refuses to believe your Ministerial speeches as to the new lease of life granted to the Turkish Power.

The outlook is not less gloomy abroad. In place of friends gathering for his protection, the Sick Man sees vultures impatiently waiting for their repast. Even in Russia we did not know how desperate was the condition of the Sultan until we heard he had sunk so low that Lord Beaconsfield had ventured to insult him, and, without even waiting for 'the mandate from Heaven' which was lacking in 1877 for the liberation of Bulgaria, had coerced the Turk with his ironclads to send Baker Pasha on a fool's errand into Asia Minor.

Surely, then, I may be permitted to quote the words which our Emperor Nicholas addressed to the English Ambassador at St. Petersburg in 1853. We need not alter one word, not even one syllable, to adapt them for the situation in 1879. Spoken in confidence—which you violated—twenty-six years ago, we repeat them to-day without reserve as embodying the wisest counsel that Russians can offer to Englishmen.

'The affairs of Turkey are in a very disorganised condition, the country itself seems to be falling in pieces, and it is very important that England and Russia should come to a perfectly good understanding upon these affairs. We have on our hands a Sick Man, a very Sick Man; it will be, I tell you frankly, a great misfortune if one of these days he should slip away from us, especially before all necessary arrangements were made; and, if the Turkish Empire falls, it falls to rise no more; and I put it to you, therefore, whether it is not better to be provided beforehand for a contingency, than to incur the chaos, confusion, and the certainty of an European war, all of which must attend the catastrophe if it should occur unexpectedly and before some ulterior system has been sketched. I repeat, the Sick Man is dying, and we can never allow such an event to take us by surprise. We must come to some understanding. It is not an engagement, a convention which I ask of them; it is a free interchange of ideas, and, in case of need, the word of a gentleman—that is enough between us.'[1]

Time has justified our Emperor. Not even your Ministry would now deny that the Sick Man's days are numbered; and the letter from Constantinople mentioned above contains, curiously enough, almost

[1] *Eastern Papers*, Part V., pp. 2-5.

exactly the expressions of our Monarch. And then the writer adds: 'No efforts to galvanise him permanently can possibly succeed. There will be a great deal of fighting about his inheritance'—which is precisely the probability Russia, in 1853, desired to avert. Who are to be his heirs? Surely sensible people would not defer the settlement of that question until we are all in the midst of a *culbute générale*. Why is it so difficult to come to an understanding?

Russia has no reserves. Her policy is perfectly frank and straightforward on this question. Our Emperors have repeatedly explained what our views are of the disposition of the Sick Man's estates.

I have no authority to speak in the name of Russia. I am not, as your papers so kindly declare, an agent of our Government (which sometimes I wish I were, because, then, believe me, I should know how to make my voice, not only heard, but attentively listened to!). But I am familiar with a little of our history, and with the opinions of many of our best Russians upon the subject. Under these circumstances, one is allowed, perhaps, to speak with confidence as to the Russian views on these matters.

Russia seeks no annexations on the Balkan Peninsula. Within the last sixty years we have thrice dictated treaties to the vanquished Turks, but we have not at this moment one foot more territory in Europe than we had in 1815. We have not even taken a Cyprus concession from the Sultan in this continent as the price of all our victories. Turkey in Europe, so far as Russia is concerned, is territorially as she was when the Battle of Waterloo was fought.

This fact at least gives us some claim to your confidence, when we declare that we want nothing for ourselves from the Sick Man's inheritance.

Our policy was accurately defined by Count Nesselrode, exactly fifty years ago. He wrote:—

'The Emperor will not advance the boundaries of his territory, and only demands from his allies that absence of ambition and of selfish designs of which he will be the first to set the example.'[1]

Fifteen years later, when the Emperor Nicholas visited England, he repeated this axiom of Russian policy in the Balkan. 'I do not claim,' he said, 'one inch of Turkish soil,' when he anticipated in his interview with Sir Robert Peel the confidences which he afterwards shared with Sir Hamilton Seymour. I own I admire our Emperor's foresight at that time. 'Turkey,' said he to Lord Aberdeen, 'is a dying man. We may endeavour to keep him alive, but we shall not succeed —he will, he must die.[2] That will be a critical moment. I foresee that I shall have to put my armies in movement, and Austria must do the same. Must not England be on the spot with the whole of her maritime forces? But a Russian army, an Austrian army, a great English fleet, all congregated together in these parts—so many powder barrels so close to

---

[1] *Wellington's Despatches*, vol. vii. p. 80.

[2] English politicians now speak even more frankly than Russians on this point. Sir W. Harcourt recently told his constituents: 'There is no policy which is worth discussing which does not assume for its basis, and make provision for, the inevitable dissolution of the Turkish Empire. That is a thing which must be, which ought to be, and which will be.'

the fire—how shall one prevent the sparks from catching. Why should we not, then, come to a previous understanding, that in case anything unforeseen should happen in Turkey, Russia and England should come to a previous understanding with each other as to what they should have to do in common (*que s'il arrivait quelque chose d'imprévu en Turquie, la Russie et l'Angleterre se concerteraient préalablement entr'elles sur ce qu'elles auraient à faire en commun*).'[1]

That straightforward and honest understanding, with a view to a future *concert préalable, le cas échéant*, on which the Emperor Nicholas agreed with the English Ministers in 1844, is exactly what might be established now. No more and no less. It is not to be desired the most in the interests of Russia. If there is to be a general scramble, Russia perhaps is not more unready for doing her part than the Government of Lord Beaconsfield. Kars and Batoum afford better bases of operation than Cyprus; and your difficulties in Zululand lead many to infer that the conquest of Asia Minor may be a task beyond your powers.

The Duke of Wellington, in his Memorandum on the Treaty of Adrianople, foreshadowed the concerted understanding which is now more than ever to be desired. He wrote: 'The object of our measures, whatever they are, should be to obtain an engagement, or, at all events, a clear understanding among the Five Powers, that in case of the dissolution of the Turkish Monarchy the disposition of the dominions

---

[1] *Stockmar's Memoirs*, vol. ii. pp. 106, 114.

hitherto under its government should be concerted and determined upon by the Five Powers in Conference.' After urging the importance of concerting what should be done, he points out that by such an arrangement the Powers would be 'assured that the crumbling to pieces of the Turkish Government would not create a war, and would not occasion such an accession of dominion and power to any State as would alter the general balance of power, or give reasonable cause of apprehension to others.[1]

The necessity of this '*concert préalable*' is not Russian, but European. It is urged in the interest of the general peace, and of the unhappy populations of the East.

Without a general understanding on a basis of abstention from conquests, there may arise most fatal emergencies. Let us look at the facts as they are. An *émeute* in Constantinople, or even an accident in the Seraglio, might to-morrow give the signal for a world-wide war over the inheritance of the Turk.

If there is such a thing as statesmanship in Europe, a contingency so terrible ought not to be left for solution to chance.

It is assumed by some that England and Austria have settled everything, without consulting the other members of the European concert. Such a settlement would only settle one thing, and that is—war.

No Power, and Russia least of all, will permit a question which vitally interests her as much as any, and more than most, to be settled over her head. Her voice must be heard, her legitimate interests

[1] *Wellington's Despatches*, vol. vi. p. 219.

respected, and her duties fulfilled. This is claiming for my country no more than we concede to yours. If you exclude us from the Council Chamber, you evidently prefer meeting us in the field. But there is no reason for this morbid dread of Russia's councils, unless there is some *arrière pensée* in your minds as to territorial annexations. In that case you are, perhaps, only right in shrouding your designs in impenetrable darkness. We, who have no such reserves, can speak frankly. We seek no annexations for ourselves; but this very disinterestedness justifies us in resolutely denying annexations to others.

The territorial integrity of the Ottoman Empire— that watchword of the past generation—reappears in a new form as the embodiment of Russia's policy in the East. We maintain the territorial integrity of the Ottoman Empire, but we demand, not the independence, but the elimination of the authority of the Sultan.

We extend that principle to those provinces— to Servia, Montenegro, and Roumania, from which the Sultan's authority has been finally eliminated by the Treaty of San Stefano, ratified at Berlin.

Of these States, as well as of all the territory left to the Sultan by the Berlin Treaty, Russia claims nothing and concedes nothing. The Balkan lands belong to the Balkan people. Mr. Aksakoff accurately stated the views of Russia when he wrote: 'The East of Europe belongs to Oriental Europeans; the Slav countries belong to the Slavs. It is not a question of territorial conquests for Russia; it is a question of calling to an independent existence (political and social) all these different Slav groups which people the Balkan Peninsula.' We have not freed them from the pashas of Constantinople, to see them handed over to the tax-gatherers of Vienna, or even to the Commissioners of London. Do not imagine that it is only Russians who object to an Austrian appropriation of the inheritance of the sick man. There is no more rancorous Russophobist living than Louis Kossuth, and this is his opinion as to the danger before Austria-Hungary, which, he says, 'he sees like a death-prophesying bird, with outstretched wings, fluttering over my country.' 'What will be the result of the Vienna Cabinet should it again follow this damnable policy of expediency? In the past, it has put a razor in the hand of Russia. Now, it would put this razor to the throat of Hungary and also of Austria. . . . What the Viennese Cabinet would pilfer from the Turkish Empire would only weaken us, and become eventually our death ; because it would eternally multiply and put into further fermentation all the already fermenting and dissolving elements. The Slavonians who would be caught by the Viennese Cabinet would take the latter with them. And what would be the infallible final result? The punishment of *talio*. If St. Petersburg and Vienna should divide the rags of the Turkish Empire, twenty-five years would not elapse before the Russians, the Prussians, and the Italians would divide Austria and Hungary among themselves, perhaps leaving something of the booty to Wallachia, as the reward of subserviency to Russia. This is as true as that there is a God.'[1]

M. Emile de Laveleye, I regret to see, thinks that to assure to the Slav populations liberty, autonomy, and well-being, the only practical method is to extend the influence of Austria. M. de Laveleye is a very great authority, I admit; but even M. de Laveleye's *ipse dixit* would not reconcile these same Slav populations to Austrian annexation.[2] Servians, Bulgarians, and even Roumanians (though the latter are united to the Balkan Slavs by their religion, not by their nationality) regard the prospect of Austrian absorption with only less dread than the restoration of Turkish authority.

It is curious that admiration for Austria has sprung up in the West. In the East, where Austria is better known, Austria is almost detested.

Even the terrible Russians are more popular amongst the Southern Slavs than the admirable Austrians, as you may have noticed in the contrast

[1] 'Russian Aggression,' *Contemporary Review*, December, 1877, pp. 22, 23.

[2] In the same review in which M. de Laveleye expresses this conviction, Mr. W. J. Stillman remarks:—'The very constitution, history, and organic habit of the Austro-Hungarian monarchy are such, that it must always be a source of great apprehension to a weaker neighbour. It is what the Americans call a carpet-bagger on an Imperial scale, and has no possible utility for people who are not in need of an esoteric rule. As its existence depends on its rights of conquest, its growth must always be at the expense of its neighbours. It has no *raison d'être*, except the incapacity of its subjects to govern themselves. It is purely parasitic, and any subject nationality which retains vitality as such must struggle to throw off the weight of it; nor is there any possibility of its becoming a permanent institution in the face of the development of self-government, except by its identifying itself with some national organism, after the example of the House of Savoy.'—Article 'Italy,' *Fortnightly Review*, December, 1879, p. 838.

between our welcome by the Christians in Bulgaria and the chilling reception in Bosnia. When we say 'Austria,' it is, in fact, giving a title of courtesy to the German-Magyar Government of Vienna-Pesth. If a new Austria, essentially Slavonic, were to be formed, a voluntary union of the States of the Danube might, perhaps, be established with advantage. But the Confederation of the Danube must spring from the voluntary alliance of Free States, it must not be the offspring of military conquest, and we doubt whether 'Austria' would be the name by which the Slavonic Free States would choose to be known.

General Chrzanowski, a Pole, whose antipathy to Russia was frank and vehement, is reported by Mr. Senior, in his most interesting 'Conversations,' as having uttered some remarks concerning Austria which may enable you to understand why the Servians and the Bulgarians regard her as only one degree better than the Turk. 'Austria,' he remarked,[1] 'by occupying, in 1855, the Principalities, has succeeded in making even the Russians regretted; nothing has so prepared the Moldavians and Wallachians for incorporation with Russia as their experience of Austrian rule. The pressure of Russia is heavy, but gradual. It is a screw slowly turned. The Austrians are brutal and impatient; they use not a screw, but a mallet; they insult while they rob. Russia consolidates her conquests; the subjects of Austria are always impatient; always on the brink of insurrection.' Austria, no doubt, has improved since then; but impressions produced by centuries are slowly effaced.

[1] *Senior's Conversations*, vol. ii. p. 69.

Why cannot these Balkan States be allowed, like Italy, to '*fare da se*'? That is Russia's policy. Why should it not be England's? It is, at all events, fortunately, Mr. Gladstone's policy. The natural alliance of the future is that of Orthodox Russia and Liberal England, to defend the independence and develope the liberties of the populations of the Balkan Peninsula.[1]

M. de Laveleye thinks that Austria will free

---

[1] Addressing an enormous meeting of working men at Edinburgh on November 29, 1879, Mr. Gladstone said:—'Who is to have the succession of Turkey? Gentlemen, from the bottom of my heart, and with the fullest conviction of my understanding, I will give you the reply—a reply which I am perfectly certain will awaken a free, generous, and unanimous echo in your bosoms. That succession is not to pass to Russia. It is not to pass to Austria. It is not to pass to England, under whatever name of Anglo-Turkish Convention, or anything else. It is to pass to the people of these countries, to those who have inhabited them for many long centuries, to those who had reared them to a state of civilisation when the great calamity of Ottoman conquest spread like a wild wave over that portion of the earth, and buried that civilisation under its overwhelming force. Gentlemen, I appeal to you to join me in the expression of the hope that under the yoke of no Power whatever will those free provinces be brought. It is not Russia alone whose movements ought to be watched with vigilance. There are schemes abroad of which others are the authors. There is too much reason to suspect that some portion of the statesmen of Austria will endeavour to extend her rule, and to fulfil the evil prophecies that have been uttered, and cause the great change in the Balkan Peninsula to be only the substitution of one kind of supremacy for another. Gentlemen, let us place the sympathies of this country on the side of the free. Rely upon it those people who inhabit those provinces have no desire to trouble their neighbours, no desire to vex you or me. Their desire is peacefully to pass their human existence in the discharge of their duties to God and man; in the care of their families, in the enjoyment of tranquillity and freedom, in making happiness prevail upon the earth which has so long been deformed in that portion of it by misery and by shame. But we say, gentlemen, that this is a fair picture which is now presented to our eyes, and one which should not be spoiled by the hand of man. I demand of the authorities of this country, I demand it of our Government, and I believe that you will echo the demand, that to no Russian scheme, that to no Austrian scheme, to no English scheme—for here we bring the matter home—shall they lend a moment's countenance; but

Macedonia, but Austria, with England's aid, re-enslaved Macedonia at the Congress. It would be interesting to hear of any unselfish deed done by Austria in the whole course of her history.[1] It would encourage us to hope that Macedonia may yet owe her liberation to the hand of her enslaver. At present the Slavs of the South may be pardoned if they doubt whether their brethren the Czechs have sufficient influence in Austria to prevent the exploitation of the Balkan Peninsula for the benefit of Jews, Germans, and Magyars.

Why should you distrust those rising races of the East? They are not strong as yet, neither are they rich; but they contain the seeds of a prosperous future. Their development may be retarded by diplomacy, but it cannot be prevented. Nationalities that have survived the fiery furnace of Ottoman domination will not perish because of the swaddling clothes of Western diplomacy.

It is of no use pointing to the troubles of Bul-

---

that we shall with a kindly care cherish and foster the blessed institutions of free government that are beginning to prevail—nay, that are already at work in those now emancipated provinces.'—*Political Speeches*, p. 92.

In like manner spoke Sir William Harcourt at Oxford, January 13, 1880:—'The arrangements of the Treaty of Berlin have irretrievably broken down. Ministers now pin their faith upon an Austria-German Convention. That is only a new blunder. That is to replace the old blunder by a new one. The conception of constituting Austria the gaoler of the Slav nationalities is a conception which is unworthy of practical statesmen, and altogether repugnant to Liberal principles. Russia has won the hearts of those provinces by making herself the patron of their independence. She leaves to Austria to assume the position of the conqueror of alien races and of a dissatisfied people.'

[1] Mr. Gladstone, in March, 1878, referred to the long catalogue of Austria's misdeeds, 'scarcely relieved by a solitary act done on behalf of justice and of freedom.'—'Paths of Honour and of Shame,' *Nineteenth Century*, p. 603.

garia and Eastern Roumelia. These troubles, and even worse difficulties, were expected by Russians as the natural consequence of the policy of the Berlin Congress. Instead of one strong, independent Bulgaria, Europe insisted upon making three, and gave independence only to the least advance.

You cannot say that this is an after-thought. On June 10, 1877, before our army had crossed the Danube, Prince Gortschakoff informed your Government that the separation of Bulgaria into two provinces would be impracticable, as local information proved that Bulgaria must remain a single province, otherwise the most laborious and intelligent of the Bulgarian population would remain excluded from the autonomous institutions.

A failure in Bulgaria and Eastern Roumelia would not prove the unfitness of the Bulgarians for self-government. It would merely prove our Chancellor was right in 1877, and that the Congress was wrong in 1878.[1]

[1] The following official communication, which I translate from a recent number of the *Moscow Gazette*, clears up a point on which there has been some misunderstanding:—'The ministerial crisis in Bulgaria has evoked in the press discussions about the Bulgarian Constitution, in which not only foreign but even Russian papers have maintained that the Constitution granted to Bulgaria was the work of the Russian Government. This is quite incorrect. According to the 4th and 5th clauses of the Berlin Treaty the National Assembly convoked at Tirnova had to elaborate the fundamental institutions of the principality. To help and quicken these works the Russian Commissary presented a project of a statute, simply as a foundation for further elaborations. The Russian Commissary declared positively that the final decision belonged exclusively to the National Assembly. During the discussions several points of this draft Constitution have been greatly modified. The Imperial Government carefully avoided every intervention, only advising moderation, especially in regard to the liberty of the press and of the right of public meeting. Therefore the responsibility for the existing

The English observers who speak most disparagingly of the Bulgarians only know those north of the Balkans. Those who—like the late Mr. MacGahan, Mr. Jasper More, Dr. Sandwith, Major Baker, and Sir George Campbell—knew the Bulgarians of the South, always spoke of them in the very highest terms.

Sir George Campbell, indeed, places them high above the Russians, who, he says, 'can claim none of the elements of an Imperial race.' I admired my countrymen more than ever after reading this declaration of Sir George Campbell's. It is wonderful to make bricks without straw; and it is a feat no one else but Russians could have accomplished, to create and govern the largest Empire in the world without possessing any single element of an ' Imperial race.'

But on one point I agree with the hon. member for Kirkcaldy. The Bulgarians are really a very superior race. I well remember that General Tchernayeff, who is as patriotic a Russian as he is a devoted friend of the Southern Slavs, declared to me, on his return from a tour in the Balkans, 'Believe me, these Bulgarians are a capital people. Give them ten years of good government, they'll astonish every one by their progress.'

Similar testimony, not less emphatic, has been given by your Consuls. Tell me, if we poor Russians, who, 'without any of the elements of an Imperial race,' have contrived to build up the greatest Empire the world ever saw, why can you not believe that

institutions rests entirely on the Tirnova Assembly. The modifications which experience advises are not in the least opposed to the views of the Imperial Government, whose chief object is the consolidation and welfare of the Principality.'

these richly gifted Bulgarians, if freed from the intermeddling of the Turks of Constantinople and of the Turks of diplomacy, will at least be able to manage their own affairs?

I shall be told that the rival races of the Balkan Peninsula hate each other almost as much, to judge from English descriptions, as the Neapolitans used to hate the Piedmontese, in the descriptions of those who advocated the maintenance of Austria's influence in Italy.

There are differences, no doubt.[1] Boundary lines

[1] The difference between the Bulgarian Exarch and the Patriarch of Constantinople is now happily in a way to be healed. The separation of the Bulgarian Church from the Patriarchate was purely administrative, and exclusively temporal. There are no differences as to dogma or purely spiritual matters, and the Bulgarian Church occupies the same position to the Patriarchate as the Churches of Russia, Servia, and Wallachia. The quarrel about the Church of Sveta Petka in Philippopolis would never have arisen but for the differences between the Patriarch and the Exarch. The Church of Sveta Petka was built by the Bulgarian Voulco Théodorovitch, at a cost of 50,713 piastres; 43,013 were subscribed by Bulgarians, and only 1,700 by Greeks. Its title deeds declare it to be communal property, and to be controlled and maintained by the elected representatives of the commune. In that commune 250 out of 305 families are Bulgarians of the Bulgarian Church; fifty are Bulgarians who side with the Patriarch, and only five are Greek. When the independence of the Bulgarian Church was recognised by the Sultan's decree in 1872, the Bulgarians were allowed to hold all their churches wherever they possessed a majority. Whenever Bulgarian apathy permitted it, the influence of the Patriarch was exerted to prevent the churches passing out of his jurisdiction. In this way the Church of Sveta Petka, and another called Sveta Nédélia remained in the hands of the Greeks. The other day the Bulgarians forcibly possessed themselves of the former church, maintaining that by its origin, by its title deeds, by the majority of the commune, and by the Firman of 1872, it belonged to them, and ought to be under the jurisdiction, not of the Patriarch, but of the Exarch. Disturbances ensued, and Prince Vogarides locked up the church and sent the case for trial. So much has been made of this dispute to the prejudice of the Bulgarians, that it may be useful briefly to state these facts, and to point out that the quarrel arose, not so much out of a rivalry of race, as from an ecclesiastic difference, which shortly will be removed. A full account of the Sveta Petka will be found in the ably conducted organ of the Southern Bulgarians, the *Maritza*, February 5, 1880.

would have to be traced, and many other things would have to be done. But all these are mere trifles. The peril of the Eastern Question does not lie in the antipathies of local populations, but in the rivalries of mighty Empires.

If the Powers honestly forswear individual aggrandisement, a settlement of these topographical details would be easy. The principle of the Treaty of San Stefano, that the frontiers should be settled after local examination on the spot, in accordance with ethnographical facts, would suffice to settle these small questions.[1]

You will object that in some districts the population is too inextricably mixed up for division on ethnographical principles. Well, it may be so. In that case the obvious arrangement would be to adopt the Eastern Roumelian expedient, without the intervention of the Sultan. Eastern Roumelia is Bulgaria.[2] So is a large—possibly the largest—part of Mace-

[1] Article VI. of the Treaty of San Stefano runs as follows:—
'Bulgaria is constituted an autonomous tributary Principality, with a Christian Government and a national militia. The definitive frontiers of the Bulgarian Principality will be laid down by a special Russo-Turkish Commission before the evacuation of Roumelia by the Imperial Russian army. This Commission will take into its consideration, when considering on the spot the modifications to be made in the general map, the principle of the nationality of the majority of the inhabitants of the districts, conformably to the Bases of Peace, and also the topographical necessities and practical interests of traffic of the local population. The extent of the Bulgarian Principality is marked in general terms on the accompanying map, which will serve as a basis for the definitive fixing of the limits.'

[2] The overwhelming numerical preponderance of the Bulgarian population in Eastern Roumelia, is proved by the result of the elections for the first Provincial Assembly which were held in autumn 1879, under the provisions of the Organic Statute drawn up by the International Commission. The Bulgarian deputies outnumbered those of all other nationalities by nearly six to one. The Greeks only elected four members, the Turks *three*, and the Jews and Armenians two each.

donia. This view was supported by Lord Salisbury and his diplomatic colleagues at the Constantinople Conference.[1] But outside the limits of the Bulgaria of the Constantinople Conference there may be a region, stretching from Adrianople to beyond Salonica, including the south of Macedonia and the extreme north of Epirus and Thessaly, not sufficiently Hellenic to be annexed to Greece, or Bulgarian to be annexed to Bulgaria, which might be governed on the plan, which is little better than a vexatious absurdity when applied to the sub-Balkan districts of Bulgaria.

In time the races would amalgamate, or one would acquire sufficient ascendancy to decide the destinies of these narrow strips of border land, through which, of course, both Servia and Bulgaria should have access to the Ægean—Servia by an international railway to Salonica, and Bulgaria by a port at Enos, at the mouth of the Maritza.[2]

Albania is tolerably autonomous already; but Greece should receive Epirus, Thessaly, Crete, and the Hellenic Islands, which may, perhaps, include Cyprus, when you get tired of it.

The rightful heirs of the Sick Man are his long oppressed subjects.

There remains the Last Word of the Eastern Question—Who is to have Constantinople?

---

[1] See Map, p. 120.

[2] Opinions differ as to the most suitable port for Bulgaria. The Treaty of San Stefano suggested Kavalla; others have pointed to Salonica, which, however, is more likely to become a free town, a neutral sea-port. The advantages of Enos over both are obvious, as being at the mouth of the Maritza, the chief river of Southern Bulgaria. They were very forcibly pointed out by the late Mr. MacGahan, in one of the last letters which that indefatigable and well-informed correspondent ever wrote.

CHAPTER IV.

'THE LAST WORD OF THE EASTERN QUESTION.'

'THE last word of the Eastern Question,' said Lord Derby, ' is—Who is to have Constantinople?'

Lord Derby may be right; but it seems, after all, that the importance of Constantinople has been strangely, even ridiculously, exaggerated. The popular conception of the city as a kind of talisman of Empire is really as absurd as the other superstitions about talismans which flourished in the age from which the superstition about Constantinople is a somewhat grotesque revival.

Constantinople has long since ceased to play the most important part in the history of the world. The idea of its importance dates from the time when civilisation and commerce were almost confined to the shores of the Mediterranean. When Constantinople acquired its domination over the imagination of men one-half of the capitals of modern Europe did not exist; and, with the exception of Rome, none of those which had begun to live could venture to rival the position of the city of Constantine. All that is changed. Alike in commerce and in war, in science and in religion, the world's centre is no longer on the Bosphorus.

A company of London merchants have created at the other side of Asia an Empire more splendid than that of Amurath ; and our Peter the Great reared on the icebound shores of the Northern Seas a capital whose monarchs dictate the terms on which the rulers of Constantinople are permitted to hold their Empire.

The whole world has been transformed since our ancestors, crusading with the Lion-heart or conquering with Sviatoslaf, learned to regard Constantinople as the natural seat of universal Empire.

Constantinople is no longer even the commercial emporium of the world, standing midway between two continents, and essential to both. Since the days of Constantine, an Englishman, a Portuguese, and a Frenchman have changed everything. Constantinople resembles a seaport from which the ocean has receded, for the Steam Engine, the Cape route, and the Suez Canal have dried up the ancient channels of trade between Asia and Europe. The road to the Indies no longer runs through the Bosphorus, and the commercial glories of Constantinople are now almost as faded as those of Trebizonde.

'The Empire of the world' is so far from belonging to the owners of Constantinople, that even the appointment of their officials is dictated to them by telegrams from London, emphasised by ironclads at Malta. Stripped of this romantic halo of superstition and exaggeration, what is Constantinople?

Constantinople is a city commanding the narrow straits by which alone the dwellers on the shores of the Black Sea and the vast populations on the rivers draining into that ocean can gain access to the Mediterranean. To Russia, Austria, Hungary, Roumania, and the Balkan States, the ownership of Constantinople can never be the matter of indifference which it might be to the other European States. Constantinople is the gate of the Euxine, and the question, Who shall keep its keys? is of vital interest only to Euxine and Danubian States, and therefore primarily to Russia.

Commercially the ownership of Constantinople, as commanding the Bosphorus, which has been described as the real mouth of the Danube, is almost as important to Austria as to Russia. Politically, however, it is of more importance to Russia. Austria has no seaboard on the Black Sea; no ironclads can threaten her from the Euxine, while the Russian seaboard lies open to every attack. It is, therefore, doubly important for us that the keys of the Black Sea should be in the hands of—if not of a friendly Power—then of a Power too weak to be a menace to the safety of our ports or the security of our commerce.

From a commercial and political point of view, the Sultan is as good a gatekeeper of the Euxine as Russia could wish to have. As Emperor Nicholas told Sir Hamilton Seymour, 'Nothing better for our interests could be desired.' In former times the Sultan closed the Black Sea to all the commerce of the world, and menaced Europe with conquest. Russia has effectively opened the Black Sea to trade, and at the present day Russia could not possibly have a more submissive doorkeeper than her helpless debtor, the Sultan, although if he has a fault it is that he is a little too weak to uphold his treaty rights against the encroachments of England.

In Constantinople, under the eye of the Ambassadors, the Sultan cannot do much harm, and he need not have more than a 'cabbage garden in Europe.' This arrangement is practicable enough. It was nearly a century after the Turks made Adrianople the capital of their European dominions, that they succeeded in taking Constantinople, which from 1361 to 1453 preserved its independence.

Russia has repeatedly approached Constantinople. She has never entered it. The only entrance with which we have been credited was due to English ignorance of the French language. While the discussion of Mr. Forster's amendment in the House of Commons hostile to the six millions war vote was proceeding, Count Schouvaloff, talking to a lady at an evening party in London, observed in passing, 'Oh, mon Dieu! quant à Constantinople, nous sommes dedans,' a colloquial French expression meaning, 'We have been taken in or deceived.' It passed from mouth to mouth, and was construed as a positive announcement by the Russian Ambassador that our army had entered Constantinople!

Next morning several London papers appeared with excited articles, commencing, 'Nous sommes dedans!' The Russians are in Constantinople—such was the categorical declaration of Count Schouvaloff, the Russian Ambassador!' and then followed the usual inflammatory nonsense concerning Russian 'perfidy' and Muscovite 'greed,' of which the London press always keeps so large a quantity in stock, and whilst Count Schouvaloff, with difficulty preserving his gravity, was endeavouring to explain French phrases to English Ministers, Sir A. Layard's misleading telegrams about the alleged advance of Russian troops on Constantinople, seemed to the masses to confirm the English interpretation of ' Nous sommes dedans,' and, in the explosion of excitement which followed, Mr. Forster's amendment was withdrawn.

That, however, was the only Russian entry into Constantinople recorded in history. In 1829 a Council of the Empire decided that as no arrangement could be more advantageous to Russia than the maintenance of the Sultan in Constantinople, he should be left on his throne. Russia, in 1833, and again in 1840, interfered to save the Sultan from destruction, and it is possible events may again call for her intervention against another foe. It was said to be 'against the well understood interests of the Russian Empire' that Turkey should be destroyed.

I was told the other day that a belief prevails in high official quarters among the Turks that the English Government intended to invite Austria to occupy Constantinople when the collapse comes. Lord Salisbury's 'sentinel of the gate' is to be placed in possession of the city, and the Government of Vienna and Pesth is to hold the keys of the Black Sea.

It is well to be plain spoken. Unless one admits that Austrian statesmen have altogether taken leave of their wits, one should acquit them of any desire to reign on the Bosphorus. Is it not only to Lord Salisbury that we should say, '*Pas trop de zèle; surtout pas trop de zèle?* Poor 'Austrians' have sins enough on their conscience without our adding to them all that the English Minister can meditate for them to perpetrate. But should a design like this really be contemplated, it could evidently be executed only by war. Russia could not humbly submit to see the key of the Black Sea conferred upon a rival Power without her becoming the laughing-stock of the whole world. 'England understands,' said Count Nesselrode in 1853—what Austria understands to-day —'that Russia cannot suffer the establishment at Constantinople of a Christian Power sufficiently strong to control or disquiet her. The Emperor disclaimed any wish or design of establishing himself there, but he has determined not to allow either the English or the French to establish themselves there.' In those days an Austrian occupation of Constantinople was too absurd even to be talked of. Russia desires to see at Constantinople what your Ministers pretended to desire to see at Cabul—a strong, a friendly, and an independent Power. There is, however, this difference; that for you such a state of affairs was a superfluous luxury, whilst to us it would be an imperative necessity.

It is the inveterate superstition of Russophobists that we desire to annex Constantinople. Our history does not justify the suspicion. But it is quite true that Constantinople occupies such a place in the Russian imagination that, questions of self-preservation apart, no Russian Emperor could tolerate the Austrians on the Bosphorus.

The Italian Peninsula until twenty years ago was the amphitheatre in which France and Austria struggled for ascendancy. Austria represented the power of the conqueror. France fostered the national idea. The interest of the European drama has been shifted eastward. The Balkan Peninsula takes the place of that of Italy. Austria again represents foreign conquest; but the representative of nationality and independence is no longer France, but Russia— 'a Power,' as was observed the other day by a very intelligent diplomatist, 'which never gave up in the course of all this century any step which she thought it her duty to pursue, though she sometimes consented to intervals of halt.' In both peninsulas the Imperial city exercises a strange fascination. To save the Eternal City from falling into the hands of Austria, the French Republicans stifled in blood the Republic of Rome. Said M. Thiers, 'You can scarcely estimate the importance we attach to Rome. As the throne of Catholicism, as the centre of Art, as having been long the second city of the French Empire, it fills in our minds almost as great a space as Paris. To know that the Austrian flag was flying over the Castle of St. Angelo is a humiliation under which no Frenchman could bear to exist; and,' then exclaimed the impetuous Frenchman, 'rather than see the Austrian eagle on the flagstaff that rises above the Tiber, I would destroy a hundred Constitutions and a hundred religions.'[1]

If the thought of Rome falling into the hands of Catholic Austria excited such passions in the heart of Catholic and Voltairean France, can you wonder if the thought of Catholic Austria in possession of St. Sophia kindles feelings of ungovernable indignation in the minds of Orthodox Russia? Constantinople fills an even greater space in our imagination than Rome in that of the Frenchman. Our religion is Byzantine, our laws, our Constitution, our architecture have all more or less been influenced by Byzantium.

Russia may endure the *status quo*. She has certainly no desire to possess Constantinople. But she never could consent to Constantinople passing either to Catholic Austria or Protestant England.

Russia's relations to Constantinople take their rise in the heroic ages of her history; nor should Russians hesitate to admit that they began in a series of attempts on the part of our early rulers to possess themselves of Constantinople—that is, of Tzargrad, or 'King of Cities,' as it was then popularly described in Russia.

No fewer than five several times in the course of two centuries Russia attempted to conquer Tzargrad, and this, no doubt, is sufficient to convince our

[1] *Conversations with M. Thiers, M. Guizot, and other distinguished Persons*, Nassau W. Senior, vol. i. pp. 53, 61.

enemies that we are animated by a never-dying desire to possess Constantinople. The argument, I confess, seems to me somewhat weak.

The attempt to conquer the East at the dawn of the Middle Ages was almost exclusively Scandinavian. Whether it was directed from the North-East or the North-West of Europe, the restless valour of the Norse Vikings impelled alike all the Russian expeditions under our Variag[1] Princes against Constantinople and the Crusades of the Western monarchs. Oleg was no more a Russian than Richard was an Englishman. The impulse which drove the Franks to plant their standard on the walls of Jerusalem, although to a large extent religious, was greatly due to the same fierce Norman fever for conquest which drove Sviatoslaf to capture the city of Philippopolis and Oleg to hang his shield on the Golden Door at Byzantium. If these early Variag expeditions of ours in the tenth century against Constantinople prove that Russia to-day desires to seize the city of the Sultans, much more does the conquering of Constantinople in the twelfth century by the Crusaders from the West prove that Tzargrad is in danger from the descendants of those who made the Third Crusade.

The first attack was made by Askold and Dir, who, true to their Viking instincts, conducted a naval expedition against Byzantium. They perished, with their two hundred vessels, in a tempest.

The second attack was more successful. Oleg, in 907, with 2,000 vessels, invested Tzargrad by land,

[1] In English usually called 'Varangian.'

and dictated terms of peace at the gates of the city. An indemnity was exacted from the Greek Emperor, a commercial treaty was signed, and Oleg suspended his shield from the Golden Door. His successor, Igor, was less fortunate. His flotilla was destroyed by Greek fire in his first attempt, but in 944 the menace of a second invasion induced the rulers of Byzantium to pay an indemnity and sign a new commercial treaty. The most memorable war of early Russia against the Lower Empire was that which resulted in the annihilation of the army of Sviatoslaf by the forces of John Zimisces. The origin of the war was curious. The Byzantine Emperor, finding himself in danger from Bulgaria, then an independent kingdom under its own Tzars, called on the Russians to defend his capital against the nationality on whose behalf Russia fought her war of 1877-8. Sviatoslaf, with an army of 60,000 men, subsidised by Byzantium, crushed the resistance of the Bulgarians, captured their capital and all their fortresses, and practically annexed their country. John Zimisces demanded its evacuation. Sviatoslaf replied by threatening Constantinople. War ensued between the late allies, and after displaying marvellous bravery at Silistria the Russians were completely defeated, and the remains of their heroic army evacuated the Balkan. This was in 972. Seventy years afterwards, Yaroslaf the Great, the Charlemagne of Russia, sent an expedition against the Greek Empire, which met a disastrous fate. The stormy Euxine, Greek fire, and the sword of Monomachus destroyed it to the last man. Only 800 Russians, blinded by their captors, survived as prisoners in Byzantium. Seven centuries had to pass away before a Russian army again encamped in the Balkan Peninsula. It was not until 1772 that Russians again crossed the Danube, and the war which was ended by the Treaty of Kainardji certainly did not aim at the conquest of Constantinople.

The only war which Russia entered upon with the design of changing the ownership of Constantinople was that which sprang from 'the Greek project,' arranged between Catherine the Great and Joseph II., and which was begun by the Turks in 1787. But although it was agreed by Austria and Russia to place Constantine, the second son of Paul I., on the vacant throne of Tzargrad, it was expressly declared that Constantinople should not be annexed to Russia.

This arrangement was a strange one, and under present circumstances it may be interesting to reproduce it, as it proves that, in the eighteenth as in the nineteenth century, Austria's appetite for the inheritance of the Sick Man was far greater than that of Russia.

Austria was to have Servia, Bosnia, and the Herzegovina, as well as Dalmatia, which then belonged to Venice, recouping the Venetians for Dalmatia by ceding them the Morea, Candia, and Cyprus. Russia was only to have Otchakoff, the strip of land between the Bug and the Dnieper, and one or two islands of the Archipelago. If the war were crowned with such success that the Turks were expelled from Constantinople, the Greek Empire was to be re-established in complete independence, the throne of Byzantium to be filled by the Grand Duke Constantine Pavlovitch, who was to renounce all claims to the throne of Russia, so that the two kingdoms might never be united under the same sceptre.[1]

When the ambitious schemes of Catherine are referred to as proving the desperate determination of Russia to annex Constantinople, it is well to remember that that monarch laid it down as an imperative direction for the policy of Russia that Constantinople and Moscow should never be united under the same sceptre.

The war did not prosper as was expected. Poland was partitioned instead of Turkey, and Russia contented herself with Otchakoff.

During the Napoleonic wars, Alexander I. submitted to England a scheme for the partition of the Ottoman Empire, in case of its existence becoming incompatible with the present state of Europe. England was not cordial, but she concluded a treaty of subsidies with the Emperor against Napoleon. A few years afterwards, when Napoleon and Alexander met at Tilsit, there occurs the only occasion in history in which a Russian Emperor expressed a wish to secure possession of Constantinople. *Napoleon declares* that Alexander urged strongly a claim to Constantinople, but that he refused to hear of it. The arrangement that was arrived at provided that Russia and France should 'come to an understanding to withdraw all the Ottoman provinces in Europe—Constantinople

[1] Rambaud's *History of Russia*, vol. ii. p. 160.

and Roumelia excepted—from the yoke and tyranny of the Turks.' That desirable consummation even now is not yet completed, although the Treaty of Berlin, in this respect, does not fall far short of the provisions of the Treaty of Tilsit.

Since that time our Emperors have not only persistently repudiated any intention to annex Constantinople, but they have as consistently refused to take any step to deprive the Sultan of his capital.

In 1829, when our armies were at Adrianople, it was decided that it would be detrimental to Russia's interests to overthrow the Government of the Sultan on the Bosphorus, but if such a contingency could not be averted they proposed that Constantinople should be made a free city.

The contingency did not arise, and the city remained in the hands of the Sultan, to the regret even of Conservative Englishmen. 'There is no doubt,' said the Duke of Wellington, ' that it would have been more fortunate, and better for the world, if the Treaty of Adrianople had not been signed, and if the Russians had entered Constantinople, and if the Turkish Empire had been dissolved.'[1] Lord Holland was even more outspoken. In the session of 1830, in his place in Parliament he exclaimed, ' As a citizen of the world, I am sorry that the Russians have not taken Constantinople.'[2]

In 1833, when the success of Mehemet Ali threatened the Ottoman Empire with sudden dissolution, a Russian army occupied Constantinople for the defence

---

[1] *Wellington Despatches*, vol. vi. p. 219.
[2] *Thirty Years of Foreign Policy*, p. 115.

of the Sultan against his rebellious vassal. Lord Palmerston, in the debate on the presence of Russians at Constantinople, to which the English Government had consented, said :—' I very much doubt whether the Russian nation would be prepared to see that transference of power, of residence, and of authority to the southern provinces which would be the necessary consequence of the conquest by Russia of Constantinople; and if we have quietly beheld the temporary occupation of the Turkish capital by the forces of Russia it is because we have full confidence in the honour and good faith of Russia, and believe that those troops will be withdrawn in a very short time.'[1] Lord Palmerston was justified in his confidence, and our troops were withdrawn when the capital was out of danger.

If only a similar just confidence had been displayed in 1878 Europe would not have been brought to the verge of a gigantic war.

In the Crimean War I only need to refer to Mr. Kinglake's authority to prove that ' it would be wrong to believe' that when the steps were taken which brought about the war ' Russia was acting in furtherance of territorial aggrandisement,' much less from a design to annex Constantinople.

In 1876, and still more signally in 1878, Russia remained true to her traditional policy. The words of our Emperor to Lord Augustus Loftus, at Livadia, may here be given as the latest authoritative expression of Russia's will on this subject.

[1] Sir Tollemache Sinclair's *Defence of Russia*, p. 6.

The Emperor said he had not the smallest wish or intention to be possessed of Constantinople. 'All that had been said or written about a will of Peter the Great and the aims of Catherine II. were illusions and phantoms, and never existed in reality; and he considered that the acquisition of Constantinople would be a misfortune for Russia. There was no question of it, nor had it ever been entertained by his late father, who had given a proof of it in 1828 when his victorious army was within four days' march of the Turkish capital. . . . His Majesty pledged his sacred word of honour, in the most earnest and solemn manner, that he had no intention of acquiring Constantinople.

'His Majesty here reverted to the proposal addressed to Her Majesty's Government for the occupation of Bosnia by Austria, of Bulgaria by Russia, and of a naval demonstration at Constantinople, where, he said, Her Majesty's fleet would have been the dominant power. This, His Majesty thought, ought to be a sufficient proof that Russia entertained no intention of occupying that capital.

'His Majesty could not understand why there should not be a perfect understanding between England and Russia—an understanding based on a policy of peace—which would be equally beneficial to their mutual interests and those of Europe at large.

'"Intentions," said His Majesty, "are attributed to Russia of a future conquest of India and of the possession of Constantinople. Can anything be more absurd? With regard to the former it is a perfect impossibility;

and as regards the latter I repeat again the most solemn assurances that I entertain neither the wish nor the intention." '[1]

Not less categorical was the more formal declaration of the Russian Government. Prince Gortschakoff, on May 18, 1877, defined the position of Russia towards that city. He wrote :—' As far as concerns Constantinople . . . the Imperial Cabinet repeats that the acquisition of that capital is excluded from the views of His Majesty the Emperor. They recognise that in any case the future of Constantinople is a question of common interest, which cannot be settled otherwise than by a general understanding, and that if the possession of the city were to be put in question, it could not be allowed to belong to any of the Great Powers.'

The Treaty of San Stefano—signed when Turkey was absolutely in Russia's power—proved that Russia had no intention of dispossessing the Sultan of Stamboul; and it is probable that 'the well understood interests of the Russian Empire' are still believed to require the maintenance of his authority as custodian of the Straits.

Constantinople, though it possesses great religious and historical attractions to Russians, has not that exaggerated importance in our eyes that is held in the minds of both English and Turkish statesmen. Mr. Gladstone, at St. James's Hall, and again at Midlothian, declared that if England had been in Russia's place ' she would have eaten up Turkey long ago.' Fuad

[1] *Blue Book*, Turkey 1 (1877), p. 643.

Pasha, in that political testament which affords so singular an illustration of a statesman-like perception on the part of a Turkish Minister, declares, 'If I had been myself a Russian Minister I would have overturned the world to have conquered Constantinople.'[1] Russian Ministers do not share the idea of Fuad Pasha, that the possession of Constantinople is worth the overturn of the world. If we transferred our capital to the Bosphorus, Constantinople would be the Achilles' heel of the Russian Empire.

I was discussing this subject a short time since with a brilliant Frenchman. 'I do not see,' he remarked, half jokingly, half seriously, ' why Russia should not have Constantinople. I desire nothing so much as to see you there.' 'But,' I remonstrated, 'we do not share your desire. The day we established ourselves on the Bosphorus our decline would begin.' 'Certainly,' rejoined my sarcastic friend; 'and that is precisely why I wished to see you there!'[2]

[1] Farley's *Turks and Christians*, Appendix III. p. 239.
[2] Emperor Nicholas told Şir Hamilton Seymour: 'If an Emperor of Russia should one day chance to conquer Constantinople, or should find himself forced to occupy it permanently and fortify it with a view to making it impregnable, from that day would date the decline of Russia. ... If once the Tzar were to take up his abode at Constantinople, Russia would cease to be Russian. No Russian would like that.' Even Mr. Cowen, M.P., in his lucid interval recognised this truth. Coming from such a Russophobist, the following remarks are perhaps of some little interest. 'Many intelligent Russians,' said Mr. Cowen—speaking at Blaydon on September 30, 1876—' entertain strong objections to the extension of the Russian rule to Constantinople. And for this very sensible reason. ... The Russians, whose number is considerable, and I believe increasing, are of opinion that it would be unwise to remove the capital of Russia from Petersburg to Constantinople. On these grounds, then, I dismiss this question of Russian extension as

If, however, sudden collapse should occur, and the ownership of Constantinople should come up for settlement, it seems to me that there are, perhaps, only two solutions which Russia can even so much as discuss.

The first is the conversion of Constantinople into a free city under the guarantee of Europe, governed by an International Commission. To this there is the grave objection that Constantinople carries with it the sovereignty of Asia Minor, which can hardly be vested in either an International Commission or in the civic authorities of a single city.

The other solution is the establishment under the tutelage and guarantee of Europe of a European Prince, a *persona grata* to all the Powers as Sovereign of Byzantium and Asia Minor.

Time is not yet ripe for making Constantinople the seat of a Balkan Confederation. It would be absurd and dangerous to entrust it to Greece, and the veto of Russia is recorded in advance against any scheme of placing Constantinople in the hands of any of the Powers.

Our position is clear and unambiguous. If England is equally free from all *arrières pensées* as to the last word of the Eastern Question, why should we not come to a perfect understanding on the subject based on 'a policy of peace which would be equally beneficial to our mutual interests and to those of Europe at large'?

unworthy of consideration. The fear of Russian aggression is an exploded illusion.'

PART III.

MISUNDERSTANDINGS AND PREJUDICES.

1. SOME ENGLISH PREJUDICES.
2. POLAND AND CIRCASSIA.
3. SIBERIA.
4. RUSSIAN AUTOCRACY.
5. CONSTITUTIONALISM IN RUSSIA.
6. THE ATTEMPT ON THE EMPEROR.

CHAPTER I.

SOME ENGLISH PREJUDICES.

ALAS! poor Russians! we seem to have no chance, no chance whatever, of obtaining justice among the English in England. No sooner do we flatter ourselves that at last we have met with a friend—with at least one person who has the wisdom to question the truth of accusations brought against us without positive evidence, and to refuse to regard separate cases as general absolute truths—than a rude rebuff recalls us to reality, and an act of pure unmistakable hostility dissipates in a moment the pleasing illusion that at last we had found an unprejudiced judge.

Fear can surely have no share in the production of so persistent an animosity! The menace to your Indian realm exists only in the imagination of those who fancy that it is but a stone's throw from the banks of the Oxus to the southern slopes of the Himalayas. In Russia we cannot understand why Englishmen should permit a dread of Russian power to colour all the speeches of your Conservative politicians, and to bias the policy of your Ministry. We know too much of the power of England to accept such a compliment as quite serious. We see that

England annexes new territories every year with a facility which betrays to foreigners little evidence of reluctance on her part to extend the boundaries of her Empire. We know that she is all-powerful at sea, and her financial position is first-class. Russia, on the other hand, is not wealthy. She is only morally rich, which, according to old-fashioned Russian views, is not altogether to be despised. But that moral wealth can neither threaten India nor annex Great Britain. Why, then, this irrational panic, which haunts the imagination of what used to be the most self-confident, self-reliant, and fearless race in the world? If I were an Englishman I should blush for shame if I entertained this coward fear of any Power on earth.

It is impossible to believe that fears so groundless can really occasion all the hostility with which my country is regarded by many Englishmen. If it is not fear, to what unknown source, then, can we trace the origin of Russophobia? To poor, simple-minded Russians it seems hopeless to undertake such an inquiry. One involuntarily recalls Hamlet's remark, 'There are more things in heaven and earth, Horatio, than are dreamt of in your philosophy.' But perhaps I may be pardoned if I suggest that ignorance, pure, sheer, downright ignorance,[1] has not a little to do with it.'

[1] The *Statesman* of December 13, 1879, referring to this prevailing ignorance says:—' A few years ago, Father Coleridge earnestly warned us in *The Month* that the English temper towards Russia was such that we were ready to attribute to her machinations the very physical disturbances of the earth. If Mount Etna breaks into eruption, the temper of our news-

Let me give an instance of this ignorance in places where it might least be expected to exist. The other day a friend mentioned, in the course of conversation, that your great English poet, Mr. Tennyson, hated Russia.

'Indeed,' said I; 'that is most unfortunate. But can you tell me why?'

'Oh,' was the response, 'we English people, you know, cannot tolerate your knout system!'

'How good of you!" I exclaimed; 'upon this we perfectly agree. But tell me, why should your Laureate live only in the past and take no notice of the present? Poets are not confined to the contemplation of the past; the future itself is sometimes disclosed to their ken.'

With a puzzled look and hesitating accent, he

papers is such that they are ready at once to ascribe it to Russian agency at the bottom of the crater. We tell our countrymen, almost with passionate earnestness, that while they permit themselves to be deluded as they are, by German, Magyar, and Jewish hatred of Russia, there is no hope of wise and noble guidance of the foreign policy of the nation. The metropolitan press pours forth an incessant stream of the wildest delusions concerning the great and simple-minded people whom it is our misfortune to have made our enemies by the abuse and calumnies we have poured upon them for years. It is most unworthy and most guilty; and until the English people are enlightened enough to judge of Russia for themselves, instead of looking at her through the spectacles of German Jews, Magyar patriots, and Romish priests, they will never understand what Russia really is.' And again, on January 3, the *Statesman* says:—' These Continental scribblers have made the masses of our countrymen insane about Russia. ... Russia and America are marked out, by every fact of their being, as the two natural allies of this country in the great work of regenerating Asia. Neither Tory statesmen nor publicists will permit the nation to cherish any other feelings than those of hostility and jealousy towards both. ... Russia is at this moment our natural ally, and it is nothing but our own evil temper as a people towards her that prevents our discerning it. But the guilt of it is not the people's—it is the publicists',

observed, 'But you do not mean to say that the knout is a thing of the past, not of the present?'

'That is exactly what I do mean to say,' I answered. 'If I wish to stick to facts I can say nothing else. The knout has ceased to exist in Russia—even in the navy,' I added, ' which perhaps is also the case with the cat-o'-nine-tails in the navy of England! Is it not so?'

Without answering my question, my friend said, 'Since when?'

'Shortly after the emancipation of the serfs,' said I. 'Russia is a long way off; but is seventeen years not long enough for such a reform to reach the ears of England's Laureate?'

We may be 'barbarians,' but our criminal code, judged by the standard of the Howard Association, is more humane than that of at least one other nation, which retains the lash in the army and navy,[1] applies the cat-o'-nine-tails to the garotter, and secretly strangles murderers in the recesses of her gaols.[2]

Well, perhaps that does not improve matters. Is ignorance not invincible? Does not Schiller say 'against stupidity the gods themselves contend in vain'? If Englishmen, seventeen years after the knout has disappeared from Russia, persist in

---

[1] Recent debates in Parliament almost lead one to believe that, in the opinion of the English Government, at least, the Army Cat is quite a pillar of the British Constitution.

[2] When this letter first appeared exception was taken to this phrase, perhaps not without some ground. Newspaper reporters, it was said, were *always* present at English executions. Since then, however, the Home Secretary, Mr. Cross, has excluded reporters by an Ukase, and so the phrase can now remain unaltered.

denouncing Russians for using the knout, what can we hope? And here again we Russians labour at a great disadvantage. We shrink from the task of vindicating ourselves even from the most unjust reproaches. Some accusations appear to us so inconceivably absurd that we cannot understand how any answer can be required.

Let me illustrate this. Last year a curious collection of calumnies against Russia was anonymously published in England. My English friends were anxious that it should be refuted. I applied, and applied in vain, to one after another of my literary friends in Russia to undertake such a task. 'How can you ask such a thing! No Russian with any self-respect could stoop to notice such monstrous libels. Your beloved England is evidently demoralising you, or you would never pay attention to such attacks.'

Is it either right or generous to declare that because no reply is made no reply can be made? The *Golos* in 1876 published a long and circumstantial story of the way in which Lord Beaconsfield abused his position as Premier to influence the Money Market. Nobody in England dreamed of categorically refuting it. They regarded the calumny as beneath contempt. Has not a Russian as much right to silence when accused as Lord Beaconsfield?

I am the more disposed to attribute this strange antipathy to ignorance, because those Englishmen who really know us are among the best friends we have. If there were really some secret antipathy between the nations this would not be so. In cases of mutual repulsion the repulsion is most marked when the two objects approach. But English residents in Russia rarely manifest the irrational antipathy which is so strongly shown on the banks of the Thames.

Examples of an exactly opposite feeling are present to our memory—such, for instance, as the warm-hearted letters which appeared in the *Daily News* and the *Times* in 1876, from well-known English residents in Moscow; and, frankly speaking, I think they are only paying us with our own coin.

The position of Russian visitors in England is, unfortunately, not always so pleasant. When England is determined only to recognise in every Russian a concealed enemy, intriguing against English interests, it is not to be wondered at if Russians shrink from visiting England, and if the two nations are somewhat estranged. Permit me to illustrate this by a little personal detail. As many Russians generally do, I was going to spend my summer and autumn abroad. Several people came to take leave of me, and we began discussing the projected journey. No sooner did I say 'I hope to go for a few weeks to England' when I was interrupted by several voices. 'It's impossible! Can you really go after what has happened? Why should you not rather go to China?' 'What do you mean?' I asked. 'How can one take the place of the other?' 'Oh,' they replied; 'one is preferable to the other. The Chinese are less afraid, less suspicious of foreigners, than the English; and besides, what the Chinese say and think of us we at least do not know.' 'But then, the few friends we have, why should I not be allowed to see them?' I asked. 'We have no friends,' they exclaimed; 'you are under a delusion!' And they but honestly expressed the general conviction. How can it be otherwise, when it is impossible for a Russian to pay a friendly visit to London without being regarded as a Russian partisan or even as a Russian agent?

Thousands of Russians go to France. Every Frenchman noticing the fact looks rather pleased, and finds it only natural: '*Ma foi, comme de raison, on adore Paris, c'est tout simple!*' But if a Russian comes to London it produces quite a different impression upon Englishmen. 'What can be his or her object in coming here? It looks very bad, the very fact of these frequent visits—very bad indeed!' The unfortunate foreigner tries to explain that he has a great liking for the country, its peculiar qualities, for some friends who have always been the same, equally kind and intelligent. But, after he has said all this, it remains as incredible as before! And yet, why should it be impossible for a Russian to visit England except as an 'agent'? You are really too modest.

The evidence of war correspondents[1] of the Eng-

---

[1] As so much has been said of the ferocity of our soldiers, may I ask credulous believers in Rhodope and other fables to read the following testimony by a distinguished British officer who bears an illustrious name in English history? Addressing his constituents at Sunderland in 1877, after three months' sojourn in the Russian camp, Sir Henry Havelock,

lish press is not without some little weight. Colonel Brackenbury, Mr. MacGahan, Mr. Forbes, Sir Henry Havelock, Mr. Boyle and others, less well known, made the acquaintance of Russians in Roumania and Bulgaria under circumstances which render concealment of realities impossible. I desire no better verdict for my countrymen than that pronounced by those witnesses selected at random, although some were hostile and others did not spare their reproaches against what they believed to be wrong—for, after all, we cannot be vexed with people, although they do not arrive at exactly the right result, if they honestly do their best.

This habit of always reproaching us with past, present, and future crimes is unjust and impolitic. Just put yourself in our place, and imagine a foreigner never uttering or writing a word about England

M.P., said he found the Russian soldier docile, gentle, tractable, he had almost said sheepish to a degree in his gentleness. During the time he was with the Russians, he came into contact in one way or other with 200,000 soldiers. Instead of finding them a degraded people, he only saw three drunken men during the whole time! In the dealings of the Russians with the Bulgarians, he remarked at all times the greatest gentleness and abstinence from violence. He not only saw them in large masses, but in distant villages, at the roadside, where soldiers were under no control, and the presence of a stranger like himself would have no effect on their action. Their conduct was the most admirable he had ever seen in his life. In their treatment of their enemies, were they the bloodthirsty people they had been represented? He was associated with the Cossacks for about three months. He never saw a tamer set of people in his life. He would challenge anybody to produce one single well-authenticated instance of violence, even of a minor degree, perpetrated by a Russian officer or soldier, either north or south of the Balkans, during the whole time of their occupation of that country!' Those who desire other testimonies will find them in the admirable papers on 'The Rhodope Commission and the *Pall Mall Gazette*, reprinted from the *Spectator* by Chatto and Windus.

without exclaiming, 'What a disgrace your Opium Trade with China is, in these days of Christianity and progress.' What would you feel?—although the reproach is, perhaps, not so unfair as many you cast at us. Suppose he even went further, and declared, 'You cannot care a straw for civilisation and liberty as long as you continue to tolerate the Opium Trade,' would he be worse than many Englishmen who disbelieve our sympathies with the Slavs, because of the shortcomings with which they reproach Russia?[1]

In Russia, when it happened to me to draw the attention of my countrymen to some friendly notice written about our people, and to read aloud some few favourable lines, I generally was interrupted with 'Well, well, when is the "but" coming? When are you coming to "Poland," "barbarism," the

[1] This point is put very forcibly by Mr. James Annand in one of his excellent *Campaigning Papers*. He says: 'Suppose England were in a condition similar to that of Russia, with more territory than wealth, and comparatively unknown among its neighbours, and suppose a set of people, say in Germany, were to devote themselves to telling how we blew Sepoys from guns in India, how we gag the native press, how we forced on an opium war, how we fought small potentates with little provocation, and how wherever we go the aboriginal inhabitants perish before us; suppose it were told that our people are divorced from the soil, that every thirtieth person we meet is an actual pauper, and every sixth or seventh an occasional one; suppose it were preached abroad that our law holds a man innocent until he be proved guilty, and yet he may be imprisoned like a common felon before his guilt is proved. All these are facts, or rough semblances of facts, and yet they would give an utterly inadequate idea of the kind of country England is, and of the kind of people of whom it is composed. Suppose the fact of our liberation of the West Indian slaves were suppressed or never referred to as the Russian liberation of the Serfs is, and suppose all the evil we ever did from the days of our barbarism upwards were continually brought before us whenever we made a movement to do well: we should be somewhat in the position in which certain people placed Russia during the late negotiations.'

"cherished knout," and the quicksilver mines, or at least the latest series of atrocities which need to be refuted?' Discouraged, I often had to give up my conciliatory attempt. Quicksilver mines, and Poland, and the famous knout actually seldom failed to appear, and my poor efforts to describe English sympathies or to explain my Anglomania generally terminated in a ridiculous *fiasco*.

No Englishman is asked to forget the duties which he owes to his own country: all that is wanted is that he should speak out his friendly feelings—when there are such—without trembling for being taken for a partisan or an agent, and even might I hope, without the everlasting 'but' which now qualifies and spoils almost every expression of your sympathy.

After the knout, Russia is most abused for her treatment of her subject races, and with as little reason. We have, for instance, many Mohammedan subjects. They are not oppressed or persecuted. They have all the liberty enjoyed by the Mohammedans in Turkey, except the liberty of oppressing their Christian neighbours. They certainly enjoy a far better government than their co-religionists in Asia Minor. In the Baltic provinces there are many local municipal institutions; and no race has less reason to complain of ill-treatment than the Germans, who enjoy so large a share of the administration of the Empire. It is a characteristic of Russia that we open even the highest branches of our service to all our subject races—an example which England, I think, does not follow in India. General Melikoff and General Lazareff, who have covered themselves with glory in Armenia, are both Armenians. Todleben and Heimann are Germans of the Baltic Provinces. Nepokoitschitzky is a Pole, as also is Levitsky.

'Ah, Poland!' you exclaim. Of course it is in vain for a Russian to appeal for a hearing of his defence about the Poles, even to those who deny Home Rule to the Irish.

Have you studied the facts—'those engrossed hierograms,' as Mr. Carlyle says, of which so few have the key? Have you tried, before framing your bill of indictment against a whole nation, at least to read what is written by our few, but honest, courageous defenders.

M. Emile de Girardin, in spite of his intimacy with the Bonapartes, felt indignant at the sheer ignorance of our accusers, and wrote his famous 'La Pologne et la Diplomatie'—full of authentic documents and historical proofs of the groundlessness of the prevailing prejudices. But this book, I fear, is not extensively circulated in England.

In another chapter I shall refer to this Polish Question, but now I content myself with saying that Poland would have had a Constitution of its own for the last sixteen years if the Poles would have been content with the boundaries of the kingdom of Poland. But when they insisted, even at the sword's point, that we should not only give Home Rule to Poland but Polish rule almost to half Russia, which they claimed to be theirs, then a reaction set in, and the reforms which the Grand Duke Constantine went to Warsaw with such high hopes to establish remained a dead letter.

Constitutions are not unknown in Russia, nor is it beyond the boundaries of Russian policy to grant Home Rule to its subject provinces. Those who think so should go to Finland. In that important maritime province they would find the Finns in possession of a very large measure of administrative independence. The Russian language is not employed in Finnish courts or in Finnish official documents. Am I wrong in saying that in Wales the Welsh language is not so favoured?

The Lutheran, and not the Russian Orthodox Church, is the established religion of Finland. Nay, even the Russian rouble will not circulate in that Russian province—which lies almost at the gates of the Russian capital. Finland has its own laws, its own legislature, its own Church, its own coinage, its own language, its own budget, and its own national debt.

M. de Circourt, one of the most distinguished Frenchmen of this century, whose stores of information were as exact as they were vast, in his conversations with Mr. Senior,[1] referred to this subject in terms which must horrify those who delight to represent Finland as one of the many victims of 'Russian aggression.' 'The Swedes,' said M. de Circourt, in 1863, 'must know that Finland is irrecoverably lost to them. They ruled it oppressively. Not a Fin was allowed to take part in the management of his own

[1] *Fortnightly Review*, January, 1880, p. 115.

country. It is now one of the best governed countries in the world. The population consists of about 50,000 Russians, 250,000 Swedes, and 1,600,000 Fins. The Finnish population has doubled since Finland became Russian. They detest Sweden, and are loyal Russians.' When asked by Mr. Senior, 'How do you account for the popularity of Russian rule in Finland and its unpopularity in Poland?' M. de Circourt replied, 'The causes are religion and race. The Fins are Lutherans, enjoying the best form of Christianity. The Poles are Roman Catholics, subject to the worst. Lutherans are tolerant, and are satisfied with toleration. Roman Catholics require supremacy. In Russian and Prussian Poland and in Lithuania they are merely on a par with the other Christian sects. The Lutheran Fins are not merely unpersecuted, their clergy are paid by the State. Then they are an admirable race: honest, diligent, quiet, and moral. They are among the happiest people in Europe, as the Poles are among the unhappiest.'

Nor does the recognition of local independence destroy the loyalty of our Finns. During this war their enthusiasm has been very great, although they are connected neither by race nor religion with the Southern Slavs. There is no conscription in Finland. Its system of raising soldiers is the same as the English. A few weeks ago a call was made for volunteers in one district in Finland.[1] In three days the list was more than filled by gallant men who were eager to be led to the liberation of Bulgaria. That

[1] This letter was written in November 1877.

they knew it was no holiday work upon which they had entered was shown by one grim little fact. Every volunteer before joining the ranks provided himself with a dagger, in order that he might have the means of saving himself by a swift death-stroke from the mutilation and torture that awaits the wounded who fall into the hands of the Turks! Have we not reason to be proud of men who go out joyfully to risk their lives in such a war?

It is difficult to convince those who are not familiar with Russia how willingly the whole population of my country will surrender all that they have, even life itself, if it be required by the Tzar, in order to carry on the war which he has undertaken for the oppressed Slavs. The declaration in the petitions which flowed in to the Emperor after the Moscow address—'We place our fortunes and our lives at thy disposal'—was no meaningless phrase. The records of Russia's history prove that it is a simple statement of a fact.

The calculating, sceptical, selfish part of Europe may look upon the addresses and petitions to the Emperor merely as a species of new-fashioned eloquence. But in burning, decisive, historical moments such Russian words have always been synonymous with deeds. An offer of 'life and fortune' can only be voluntary. We Russians are sometimes prevented from having this will categorically expressed and carried out; but after we have almost implored to be allowed to sacrifice them in a holy cause we never fear to be taken at our word—we never shrink from its consequences. The mighty voice of the Russian people has never been heard in vain.

Permit me to recall one instance alone out of numbers which might be mentioned to illustrate this characteristic of my countrymen. In the time of Peter the Great, whilst Russia was fighting, not for the tortured Slavs, not for her persecuted co-religionists, but merely for the possession of the Baltic Provinces—a question of comparatively small moment to the Russian people—the Emperor sent a ukase to the Senate fixing new taxes upon salt. No sooner was the Imperial decree read than Prince Jacob Dolgorouky sprang from his chair, and in the presence of a numerous assemblage, to the bewilderment of everyone, tore it to pieces.

'Emperor!' exclaimed he, with a trembling voice, 'you want money? We understand it! But why should the poor suffer and pay for it? Have you no wealthy nobility to dispose of? Prince Menshikoff may build a ship at his private expense, Apraxine another one, and I will certainly not remain behind my countrymen!'

Such was the spirit displayed by the Russians in those days, and since the time of Peter the Great Russians have not degenerated.

CHAPTER II.

POLAND AND CIRCASSIA.

Russia, writes a gifted friend of mine, 'Russia like England has her faults: their faults are identical.'

Without endorsing this view, it strikes me that there is, at all events, a great similarity in the complaints which each makes of the other. If you lived in Russia, you would see the other side of the shield, which is not visible in England. Sometimes at Moscow, when fresh from my English visit, when I hear good Russian patriots declaiming against England's shortcomings, their words sound to me like an echo of the denunciations of Russia with which I am sometimes favoured by my Turkophile friends. One cannot help smiling sometimes, for the indignation in both cases is just as intense, the accusations are just the same: only the names are changed. At Moscow they say England where at London they say Russia, but with that exception the philippics are almost identical.

While admitting that Russian patriots are sometimes mistaken, I must submit that English patriots are not always well informed about Russia.

Take, for instance, the charges which rise to the

minds of these mutual accusers when they utter the words 'Poland and Ireland.' Counting upon your love for straightforwardness, I must say that we can never understand why you should be so horrified with Russia for taking one share of partitioned Poland, while England never seems ashamed of having conquered Ireland by the sword. There are many points in common between the Poles and the Irish. Was it not your Prince Consort who said ' The Poles ! they are the Irish of the Continent.' ?

And here I may make just a passing remark, that it seems to a Russian somewhat strange that of the three Powers which divided Poland, your wrath is entirely expended upon the one which had the best historical justification for her action, whilst the worst of the partitioning Powers is the special favourite of English Conservatives.[1]

Of course I know that you have been induced by Mr. Gladstone, and other Liberal statesmen before his day, to improve the condition of the Irish. But just as your Poet Laureate still complains of the knout in Russia, which we abolished many years ago, so Russian readers are sometimes apt to be so far misled by the complaints of the Irish Home Rule obstructionists as to believe that Ireland still writhes an unwilling victim in the grasp of the England—say of 1798.

If our past in Poland is to be perpetually revived

[1] 'The manner in which Austria acted was perhaps the worst of the three confederates. Frederick and Catherine might be considered open foes; but the blackness of Austria was double-dyed, for she was treacherous and cowardly.'—*Thirty Years of Foreign Policy*, p. 32.

to inflame English animosities against Russia, can you wonder if your past in Ireland should occasionally be used in Russia to justify invectives against England, as 'a merciless oppressor of helpless nationalities'? Is there not somewhere a saying justifying the same measure you mete out to others being meted out to you? It is quite as unjust for Englishmen to abuse Russia of to-day for the sack of Warsaw, and to excite prejudice against us by reciting Campbell's rhapsodies about Kosciusko, as it is for Russians to denounce England's doings in Ireland as if the Penal Laws were still in force and 'flogging Fitzgerald' were still committing atrocities upon the Irish peasantry.

Despite Polish legends and Irish grievances, both Poland and Ireland, I believe, are getting on tolerably well under the respective heels of the Muscovite and the Saxon. As to Poland, let me, as usual, revert to English testimony, for I carefully avoid quoting our own, lest it should be said we are acting as judges in our own case. Mr. William Mather, of Salford, returning home in May 1878, from a lengthened tour in Russia, wrote to the *Manchester Examiner*: 'Poland is now one of the most prosperous and rapidly developing parts of the Empire. This I know to be a fact. In all business and industrial pursuits, Poland is developing more soundly than any other part of Russia.'

Recent reports of your consuls give the same flattering accounts of the present condition of Poland. They say, 'there is a very remarkable progress in commerce, agriculture, and manufacture,' and further, that 'the country is becoming rich and prosperous beyond all expectation.'[1]

Whatever wrongs the Russians may have done to the Poles, they were by no means the unoffending neighbours that some people believe.[2] That 'Sarmatia fell unwept without a crime' is, I believe, an article in the English creed; but the Poles took Moscow before we took Warsaw, and there was more excuse for rectifying our frontier at the expense of Poland a hundred years ago than there is for Lord Beaconsfield's scientific rectification of the north-west frontier of India at the expense of Afghanistan.

Mr. Cobden's testimony is well known.[3] But I can

[1] See Mackenzie's *The Nineteenth Century*, p. 379.

[2] I wish that some of my countrymen who possess that earnest love of truth and superiority to popular prejudices which so eminently distinguish your great historian, Mr. Froude, would render the Russians in Poland the inestimable service which the latter has rendered 'the English in Ireland.' Believe me the responsibility of the Poles for the miseries of Poland is at least as great as that of the Irish for the sufferings of Ireland.

[3] Mr. Cobden, in 1836, declared that there had been 'lavished upon Poland more false sentiment, deluded sympathy, and amiable ignorance, than on any other subject of the present age;' and he proved that, whatever might be the wickedness of the partitioning Powers, their act had been fraught with incalculable blessings to the Poles. He says:—'Down to the partition, nineteen out of every twenty inhabitants were slaves belonging to the very worst aristocracy of ancient or modern times. The Poles, who are now viewed only as a suffering and injured people, were, during the thirteenth, fourteenth, and fifteenth centuries, a most formidable and aggressive enemy to the neighbouring empires. They knew no other employment than that of the sword; war, devastation, and bloodshed were the only fashionable occupations for the nobility, whilst the peasants reaped the fruits of famine and slaughter. . . . . From the death of Sigismond, Poland became one universal scene of corruption, faction, and confusion. There is nothing in the history of the world comparable for confusion, suffering, and

call another witness whose voice ought to be heard with respect by those who refuse to listen to Mr. Cobden. There was a debate in the House of Commons on March 16, 1847, upon the annexation of Cracow, in the course of which a very remarkable speech was made from which I make no apology for making the following lengthy extract.

If there be any assembly in Europe which should be the last to criticise the conduct of the Powers with regard to Poland it is the Parliament of England. Before the partition of Poland took place the Minister of England was perfectly aware of what was contemplated. He was in communication

---

wickedness to the condition of this unhappy kingdom during these two centuries. The republic of Poland was a despotism one hundred thousand times worse than that of Turkey at this time, because it gave to 100,000 tyrants absolute power over the lives of the rest of the community. The historian of *The Anarchy of Poland* (in four octavo volumes) exclaims— "Oh, that some strong despot would come, and in mercy rescue these people from themselves." The fate of Poland was but a triumph of justice, without which its history would have conveyed no moral. . . . . The dismemberment of that empire has been followed by an increase in the amount of peace, wealth, liberty, civilisation and happiness enjoyed by the great mass of the people. Slavery no more exists, the peasantry now possess the control over their own persons and fortunes, and are at liberty to pursue happiness according to their own free will and pleasure, which is nearly the amount of freedom that can be *felt* to be possessed by the great mass of any nation. Under Russian rule, the condition of the country has continued to improve beyond all precedent; at no former period of its history was the public wealth so great and so generally diffused. The happy countenances of the inferior classes of society exhibited a wonderful contrast to what had lately been. To restore the Polish nation to its condition previously to the first partition in 1772 would be to plunge nineteen-twentieths of the inhabitants from freedom into bondage, from comparative happiness into the profoundest state of misery. *In all cases where neighbouring States have been annexed to Russia the inhabitants have thereby been advanced in civilisation and happiness.* Poland has undoubtedly benefited more than any other country by its incorporation with Russia. The spread of Russian Empire has invariably increased instead of diminishing the growth of civilisation and commerce.'—Cobden's *Political Writings: Poland*, pp. 92-97 and 101.

with the Government of France, and France offered to unite with England to prevent that partition. That Minister was second to none of those who have regulated the affairs of this nation in his knowledge of the Continent; and what did the Parliament do? On the very eve of the partition of Poland they turned that Minister out of office, and Poland was partitioned.

Many events have happened since then. Who can now deny that the spoliation of Poland has ceased to be a political catastrophe, and must be regarded as an historical fact? There must have been some good cause for a great and numerous race having met the doom we all acknowledge they have encountered. We hear much of a great nation. The hon. Member for Bolton tells us of twenty millions of people; but it is not the number of the people which makes a great nation. A great nation is a nation which produces great men. It is not by millions of population that we prove the magnitude of mind; and when I hear of the 'infamous' partition of Poland—although as an Englishman I regret a political event which I think was injurious to our country [1]—*I have no sympathy with the race which was partitioned.* It is just 100 years ago that it was proposed to partition another Empire. Look at the proceedings that took place at Frankfort against Maria Theresa of Austria. Look at the arch-conspirators that were there leagued together, at the head of whom was the King and the Republic of Poland. Why was not Austria partitioned when Poland was at the head of the conspirators to destroy her? I tell you it was the national character that saved Austria. She was not twenty millions then, and yet she baffled Prussia, she baffled France, she baffled Poland—that Poland which always comes before us as if she had been the victim of Europe instead of having been a ready conspirator on every occasion, and the pamperer of the lusts of an aristocracy

[1] The cynical doctrine of 'British interests,' which was applied to Bulgaria in 1877, had been applied by its author, it would seem, to Poland thirty years ago.

which ultimately betrayed her. Is it the suffering people who raise the commotions which are constantly taking place in Italy, in Poland, in Spain? Are they the parties to those movements? No. In every country it is the remnant of a subverted aristocracy—subverted because they were false to their trust, and never placed themselves at the head of their people. The men who really caused the fall of Poland were not the great Powers whom you denounce in your hustings' speeches. It was this order of men who never supported the people, under whom the people, indeed, were serfs and not free men. In Russian Poland the peasantry are in a far more easy condition than they were under independent Poland. Are you surprised, then, that the men who found themselves no longer serfs, but placed in this improved condition, should adhere to the arbitrary constitution which you denounce, and shrink from the aristocratic conspirators whom you patronise? If you assume to school the potentates and guide the populations of Europe, it is at least expected of you that your counsels should be founded on knowledge; it is at least expected that they should be expressed in the decorous language of a dignified conciliation.[1]

That testimony is very strong, coming from any Englishman at a time when, as a bitter enemy of Russia's declared, but a few months before 'the blood of the aristocracy of Galicia had been poured out like water in a common massacre,' but its weight will no doubt be immeasurably increased, when I add that the speaker was then Mr. Disraeli, who as the Earl of Beaconsfield is now Prime Minister of England.

Fifteen years ago the Grand Duke Constantine went to Poland to give her a Constitution. He was ardently supported by the Marquis Weliapolsky and Count Zamoisky, but the Marquis almost

[1] Hansard, vol. xci. pp. 67–91.

miraculously escaped death from assassination, and the offer of a Constitution was responded to by rebellion. Demands were made that autonomous Poland should extend almost beyond Smolensk, and in the troubles that ensued the Constitution was abandoned. The facts are notorious, but if you refuse to receive them on Russian testimony, Mr. Butler Johnstone, who is fanatically Turkophile, states them in the letters which he wrote from Russia two or three years ago.[1]

But do you know that if the Poles have not a national Government of their own, it is to some extent due to English diplomacy? After the overthrow of Napoleon, our Emperor was most anxious to reestablish the Polish Kingdom, and, if he failed, it was due to the representations of Austria and Prussia, supported by the English Plenipotentiaries. It is not only at Berlin that English Plenipotentiaries play a very different part from that demanded by the English people. Lord Beaconsfield had a good precedent for opposing the resurrection of Bulgaria, for, more than

---

[1] 'Political opinion in Russia would have been quite willing to grant autonomy with reference to Poland proper—*i.e.* the Grand Duchy of Warsaw. The chief organ of public opinion in Moscow was allowed openly to advocate this solution of the Polish difficulty. It was the Poles themselves who rejected it, . . . and insisted on their ancient provinces of Lithuania sharing their future. This claim of the Polish people to what the Russians call *their* Western Provinces was the tocsin which roused the patriotism of the nation, and the unequal struggle commenced. It was essentially and distinctly a struggle, not for Poland, but for Lithuania, where the minority, the proprietors and ruling classes, are chiefly Polish, but the majority, the peasantry, belonged to a different though kindred branch of the great Slav and Sarmatian family.'— *A Trip up the Volga.* By F. Butler-Johnstone, p. 7.

sixty years ago, had not Lord Castlereagh opposed the resurrection of Poland?

Addressing the Marquis of Londonderry on August 31, 1831, on the discussions which took place between the powers in 1814–15, the Duke of Wellington wrote as follows:—

> I think the principal subject of the discussion between Lord Castlereagh and the Emperor Alexander, who was then in a liberal mood, was the desire of the latter to constitute a Kingdom of Poland by adding to the provinces which had formed the Duchy of Warsaw the Polish provinces acquired by Russia by different treaties of partition; of which Kingdom the Emperor of Russia was to be King. The scheme created great alarm in the Courts of Austria and Prussia, who felt that their Polish provinces would be but insecure possessions if it were adopted, and *your brother took up the cause for them.* The affair ended by the partial adoption of the plan: that is to say, the Emperor became the King of Poland, consisting of those provinces which had constituted the Duchy of Warsaw, with the exception of certain cessions to Prussia and Austria respectively. The Emperor reserved to himself the right of increasing the Kingdom of Poland by adding thereto such Russo-Polish provinces as he might think proper, and he stipulated for a national Government for the Poles, not only by the King of Poland that was himself, but by the Emperor of Austria and the King of Prussia. Russia is the one of three Governments which has executed this last-mentioned article of the Treaty of Vienna with most strictness.[1]

M. Adolphe de Circourt, Ambassador of the French Republic of 1848 at the Court of Berlin, gave to Mr. Senior in 1863[2] some facts about

---

[1] *Wellington Despatches*, vol. vii. p. 500.

[2] See *Fortnightly Review*, January, 1880: 'Conversations with Adolphe de Circourt.'

Poland and the Poles which I take the liberty of quoting here. M. de Circourt was, as M. Scherer testifies, a man of 'prodigious erudition,' 'a living dictionary,' whose extraordinary attainments and intellectual gifts gave him a European reputation. Referring to the insurrection of 1863, M. de Circourt told Mr. Senior that it was almost entirely the work of the low townspeople, the poor nobles, and the retainers of the richer proprietors. Hardly any of the noble proprietors, or of the *bonne bourgeoisie*, or of the peasants had taken part in it. The rising was not much more important than the brigandage of Naples. Referring to the aristocratic class which gives to the Poles their national character, M. de Circourt says:—

They sigh, and as long as they are kept poor by their idleness, and idle by the want of education and by the prejudices of caste, they will sigh for the good old times, when they were the human beings of Poland and the peasants mere domestic animals; when any one of them had power to stop by a *liberum veto* the legislation and the policy of the kingdom. They hate the improvement which has followed the Russian Government. The bulk of the peasants are indifferent, or opposed to the insurrection. The Russian Government has not been a bad one to them. Even despotism is better for the lower classes than an ignorant aristocracy.

The whole Polish population is six millions seven hundred and ninety-two thousand— 3,872,100 in the Kingdom of Poland, 1,100,000 in Galicia, 1,140,000 in White and Little Russia, to the west of the Dnieper, to whom must be added 1,615,000 Roman Catholic Lithuanians, who, though not of Polish race, sympathise with the Poles as co-religionists. But of this total of eight millions and a half only the 3,872,000 of the Kingdom of Poland are compact enough to form a separate State. In the Russian provinces to the west of the Dnieper there are 5,950,000 Russians of the Greek Church, 1,140,000 Jews, and 115,000 Wallachs—that is, 6,215,000, as against 2,661,000 Poles and Catholic Lithuanians. In Galicia the Poles are only 1,100,000; the Ruthenians and others of Russian descent and religion are 3,100,000. So that in these outlying provinces the portion of the population which is not Polish or Catholic is 9,315,000; that which is Polish or Catholic is only 3,661,000.

When the Poles penetrated into Western Russia, the Poles—that is to say, the Polish nobility—seized the land and gradually reduced the peasants to the state of serfs. From Poland the malady of serfdom spread over Russia, but was not finally established in Russia proper—that is to say, in Muscovy—till about the year 1618. It was not a Russian institution.

On the whole the Poles are the worst nation in civilised Europe: the most turbulent, the most unscrupulous, the least capable of doing good to themselves or to anybody else, and, after the French, the most capable of doing harm. And, as is the case with all weak, silly, ill-conditioned nations, they have been always ill-treated since the time when they were strong enough to ill-treat others. I know that the Russian Government is anxious to do for the Poles all that can be done for them without injustice to its subjects. It cannot surrender to Poland a population of five millions of Russians in its western provinces, in order to please scarcely more than one million Poles.

Independence means the right of eighty-five thousand families to oppress four millions of their fellow-countrymen, and six or seven millions more of people who differ from them in race or in religion, and belong to them only because they inhabit countries which two or three hundred years ago went by the name of Poland.

Russia will fight to the knife rather than create an independent Poland. It would be a mere *avant-garde* of France in her next war against Russia.

M. de Circourt then reverts to a subject which should not be lost sight of by those who are content to derive all their ideas of Russia and the Russians from Polish sources. Mr. Senior having asked whether the Poles really enjoyed religious liberty as M. de Circourt asserted, and referred to the famous legend of persecution under Nicholas, and the outrages inflicted on the abbess and the nuns of a convent at Minsk, to force them to apostatise to the Greek creed, M. de Circourt replied :—

'I do not believe a word of those stories. I do not believe that there ever was such an abbess or such nuns or such a convent. The lies of the Poles are beyond description or enumeration. Never believe a word a Pole tells you. He secretes and then pours out falsehood naturally, almost unconsciously.'

I do not pretend to write a treatise on the subject of Poland. I merely jot down one or two things that it strikes one are not always remembered by our accusers. Believe me, we are not undesirous to do 'Justice to Poland,' but our efforts are made none the easier by unjust invectives from those who are unacquainted with our difficulties.

There is another sore subject with Englishmen when they speak of Russia—that of Schamyl and the Circassians. They formed a stock subject of English attacks some years ago, but is it not time you reconsidered your ideas in the light of recent facts?

In 1876, Lord Beaconsfield described the Circassians as peaceful, law-abiding, industrious settlers in European Turkey. Mr. Sedley Taylor wittily observed that he might as well have said that 'the man-eating tiger has become a strict vegetarian, and is engaged in drawing children about in go-carts, without any imputation of ungraminiferous behaviour resting on his character:' but everyone was not so well informed as Mr. Taylor, and your Premier no doubt expressed a common delusion about that interesting race. But even Lord Beaconsfield, unhesitating as he is in all his statements, would not now insist upon the high moral excellence of the Circassian character.

Instead of blaming us, we rather deserve your sympathy for having had to establish peace and order in regions inhabited by such untameable savages as the Tcherkess, whose real character has been so terribly attested by desolated Bulgaria. Even the Turks have denounced them, and all the correspondents of your journals agree as to their unenviable disposition.

As for Schamyl, 'the patriot chief defending in his majestic mountains the freedom of his race,' the conception no doubt is poetic, and interesting, only it is puzzling to see how vividly it appeals to the imagination of the people who are now making war on the Amir.

Schamyl's son entered the Russian army and became an officer of rank in our European service. I wonder if there is any chance of seeing a son of Yakub Khan as an officer of the Guards in attendance on the Empress of India?

CHAPTER III.

SIBERIA.

'THERE are at this moment millions of Poles being tortured to death in the quicksilver mines of Siberia solely because they are Roman Catholics.'

Such is one of the startling assertions with which all attempts to create an *entente cordiale* between Russia and England are so often rudely repulsed. It is more dignified, of course, to let stories of that kind pass unnoticed. One scarcely admits that anybody earnestly craving for truth can accept every absurdity. But it is no easy task for English people to find out what is the real state of things in Russia, our language being not an easy one to learn,[1] and we publish so seldom any refutation in our self-defence in any foreign tongue. I think my countrymen are wrong in never caring for what is said of them abroad, the moment

[1] On this point Prince Bismarck is an authority. In Busch's remarkable book, *Bismarck und seine Leute*, the German Chancellor expresses himself as follows:—'I cannot conceive why Greek should be learnt at all. If it is contended that the study of Greek is excellent mental discipline, to learn Russian would be still more so, and at the same time practically useful. Twenty-eight declensions and the innumerable niceties by which the deficiencies of conjugations are made up for are something to exercise the memory. And then, how are the words changed! Frequently nothing but a single letter of the original root remains.'

they perceive that ill-faith has anything to do with this or with that calumny. There is too much pride in our systematic contempt for injustice. I see no humiliation in trying to explain the very little I know.

I wish I could be eloquent and persuasive. But I can only be true and outspoken. Nor is there any great merit in reporting what has already become a commonplace. That, surely, requires little civic or moral courage! But there is a reason which often prevents Russians from protesting, with which I heartily sympathise. As a rule, the more you have to defend yourself the more you come to the ungenerous ' Tu quoque!' Now, there is very little consolation in thinking that we both are equally bad; but how are you to realise our difficulties if you are not reminded of your own?

When you accuse us, for instance, of our 'atrocious convict system,' how are we to avoid reminding you that you exiled your convicts to the Antipodes as late as 1853, and that your convict establishments at Norfolk Island and Macquarrie Harbour were not supposed to be exactly what philanthropists could wish for? Indeed, Russians have been often told stories of horror of the chain-gang and the lash at the Antipodes which rival even the worst your libellers have invented about our quicksilver mines.

England made a point of disbelieving the reality of our good feelings because of our shortcomings. Are we to apply the same system in judging you? When we honestly sought your alliance in supporting the Eastern Christians, you not only refused your help but strengthened as much as you could the Turkish resistance. Your Government brought upon us a war which cost us not only millions of money, but many, many lives, whose loss will always be present to our memory, in spite of the lapse of time and in spite of all the advantages which a successful war could gain. Your Government has done us a great deal of harm; and that it did not go further was simply because it felt convinced that no sacrifice, no danger could stop us the moment we thought it our duty to resist its concealed or open attacks. And in order to calm some generous, straightforward Englishmen, your officials tried to estrange them from us by inventing 'Russian atrocities' in Southern Bulgaria and elsewhere; and the ridiculous story about the millions of Poles exiled on account of their religion to Siberia is one of the snares set for English credulity.

The fact is this: Since this century commenced there have been (taking the most exaggerated numbers) about five hundred thousand persons exiled to Siberia, or less than ten thousand a year, but the majority of these were not Poles but Russians; nor were the Poles exiled on account of their religion —unless ordered to be rebels by their religion, as has sometimes been the case: but even then they were exiled for their rebellion, not for their religion. Imaginary geography is, I dare say, well studied in England, but the real one is decidedly not. Allow me, therefore, to remind you of what Siberia really is. Siberia is the northern half of the continent of Asia, exceeding in size the whole of Europe, and, as such, not easily described in a single formula. In the extreme north it is almost uninhabitable, and it is not thither that we send our criminals, for obvious reasons. It is too far off, and if we sent them into these dreary expanses of snow and ice, we should have to feed them at a ruinous expense. As you see, I do not want to idealise the measures taken by our Government. But, sending our criminals to Siberia, as we do, in order to get rid of them cheaply, it would defeat our object to send them into the confines of the Arctic Circle. When you say Siberia, you imagine only the desolate north. Siberia, to exiles, with few exceptions, in reality means the fertile south, so fertile, indeed, that when set at liberty the exiles very often prefer to remain on its rich and cultivated soil. A university is going to be established at Tomsk, which will enable their children to profit by all the results of culture and civilisation. Only the worst criminals, murderers, and desperate enemies of the State are sent to the mines and there employed in hard labour. But they form a small minority. In nine cases out of ten, exile to Siberia means enforced emigration to a fertile and scantily-peopled country. Transportation with us does not necessarily imply penal servitude. In many cases we simply convey the convicts across the Oural range, and then turn them loose to help themselves. Once in Siberia they are free to go where they please, as long as they do not return to European Russia.

As the Governor-General of Western Siberia reports only the other day, the English convict system differed from the Russian chiefly in severity. The English convict was compelled to work on penalty of the lash or gallows; the Russian convict—I quote General Koznakoff's exact words, as I have good reasons for trusting his word—is pitchforked into Siberia, and permitted to do whatever he likes short of actual crime. Many weighty voices are heard against 'the too great liberty accorded to convicts.' But foolish kind-heartedness, however absurd such an assertion may appear to you, is one of our national features. We often bear in mind what our great Empress, Catherine the Second, used to say:—' Better pardon ten criminals than punish one innocent.' We feel these words, and act accordingly, and I would prefer being still more foolish to introducing the slavery of English convict prisons into Siberia. To accuse and find fault is always an easy thing. To accuse with indisputable good ground is more difficult, but to understand entirely those we judge is almost beyond our power. So, as you see, it is only natural to distrust our judgment if its object is to torture those who depend upon it. But is it such a cruel thing, so revolting to English humanity, when a man has committed even a crime to give him a new start in life in a new and more fertile country?

Mr. Barry, in his 'Russia in 1870,' declares that in many districts the climate of Siberia has the mildness of that of Italy, lying, as it does, in the same latitude as Venice. The soil is a rich, deep black loam, capable of yielding prodigious harvests. Fruit grows wild in any quantity. Game is in abundance, and food is exceedingly cheap. 'I can think of no country in the world,' he concludes by asserting, 'which offers the same advantages to a young man with a small capital as Siberia. Whenever I travel in Siberia I always think—Why is it that our countrymen are sent away to the Antipodes in search of a colony? Here they would be nearer home; they can get better land, cheaper than in many of our colonies! They could live more cheaply, get cheaper labour, and enjoy many advantages of civilisation which they would want in the colonies.'

That is not Russian—that is English testimony. Another Englishman who employed many workmen in Russia recently remarked: 'Many of our hands come from Siberia, but they never remain very long. After two or three years they begin to pine for home, and when they leave they give no reason except—"It is very good, but not like Siberia!"'

Many Englishmen seem to think that Siberia is a large torture chamber—a gigantic quicksilver mine—where we send innocent persons to be slowly murdered. It is, on the contrary, a huge emigration field, whither we send criminals with the double object of getting rid of them and of supplying a sparsely-peopled province with colonists. It may not be a good way of dealing with criminals according to your view, but at least the charge of too great leniency is quite the reverse of what we are usually blamed for. To some the sentence ordering them to go to Siberia inflicts no disgrace. In their case it is simply equivalent to a compulsory passage to one of your colonies.

The number sent to Siberia, according to the latest official report, averages since 1860 about 20,000 per annum—not a very large proportion out of a population of 84,000,000. In England and Wales, with little more than one quarter of the population, you have 12,000 criminal convictions every year. The evils of which General Koznakoff complains are precisely those which would never arise if the facts corresponded to the English notion. So little limitation is placed upon the liberty of our convicts that numbers escape. In Tobolsk, in January, 1876, out of 51,122 exiles only 34,293 could be found. In Tomsk nearly 5,000 were missing out of 30,000. The great mischief of our system of pitchforking convicts into Siberia, and telling them to do what they please, is that very few of them take to honest labour. The country is so rich that they can live without hard work, and they become idle, good-for-nothing vagabonds. It is an easy way of getting rid of convicts, but it is not good for Siberia. M. Koznakoff, the Governor-General, declares that millions are spent in governing them without there being the slightest return for the expenditure in the shape of private or public works. Since 1870 about four thousand persons a year have been exiled for ' offences against the Administration,' some of whom, of course, are political offenders. But no mistake could be greater than to suppose that all these political offenders were sent to the quicksilver mines. For the most part they are left free to do as they please in certain districts, subject to police surveillance. As to the quicksilver mines, they are solely reserved for murderers and political criminals of the worst kind—people many of whom in England you would have hanged offhand. But as we have abolished capital punishment, we must do something with our murderers, &c., so we send them to the mines.

Of course, there may be great abuses in our establishments—I wish I could deny that—just as there were in New South Wales and Van Diemen's Land before you discontinued transportation. I admit injustice and mistakes on the part of our authorities —authorities are not infallible. But you would be wise in not accepting implicitly every libel told against us by Polish rebels. A few months ago a friend sent me a report of the most dreadful cruelties which a Fenian prisoner said he had suffered in your convict prisons. Believe me, our Poles, when instigated by their father confessors, are not behind your Fenians in the compilation of a catalogue of horrors. If merely Russophobes attacked us I would not make even the shortest reply. But the minds of some of our friends are evidently put out of ease with these horrible legends, and I do not like to strengthen our enemies' hands by refraining from stating the truth.

If it is complained that 'I idealise even Siberia,' I may quote from an article embodying the results of Recent Exploration of the Siberian Coast,' by Captain Wiggins, the adventurous explorer of the Arctic regions, whose enterprise in opening up a trade route by sea to Siberia has attracted much

attention in Russia. As the testimony of an independent witness, I make the following extract:[1]—
'Captain Wiggins has had many opportunities during his visits of thoroughly studying the system of exile from other parts of the Russian Empire, which is such a prominent subject in connection with Siberia, and, like others who have personally investigated it, he has arrived at conclusions very different from those popularly entertained. The captain declares that not one-third of these time-service exiles elect to make the return journey to their former homes; they find that life is easier and pleasanter in the land to which they have been forcibly sent, and they end by becoming free settlers in the country of their adoption. Desperate criminals only are sent to labour in the quicksilver mines and for these there is a specially severe discipline provided, and "horrors, without doubt, exist."'

The explorer goes on to say, for many years past the desire of the Russian Government has been to forward, by all means in their power, the settlement of this portion of their territory, and they have learnt that it is good policy to take the utmost possible care of the lives of the exiles, and to place them in the best possible positions for self-maintenance at the earliest opportunity. With the exception of the robbers and cut-throats specially condemned to the mines, the exiles are spread about in the towns and agricultural districts soon after their

[1] From an article published on Nov. 21, 1878, by the *Newcastle Chronicle*, the organ, I am told, of one of the most prejudiced of English Russophobes.

arrival, and, as a rule, they are left to shift for themselves. The supervision over them is slight, but tolerably effectual. The exiles, when quitting for any length of time the district to which they are assigned, must report their project to the head man, and they are then at liberty to go where they please, up or down the great river systems of the country, but they must not attempt to pass westward towards European Russia. A great number of the Russian exiles and immigrants employ themselves in the mines, and Captain Wiggins' experience of the people convinces him that they are 'a happy, rollicking, joyous community—well clad, well fed, and well cared for.' During the summer months they are able to earn sufficient money to provide for the wants of their respective households in the long winter; and the commencement of the cold season, when they visit the town to make their purchases, is generally a time of high festivity amongst them. Captain Wiggins declares that some exiles are now settled in the north by the Russian Government, which, in this particular kind of banishment, undertakes certain responsibilities with regard to the maintenance of the convicts. Supplies of rye meal are, in the summer season, forwarded to the furthest northern limits where the head men are appointed. These officials dispense the stores, during the winter, on a sort of credit system, to such exiles (or even families of the native tribes) as may need it, and in the succeeding summer the indebted parties must liquidate the cost price of the food they have received in furs, skins, or dried fish.

Captain Wiggins, unlike most writers on Russian questions, has visited Siberia and seen the country with his own eyes. It was, therefore, but natural that his evidence should be favourable. More surprising and unexpected is the testimony as to the falsity of the prevailing prejudices which appeared in November, 1879, in the Conservative *Standard*, entitled, 'The Future of Siberia.' It really is encouraging to find such truthful remarks as the following in the columns of a Ministerial organ :—

Siberia, to the mind of Europe, is associated with nothing but horror. One connects it with the crack of Bashkir Cossack's whip, with the groans of wretched exiles dying—or, worse still, living—in the mines of Nertchinsk, and with cold and misery. In reality these ideas, though firmly imbedded in the English mind, are altogether erroneous if they are to be accepted as true of Siberia at large or of the state of matters in that country at present. The truth is Siberia is a country of such extent that no general description can apply to all of it, and even when the accounts which have reached Europe have been true, which in the vast number of cases they were not, they related only to the northern part of the territory. Siberia is an infinitely richer and finer country than Canada or the northern part of America generally. Though the Polish exiles and others of a literary turn have not unnaturally given it a bad name, they have allowed their own sufferings to colour their narrative. In Siberia the Russian peasant can get the ' black earth ' soil, and he escapes, under certain conditions, the military service. Doubtless the ' unfortunates' who are sent on an average at the rate of 13,000 per annum to the penal colonies of Siberia are not pampered to any alarming extent. But that they are nowadays treated with the severity they were in the times of Peter, Catherine, Paul, and even Nicholas, is entirely untrue. Indeed, since the accession of the present Tzar, who in early life visited the penal settlements, the bureaucrats' complaint is that so mild has the punishment of expatriation become that Siberia is losing its terrors. It is, indeed, the locality into which the Russian gaols are annually emptied, and an offender is sent to that country who would in any other be simply sentenced to a few years' imprisonment. In the vast number of cases exile to Siberia is a very different matter from what banishment to Tasmania or New South Wales used to be. In the first place, as a rule, the Russian convicts go from a bad climate to a better, and are in such good company that the disgrace of transportation gets much modified. Only the third class—criminals of the deepest dye—work in the mines. These mines are, however, not all underground: they may consist of gold washeries, or the exile may be set to the almost pleasureable excitement of searching for gems. At one time the worst class of convicts —usually murderers and particularly offensive politicians— were not only compelled to work underground, but they had to live there, and—horrible thought—were buried there also. No wonder that Siberia got a bad name. But not over one-fourth of the Siberian miners are convicts, and a recent explorer is even of opinion that the latter are in better circumstances physically, and lead quite as comfortable and more moral lives, than the corresponding class of free men in America, England or Australia. Society in the large towns is pleasant and polished. Banishment to Siberia has been overdone, and thus the mischief is righting itself by the natural law of compensation. It has long ceased to be a disgrace; it is rapidly ceasing to be a punishment.

No country in the world, except, perhaps, the valleys of the Amazon and the Mississippi, has such a perfect system of water communication as Siberia. The rich meadows near the mouth of the Yenessei, even though far within the Arctic Circle, astonished the Norwegian walrus-hunters who accompanied Professor Nordenskjöld. 'What a land God has given the Russians!' was the half-admiring, half-envious exclamation of a peasant seaman who owned a little patch among the uplands in the Scandinavian Nordland. Yet these few pastures are uncropped and unscythed. The river has good coal-beds and fine forests, and south of the forest region level, stoneless plains, covered for hundreds of leagues with the richest 'black earth' soil, only wanting the plough of the farmer to yield abundant harvests. Still further south the river flows through a region where the vine grows in the open air. Altogether it is believed that by the expenditure of about one hundred thousand pounds the Yenessei could be made navigable, though its tributary, the Angora, on the Lake Baikal—an inland sea not much smaller than Lake Superior—and the Obi could be connected with the Yenessei, and the Yenessei with the Lena.

Leaving out of account the numerous other Siberian rivers all more or less navigable, a country could be thus thrown open equal to the combined territories of all the rivers which flow into the Black Sea, the Sea of Marmora, and the Mediterranean. Yet from these rivers flowing into the Arctic Ocean, so cheap is produce in their valleys, one of which contains over two millions of people, that Captain Wiggins ballasted his ship with black lead of fine quality. The valleys are full of the most magnificent timber, larch, spruce, &c., which is so little in demand that at the town of Yenesseik, a ship's mast, 36 inches in diameter at the base, 18 inches diameter at the top, and 60 feet long, can be bought for a sovereign, and any number supplied in a few days; beef costs $2\frac{1}{2}d.$ per lb., and game of all kinds may be got in such abundance as to render mere living cheap enough. So abundant is corn and hay on the great steppes between Tomsk and Tjumen that horses are hired for one halfpenny per mile. A ton of salt, which costs in England 15s., is sold on the Yenessei for 15l.; and wheat, which commands 15l. or 16l. per ton in London, may be got in any quantity for 25s. per ton. To use the words of Mr. Seebohm, 'a colossal fortune awaits the adventurer who is backed by sufficient capital, and a properly organised staff, to carry on a trade between this country and Siberia, *via* the Kara Sea.' To-day, a fresh market for the disposal of our manufactures, is as much required as it was three centuries ago. Here in 'frozen Siberia'—miscalled—is a field richer than Central Africa, and about as little cultivated as Corea, waiting his energy and his knowledge.

CHAPTER IV.

RUSSIAN AUTOCRACY.

IF I were English I would probably be a Liberal; were I an American I would undoubtedly be a Republican; as I am a Russian I am, after all—and '*Honi soit qui mal y pense*'—a believer in the Autocracy.

This is no paradox, nor am I inconsistent. At Liberal meetings in this country nothing is more common than an appeal to the results of Liberalism. The greatness and the glory of the Empire of England are referred to as a proof of the success of Liberal principles. It seems to me quite true. But it is equally true that the greatness and glory of the Empire of Russia have been indissoluble from the autocracy.

Mr. Wallace, after several years' close study of my country, declares quite truly: 'Never was the autocratic power stronger in Russia, or more secure, than it is to-day.' Can you say as much of Liberal principles in England? Are you not rather inclined to approximate to Russian doctrines? Is your Premier not exalting the Royal prerogative, and your Parliament only allowed to discuss trivialities and *faits accomplis?* Your example gives moments of serious hesitation and doubts even to those in Russia who dream of a Constitution.

Autocracy has been good for Russia. I doubt whether it would be as good for England. Autocracy without an autocrat, or a constitutionalism reduced to a despotism *plus* humbug, is not attractive to me, and I hope no unkind friend will accuse me of endeavouring to popularise absolutism in England. 'In submission to despotism,' wrote M. de Tocqueville,[1] ' after having enjoyed liberty, there is nothing but degradation; but there often enters into the submission of a people who have never been free a principle of morality which must not be overlooked.'

The great obstacle to good understanding between England and Russia is that there is no understanding at all of each other's political views. I wish somebody else, abler and better informed than I, desired to throw some light upon the relations existing between the two countries; but unfortunately amongst my countrymen it is considered a positive folly to write a word of self-defence or explanation for English readers, who are generally supposed not to care really for our intimate acquaintance. I beg, therefore, the permission to explain as simply as I can how it is that we Russians cannot understand why our devotion to our Emperor—which in the lower classes is certainly not weaker than in the higher—should be looked down upon by constitutional peoples. If we introduced universal suffrage and vote by ballot to-

[1] *Remains of Alexis de Tocqueville*, vol. i. p. 255.

morrow it would strengthen, not diminish, the Imperial power in Russia.

We believe in our Emperor because we owe to the autocracy our national existence and the progress of our civilisation.

When Europe emerged from the dark ages there were two Slav nations struggling into being—one was Poland, the other Russia. At first both were almost equally anarchic. Poland was richer, more populous, nearer to 'Europe,' and had a lustre of civilisation which was lacking to Russia. The latter was exposed for centuries to the withering blast of Tartar invasions, from which she sheltered her western neighbour. To-day Poland no longer exists, especially in Germanised Posen, whilst Russia is one of the greatest empires of the world. Why? Because Russians, tutored in the terrible school of adversity, learned the lesson of identifying themselves with an autocracy, and thus formed one strongly-united body; whilst anarchic Poland, which clung persistently to her divided aristocracy, has been blotted out of the map of Europe. Of course we are blamed for that. But the Poles attacked Moscow before the Russians took Warsaw; and even if Russia had as little excuse for conquering Poland as England for conquering Ireland, the fate of Poland demonstrates the weakness of anarchy and the strength of the opposite principle.

Anarchy was the besetting sin of the Slavs. Russia passed through a frightful experience before she learned the necessity of creating that strong central power to which, to a very great extent, she owes all that she has. At the dawn of our history the consciousness of this national weakness led the Russian Slavs, after driving out the Variags, to call them back across the Baltic to maintain order and exercise authority in Russia. If Rurik and his successors had not divided and re-divided their soldiers and their lands amongst their children, Russia might have escaped both the horrors of intestine war and the scourge of the Tartar conquest, as well as the necessity, born of these troubles, of establishing the autocracy.

Unfortunately, the law of division prevailed. No strong central power existed. In little more than a century, as M. Rambaud remarks,[1] Russia saw no fewer than sixty-four principalities with 293 rival princes, whose feuds occasioned no less than eighty-three civil wars. Our unhappy country, convulsed by their incessant strife, was the prey of all her neighbours. In that period the Polovtzi alone invaded Russian territory forty-six times. At the close of that terrible time retribution came in the shape of the Tartar conquest. Russia was submerged by a tide of Asiatic barbarism, and for more than two centuries the Russian State almost ceased to exist.

In the darkness and despair of these awful centuries Russians learnt the necessity of creating and obeying implicitly a strong central Government. To smite down the Infidel, Russia's sword must be placed in a single hand, and that hand must be

---

[1] *History of Russia*, vol. i. p. 93.

nerved with the strength of the whole nation. While under the Tartar domination that sword was slowly 'forged by adverse fates,' until at length it was keen and strong for its work. Not until the autocratic power was founded were the Tartars vanquished and Russia freed.

Some people define Russian autocracy as a Dictatorship *en permanence*. Granted; and the ancient Romans found dictatorship necessary. Machiavelli even believed that the dictatorship alone rendered possible the continuance of the Roman Republic. Nothing but a dictatorship could have saved Russia from her foes. That dictatorship, founded to rescue Europe from Asia and Christendom from the Moslem invasion, will not have completed its task until the Sultan ceases to rule in Europe, and the last results of the Tartar conquest have been obliterated.

At present neither of these results have been attained, although one, fortunately, is not far distant.

While we stood sentinel on the ramparts of Europe, you Westerns, protected by our sacrifices, were making rapid progress in civilisation. To overtake you we found the dictatorship as necessary as it was to get rid of the horde. Before we even could start in the race we had to gain elbow-room by beating back enemies that threatened to extinguish our national existence. As late as 1571, a Tartar Khan burnt Moscow and swept 100,000 of her inhabitants into slavery. Forty years later our ancient capital was destroyed by Poles. The Zaporogues and the Cossacks of the Don ravaged our country, and all the outlying provinces were given over to anarchy. The Swedes established themselves at 'Novgorod the Great.' Thus, when the English were beginning to defend Parliamentary Government against the Stuarts we were still locked in a life-and-death struggle for the right to exist. In that struggle, but for the absolute power of our Tzars, we had been for ever undone. Thanks to that principle, Russia emerged, bruised and bleeding, but still a nation and a State.

In England civilisation has come from below—the people led, the rulers followed. In Russia the process is reversed. I shall be told that that is to admit that the Russian people were ignorant and destitute of civilisation. Yes, they were! Who ever denied it? What better would you have been if you had had a Tartar Conquest instead of a Magna Charta, and Englishmen had seen London burnt by Mongols instead of witnessing the dispersion of the Armada?

But Russian civilisation has to contend against another difficulty, from which you are entirely free. Civilisation, from its name, is the product of cities. Russia is an Empire of villages. The enormous expanse of territory over which our population is scattered—an expanse all the more formidable by the scarcity of good roads—renders spontaneous civilisation impossible. Russia thus could only be civilised from above, and it is the glory of our Emperors that they applied themselves strenuously to the work.

One of my English friends—who is, perhaps, a little tinged with Republicanism—declares that for three centuries there has been only one King in England who was worth his rations, and he was a Dutchman; and he added that since William of Orange, when they did more than draw their rations they always did mischief. My friend, no doubt, exaggerates. But with us it is quite different. Of course there have been exceptions; but our Emperors have been the real reformers of Russia. Peter the Great— 'that noblest example of history,' as Mr. Cobden styled him—was but the most striking figure among many Emperors and Empresses who laboured without ceasing to the best of their ability to elevate, to educate, to civilise their people. And amidst what difficulties! As a rule the Russian worships his old traditions and customs of former days; he idolises his past, he distrusts innovations. 'Novelty brings calamity' was not merely a proverb, it was almost an article of faith. Yet upon such people Peter turned the full light of Western civilisation. Even in our days you often meet Russians who reproach him for having done so, for not having simply developed our own national elements, without any attempt to wrap us up in Western mantles. 'Why should we imitate other nations?' they exclaim; 'Their superiority is more apparent than real,' &c. Peter the Great, however, pursued his own views upon the matter, and it is not for Westerns to ignore his innovations. There was nothing too great or too small to escape his attention. It was he who published the first Russian newspaper, and created the modern Russian civil alphabet. Like some mythic hero of the dim and distant past, this man of the seventeenth century appeared to incarnate all the energies of a mighty nation. Deserted by friends, betrayed by those of his own household, confronted alike by foreign foe and internal rebellion, he never wavered, he never flinched. Sometimes a despairing cry broke from him, when baffled by some more than ordinary display of stupidity, but it was only for a moment; the next he was hard at work, receiving Prussian Ambassadors at the topsail of the mainmast, digging canals, publishing books, building ships, never resting in his efforts to civilise his country. By turns pilot, smith, labourer, carpenter, astronomer, manufacturer, artilleryman, 'he worked harder than a bourlak.' As our greatest poet, Alexander Poushkin, wrote:—

> With helm and hammer, pen and sword,
> He stamped his soul on Russia's story,
> And like a workman for reward,
> Worked night and day for Russia's glory.[1]

Peter was not the first, neither was he the last of the Emperors to whom Russia owes reforms, which she could not and would not have introduced under a Parliamentary system. In the present reign the emancipation of the serfs and the liberation of the Southern Slavs are achievements even more brilliant than the founding of St. Petersburg and the victory of Poltava.[2] Our Emperor is true to the traditions of

---

[1] Translated by Madame A. B———y in her *Translations from Russian and German Poets*, published at Baden-Baden, 1878.

[2] 'The present Sovereign of Russia, by the emancipation of serfs, said to reach forty millions in number, has placed himself on the first rank of the philanthropic legislators of the world.'—Mr. Gladstone, 'Russians in Turkestan' (*Contemporary Review*, Nov. 1876, p. 877).

the autocracy; and in the future, as in the past, we expect confidently the power of the Emperor will enable Russia to take even larger strides in civilisation than if we substituted for him a Parliament elected on an English model.

We firmly believe that had it not been for the concentration of power, which enabled us with greater ease to introduce at once desired reforms all over the realm, we might never have been able to play the grand *rôle* befitting the only Slav country at once free, independent, and strong.

Russians are not easily forgetful. If they remember well the harm done, they also keep in mind all their obligations. Now, the magnificent reforms introduced by our present Emperor have claims upon our confidence. He is as good a Russian, as devoted to the grand destinies of his country, as the best amongst us. We only want to add to his omnipotence the advantages of omniscience. In our history we have examples of how this might be done which might be known by anybody who cares to study the subject. The Zemskie Sobory to which I refer were a natural development of our political growth. The so-called Zemskie Sobory were a kind of Assembly of different representatives—of deputies—not a legislative, but a consultative body, composed of the high clergy, nobility, and merchants. When the Tzar John the Fourth, three hundred years ago, had to give an answer to Poland, and to accept or refuse the truce proposed by the King, he consulted the Assembly, or Sobor, which rejected the truce, advised the prosecution of the war, and offered the Tzar men and money to bring it to a successful conclusion. These Zemskie Sobory played a great and interesting part in our country. To mention only one instance, in 1598, on the death of Feodor, it formed a kind of Diet, and offered Boris Godounoff the throne of Russia.

There is a nobility in Russia—it never had, however, the privileges of your aristocracy: the privileges it had have disappeared almost entirely since the emancipation of the serfs and the general military conscription. In reality, Russia now is a democratic country,[1] and a 'House of Lords' in Russia would be a very ridiculous innovation indeed. In the democracy lies the great strength of the autocracy. Alexis de Tocqueville says:—'A democratic people tends towards centralisation as it were by instinct. The citizens being so nearly equal among themselves, are naturally led to place the details of administration in the hands of the only power which stands forth conspicuously in an elevated position above them all, viz., the central government of the State.'[2]

Under Anne Ivanovna, an oligarchic Constitution, framed by the Princes Galitzine and Dolgorouky, which destroyed the autocracy, was set

---

[1] Mr. Kinglake, in the preface to the sixth edition of his *Invasion of the Crimea*, says: 'A very able and interesting account of the political Russia of the present day was given to the world on October 26, 1876, by Prince M. Mestchersky. The Prince assures his readers that Russia is now a Democracy, with "liberty, equality, and fraternity" all complete; but it is loyal, he says, and religious, and not therefore deserving to be confounded with the Democracy of the French Revolution.'

[2] *Remains of Alexis de Tocqueville*, vol. i. p. 242.

aside by a popular movement, which demanded the re-establishment of the autocracy in the name of the people and in the interests of progress. In Poland the aristocracy crushed the people beneath the yoke of 100,000 despots. In Russia they had only one master, and that master was, and is at this moment, regarded as the Tribune of the People, to whom they only need to make known their wrongs to obtain immediate redress.[1] If they suffer injustice it is not because it is the will of the Emperor, but because, as the popular proverb says, 'Heaven is high, and the Tzar is too far off.' That this deep, unalterable, unshaken conviction of the Russian peasants in the goodness of their Emperor has been without cause is as much opposed to the teachings of history as it is logically absurd.

The example of the Polish Constitution strengthened the advocates of autocracy in Russia in former days, just as Lord Beaconsfield's unceremonious policy paralyses now in Russia people who once had faith in Constitutionalism. Whenever any attempt was made to limit the autocratic power of our Emperors in the past it was checked by a reference to the anarchy which the Pacta Conventa occasioned in Poland. The nation at large not only was not opposed to autocracy, but defended it and supported it with all its energy and power.

To-day in Russia Liberals are often silenced by a reference to the Nihilists. The Poles in the seven-

---

[1] For a striking English testimony to this effect, see Herbert Barry's *Russia in* 1870, p. 201.

teenth and the Nihilists in the nineteenth are the drunken helots employed by Russian Conservatism to deter the natives from drinking the dangerous waters of Liberalism and reform. The first can easily be understood; the second is quite unjust. Nihilism is not Liberalism. A Liberal has a positive code of principles before him, a political religion, a stern national duty. A Nihilist scorns and derides those who care either for their country or for those things which constitute the greatest blessings of all civilised countries. A Nihilist is an anarchist in the widest sense of the word. To those who are opposed to every reform, every real progress, it naturally appears as an easy way of making a terrible mess of all the different schools and tendencies of Liberalism by declaring they all lead to Nihilism. Does it not happen sometimes in England that the Conservative party does not disdain to describe as Republican and Revolutionary every measure which threatens a cherished abuse or attacks a vested interest? So with us, men who would die for their country and their Emperor are represented sometimes as dangerous and most wicked merely because they dare to have their own views upon some separate questions.

The great democratic principle which it needed a French Revolution to establish in the West, '*La carrière ouverte aux talents*,' was established in Russia almost by itself, and always supported by our crowned heads. Our history abounds with instances in which men and women have risen from the lower ranks to the highest offices of State. Peter the Great's wife, Catherine I., was taken from the humblest spheres; Lomonossoff was a peasant; Menshikoff began life as a pastrycook; Speransky was the son of a poor village curate, &c. Nor was the career closed to talented men because they were not Russian. Our autocracy, more free from prejudices than some more constitutional systems, has thrown open the highest offices in the State to men of all nationalities. Le Fort, Peter's admiral, was a Swiss; Bruce and Gordon, his trusted generals, were Scotchmen; Münich was a German. In Catherine's reign the officer who led the attack which annihilated the Turkish fleet in the Bay of Chesma was an Englishman. In the last war, as in the Crimean, high commands were held by Armenians and Poles, and the army before Batoum was said to be commanded by a Montenegrin, not to speak of Germans and Finns who abound in our State service.

On the field of Poltava, at which, as M. Rambaud says, 'the Slav race, so long humiliated, made a triumphal entry on to the stage of the world,' Peter the Great addressed his soldiers in words which truly described the relation between our Emperors and the people :—' You must not think it is for Peter you fight; no! it is for the country, it is for our orthodox faith, for the Church of God! As for Peter, know that he is ready to sacrifice himself for a prosperous and glorious future for Russia.' Catherine the Great instructed the Assembly of Representatives which she summoned to draw up the new code that 'the nation is not made for the Sovereign, but the Sovereign for the nation.'

The autocracy is a weapon by which democracy

smites down its enemies, and it is the instrument which, after securing the emancipation of the serf, is destined to achieve still further reforms.

Nor, pardon me, do I see why we should be described as 'inappropriate instruments'[1] for securing the liberation of our co-religionists, the Slavs of the Balkan, because we believe in a system of government which freed Russia from the yoke of the Tartars, and enabled us to take giant strides in civilising and educating our people.

We believe, with Goethe, that the best of all Governments is that which best teaches self-government, but a permanent head of a strong centralised Administration is sometimes a necessity even for the development of self-government. In this respect Russia may compare favourably with England, for we have rural municipalities elected by universal suffrage, established by the Emperor Nicholas, and I suppose I am not wrong in saying that you have no such elective authorities in your country districts.

The centralised administration of Russia is complained of by many who complain still more bitterly

---

[1] 'A great work of liberation has been done in which we have had no part. But bitter as is the mortification with which I for one reflect upon that exclusion, I thank God that the work has been done. It has been done in one sense, perhaps, by the most inappropriate of instruments.' Curiously enough the newspaper which reported that speech by one of your statesmen contained a despatch from Bulgaria, mentioning that the liberated Bulgarians had just passed an address of gratitude to those said 'inappropriate instruments' of their emancipation. Compare the Duke of Argyll:—'Russia's ancient and hereditary hostility to the Moslem Empire of the Turks has made her power *a fitting instrument* in the gradual destruction of the most desolating dominion that has ever cursed the world.'—*Eastern Question*, vol. ii. p. 254.

of the excesses and abuses which spring from the independent powers given to the rural communes. Russia needs a strong Executive in order to civilise her people; but our democratic Empire is not so centralising or so despotic in many respects as the democratic Republic of France. In France *le personnel administratif* changes; *le pouvoir administratif* remains much the same under Empire, Republic, or any shape of Monarchy. English people are always abusing centralisation, and always centralising; but decentralisation is not always a proof of civilisation. M. Thiers, whose words deservedly command attention in England, was an enthusiastic eulogist of a system of centralisation to which that of Russia cannot be compared for stringency. 'The wisest and most complete system of administration,' he told your Mr. Senior,[1] 'is that of France, where there is not a single independent local authority; where the central power knows and superintends, and, in fact, regulates, the concerns of every commune, and where every pulsation of the heart of France is instantly felt in the Pyrenees and on the Rhine.'

As believers in progress and in liberty, we think that more progress and more freedom is possible in Russia at the present time, by placing supreme power in the hands of an enlightened autocrat, than by vesting it in an assembly which either must be elected by a minority of the people or by a majority which can hardly read and write.[2]

[1] *Conversations*, vol. i. p. 135.
[2] Even in England the opinion of the majority is not always the

'It is the everlasting privilege of the foolish to be governed by the wise; that,' says Mr. Carlyle, 'is the first right of man.' Russians are almost always of the opinion of Mr. Carlyle.

As for the power of the Crown, 'the majesty of the people,' and the other catch-words of our judges, does not Lord Beaconsfield declare, ' The House of Commons is the House of a few; the Sovereign is the sovereign of all. The proper leader of the people is the individual who sits upon the throne'?

wisest. Indeed the Duke of Somerset, in his recent 'Reflections,' goes so far as to say: 'Until a late period in the history of the country, a real representation of the majority of the people would have been a national calamity.'

CHAPTER V.

CONSTITUTIONALISM IN RUSSIA.

THE other day I was favoured with a call from one of your M.P.s. My visitor looked very solemn and dignified, and spoke in a monotonous, didactic way concerning Russia and her many shortcomings. It was rather amusing at the first, for he displayed such a wonderful ignorance of the most elementary facts that he might have been taken for Robinson Crusoe, fresh from the desolate island where he spent so many years with no other company than that of his famous Friday.

He began: 'We must keep a very sharp look out; Russia is not to be trusted. She is a standing danger to us, both in India and in this country.'

'Oh, yes,' I replied, for I am now quite familiar with such pleasant observations. 'Why should you not keep a sharp look out? Only I do not see why you should think England so very weak, both in Asia and in Europe, that she is in such danger from any foreign country.'

'Russia is dangerous,' answered my visitor, 'because she has no Constitutional Government.

We, in England, can only have confidence in Constitutional States.'

'Yes; I know your views on these matters,' I replied. 'And I dare say your dear ally Turkey has prospered amazingly since she adopted your institutions!'

'Why, of course, it's better to have a Constitution,' rejoined he. 'It makes countries strong and powerful.'

'Then, it is because you want to see Russia stronger and more powerful,' I timidly ventured to suggest, 'that you wish us to adopt a Constitution? I thought she was too strong already for your moral comfort.'

The inconsistency of my visitor was common enough to pass unnoticed here, but it often strikes foreigners. Those who profess to fear us most, and who certainly seem to entertain anything but friendly feelings towards us, are the most imperious in tendering their unasked-for advice to adopt Constitutionalism as a sovereign remedy for all our ailments, real or imaginary. The advice may be good, but it comes from a suspicious source. Nor are counsels accepted the more readily when prefaced by insults.

Do you know that in Russia there is a conviction widely spread all over the country that the reason why European Governments insisted so strongly on a Constitution for young Bulgaria was in order to embarrass her development, and as much as possible to mar Russia's work?

Nevertheless, it is true that, if the Russian people

had been consulted last year, it would have been the worse for the English Cabinet. No power but the autocracy could have compelled our victorious army to halt within sight of Constantinople. Russians did not wish to retain Constantinople; but they longed to dictate peace there, and march in triumph through its streets.

It was a national aspiration, and the disappointment has occasioned natural regret amongst all Russians.

Last year I met General Grant, the American ex-President, in Paris. Almost the first thing he asked was, 'Can you explain how it happened that the Russians did not occupy Constantinople, when they had it entirely in their hands?'

'Alas!' I replied, 'I have no good explanation to give. We never expected such a voluntary abdication of power. In fact, some of our military people telegraphed to Moscow, saying, "To-morrow Constantinople will be occupied for several days!" It is difficult to give you an idea of the disappointment throughout all Russia when it was found out that Constantinople, after all, was not to be the place where we were to dictate peace. The general conviction in Russia is, that our Government, misled by news from abroad, telegraphed orders to our generals not to advance.'

General Grant, who was listening attentively, smiled and said, 'Well, I can only say one thing; had I been one of your generals I would have put the order in my pocket and opened it at Constantinople three or four days later.'

'Yes,' I rejoined, 'it was a great trial for our national feelings, and we feel sure that nobody on earth will ever thank us for that unnecessary concession.'

The same day I dined with M. Emile de Girardin, where several eminent guests were assembled. I repeated General Grant's conversation. 'Are you surprised at his remark?' several persons asked me at the same time, and using almost the same expressions. 'It's unnecessary to say how little we liked the German promenade through Paris, but we understood, nevertheless, that the German Government could not deprive its troops of so legitimate a satisfaction.'

I heard, on very good authority, that Prince Bismarck, on learning that Russia, after all, was not going to occupy Constantinople, exclaimed with rather an uncomplimentary emphasis, '*Nein, mit den Leuten ist nichts anzufangen*' (No, there is no doing anything with those people!). The German Chancellor, in his heart of hearts, was naturally pleased with every mistake on our part, but as a good political chess-player, he felt impatient at anybody taking a wrong step.

All these remarks often come back to my memory. Had the Russian people been consulted, the English Government would never have had the glorification of getting from the Russian Government the concessions which it longed for so much, but for which it is so little grateful.

Some St. Petersburg officials laugh at our regrets, and call it childish sentimentalism. 'Russia,' they exclaim, 'has got what was really important, and does not care particularly about what are, after all, only apparent victories.' Now we, Russian Slavophiles, have notions of our own, as far as victories are concerned, and what practical people care for is not exactly our chief object in life. But I grant that English Russophobes did not gain much by our concession either from their point of view or from the point of view of our diplomatists.

You could not indulge in a greater delusion than to imagine, because we Russian Slavophiles support the autocracy, that therefore we have no opinions of our own, and do not care to express them. We do not share your implicit faith in Constitutional Government. We abide by our national traditions. We are guided by the teachings of our history, to which most of our advisers are quite indifferent. We trust our Emperor. We know his readiness to serve his country, and our trust in him has not been rooted in our hearts without strong arguments and eloquent facts. We obey him even when, as in the hoped-for temporary occupation of Constantinople, his command destroys our most cherished aspirations. But, at the same time, we wish to make known our sentiments, and therefore we desire the complete freedom of the press and the re-establishment of the Zemskie Sobory.

Of the former I need say nothing, excepting that

the strange use you make of it sometimes in England inclines some Russians to make the mistake of congratulating themselves that they are without it.

Of the latter, so little is known in England, that I may be pardoned if I explain how modest are the wishes of the Russian national party. The word '*Sobor*' means an assembly, a gathering; '*Zemskie Sobory*,' assemblies from all the land, a kind of national assembly, generally summoned when the country was in want of an honest, frank advice. It was not a permanent institution like your Parliament, which to us appears to be more a kind of chatting club, where people are obliged to make speeches, though they know very often that they have very little to say and that they are scarcely listened to. We admire that institution of yours, but merely from a literary point of view.

There is not one country in the world whose example could be blindly followed by Russia. Each has its drawbacks; and Russians believe they will do well to remain faithful to their own institutions.[1] Our

[1] A well-informed Englishman, writing on Italian affairs in the *New Quarterly Review* for January, 1880, makes some observations on Parliamentary government, which contain truths too often ignored in English criticisms of countries without Parliamentary institutions. He says:—
'Among a people where the habit of working together for a common public end is little developed, Parliamentary institutions may themselves become the very best school of selfishness and corruption. Those who hold the comfortable theory that if once you give a people free institutions all the rest will come of itself, have only to look at the Italian Chamber to be undeceived. It is not the off-hand judgment of a hostile criticism, but it is the deliberate opinion of the best and most serious and most experienced Italians, expressed over and over again of late years in books, in pamphlets, in speeches, in newspapers, and in conversation, that the Italian Chamber, as it now stands, does not answer the ends for

present Emperor has never deceived us. As I said in my last letter, we do not want to impair his omnipotence, we only wish to confer upon him the advantage of omniscience. We want him to come into closer contact with his people, to see our wants, our shortcomings, to know the failure of some of his officials, their bad faith, and their neglect of their duties. The latter naturally are afraid of that close contact, and do their best (and for us their worst) to conceal facts which it is for the honour and welfare of Russia our Emperor should know. The Zemskie Sobory would answer that purpose.

It is only those ignorant of Russian history, or men estranged by foreign influence from their own country, who see in the plea for the re-establishment of the Zemskie Sobory an attack upon the autocracy. History proves, on the contrary, that the will of the whole Russian people has always been directed to the support

which Parliamentary government is established. Unless there is a change, it is not too soon to say that Parliamentary institutions cannot possibly last in Italy. The feeling of indignation at the futility of them as they have been worked of late is one that is spreading. The disbelief in them as a means of solving the social and economical problems which are the most urgent questions for the country is becoming more general. The fact is that Parliamentary government, in its modern form, is about as much a national product as is the Church of England. To suppose that when transplanted to a wholly different soil, among a race whose character, sentiment, history, and traditions are thoroughly unlike our own, it will produce the same results, is against all experience. It is not wonderful that the prestige of the English Parliament should have imposed itself on other nations. But to copy its practice without wide alterations and without careful adaptation to the needs of each country can only work mischief. It needs no conjuror to tell us that either there must be a radical change in the mode in which the Italian Chamber discharges its duties, or else that the existence of Parliamentary government in Italy will shortly be in the gravest peril.'—*New Quarterly Magazine*, No. 26, New Series, pp. 71, 90, 91.

of that form of government, even when an aristocratic faction tried to undo it.

There was a striking illustration of this at the beginning of the reign of the Empress Anne Ivanovna. She was living at Mitau, when an aristocratic deputation offered her the Russian throne on the condition that she should accept an oligarchic Constitution. She accepted it on these terms. Some time after reaching Moscow she summoned a Zemskie Sobory. 'Let her keep to our institutions!' exclaimed the Assembly, and they pressed upon her to resume the absolute power. 'What!' she exclaimed to one of her minister-conspirators, 'then the conditions sent me through you were not the will of the nation? Then you have deceived me?' And thus, by the will of the people expressed through the Zemskie Sobory, the oligarchic Constitution was replaced by the old autocracy.

No Russian Emperor can doubt of the support of his country; his greatest power lies in the confidence of his people.

Russia, like every great country which has not given up her high aspirations and lofty feelings, has moments of self-sacrifice, of a disregard of practical interests. Such was the case in the Servian and Turkish wars of the last three years; but, as a rule, Russians are not so simple as you fancy. There must be something in their devotion to autocracy; it's not so blind and irrational as people suppose, or they would not so often have insisted upon it.

There are officials in Russia who, as I said already,

are eager to prevent these Assemblies, who want to estrange the Emperor from his people, who sometimes take measures which are as nonsensical as unjust. But facts of that sort happen in the most constitutional and angelic countries in the world. We have 'red-tapists' who could be a good match for some of yours.

Do not forget that to these National Sobory, which were originated by our Tzars themselves, Russia owes the Romanoff dynasty, which was founded by one of them 276 years ago. In 1613, after the Great War, in which Prince Pojarsky and the butcher Minine delivered Russia from the Poles, the Sobor assembled at Moscow and placed Michel Romanoff on the throne. Five years later, when the Poles were threatening again to attack Moscow, the Sobor again assembled, and the unity between the Tzar and the people was strikingly demonstrated. 'I am ready,' said the Monarch, 'to suffer hunger in besieged Moscow and to fight the aggressors, but you must do the same for me.' The Assembly, with true Russian spirit, responded enthusiastically to the appeal, and preparations were at once made for a national resistance to the common enemy.

The important part played by the Sobory is sometimes forgotten, even in Russia. In 1627 the Cossacks of the Don, having captured Azoff, offered it to Russia; our Tzar would not accept it until he had ascertained the opinion of the Sobor. It was summoned. The nobles were in favour of accepting the proposed gift;

the clergy and the merchants, on the other hand, opposed its acceptance. The voice of the Sobor was then given against the annexation of Azoff, and the annexation was accordingly refused. This was 250 years ago, and in 'barbarous, despotic, aggressive Russia!'

Tell me, when last year your Government seized Cyprus, was there as much regard paid to the Parliament of civilised, constitutional, unaggressive England?

After the seventeenth century the Sobory were not often summoned. In the latter part of the eighteenth, however, a remarkable assembly sat in Moscow discussing the new code which Catherine the Great was anxious to compile. It was not called Sobor, but the Great Legislative Commission, and it was virtually a Russian representative Parliament, only not a permanent one. Curiously enough it contained exactly the same number of members as your present House of Commons. The following is the description of its constitution from M. Alfred Rambaud's History:—

> The Commission was composed of deputies from all the services of the State, from all the orders and all the races of the Empire. Besides the delegates from the Senate, the Synod, and the colleges, and the Courts of Chancery, the nobles elected a representative for each district, the citizens one for every city, the free colonists one for every province, the soldiers, militia, and other fighting men also one for each province; the Crown peasants, the fixed tribes, whether Christian or not, equally elected one for each province. The deputation of the Cossack armies was fixed by their atamans.

Six hundred and fifty-two deputies assembled at Moscow, officials, nobles, citizens, peasants, Tartars, Kalmucks, Lapps, Samoyedes, and many others. Each man was to be furnished with full powers and with papers compiled by at least five of the electors. They were exempted for ever from all corporal punishments, and were declared inviolable during the session.[1]

It held 200 sittings and many important discussions upon economical, municipal, social, and political matters. After sitting for two years, the Empress was reluctantly compelled, by the outbreak of the Turkish war, to break up the Assembly. In dismissing it, she bore testimony to its utility.

The Commission for the Code has given me hints for all the Empire. I know now what is necessary, and with what I should occupy myself. It has elaborated all parts of the legislation, and has distributed the affairs under heads. I should have done more without the war with Turkey, but a unity hitherto unknown in the principles and methods of discussion has been introduced.

That remarkable Commission, in which, as Catherine wrote to Voltaire, ' the Orthodox was sitting between the heretic and the Mussulman, all three listening to the voice of an idolater, and all four consulting how to render their conclusion palatable to all,' was the last representative assembly of that kind which has met in Russia.

In Poland, however, the Emperor Alexander, after the war with Napoleon, established a Constitution with a representative Diet. In opening that Diet, in 1818, the Emperor spoke in praise of representative institu-

[1] *History of Russia*, vol. ii. p. 139.

tions. He said: 'I hope to prove to the contemporary kings that the liberal institutions, which they pretend to confound with the disastrous doctrines which in these days threaten the social system with a frightful catastrophe, are not a dangerous illusion, but that, reduced in good faith to practice, and directed in a pure spirit towards conservative ends and the good of humanity, they are perfectly allied to order, and the best security for the happiness of nations.'

We are certainly not going to throw mud upon our Constitutionalists. Some of them misunderstood their country, but they were men of very noble, self-sacrificing principles, of very high and lofty ideas—especially the majority of those who were known as the Decembrists. But, unfortunately for them, they mistook the spirit of their nation. When they urged the people to cry for a Constitution, some of their followers understood Constitution to refer to Constantine's wife—a Polish lady for whom he had given up his claims to the throne!

Our ideas are much more reasonable and much more practical; and the re-establishment of the Zemskie Sobory perhaps would be not less useful than the imposing Constitution generously sketched out for us in some foreign newspapers.

We Russians may be very mistaken in our adhesion to the autocracy; but that is not the opinion of your Prime Minister, for he wrote long ago: 'The tendency of advanced civilisation is in truth to pure Monarchy, and in an enlightened age the Monarch on the throne, free from the vulgar prejudices and the corrupt interests of the subject, becomes again Divine.'¹ And, again, he says: 'There is a whisper rising in this country'—even in England—' that Loyalty is not a phrase, Faith not a delusion, and Popular Liberty something more diffusive and substantial than the profane exercise of the sacred rights of sovereignty by political classes!'²

[1] The passage from which I take this extract is placed in the mouth of Sidonia in 'Coningsby.' It is curious as showing that in the opinion of the English Prime Minister, so far from the freedom of the press undermining the Monarchy, the establishment of an autocratic government follows as a natural consequence from the growth of the power of the press:—' The tendency of advanced civilisation is, in truth, to pure Monarchy. Monarchy is, indeed, a government which requires a high degree of civilisation for its full development. It needs the support of free laws and manners, and of a widely-diffused intelligence. Political compromises are not to be tolerated except at periods of rude transition. An educated nation recoils from the imperfect vicariate of what is called a representative government. Your House of Commons, that has absorbed all other powers in the State, will, in all probability, fall more rapidly than it rose. Public opinion has a more direct, a more comprehensive, a more efficient organ for its utterance than a body of men sectionally chosen. The Printing Press is a political element unknown to classic or feudal times. It absorbs in a great degree the duties of the Sovereign, the Priest, the Parliament; it controls, it educates, it discusses. That public opinion, when it acts, would appear in the form of one who has no class interests. In an enlightened age the Monarch on the throne, free from the vulgar prejudices and the corrupt interests of the subject, becomes again Divine!'—*Coningsby*, book v. ch. 8.

[2] *Sybil*, book vi. ch. 13.

CHAPTER VI.

THE ATTEMPT ON THE EMPEROR.

No words, written or spoken, can express, even slightly, the feelings of horror and indignation felt by Russians at the news of the monstrous attempt to destroy our Emperor's life. To us such a crime is almost parricide. That a second time within a single year such an attempt should be made fills our hearts with humiliation and covers us with shame.

In the midst of our distress it adds little to our comfort that in some parts of Europe such deeds are hailed with unconcealed satisfaction. In England there is perceptible behind the conventional expression of indignation a sardonic chuckle of satisfaction. Of course, it is very wicked, all your papers say, this attempted assassination; but it is to be hoped that it will lead to the abandonment of Russia's Slavonic mission, the modification of Russia's autocratic Constitution, or some other result desired by our censors. They would not commit the crime, oh no! But, as it is committed, they do their best to extract political capital out of it.

This eager moralising has naturally a very bad effect in Russia. You do not know how widely the suspicion prevails amongst our people that these Nihilist outrages are due to foreign instigation. Rightly or wrongly, our people believe that the foreigners, Jews certainly not excluded, supply funds for the Terrorists.[1] Our war for the liberation of the Christians in the East rendered the Jews more hostile to us than ever.[2] In Russia we generally think them only consistent with their religion, and thus they are naturally ready to injure their religious enemies. Therefore, there is a great feeling of distrust towards them, and they do not enjoy all the civil rights of the Christian natives. Those who defend them in this country, for instance, generally declare them to be inconsistent, and friendly to the Christians in other

[1] Some English friends protest that it is incredible that the Jews could be allied with the Nihilists or Anarchists. Permit me to remind them what the Earl of Beaconsfield wrote of the part played by the Jews in 1848, in his political biography of Lord George Bentinck. Speaking of that still recent 'outburst of destructive forces which had ravaged Europe,' Mr. Disraeli, himself of Jewish descent, declared that outbreak would never have attained such proportions but for the 'fiery energy and teeming resources' of the sons of Israel. Men of the Jewish race were found at the head of all the provisional Governments in Europe. 'The people of God co-operate with Atheists; the most skilful accumulators of property ally themselves with Communists; the peculiar and chosen race touch the hand of all the scum and low castes of Europe, and all this because they wish to destroy that ungrateful Christendom which owes to them even its name, and whose tyranny they can no longer endure.' *Lord George Bentinck: a Political Biography*, by B. Disraeli, p. 499.

[2] Dr. H. Sandwith refers to this subject in his article in the *Fortnightly Review* for December, 1879. He says:—'I had (during his journey "from Belgrade to Samakov") an ample explanation of the intolerance shown to the Jews by the Christians of the East. During all these horrors they played the part of jackal to the Turkish lion. They hunted out and betrayed the Christians; they were the most zealous volunteer spies; and they were always ready to purchase the plundered property of the rayahs. The dislike of the Eastern Christians to the Jews is not merely the result of religious intolerance.'—P. 898. See Appendix, *The Jewish Question*.

countries. Our experience has taught us differently. Amongst our Nihilists there are many of Jewish origin. But forgive me for giving you another detail, which can surprise no Russian, but which, I dare say, may shock you. Even more deeply rooted is the conviction that the Nihilist agitation is supported not only by the *Internationale*, but that the Nihilist paper is published at one of the servant's rooms of the Embassies of St. Petersburg—whether Austrian, Turkish, or British is not particularly specified. Ambassadors, of course, have their immunities. I have heard some declare that if they had the right of search in foreign Embassies the publication of the Nihilist organs of assassination would speedily be stopped.[1] This suspicion is not dispelled by the evident pleasure with which our foreign critics seize upon every outrage to emphasise their advice, and find a new reason for pressing their counsels in every murder.

It sickens one to read the conventional twaddle about 'the ruthless despotism' which is supposed to be responsible for such crimes. No Monarch in Europe has been fortunate enough not to have been chosen as a target more than once, and if anyone deserved it less than the others it was certainly our present Emperor.

The shortcomings, the mistakes, the abuses of our officials can neither explain nor justify these

[1] This remark seems to have displeased the *Times*. In a leader of December 17, 1879, it describes my statement as one of the maddest of myths. Let us hope that, by a happy chance, the *Times* this time is right.

monstrous attacks upon the Monarch himself. We look to him for their removal, and we feel certain that whenever mismanagements are discovered and malpractices are proved, the criminals will be punished without even the chance of being recommended to friendly countries as trustworthy reformers.

The Emperor is absolute. He is the representative of the people, to whom we look for the remedy of abuses and the reform of the administration. Until you can realise that, you understand nothing about our Government. I wish our critics would apply to themselves the words Mr. Gladstone at Glasgow addressed to the historian. If they would ' lift themselves out of their environment, and assume the points of view and think under the entire conditions which belong to the person (or nation) they are calling to account,' they would not, as at present, ' pervert judgment by taking their seat in the tribunal loaded with irrelevant and misleading matter.'[1]

To replace the Emperor by a Russian House of Commons would not substitute for the autocracy the government of the elected representatives of the people. The autocracy would merely be replaced by the bureaucracy, and the representatives of the people, unfamiliar with political affairs, and returned by constituents largely under the influence of the officials, might not be so effective a check upon misgovernment as is the Emperor.

[1] Rectorial Address, Glasgow University, Dec. 1879.

It is not by attempted assassinations that Russians will be persuaded to alter their institutions in the Constitutional direction. The tendency of such crimes is just the opposite. Even in Ireland far less offences lead to the suspension of Constitutional safeguards, and the crimes of the Anarchists would justify the creation of a Dictatorship rather than the proclamation of a Constitution.

The Anarchists[1] care as little for a Constitution

[1] The Nihilists believe, as their name implies, in nothing. 'We say, No law, no religion—Nihil,' and the only article of the no-faith in which they believe is, that everything must be destroyed. The following extracts from the manifesto of Bakunin exhibit Nihilism as pourtrayed by its founder in 1868:—'Brethren, I come to announce unto you a new gospel, which must penetrate to the very ends of the world. This gospel admits of no half-measures and hesitations. The old world must be destroyed, and replaced by a new one. The *Lie* must be stamped out and give way to Truth. It is our mission to destroy the *Lie*; and, to effect this, we must begin at the very commencement. Now the beginning of all those lies which have ground down this poor world in slavery, is God. Tear out of your hearts the belief in the existence of God; for, as long as an atom of that silly superstition remains in your minds, you will never know what freedom is.

'When you have got rid of the belief in this priest-begotten God, and when, moreover, you are convinced that your existence, and that of the surrounding world, is due to the conglomeration of atoms, in accordance with the laws of gravity and attraction, then, and then only, you will have accomplished the first step towards liberty, and you will experience less difficulty in ridding your minds of that second lie which tyranny has invented.

'The first lie is *God*. The second lie is *Right*. *Might* invented the fiction of Right in order to insure and strengthen her reign. *Might*, my friends, forms the sole groundwork of society. Might makes and unmakes laws, and that might should be in the hands of the majority. Once penetrated with a clear conviction of your own *might*, you will be able to destroy this mere notion of *Right*.

'And when you have freed your minds from the fear of a God, and from that childish respect for the fiction of *Right*, then all the remaining chains which bind you, and which are called science, civilisation, property, marriage, morality, and justice, will snap asunder like threads.

'Let your own happiness be your only law. But in order to get this

as they do for the Slavonic cause. They openly declare they despise it as much as the honour of their country or its moral development. Their religious, or rather philosophical, tenets allow them to do whatever they like or can to crush, not merely the Government, but the family, property, and, above all, the Christian religion. They are Russian Communards, and no society, no Government on earth, in defending all that is precious and holy to man, could allow them to have a free hand.

No Government in Europe, and certainly not the Government of England, would have been more forbearing than the Russian with such deadly enemies. Since the murder of General Mezentzoff, and the attempted assassination of the Emperor on April 14, down to October, when I heard the matter discussed by people entitled to speak with authority, not more than twelve Nihilists have been put to death, although the number of murders, and attempts to murder Government officials, have been far greater.

The French Government, dealing with enemies far less unscrupulous, after crushing the Commune of Paris, shot 3,000 Communards; and even in England you usually hang more murderers every year than we have executed Terrorists since they resorted to

law recognised, and to bring about the proper relations which should exist between the majority and minority of mankind, you must destroy everything which exists in the shape of State or social organisation. Our first work must be destruction and annihilation of everything as it now exists. You must accustom yourselves to destroy everything, the good with the bad; for if but an atom of this old world remains, the new will never be created.

'Take heed that no ark be allowed to rescue any atom of this old world which we consecrate to destruction.'

assassination.[1] The majority of the Nihilists convicted of crimes have been sent to Eastern Russia or Western Siberia, where the climate is as healthy as that of Moscow. About 400 men and women have been sent to Saghalien, but only a small part of them belonged to the Nihilists. Compare these measures with those of Napoleon, who, after December 2, sent about 2,000 men to a lingering death in Cayenne.[2] No society has the right to tolerate certain deeds, and if the Russian Government is guilty of anything, it is of a most unwise leniency.

That, at all events, is the opinion of Russians. A hurried note from St. Petersburg, written the day after the attempt on the Emperor, thus describes the feeling excited in the capital:—'The people, especially the lower classes, are very angry with the leniency of the judges towards the Nihilists. The house from which the mine was fired has been partially destroyed by the populace. The police had to interfere to prevent its total demolition. Should any catastrophe occur (which Heaven forbid !) to the Emperor and his son, the Grand Duke Tzarewitch —between whom, I need hardly add, there are the closest ties of affection and confidence—there will be

---

[1] In England, in 1879, twenty murderers were sentenced to death and fifteen were hanged.

[2] This is a very moderate computation. Mr. Kinglake says:—'None will ever know the number of men who at this period were either killed or imprisoned in France or sent to die in Africa or Cayenne; but the panegyrist (Granier de Cassagnac) of Louis Bonaparte and his fellow plotters acknowledges that the number of people who were seized and transported between the few weeks which followed the 2nd of December amounted to the enormous number of twenty-six thousand five hundred.' —*Invasion of Crimea*, sixth edition, vol. i. p. 312.

witnessed a popular outburst of the maddest and most terrible character. No power could then restrain the people from attacking and punishing without mercy every individual whom they may suspect of Nihilist sympathies.'

Have we not some justification for our indignation? Mirsky's life was granted, at the request of General Drenteln, his would-be victim. Within three days the answer to this from the Nihilist camp was the attempt to kill our Emperor!

PART IV.

THE ANGLO-RUSSIAN ALLIANCE.

———◆◦◆———

1. FRIENDS OR FOES?
2. ENGLAND'S 'TRADITIONAL POLICY.'
3. RUSSIA AND ENGLISH PARTIES.
4. RUSSIA'S FOREIGN POLICY:—A REPLY TO MR. GLADSTONE. LETTER FROM M. EMILE DE LAVELEYE.
5. RUSSIAN AGGRESSION.
6. RUSSIA AND THE AFGHAN WAR.
7. RUSSIANS IN CENTRAL ASIA.
8. TRADITIONAL POLICY OF RUSSIA.
9. SOME LAST WORDS.

CHAPTER I.

FRIENDS OR FOES?

'I DESIRE nothing from you; I do not come to you in a precarious way, *non ut cliens, sed ut amicus*. My business is to make you an offer of that which is worthy of acceptance by any prince in Europe, the friendship of the English Commonwealth, which, if you please to embrace it on just and honourable terms, will be for your advantage as well as ours. If not, you yourselves will have as much prejudice as any other by the refusal.'

Such was the straightforward declaration made by an English Ambassador[1] when the Swedish Chancellor, Oxenstierne, asked him what England desired from Sweden.

This is one of the numerous cases in which Russians could have nothing better to do than to follow the English example. I am not in any sense an ambassador, I simply state my own views, as well as those of many Russians, but were I to speak in the name of Russia to England, I could not find better terms of expressing the feeling which alone can guarantee a real, cordial alliance between us.

[1] Bulstrode Whitelocke, 1654.

We do not want your patronage any more than you want ours. But the Russian Government as well as the Russian people have taken more than one step to secure your friendship, and have gone further—I openly say—than was compatible with our national dignity, especially in the course of the last three years. We made concession after concession; we sacrificed our prestige;[1] we forgot not only our own interests, but those of people depending solely upon us, in a manner which was altogether incompatible with our duty. With what results I need not say, but, believe me, the insults, the injuries of these last times have not increased the enthusiasm or the number of your friends in Russia.

If this policy is still to be persisted in, I am afraid things will not improve in that respect. The irritation already occasioned is as sore as a bleeding wound, and it will only become sorer, if no energetic attempt is speedily made by Englishmen whose personal views and sympathies are favourable to the Slavonic cause. And here, let me say, that while I hold Lord Beaconsfield's 'triumphs' of infinite insignificance, there is one victory which I really regret. He certainly has achieved a great success in

---

[1] This, perhaps, was not so much matter. We can afford to regard Russia's prestige as Mr. Carlyle regards that of England when he says: 'The prestige of England on the Continent, I am told, is much decayed of late, which is a lamentable thing to various editors; to me not. Prestige, præstigium, magical illusion—I never understood that poor England had in her good days, or cared to have, any prestige on the Continent, or elsewhere. The word was Napoleonic, expressive enough of a Grand-Napoleonic fact; better leave it on its own side of the Channel; not wanted here!'—*Shooting Niagara*, p. 377.

paralysing the England which was so heartily in accord with our efforts for the emancipation of the Christians. To judge from much that is said, and even done now, it seems as if consistency, perseverance in a course held to be but natural and just only two years ago, is now regarded as almost a treason to England. Yet if these people were really traitors to their own country, who could trust their professions, who could esteem them, who could ever care for their friendship? Not we Russians, certainly not.

But has it really come to this, that friendship to Russia is treason to England? What a monstrous conclusion! But before accepting it as an absolute truth, would it not be well to hear what can be said on the other side?

Has the experience of the last three years been so very satisfactory as to justify a persistence in a policy of systematic animosity? Do you like the results at which we have already arrived? Are you in a better position now than if St. James's Hall, instead of Guildhall, had dictated England's answer to our friendly advances? No matter what Russia proposed, England rejected it, while the one thing you proposed—the Constantinople Conference—we cordially accepted. Lord Beaconsfield adopted a policy of isolation from his devotion to 'English interests.' Tell me, has it been so much to your interest to care for nothing but 'interests.' Has anyone gained by it?

Of course Russia has suffered. We have lost two hundred thousand lives, not to speak of money; but is that an adequate compensation to you for having made enemies of a hundred millions of Slavs? Perhaps it might, if you had really succeeded in regenerating and re-establishing the Ottoman Empire. Russia has her compensations even more moral than material for her sacrifices. Where are those of the Sultan, or—may I add—your own? Your promised 'Three Campaigns' were only fought at the Guildhall, and—whilst the poor Sultan was sighing if only for one—our armies crossed the Danube, crossed the 'impregnable' Balkans, reached Constantinople, and dictated peace!

I repeat, who, then, has gained? This policy of antagonism has kept Europe in perpetual anxiety. Greece has trusted you only to be betrayed, in common with those simple souls who put their trust in the singular Salisbury Circular. Even Austria, in spite of her large compensation for—well—I do not know exactly for what—does not seem over grateful. Has England then benefited herself? Have you reaped any material advantages? But if not materially, perhaps you have gained much morally? Have you added much to your prestige? Does your national honour stand higher since your secret agreements and your Cyprus concessions?

Your glory in the past was to have been the friend of the oppressed, the refuge of the persecuted, the emancipator of the slave, and the champion of the weak against the strong. Has that glory, which we sincerely envied you, been enhanced by your recent policy in the East, or have you not conferred upon us the proud position of standing forth as the vindicator of liberty and humanity in the Balkan Peninsula?

Honestly speaking, I do not think that the results of the policy of antagonism have been encouraging, and I am not without hope that many Englishmen share my conclusion.[1]

---

[1] Mr. Gladstone, writing in the *Nineteenth Century* for August, 1879, on 'The Country and the Government,' says:—' In no form whatever is there any sensible counterpoise to the immense mass of folly and of mischief which is now crowning us so richly with its natural fruits. Having had in former days a tolerable character for unselfishness, we have now nauseated the world with the doctrine that "British interests" supply the final criterion of right and wrong. Upon every contested question that has arisen in the councils of Europe we have been the champions not of freedom but of oppression. Not an inch has been added to free soil through our agency, or with our good will. Servia, Montenegro, Bulgaria, Greece, perhaps Roumania—every one of them are smaller through our influence than they would have been without us. For the first time it can now be said with truth, that in the management of a great crisis of human destiny it would have been better for the interests of justice and of liberty if the British nation had not existed. . . . Our only gain has been that we were supposed to have "peace with honour;" the honour of providing the Sultan with a line of fortresses along the Balkans; the honour of arresting the southward march of freedom at the mountain passes, and leaving on the map the ill-starred testimony—on the northern side, "This is free land, liberated by the Despot of Russia;" on the other hand, "This is Turkish land, recovered for the Ottomans by the Tory Ministry and Parliament of England." . . . There is not a nation upon earth with which we have drawn the bonds of friendship closer by the transactions of these last years; but we have played perilous tricks with the loyalty of India, have estranged the ninety millions who inhabit Russia, and have severed ourselves from the Christians of Turkey, Greek and Slav alike, without gaining the respect of the Moslem. And all this we have done not to increase our power, but only our engagements; not to add at any point to our resources in men and money, but only and largely to the claims which may be made upon them. Assertions so broad as these must bear, in the eyes of those who have not carefully followed the facts, the aspect of exaggeration. Yet they are simply the summing up of ample Parliamentary demonstrations; they nowhere exceed the truth, and in some cases fall within it.'

How different it might have been if there had really been established that perfect understanding between England and Russia which our Emperor, representing the best aspirations of his people, urged upon Lord Augustus Loftus at Livadia in 1876. 'It would indeed,' as he so truly said, ' have been equally beneficial to their mutual interests and to those of Europe at large.'

Is it now too late? Alas! too many of my countrymen have lost all faith in the possibility of any friendly understanding after the painful disappointment occasioned by the success with which Lord Beaconsfield has paralysed our friends. The St. James's Hall Conference and the hearty support of the Slavonic cause, by such men as Mr. Carlyle, Mr. Gladstone, Mr. Bright, Mr. Freeman, the Duke of Argyll, Canon Liddon, and many others, whose names will ever be precious to us, raised hopes of co-operation which were rudely dashed to the ground by the conduct of your Government. Nor is this the only obstacle in the way. Not only is there a feeling of the hopelessness of removing English suspicion, but the irritation and resentment occasioned amongst all classes of the Russian people by your menaces and insults have created a formidable barrier between the two nations. This, however, was one of the consequences of the policy adopted by your Ministry, and it was urged in vain upon them as a reason for adopting an opposite course.

Five days before Lord Beaconsfield made his immortal Speech of the Three Campaigns, Lord Augustus

Loftus was writing at Yalta a report of a conversation which he had with an independent Russian nobleman, 'of high rank and influence, who is known for his admiration of England and everything English.' In his despatch occurs the following passage, which I quote from your Blue Book:—

> He said he hoped England would act in co-operation with Russia. There was every motive, political or otherwise, to engage her to do so for her own interests, and for those of Europe. England would then reap with Russia the gratitude of the Christian Eastern races, and augment her influence with them. It was an opportunity which might not easily occur again, and if once lost, would not be regained. Moreover, he expressed a great anxiety that the present occasion should be profited of to establish a cordial understanding between the British and Russian nations. It would be the means of dispelling that mist of distrust which has so long disturbed the friendly feelings between the two countries, for their mutual disadvantage. He feared that if England should now continue an antagonistic policy to Russia there would arise in this country an Anglophobia far surpassing what had hitherto been known in England under the name of Russophobia.[1]

Disregarding all our appeals, your Government persisted in its antagonistic policy, with the results which were anticipated. And yet, my firm impression is, that if England determines upon a new departure in her dealings with Russia, your advances will receive a warmer welcome from us than you extended to ours. The initiative this time must come from you; we can do no more.

---

[1] *Affairs of Turkey*, No. 1 (1877), p. 646.

Sir Charles Trevelyan, writing to the *Times*,[1] confirms my hope, he says :—

I should despair of the present state of feeling towards Russia if I did not remember the time when it was part of an Englishman's religion to hate the French. England used to be on the side of every oppressed nationality; but the wrongs of Bulgarians, Greeks, Armenians, even our detestation of slavery, seem to be swallowed up by our fear and hatred of Russia. Nevertheless, I look forward to a time when we shall awake from this delusion also. England and Russia have a great work of Christian civilisation to perform, and, instead of counteracting each other, they ought, in no grudging or ungenerous spirit, to give each other mutual help.

And—who knows?—instead of war, perhaps, at last England will join her in that sacred work, and the two great united and confident peoples will begin a new era worthy of them both, and renew the intimacy which existed after the fall of Napoleon the First.

Mr. Bright, in his speech on the Six Million Vote,[2] made a declaration which supports my hope that in the future we may be Friends not Foes. Speaking with all his usual eloquence, he said :—

The Government of this country ought to declare, and the time is not far distant, I believe, when they will declare it—it is now pretty much the mind of the people of England —that we have no interest in any longer taking any step whatever to maintain the Ottoman rule in Europe, and that we have no interest in maintaining a perpetual enmity with Russia. There are two policies before us—an old policy which, if we leave it to our children, will be a legacy of

---

[1] December, 1878.   [2] January 31, 1878.

future wars; and a new policy for which I contend and which I preach, by the adoption of which we shall leave to our country, not a legacy of war, but a legacy of peace and of a growing and lasting friendship with one of the greatest Empires in the world.

To that, with all my heart, I subscribe!

CHAPTER II.

ENGLAND'S 'TRADITIONAL POLICY.'

'WE must support the Turk, for it is our traditional policy,' is the motto of England. No, not of England, but of many Englishmen. The tradition, however, does not go very far back—not much farther, in fact, than the Crimean war[1]—a war the wisdom of which many of its authors now seriously doubt.

But I will not raise that question now. Grant it

[1] The vehemently Russophobist author of *Thirty Years of Foreign Policy*, writing in 1855, says:—'It is forgotten that this violent sympathy for the Turkish cause is of a very recent date. Among Liberal politicians especially it is only within the last few years that the existence of Turkey has ever been admitted to be a political necessity. The statesmen of the last generation, with perhaps the exception of William Pitt, utterly detested the Turkish Government. Even Burke called the Turks a race of savages and worse than savages, and said that any Minister who allowed them to be of any weight in the European system, deserved the curses of posterity. Thirty years ago the English Whigs and the Tzar were both bent on wresting Greece from Turkey and doing all the harm they could to the Sultan. After Navarino, the English Opposition bitterly reproached the Ministers for declaring it was necessary to maintain the Turkish Empire. In 1828, Lord Holland could scarcely find words to express his horror at any expression of sympathy for the Ottoman Empire. Had Lord Aberdeen and the Duke of Wellington declared war in 1829 in defence of Turkey, they would have been strongly opposed by a more formidable section of Liberal politicians than ever resisted Pitt when he commenced hostilities against the French Republicans. Religious fanaticism, popular prejudices, and liberal enthusiasm were all against the cause of the Sultan.'—Pp. 107, 110, 113, 116, 117.

if you will, that the Pasha and the Bashi-Bazouk are the traditional allies of free England. Must what has been always continue? Must the past bind for ever both the present and the future? The history of every nation is nothing but a record of the changes in its traditional, internal, and external policy.

Policies must be adjusted to facts, not facts to policies. No rule of conduct can be immutable. The wisdom of yesterday is often the folly of to-day. To be truly consistent as to one's object, one must often be completely inconsistent as to the means.

The truth is not a paradox. It is a truism of politics. Two or three years ago a clerical member of the Prussian Herrenhaus attempted to overwhelm the German Chancellor by quoting at great length from a speech delivered by M. Bismarck some twenty years previously, in which he vehemently attacked the policy he had subsequently adopted as his own.

Nothing daunted by hearing the recent policy of his Government denounced so vehemently from the tribune in extracts selected from his former speech, Prince Bismarck listened attentively, and with a slight smile upon his strongly-marked features. When his assailant, with an air of triumph, had resumed his seat, Prince Bismarck said, 'I have listened attentively to the speech which I delivered twenty years ago. I heard it with pleasure, and I am delighted to see that twenty years ago I understood the situation so well. At the present moment it would be all wrong, but then it was exactly what was needed. It is impossible now to secure the safety of the State except by departing from the tradition of that time.'

Other statesmen have shown even less anxiety to justify the change of policy forced upon them by altered circumstances. The Duke of Wellington, when on one occasion he was challenged in the House of Lords with an apparent inconsistency, simply replied, with charming frankness, 'I have changed my mind!'

Every reform is more or less of a protest against the policy bequeathed to us by our ancestors—a revolt against the established traditions of the past. When the reform is accomplished, men marvel at the opposition which it encountered. Of numberless instances take a case which was mentioned to me the other day, when we were talking of the universal satisfaction with which the abolition of the Concordat was regarded in Austria-Hungary. When the Council of the Vatican proclaimed the infallibility of the Holy Father, the enunciation of that dogma effected a change in the relation between the Papacy and the Courts of Europe. Count Beust, at that time Chancellor of Austria-Hungary, recognised, with the keen perception of a statesman, that the time had come for breaking with the traditional policy of the past. Count Beust abolished the Concordat, and boldly initiated the new policy which the occasion required.

There is a significance about that last fact which should not be lost. The Sultan has not proclaimed in set terms the dogma of his infallibility, but he has done worse. At the Conference at Constantinople he asserted, for the first time for many years, his deliberate intention to defy the councils of all the Powers. Unanimously they urged him to accept the irreducible minima, and pertinaciously he refused. That refusal in itself changed the whole situation. It was the Mussulman counterpart to the decree of the Vatican —an act of defiance to Europe and to civilisation. To some extent the English Government has recognised the impossibility of carrying out the old policy under such new conditions; but, unlike Count Beust, it has not boldly broken with the past, and annulled the unwritten Concordat which bound England to the Turk.

The reasons which led England to fight Russia in 1854 no longer exist. The whole situation is transformed. Is it not necessary to abandon the mistaken attempts to secure the peace of Europe by maintaining a government always and unavoidably at war with its own subjects? Peace, said Lord Derby, is the greatest of British interests. Why sacrifice it, then, by maintaining so obstinately a policy which has become an anachronism? Can you quick-moving Westerns, who invent the locomotive and talk by the telephone, be so absorbed in the trivial details of each day's business as to ignore two of the greatest facts of modern history? What are these facts? The first is the evident progress of Russia under our present Tzar.[1] The second is the establishment of

[1] I thought this was undisputed, but of late some people seem determined to dispute everything to our credit, and I therefore may be pardoned if I quote in support of this statement the evidence of one of our most determined enemies, Mr. Butler Johnstone, who can never forgive Lord Beaconsfield's Government for not making war upon Russia in 1877. Writing in 1875 on 'Russia as it is,' he says:—'One thing is quite

the German Empire. By the first, Russia gained new claims upon the sympathies of the civilised world. The second saved the Continent from the dread of the absolute predominance of Russia. The Turk is the only unprogressive Power left in Europe, and Turkish oppression is a worse menace to peace than 'Russian aggression.'

The Sick Man is sick unto death. England has tried to galvanise him into life; but the task exceeds even the resources of English wealth. And yet there are some who say, 'Let him have one more chance!' But what is the meaning of this phrase? What can be the relations between the Turks and the Christians after the events of the last two years? But it is possible that the Turk may be spared.[1] English diplomatic influence may succeed in maintaining the Turkish Empire against the determination of the whole of Russia. If so, while apparently adhering to the traditional policy of England, Lord Beaconsfield will have sacrificed the object for which that policy was invented, viz., the maintenance of a Power at Constantinople strong enough to keep peace in the East.

clear, the Russia of 1874 is no more the Russia of the Crimean war than it is the Russia of Boris Godounoff. That war ruined Turkey and regenerated Russia. . . . Every branch of Russian administration has been reformed. Corruption is not absolutely rooted out, but has at any rate been checked and compelled to hide its head; a network of railways has been undertaken, and, greatest triumph of all, the emancipation of the serfs was resolved upon, and, in spite of the obstacles, has been successfully carried out. In fact, there has been progress—great, rapid, and astounding progress—material and social and moral progress—along the whole line.'—*A Trip up the Volga*, pp. 5-6.

[1] This letter was written in November, 1877.

CHAPTER III.

RUSSIA AND ENGLISH PARTIES.

IT sometimes amuses me to see your papers declaring that Russians place all their hopes in the accession of the English Liberals to office.[1] Russia is

[1] In his first Midlothian speech, Mr. Gladstone emphatically admits that the English Liberals did little to excite the confidence with which it is mistakenly assumed they are regarded by Russians. He said:—
'Down to the end of the session 1876, although the Government had been adopting measures of the utmost importance in direct contradiction to the spirit and action of the rest of the Powers of Europe, there was not one word of hostile comment from the Liberal party. Was it faction in the Liberal party to remain silent during all these important acts, and to extend their confidence to the Government in the affairs of the Turkish Empire, even when that Government was acting in contradiction to the whole spirit, I may say, of civilised mankind—certainly in contradiction to the united proposals of the five Great Powers of the continent of Europe? Far more difficult is it to justify the Liberal party upon the other side. Why did we allow the East to be thrown into confusion? Why did we allow the concert of Europe to be broken up? Why did we allow the Berlin Memorandum to be thrown behind the fire, and no other measure substituted in its place? Why did we allow that fatal progression of events to advance, unchecked by us, so far, even after the fields of Bulgaria had flowed with blood, and the cry of every horror known and unknown had ascended to heaven from that country? Why did we remain silent for such a length of time? Gentlemen, that is not all. It is quite true that there was soon after a refusal of the great human heart of this country, not in Parliament, but outside of Parliament, to acquiesce in what was going on, and to maintain the ignominious silence which we had maintained on the subject of the Bulgarian massacres. In August and September, 1876, there was an outburst, an involuntary outburst, for the strain could no longer be borne, from the people of this country, in every quarter of the country, denouncing those

not so weak as to place all her hopes even in 'good tidings of great joy' from foreign capitals. Russia has her own policy, and to fulfil it she relies upon herself. No doubt Russians would gladly see a change in the position of parties in England—not because they hope much from the Liberals, but because they have been convinced by years of abuse and bad faith that no tolerable *modus vivendi* is possible with the present Conservative Government. Those who desire to see peace maintained in Europe and Asia would welcome the accession of any fresh Ministry to power. It might be better, and could not possibly be worse. But to imagine that Russians generally entertain great hopes of the *entente cordiale* with England if the Liberals return to power is decidedly a mistake. The majority attribute the speeches of the Opposition to party spirit, and, I regret to say, are very sceptical as to the reality of Liberal devotion to the cause of the Christians of the East.

Some Russians do not even desire any change. Convinced by the speeches of your Ministers that war is inevitable, they wish for nothing better than that Lord Beaconsfield should remain in office. As Mr. F. de Martens, Professor of International Law at the University of St. Petersburg, truly remarks in his excellent pamphlet on 'Russia and England in Central

---

massacres. But the Liberal party was not, as a party, in the field. And it was not till after nearly two years—viz., late in the spring or during the spring of 1877—it was not until nearly two years after the Government had been busy with the Eastern Question that the Liberal party first began somewhat feebly to raise its voice in the House of Commons.

Asia': 'Russian Anglophobists are extremely grateful to the Administration of Lord Beaconsfield, because it has, at a single stroke, brought England's Indian possessions into close proximity with the Asiatic territories which acknowledge the supremacy of Russia.'[1] England is much more vulnerable than before ; and, as I said last year, if England and Russia are to be foes, it would be unpatriotic in a Russian to write one word against Lord Beaconsfield, who has thrown away Britannia's shield, and left her exposed to hostile attacks.

It is very difficult, indeed, for foreign nations to understand the working of English parties. To the average Russian Lord Beaconsfield is England, and the Opposition attacks upon his policy are mere party attacks upon their powerful opponent—party attacks of no actual significance. 'What does it matter?' said one of our most influential journalists to me in Moscow, 'What does it matter ? These Liberals may say what they like in Opposition, but when they enter office they will do no more for the Eastern nationalities than Lord Beaconsfield. They are all alike, these English—some of them, taken separately, perfectly charming and well intentioned, generous, cultivated ; but, take them as a whole, as a nation, they are not to be trusted in any way. Can you seriously be so blind, so utterly under English influence, as to believe that they care a straw for the Slavs, the Greeks, or any other oppressed nationality, or for anything in the world except their own interests ; and

[1] *Russia and England in Central Asia*, Martens, p. 10.

what interests! You may point out, as you usually do, some straightforward and noble words said, or written, by Englishmen, but what is the position of these people at home? Some of them—merely because they are not rich enough to buy at an election the confidence of their countrymen, or are too frank and outspoken to conciliate the prejudices of electors —are not even in Parliament. The others, even in Parliament, are quite powerless. England,' he continued, 'is chiefly governed now, not by men of high moral principle and of commanding intellect, as she was on many occasions in former days. England is nothing but a plutocracy—the most demoralising and vulgarising shape of government known in all history. Compassion, generosity, self-sacrifice—you little know how little this adds to your pocket; but in England this is only too well known.' I protested, but in vain. A solitary voice is sometimes raised in the Russian press, expressing unshaken faith in the honour and sincerity of the English Liberals, and a deep conviction that they would pursue in office the policy advocated in opposition; but it is *vox clamantis in deserto;* and even the editor who inserts the article emphatically declares that he does not share its sentiments, 'for one is as bad as the other, and after these years no one can trust an Englishman.'

Devoted advocates of the *entente cordiale* between Russia and England sometimes almost despair of this unjust suspicion of all things English, which, however, is perhaps not altogether unnatural after the frequent disappointments of the last three years.

In the autumn of 1876, Russians, with delighted surprise, began to believe that England would work with them in securing the peaceful emancipation of the Slavs. How gladly we hailed that prospect Lord Salisbury can tell, for no one at the Conference of Constantinople, certainly not his own colleague, so cordially supported him as the representative of Russia. After the Conference, we had nothing but disappointments. The Government would not coerce the Turks; even the miserable Protocol was not signed without provisoes making it of no effect. Mr. Gladstone's resolutions were no sooner introduced than all but one or two were withdrawn,[1] and Russia was compelled single-handed to do the work of Europe.

When the war was over, and Bulgaria was freed from the Danube to the Ægean, the English Government demanded six millions to threaten war for re-enslaving Southern Bulgaria. Mr. Forster's 'amendment' was moved, but it also was rapidly withdrawn. Preparations for war went on. The English Liberals seemed paralysed. Their Russian friends were in despair. Then came the Congress at Berlin. Lord Beaconsfield and Lord Salisbury, on their return to London, were received as conquering heroes, with shouts of enthusiastic applause, making it their chief, and indeed their only, boast that they had restored to

[1] Such at least is the universal opinion abroad. I am informed, however, on excellent authority, that these resolutions were not actually abandoned, and that the operation, mistaken for a withdrawal, was 'a mere matter of parliamentary form, not easily explained to those outside.' This is another proof of the difficulty of understanding the working of English party-government.

the power of the Turk the very province whose sufferings evoked the magnificent demonstrations against the Turks in 1876. What wonder if, after that, Russians became impatient when they were told that one-half of England cordially sympathised with their sacrifices and shared their devotion to the cause of freedom in the East?

It is very painful for me to admit that Russians distrust the Liberals almost as much as the Conservatives, because it is to some slight extent the confession of my own failure. Yes, my utmost efforts have completely failed to inspire my countrymen with confidence in the reality of Liberal devotion to the cause of emancipation in the East. All that is effected is that Russians will watch with some sceptical curiosity to see whether the next Liberal Cabinet will carry out the policy professed in Opposition. They hope little, and expect less; but they are willing to admit the possibility that the Liberals may do something, however small, to work with Russia to promote the independence of the nationalities in the Balkan Peninsula.

The declaration of devotion to the engagements of the present Government is another matter that somewhat puzzles Russians; 'for how,' they ask, 'can they fulfil the Conservative treaties and remain faithful to Liberal pledges?' I understand, however, that that inconsistency is only apparent. It is possible to accept the treaties in order to modify the policy, as reformers recognise the Constitution which they seek to free from abuses. Russia also accepts existing obligations in the same sense, I suppose. Except in some few points, she cordially welcomes declarations of devotion to the Treaty of Berlin. The Treaty of Berlin is, three-quarters of it, the Treaty of San Stefano. The more faithfully it is fulfilled, the better Russia will be pleased. But in at least one important point it is not so. The partition of Bulgaria is an outrage decreed at Berlin. Against that partition English Liberals also have protested as loudly as the Moscow Slavophiles. What will they do when they return to power? I quite share my brother General Alexander Kiréeff's desires on this matter. The other day, when I was reminding him of several protests made by some friends of mine in England, 'Well,' said he, not without a tinge of regret, 'let the Liberals achieve the work we have left undone; let them, by some energetic measure, repair the harm their country has done in the course of these three years.'

Will they take this course? I am glad to see that Mr. Leonard Courtney, M.P., seems to think they will. Speaking at Liskeard, in November, 1879, he said:—

The duty of the new Liberal Government would simply be to work out what has been begun, but in a different spirit from the present Ministry, which impedes as much as possible the action of what is good, and furthers as much as possible the action of what is evil. The new Liberal Government would promote the liberation of Greece—the extension of Greece. A Liberal Government would come to the help of Greece, and would insist on the performance of the promises that have been given. A Liberal Government would take up the work that has been done, would clear it of imperfections, make perfect what has been left imperfect, and would do in no grudging spirit that which the present Government is trying to avoid doing at all.[1]

Nor is it only in the East that the Russians have been led to regard with some indifference the fortunes of political warfare in England. There is nothing that is more desired than a cordial understanding and a lasting friendship with England. Russia seeks no alliance with England so far as civilised States are concerned, for she seeks no alliance against any Power. But in Asia, and in that rapidly-diminishing section of Asia overlapping the East of Europe, the Anglo-Russian alliance against barbarism, anarchy, and fanaticism is the watchword of Civilisation, the key to the peaceful development of the Orient. Yet is it not a fact that in the party conflict of the last twelve months the Liberal party have, in pursuance of, it may be, legitimate tactics of party warfare, done much to convince Russia that with Liberal England also all hope of an *entente cordiale* is an idle dream?

What was the Liberal contention at the commencement of the Afghan War? I remember distinctly the cheers that hailed Mr. Gladstone's declaration at

---

[1] Even more categorical is the following definition of the policy which many Liberals hope to be able to pursue on their return to office:—
' Q. What will the Liberals do with the Turks? A. Labour to secure concerted European co-operation under the Treaty of Berlin, to decentralise or disintegrate the Ottoman Empire; to develop the liberties of the subject races, to permit the union of the Bulgarias, to extend the frontier of Greece, and to preserve the integrity of Turkey, by extinguishing, as expeditiously as is compatible with peace, the power of the ruling Turks.'
—*A Political Catechism*, published by Infield, 1880, p. 26.

Greenwich, that *if war had to be made*, it ought to have been made with Russia, not with Afghanistan. Mr. Gladstone, I suppose, did not believe that war should be made at all. But too many Russians ignored the proviso, and even Professor Martens places Mr. Gladstone's arguments in the mouth of 'advocates of war with Russia,' and congratulates his countrymen on the fact that the Conservative Ministers who declared that the sending of our Mission 'was perfectly allowable' under the circumstances, were wise and courageous enough to thwart 'these efforts to provoke a rupture' between the two Powers.[1] The provisoes, the limitations, are invisible at the distance of Moscow and St. Petersburg; and the effect is exactly opposite to that which is really desired.

I mention these matters with great regret. It is with almost a greater sacrifice to my own feelings that I allude to the unfortunate effect occasioned in Russia by Mr. Gladstone's article in the *Nineteenth Century* for January 1879, on 'The Friends and Foes of Russia;' for its allusions to our volunteers in Servia rendered it very precious to me, and it abounds with such generous tributes to the reality of our liberating work in Bulgaria that it is most painful to refer to it except in terms of gratitude.

In Russia Mr. Gladstone seemed so great in his magnificent advocacy of the cause of the oppressed, that we regarded him with feelings of enthusiastic admiration. When our best and bravest

[1] *Russia and England in Central Asia*, pp. 3-4.

had died for that noble cause, when every Russian home was saddened by the thoughts of those 'who went, but who return no more,' and when Lord Beaconsfield was straining every nerve to bring about a war to re-enslave the Bulgarians, we were cheered by the spectacle of Mr. Gladstone contending, almost single-handed, but with unwavering resolution, against those who wished to destroy the liberating work which our armies had accomplished.

His efforts were unsuccessful. Southern Bulgaria was 'restored to the Turk;' and Montenegro shorn of her territory; but, none the less for that, Mr. Gladstone has stamped his name in imperishable characters on every Slavonic heart. In the liberation of Bulgaria we had been allies; not foes, but friends united by a common enthusiasm and by mutual sympathies; and we believed that if ever he returned to power the memory of that great campaign for liberty would render possible that longed-for consummation—the establishment of a hearty *entente*, and the most friendly understanding between England and Russia for the complete deliverance of the Eastern Christians.

I still share that hope; but, unfortunately, the exigencies of party warfare in England have led to its abandonment by many Russians. The article on 'The Friends and Foes of Russia' was, no doubt, an effective polemic. It may have served an excellent party purpose to have retorted on the Conservatives their utterly unfounded charge of undue predilection for Russia; but its effect was anything but excellent in Russia. A slight from a friend is worse than a blow from a foe. To many Russians it seemed as if Mr. Gladstone, the only foreign statesman whom they had regarded with absolute confidence and esteem, was repudiating almost as an insult the charge that he entertained friendly feelings for their country.[1] 'Well,' they exclaimed, 'if even Mr. Gladstone regards our friendship as a stigma to be affixed upon the Conservative party and repudiated as a disgrace for the Liberals, let us not dream any longer of a good understanding with England.' It was in vain I pointed out that, even in that very article, Mr. Gladstone said, 'The standing motto of Liberals is friendship with every country,' and that the friendship with Russia, which he repudiated, was not the loyal friendship of great peoples, but an undue subserviency to the wishes of a foreign Power. I was told that Mr. Gladstone assumed, as a matter of course, that Russia would in the future naturally and inevitably pursue a policy in Europe hostile to freedom and humanity; and, of course, with such a policy no real friendship is

[1] It is a curious thing that distinguished Englishmen out of Parliament are, as a rule, much more courageous in avowing publicly their sympathies with us than those who, having evenly-balanced constituencies to humour, shrink from uttering the generous words which might risk the doubtful vote. For example, how seldom do you find an M.P. speaking like Dr. Sandwith, who recently said at a large meeting in London:—'The Conservatives accuse us of being friends of Russia. As for Russia, I here declare openly that I at least am not ashamed of being a friend of that noble and chivalrous people, who, in these degenerate times, scorning the cold calculations of prudence, rashly, gloriously rushed to the rescue of suffering humanity, not counting the cost, and dragging their more prudent Government after them. All honour be to them, while I blush with shame for the miserable part which England played in that struggle.'

possible. 'If Mr. Gladstone,' they added, 'could say such things, what chance is there of any Liberal Government entertaining friendly relations with Russia?' If Russia is to be assumed, even by those who sympathised most deeply with her great work of liberation, to be the eternal foe of freedom and humanity, 'except when she departs from herself,' of course, the only relation England should maintain towards Russia would be one of opposition.

But surely Russia, which played some little part in the liberation of Italy, in the unification of Germany, in the emancipation of Greece, Servia, Roumania, and Bulgaria, and which, without any pressure from without or any revolution at home, has liberated twenty-two millions of her own serfs—a fact too often forgotten by our supreme judges—is not justly assumed to be predestined to 'oppose freedom in all its forms'? But why assume a guilt which has not yet been committed?

The feeling in Russia with regard to the repeated rebuffs which we have received at the hands of England is one of indignation. These advances, they say, should never have been made. Russia is not going to implore anybody's friendship, not even that of England. Pardon me, but the very idea makes me smile. Boasting and blustering may not be our characteristic, but we really are not so humble as some imagine. If England wishes for our friendship it is not wise to repel every attempt on our part to promote a good understanding. Fortunately, Russia is not depending for her greatness and her existence upon the goodwill of any other country, not even on that of England.

The Future is ours!

'The Germans have reached their day, the English their mid-day, the French their afternoon, the Italians their evening, the Spaniards their night, but the Slavs stand on the threshold of the morning.'

CHAPTER IV.

RUSSIA'S FOREIGN POLICY: A REPLY TO MR. GLADSTONE.[1]

M. EMILE DE LAVELEYE, writing with his usual talent and brilliancy in the *Fortnightly Review* for December, gives a curious account of the apparently anti-Russian animus of Prince Bismarck's visit to Vienna, which does not appear, as yet, to have attracted much attention. It is rather daring to differ from so great an authority as the celebrated Belgian Professor. But since Molière submitted his literary works to the critical appreciation of a humble kitchen-maid, other simple mortals can also avail themselves of the charming privilege of plain speaking.

Is it really proved that questions of mere personalities always play such a decisive part in the policy of Powers? Is M. de Laveleye absolutely right in his conclusions either as to the mission of Austria—that is, of the present Government of Austria-Hungary—in the Balkan Peninsula, or as to the anti-Russian character of the Austro-German Alliance? Although these questions are doubtful, nevertheless he may be well informed about the *motif* of the Ger-

---

[1] *Vide* Mr. Gladstone's article in the *Nineteenth Century*, January 1879; 'The Friends and Foes of Russia.'

man Chancellor's trip to Vienna, and his story is as follows :—

In May, 1875, the military party in Germany, with or without Prince Bismarck's sanction, determined upon attacking France without any pretext but that she was becoming too strong. It was intended to demand the reduction of the French army to 200,000 men, and the immediate suspension of the reconstruction of fortresses. The ultimatum being rejected, France was to be invaded, dismembered, and destroyed. Russia, supported by England, interfered, and vetoed the projected war. Russia, says M. de Laveleye, was offered Constantinople by Germany as the price of her neutrality. The bribe was refused. Prince Gortschakoff insisted that France must be left alone. He, therefore, preserved the peace of Europe, and saved France from invasion; but he encountered the deadly animosity of Prince Bismarck. 'The visit to Vienna, which resulted in an Austro-German Alliance,' M. de Laveleye asserts, 'is the German Chancellor's revenge for Prince Gortschakoff's interference in 1875.' Yet, the Herald Angel of that 'good tidings of great joy for all who cared for the peace of Europe or the independence of nations' was a leading member of the Cabinet which then co-operated with Russia in preserving the peace of Europe, and the independence of France from the designs of Germany! 'It seems to be the destiny of Russia,' most justly remarks M. de Laveleye, 'to meet with ingratitude.' But even Russians, inured to ingratitude, recollect no precedent for this exultation by a former ally over a misfortune supposed to have overtaken us because of our share in the Peace Alliance of 1875.

This last occasion on which England and Russia acted cordially in concert in Continental politics is not encouraging for those who still hope for the triumph of common sense over absurd prejudices. The two nations have so much in common, their true interests lead so naturally to their co-operation, that if once this fever fit of suspicion passed away, a cordial understanding would be seen to be a mutual necessity.

'Nations, like individuals,' as has been observed more than once, 'may sometimes go mad,' and the prevalence of Russophobia is an illustration of national delirium. Nothing but temporary mental derangement, leading to total oblivion of their own history, could lead Englishmen to exult in an imagined effacement of Russia.[1] The best English historians have,

---

[1] I am glad to see that there is even in Lord Beaconsfield's Cabinet a staunch Conservative member who holds more rational views, and not only most kindly allows us to live, but even desires our friendship. The First Lord of the Admiralty, Mr. W. H. Smith, speaking at Sutton on January 15, 1880, said :—' Do not let it be supposed that Her Majesty's Government have any hostility against Russia. We have no desire whatever to have any other relations than those of the most perfect amity with Russia. There is no portion of the territory of Russia which we covet. There is no portion of the legitimate influence of Russia which we desire to decrease. There is no portion of the trade of Russia or the commerce of Russia that we desire to interfere with. The greatest desire of this country must be that a vast empire like Russia shall be prosperous, shall be contented, shall be well governed, and at peace with itself. We deplore as much as any individual can deplore the misfortunes—I can speak in no other terms—which have occurred with regard to the Government of Russia during the past few months. Anything which requires assassination and conspiracy and bloodshed, and acts of that character, must be wrong in itself. It is abominable and hateful to

therefore, throughout all this last Eastern crisis been on our side, beginning with Mr. Carlyle, the noblest genius of our age.[1] History proves that Russia is an element in the balance of power with which England, whether she likes it or not, can hardly afford to dispense.[2]

every human being. It is impossible that conspiracy can be right, directed against a Sovereign reigning for the benefit of his subjects. We long to be at peace with Russia, and there is no reason why we should not be at peace with Russia if Russia remains, as we trust she will be, on peaceful and honest terms with us.' Peaceful and honest terms by all means, but England hitherto has hardly regarded these stipulations with which Russia has loyally complied.

[1] On the eve of the St. James's Hall Conference, Mr. Carlyle wrote:— 'For fifty years back my clear belief about the Russians has been that they are a good and even noble element in Europe. Ever since Peter the Great's appearance among them, they have been in steady progress of development. In our own time they have done signal service to God and man in drilling into order and peace anarchic populations all over their side of the world. The present Tzar of Russia I judge to be a strictly honest and just man, and, in short, my belief is that the Russians are called to do great things in the world, and to be a conspicuous benefit, directly and indirectly, to their fellow-men.' And again in 1876 he said, with characteristic force:—' The newspaper outcry against Russia is no more respectable to me than the howlings of Bedlam, proceeding as it does from the deepest ignorance, egoism, and paltry national jealousy.'

[2] In saying this I assert no more than what has been admitted by at least one of the present Ministers. Mr. Lowther, M.P., Irish Secretary, addressing his constituents at York, Feb. 18, 1878, when war between England and Russia was believed to be imminent, said:—' He did not, however, conceal his opinion that Russia was a Power which had its uses in the world. Russia in the past had filled a position which made him think that anything which tended to remove so great an influence for weal or woe from the body politic of nations would be a calamity. He had always considered the position of Russia as one of the Northern Powers, when its attention was not directed to the acquisition of her neighbour's land, which possessed a conservative and pacific influence in Europe; for they must not forget at that moment, when there was nothing but Eastern clouds in the horizon, there was a Western question. They must remember that most of the battles of this country, in a contest which overawed all others, was not waged so much in the East as in the

Each member of the European family has its historic mission, which no other nation can perform. To efface one Power is to weaken all.

In party polemics, Liberals sometimes, with little regard for our feelings, say that Russia on the Continent has, with few exceptions, supported a reactionary policy which commanded the support of English Conservatives. Now, English Liberals tolerate free and plain speaking; they not seldom display a noble courage in confessing their error, if it is proved that any of their passing remarks are contrary to some facts which may easily have slipped from their memory at the time. This encourages me to insist upon certain truths which appear to be forgotten. Russia is not infallible, and if you are only happy in referring to our shortcomings, do so as often as you like; but, judging from the speeches of some of your best statesmen, whose opinions are weighty and well informed, our policy has been throughout the greater part of the nineteenth century more in accordance with the matured views of English Liberalism than the policy of England herself.

In the East events have vindicated the policy of Russia. The real nature of Turkish misrule is not denied now, even by Conservatives. English Liberals have, at last, realised the iniquity of supporting the Turk, which our Tzar Boris Godounoff urged upon your Queen Elizabeth, nearly three hundred years ago, in the following letter, which was, curiously

West, and in that they had Russia as their ally. At that moment, when considerable irritation was felt, they must not forget that Russia had stood them in good stead, and might do so again.'

enough, referred to Lord Robert Cecil—Lord Salisbury's distinguished ancestor and 'a friend of Russia' at that distant time. The Tzar wrote :—

We have learned that the Queen has furnished help to the Turks against the Kaiser of Germany. We are astonished at it, as to act thus is not proper for Christian Sovereigns; and you, our well beloved sister, ought not for the future to enter into relationship of friendship with Bousourman (Mussulman) princes, nor to help them in any way whether by men or silver; but, on the contrary, should desire and insist that all the great Christian potentates should have a good understanding, union, and strong friendship, and make one against the Mussulmans till the hand of the Christians rise and that of the Mussulmans is abased.[1]

Russian methods may not meet your approval, but Russian policy—the breaking down of the Ottoman Power and the emancipation of the subject races—has even in England triumphed over the old English policy of upholding the Porte. In the historical development of the East, the leading part has been played, not by England, but by Russia.

Once, and only once, by an 'untoward event,' England struck a blow for freedom in the East; but the emancipation of the Christians has been the sacred mission of Russia from the day she achieved her own liberation.

Roumania, Servia, and Bulgaria owe their liberties to us, not to you; and even for Greece the battle of Navarino would have availed little but for the victories of General Diebitch.

Tell me, as you look back across the centuries,

[1] Rambaud, *History of Russia*, vol. i. p. 344.

which policy was more truly liberal in the East—that of England, which supported the Sultan; or that of Russia, which freed his subjects?

Yes! replies one of our eloquent accusers, I admit that in the East, Russia has marched in the van of progress; but it was only a noble inconsistency. Elsewhere she has been the persistent foe of freedom, the disturber of the peace, a standing menace to the independence of nations—in short, a fitting ally of our Conservative Government.[1]

But why do they generally refuse to give any proofs of their sweeping accusations? Is it fair-play? I am referred, in answer, to Hungary and Belgium.

I do not defend our intervention in Hungary. In the first place—pardon my frankness—because we ought to have known beforehand that, in return for our help, Austria would only 'astonish the world with her ingratitude,' as was graphically described by Prince Schwartzenberg. In the second, because Hungary was not altogether wrong in complaining of her rulers. But it should not be forgotten that if it had not been stopped from the beginning, very probably the revolution would have been continued in other countries—in Russia as well as in Germany.

---

[1] 'A Power whose action in European politics has been as a rule on the side opposed to English sympathies.' (Mr. Gladstone, *Nineteenth Century*, Feb. 1878, p. 209.) And again, 'Unless in cases of pure exception, Russia has uniformly and habitually ranged herself in European politics with the antagonists of freedom.' (*Ibid.* Jan. 1879, p. 172.) 'Everywhere, except in Turkey, Russian statesmanship has headed and sustained the votaries of reaction, with the support and sympathy of English Toryism' (p. 174).

But is it not curious that our saving Austria is almost the only act of ours[1] which still finds eulogists among your Ministers, which of course is rather a bad sign?

We must, however, remember that the Emperor Nicholas—a *preux chevalier* in all his feelings, a sincere ally of his allies—in saving 'the keystone of Central Europe' from ruin prevented the subjection of the Slavs[2] of Hungary to the Magyars, and the Russian troops behaved with far greater humanity to the insurgents than did the Austrians. The question was not so very simple; it could be judged very differently indeed by men of very good faith and very generous views.[3]

The Emperor Nicholas was greatly misunderstood

[1] Mr. Gladstone writes:—'I say nothing of Hungary, for Russia's intervention there, however odious to Liberals, is, I apprehend, within the limits of the high Tory creed, is supported by the practice of older and more advanced countries, and cannot be compared in guilt of details with our intervention in the two Sicilies only half a century before.' —*Nineteenth Century*, February 1878, p. 214. (*See* Speech by Lord Beaconsfield, then Mr. Disraeli, Feb. 1, 1849). A Conservative Secretary of State mentioned our intervention in Hungary as an instance in which Russia had done good service to the cause of order and peace by saving the keystone of Central Europe from destruction.

[2] The Slavs in 1849 were not avowed as brethren, or rather were only recognised by the few so-called 'Moscow Slavophiles,' the poet Homiakoff, Pogodine, Kosheleff, the three Aksakoffs, Samarine, the two brothers Kiréefsky, Prince Tcherkassky, and some others. The Russian Government, until the Servian war, ignored them officially, but could not help feeling for them and sympathising with their unfortunate lot.

[3] Prosper Mérimée, speaking to Mr. Senior in 1859, said:—' Austria, with her usual stupidity and brutality, has made enemies, not only of Magyars, but also of the Croats, who rendered her such services in the late insurrection. The Russians, when they entered Hungary, behaved with the utmost moderation, paid liberally for all that they wanted, and when they had beaten the Hungarians, protected them against the Austrians.'—Senior's *Conversations*, vol. ii. p. 246.

abroad. He was certainly not the heartless tyrant he is represented in this country; just the opposite, and those who knew him well will gladly endorse my opinion. He was certainly not a diplomatist, as was well proved by his famous conversation with your Ambassador, Sir Hamilton Seymour. He was not a man of science. But he was devoted to his country: he was proud of her, he upheld her dignity with all his power, and he followed without hesitation wherever his duty led. He understood as well as his people that sometimes a reverse is not a disgrace, and the noble motto of his life was '*Fais ce que dois, advienne que pourra.*' Of course, this does not save a man from mistakes—but what does?[1]

If Russia made war from a mistaken idea, she demanded no compensation for her sacrifices, and also 'astonished the world,' but only because she retired without annexing a single verst of the Empire she restored to the Hapsburgs. Even our bitterest enemies do not deny that the measure was dictated 'by a spirit of austere virtue ranging high above

---

[1] Mr. Klaczko, the distinguished Polish author, in his *Two Chancellors*, says:—'It is undeniable that the intervention of the Emperor Nicholas in Hungary bears the stamp of a generous and chivalrous nature, and was in itself an undertaking that astonished his contemporaries.' Mr. Klaczki 'mentions the fact that Bismarck, then an unknown young member for the Prussian Chamber, expressed, in September 6, 1849, his admiration of the brilliant conduct of the Emperor, and expressed his patriotic regret that this magnanimous task should not have devolved upon his own country (Prussia)' (p. 25). The same author pays a well deserved tribute to the policy of the Emperor Nicholas, whose 'perfect uprightness and immovable firmness none dared contest, and which was employed, with a remarkable disinterestedness, to maintain the world's equilibrium and enforce respect for treaties' (pp. 11–13).

common ambition.' Our Emperor—'the Chief Justice of Europe'—not only believed himself 'bound in honour' (and these words, to Russians, have a very great weight) to assist the youthful Kaiser in distress, but he was convinced the explosive forces of the revolution needed his intervention, and many Englishmen shared his views.

In the case of Belgium, where we are accused of actively manifesting our displeasure against the creation of the new kingdom, I assert confidently that the accusation is unjustified, and that whatever faults there may have been in Russian policy—and the worst that can be charged against her is a lack of zeal and some indecision in the first stages of the affair—was far more than atoned for by the protection she extended to Belgium in 1851.

You will find the whole story of our shortcomings, such as they were, told at length in the Memoirs of Baron Stockmar. I do not think they bear out the sweeping charge of Russia's opposition to freedom all over the world. Belgium in 1814 and 1815 was, by England's advice, added to Holland in the Treaty of Vienna. The Belgians revolted in 1830, and Europe was threatened with a general European war. The heir to the Dutch throne was the brother-in-law of our Emperor, and Nicholas I. combined a scrupulous respect for treaties with a marked horror of revolutions. Nevertheless, he did not oppose—on the contrary, as soon as it was evident that no attack was meditated by France—he supported, with some natural hesitation and excusable vacillation, the establishment of the Belgian Kingdom.[1]

Russia was one of the five Powers to whom Belgium owed her existence.[2] The Emperor ratified both the treaties of 1831 and 1839, and although somewhat slow to move, so far from offering any opposition to the policy of England, always ultimately supported it. We should be well content if you had supported our policy in Bulgaria as we supported your policy in Belgium.

But granting that Russia did not in Belgium, as she did in the East, do more than any other Power for the cause of liberty and independence, her shortcomings were abundantly atoned for twenty years later, when but for Russia Napoleon would have annexed Belgium.

This fact is too often ignored in England, yet its authenticity is beyond dispute. King Leopold told Mr. Senior that Belgium, after the *coup d'état*, was in imminent danger of being annexed by France. He

[1] See, at the end of this chapter, the letter from the distinguished Belgian Professor, M. Emile de Laveleye, vindicating against me Russian policy in Belgium in 1830.

[2] Besides the treaties of the five Powers, to which Russia was a party, there was a separate Anglo-Russian Convention, by which Russia bound herself to do nothing in relation to Belgium without consulting England. The second article of the Convention shows that Russia, equally with England, upheld the independent neutrality of Belgium. It is as follows:—' S.M. l'Empereur de toutes les Russies s'engage si (ce qu'à Dieu ne plaise) les arrangements arrêtés pour l'indépendance et la neutralité de la Belgique, et au maintien desquels les deux hautes Puissances sont également liées, venaient à être compromis par les événements, à ne se plier à aucun arrangement nouveau, sans concert préalable avec S.M. Britannique et sans son assentiment formel.'—*Memoirs of Stockmar*, vol. i. pp. 267-8.

said: 'I have reason to know that Napoleon intended to copy the decrees by which his uncle annexed to France first Holland, and afterwards the provinces at the mouths of the Weser and of the Elbe. I believe that the decree for the annexation of Belgium was actually drawn out. He was checked by Russia. After the 2nd of December he wrote to the different Sovereigns announcing his election. The smaller Powers could only express their acquiescence. Austria offered the most friendly congratulations; Russia administered to him a grave admonition. The Emperor said he trusted that France was prepared to respect what Russia was determined to enforce—the existing treaties, the existing limits, the existing balance of power. This was a warning which he did not venture to disregard.'[1]

But for that intimation King Leopold declared that the annexation of Belgium, in spite of England, would certainly have been attempted by France.

Again, in 1870, the failure of the Benedetti project for the annexation of Belgium was largely due to Russia's arrangement with Germany.[2]

Surely, then, it is unhistorical to represent Russia as exercising an evil and reactionary policy in Europe on account of Belgium? May I not, on the contrary, fairly assert that the history of Belgium affords a signal illustration of the importance to the cause of liberty of the Russian element in the balance of Power?

[1] Senior's *Conversations*, vol. i. p. 89.
[2] Klaczko's *Two Chancellors*, p. 244.

England can surely not have forgotten the services which Russia rendered to England and the cause of Liberty in the Napoleonic wars, which even the Treaty of Tilsit cannot obscure.

In the brilliant pages of Mr. Kinglake you may read [1] of the services to Europe, and especially to England, rendered by Russia's 'loyal obedience to the great usage' which forms the safeguard of Europe and the protection of the weak against the strong. It was the Russian alliance with Austria in 1805 that broke up the camp of Boulogne, and saved England from invasion several weeks before the battle of Trafalgar. Again, in 1806, our Emperor came forward with his army to the rescue of the Continent. Although his heroic struggles were unsuccessful, his 'faithful, valorous efforts' gained him the respect of Europe and the eloquent tribute of your great historian.

Have you forgotten the glorious year of 1812—generally known in Russia simply as 'the year 12'—in which Moscow was offered up as a burnt sacrifice on the altar of European freedom? You may be proud, indeed, of the brilliant exploits of the 'Iron Duke;' but although he contributed in the Peninsular War to the defeat of Napoleon, the leading part of that great tragic drama was not taken by your Irish general and your troops, but by our Emperor and our people. After Russia had been freed from the invading army of twenty nations, Alexander the First determined on the liberation of Europe. 'Confiance

---

[1] *Invasion of the Crimea*, sixth edition, vol. i. pp. 26, 27.

en Dieu, Courage, Persévérance, Union!' were his watchwords, when, as Stein, the German patriot-statesman, says, 'with the eye of faith, which boldly and undazzled looks up to heaven, he surrendered himself to the inspiration of his large-hearted noble soul, and hurled the giant to the ground.'[1]

Alexander became the soul of the coalition which crushed Napoleon at Leipzig, and it was his indomitable resolution that led him to begin that march on Paris which freed Europe.

It was no idle boast, his proclamation of Freiburg, when he told his heroic troops, 'Already we have saved and glorified our country. We have given back to Europe her liberty and independence.' Undaunted by temporary reverses, he remained faithful to his wise resolve : 'No peace as long as Napoleon is on the throne.' When at last Napoleon was dethroned, he who had been the foremost in the fight was the most generous to his vanquished foe ! If you read Las Casas' 'Mémorial de St. Hélène' you will

[1] In a speech delivered by Mr. Canning at a public dinner in Liverpool, January 10, 1814, your great statesman, speaking of the overthrow of Napoleon, put this point in a very striking manner:—'By what power, in what part of the world, has that final blow been struck which has smitten the tyrant to the ground? I suppose by some enlightened republic, I suppose by some nation which, in the excess of popular freedom, considers even a representative system as defective unless each individual interferes directly in the national concerns; some nation of enlightened patriots, every man of whom is a politician in the coffee-house as well as in the Senate. I suppose it is from such government as this that the Conqueror of Autocrats, the sworn destroyer of Monarchical England, has met his doom. I look through the European world in vain. I find there no such august community. But where was the blow struck? Where? Alas! for theory! In the wilds of despotic Russia. It was followed up on the plains of Leipzig by Russian, Prussian, and Austrian arms.'—*Memoir of George Canning*, p. 323.

see that the captive representative of passed glories speaks in terms of admiration of his conqueror.

M. Alfred Rambaud—himself a Frenchman—bears unqualified testimony to this feature of Russian policy. He says:—' The Power which had struck hardest for the freedom of Europe was most poorly compensated. It is an incontestable fact that of all the allies Russia showed herself the least grasping. It was she who had given the signal for the struggle against Napoleon, and had shown the most perseverance in pursuit of the common end. Without her example the States of Europe would never have dreamed of arming against him. Her skilful leniency towards France finished the work begun by the war. Alexander was incontestably at the head of the European Areopagus.' [1]

The policy of Russia towards the later years of Alexander's life—from 1819–1825—although it commanded the warm admiration of the English Conservatives, I do not defend, although I would not condemn. During these six years Russia exerted herself against the assassinating Revolutionists of Germany, the Carbonari of Naples, and the Constitutionalists of Spain. It was a time of reaction at home and abroad. Europe, still shaking with the earthquake of the French Revolution, was not inclined to tolerate insurrectionary movements; and Alexander, who was the leader of the European coalition against Napoleon, believed himself bound to

---

[1] Rambaud's *History of Russia*, vol. ii. pp. 297, 300, 304. *Vide* M. Emile de Laveleye's letter at the close of this chapter.

support the Conservative cause against all the Revolutionists of Europe.

But it is rather amusing to hear the conduct of Emperor Alexander during the last years of his life alluded to as a conclusive proof that the foreign policy of an autocracy is opposed to liberty. The foreign policy of Constitutional England and of Parliamentary, though Legitimist, France was almost (if not quite) as reactionary as that of autocratic Russia. It is as great a mistake to believe that because a State possesses free institutions itself it will always support them abroad, as to believe that because a nation is governed by an autocrat it will be the eternal foe of liberty in neighbouring States.

Permit me to give a striking illustration of this. Perhaps the most illiberal act of Alexander I. was his diplomatic opposition to the establishment of Constitutional Government in Spain in 1822. But while Russia contented herself with diplomatic representations, France—that enlightened Western nation, enjoying herself Constitutional Government—marched an army across the Pyrenees, and crushed by her cannon the Constitution of Spain.

M. Thiers thirty years after justified that intervention—which, indeed, he had counselled from the first—by arguments which may be recommended to those who think that Constitutional States can be trusted to support liberty in other countries. Replying to those who declared it would be an enormity to hinder an independent nation shaking off an intolerable tyranny, M. Thiers maintained that it was necessary to do so. He argued that 'If Spain continued Constitutional the antipathy of the Spaniards towards the French would make her a rival or an enemy, instead of an ally. It was the duty, therefore, of every French Government to put down every Spanish Constitution!'[1]

After the death of the Emperor Alexander the policy of Russia ceased to deserve the denunciations of English Liberals. That it received the anathemas of English Tories may, perhaps, be a recommendation in some eyes. When we are accused of uniformly supporting the side of power, and of commanding on that account the uniform support of English Toryism, I cannot help wondering if our accusers ever read Lord Aberdeen's letter to the Duke of Wellington, in 1830, in which he says; 'It is a most extraordinary thing that the Russian policy, although at home the most despotic in the world, should have supported in every country for some time past the efforts of every party opposed to the established Government.'[2]

We are blamed for being displeased with the French Revolution of 1830, but we did not oppose it. Our displeasure was purely platonic. Remembering the Continental catastrophe which followed the preceding Revolution, it was no more a proof of a rooted antipathy to liberty than was Lord Palmerston's eager recognition of the hero of the *coup d'état*—a crime which our Emperor did not so slightly condone.

[1] Senior's *Conversations*, vol. i. p. 63.
[2] *Wellington Despatches*, vol. iii. p. 158.

If we are to go into questions of sentimental sympathy, I may be perhaps permitted to recall the fact that, in the great war of liberation in America, Russian opinion was much more strongly on the side of freedom in the North than was the case with public opinion in England. Our 'displeasure' with the Revolution of 1830 was by no means so serious an offence against the cause of liberty as the delight manifested in England at the early successes of the Southern slaveowners.

But why dwell on such trivialities? Look at the great movements of our century, and ask whether it was England or Russia that furthered most the policy which, in the opinion of English Liberals to-day, was most in harmony with the development of Liberty and the progress of Civilisation?

The first of these was the Liberation of Italy. One or two despatches of Prince Gortschakoff's criticising minor incidents in the unification of Italy have caused it to be forgotten how large a share Russia had in achieving the liberation of that country. The fact is that, next to France, Russia was the best friend of Italy.

Of this there is abundant evidence of the best kind—the evidence of a hostile witness in Mr. Martin's last volume of the 'Life of the Prince Consort.' From that valuable mine of authentic documents one might bring many conclusive extracts proving that the English Government opposed, while Russia strongly supported, the cause of Italian emancipation. Your Queen, for instance, according to Mr. Martin, declared that the war of unification undertaken by Napoleon was 'brought about by the wicked folly of Russia and France.'[1] The Prince Consort declared— 'The Russians are, of course, at the bottom of the whole thing,'[2] and mentions the suggestive little fact, that Russia placed an army of 200,000 men on her frontiers, to keep Austria and Prussia in check, whilst Napoleon was engaged in the campaign in Lombardy. I even find a characteristic *bon mot* of my old and sarcastic friend, Lord Clarendon, relative to our proposal to France that a European Congress should be summoned to secure the liberation of Italy. 'One despotic Power,' said he, 'has proposed to another despotic Power that by means of a Congress a third despotic Power should pave the way for liberal institutions.'[3]

Her Majesty's Historian-in-Waiting, Mr. Martin, himself says that English statesmen distrusted the plan by which France and Russia would play the liberators of Italy. In spite of your distrust, however, the 'two absolute despotic Powers'[4] achieved their end, and the freedom of Italy was added to the other boons which liberal Europe owes in part to autocratic Russia.

Another great movement in the North of Europe has been carried to a triumphant conclusion; nor is the Unification of Germany less remarkable as a triumph of Liberal ideas than the Liberation of Italy. Tell me who was the most potent factor in the Euro-

---

[1] *Life of Prince Consort*, vol. iv. p. 429.
[2] *Ibid.*, p. 352.
[3] *Ibid.*, p. 426.
[4] *Ibid.*, p. 349.

pean policy which rendered possible the realisation of the 'great German idea'—England or Russia? If Russia meditated schemes of aggression, or even of predominance in Europe, she ought to have opposed, not supported, the national movement in Germany. It was left to England to oppose that movement at its commencement, and to preserve a cold neutrality towards it at its close. It is needless to refer to the part played by Russia on that occasion. Wrongly or rightly, whether contrary to or according to her own interests, Russia has supported the unification of Germany. Immediately after signing the treaty, closing the war by which Germany was united, the Emperor William sent to the Emperor Alexander the following message: 'Never will Prussia forget that to you it is due that the war did not assume larger proportions. May God bless you for it! Your grateful friend for life.'[1]

A third great movement, not yet completed, owes also more to Russia than to England. I refer to the Transformation of Austria. Austria is once more becoming an 'öster-reich'—an Eastern kingdom. The war of 1859 ejected Austria from Italy. The war of 1866 converted Austria into Austria-Hungary. The ultimate result of the war of 1877-78 will be to substitute for the Dual Monarchy a Confederation of the Danube, in which the Slavonic element will assert that pre-eminence *de jure*, which already exists *de facto*.[2]

In all these stages Russia has played a great part.

[1] Klaczko's *Two Chancellors*, p. 306.
[2] See the 'Heirs of the Sick Man,' *ante*, p. 152.

'The constant security,' which Prince Bismarck could indulge as to Russia in 1866 was hardly less important for Austria-Hungary than were the Russian victories in Bulgaria. The end is not yet. But whatever may be its final shape, the Transformation of Austria, the third great beneficent revolution on the Continent, like the two which preceded it, owes certainly more to Russia than to England.

In these Russia played a part, secondary though important. In the fourth great revolution, which constitutes the glory of the Nineteenth Century Russia has done the work alone. The Emancipation of the East, the gradual overthrow of the inhuman domination of the Turk, the establishment of independent, self-governed, democratic States on the ruins of the Ottoman despotism—that has been Russia's splendid mission, and faithfully has she fulfilled it.

At the price of the life-blood of hundreds of thousands of her noblest sons, Russia has purchased the Freedom of the East. I forbear to speak of the part in that great struggle which was played by England.[1]

---

[1] On this point I may quote the following passage from the masterly work of the Duke of Argyll on the Eastern Question. Excepting three minor points in which amendments, introduced by the Congress, were accepted by Russia,—'Everything that has been gained to the cause of human freedom to the East of Europe by the Treaty of Berlin has been gained wholly and entirely by the sword of Russia. It need not have been so, it ought not to have been so. But so it is.' Vol. ii. p. 200. . . . 'All these great elements of good ought to be acknowledged, although, most unfortunately, everyone of them has been due to the interests and to the power and to the policy of Russia.' P. 213. . . . 'The voice of the English Cabinet was uniformly given against every enlargement of the " bounds of freedom," and also in favour of every possible restriction, even on the autonomous institutions, which it was compelled to sanction.' P. 180.

Even in details the same contrast may be traced. Russia supported the union of the Roumanian nationality. England opposed it: but Time recorded its decision in favour of Russia. Russia supported the union of Bulgaria. England has opposed it. Time again will prove which Power was in the right. Russia proposed to add Thessaly, Epirus, and Crete to Greece. England thwarted this. I am content to let the conscience of the Western world decide which policy was most in accordance with liberty, civilisation, and progress.

Russia's policy—against which you fought in the Crimea, and which in England was supported perhaps by a dozen men, whose names we Russians will never forget—now needs no defence. It has received tardy but ample justification at the hands of the English Government. Russia's offence in the eyes of the West was her claim, based upon an undisputed treaty, to an exclusive protectorate in the Ottoman Empire. That offence is now declared to be a virtue. The Anglo-Turkish Convention is England's official confession that, in principle, Russia was right, and the West was wrong, in the dispute of 1853.

I make no claim for my country which is not based upon facts easily verified from English sources. Russia has its faults, like the others; but, judged by the Liberal standard, her foreign policy has done more for the development of Liberty in Europe and the realisation of the aspirations of Nationalities than has been done by the foreign policy of England.

It is very odd that amongst those who declare

that between Russia and England no alliance is possible, are, as a rule, the most ardent advocates of an alliance with Austria. Yet Austria was Russia's co-partner in every reactionary measure for which we are abused. It was Austria that crushed the Carbonari in Naples; it was for Austria that we subdued the Magyars, and it was in concert with Austria that we extinguished Polish independence in Cracow—a measure of which Austria reaped all the benefit. In our good actions Austria had no share. She only participated in those exceptional measures when our influence was employed against liberty.

I must not forget one unpardonable offence which is charged against us by our enemies—the annulment of the clause of the Treaty of Paris, neutralising the Black Sea. It is rather curious, but frequently forgotten, that it was Austria that first proposed that modification in a despatch, signed by Count Beust, and dated January 1, 1867.[1]

---

[1] In view of the absurd importance which Russophobes so persistently attach to the modification of the Black Sea Clause in the Treaty of Paris, Mr. Klaczko's remarks on this point are not without interest. After pointing out that Count Beust saw that the Treaty of Paris, even in 1867, had failed to secure the integrity and vitality of the Ottoman Empire, and proposed to substitute for it a general agreement to put the Christian populations of the Sultan under obligations to the whole of Europe, by endowing them, under guarantees from all the Courts, with independent institutions in accordance with their various religions and races, Mr. Klaczko continues:—'Count Beust was all the more inclined to sacrifice to this vast conception the article concerning the Black Sea contained in the Treaty of Paris, from the fact that Austria had opposed it from the first, and also that succeeding events had since exposed its complete uselessness... Finally, the Cabinet of Vienna summed up in the following characteristic words:—"*Amour propre* ought to be set aside in the presence of such immense interests as are now at stake." And in fact we cannot give this truth a too important place; the clause

Russia has reason to be proud of her disinterested policy.

From 1814, when Alexander I. was hailed throughout the world as the Liberator of Europe, down to 1879, when Alexander II. liberated the Southern Slavs, Russia has not added to her territory in Europe one single square foot. Her trophies must be sought, not in subjugated provinces and captured cities, but in the liberties of emancipated nationalities and the destruction of oppressive and effete despotisms.

Let me sum up this rapid survey of the Continental policy of Russia. I will first take our offences against Liberal ideas :—

In 1819, at the Congress of Laybach, Alexander I., with the sympathy of the English Government, supported a Conservative policy in Germany.

In 1821, at the Congress of Verona, Alexander I., with the sympathy of the English Government, supported a Conservative policy at Naples.

In 1823 Russia supported French intervention in Spain, against the opposition of the English Government.[1]

In 1846, allied to Austria, Russia annexed to

---

on the subject of the Euxine had been for a long time past but a question of *amour propre* between the Western Powers and Russia; and M. de Beust showed himself to be clear and farsighted in his despatch of Jan. 14, 1867.'—Klaczko's *Two Chancellors*, pp. 253–5.

[1] Even in this case Russian views were shared by the English Court. 'George the Fourth did not hesitate to let France know that Canning was not agreeable to him, and secretly to encourage the French invasion, against which his Ministers protested.' See *Thirty Years of Foreign Policy*, p. 87.

Austria the Republic of Cracow, against the protest of England.[1]

There was another instance about this time when Russian and English policy was in opposition: Lord Palmerston treated Greece in the Pacifico business with a high-handed violence which led the Russian Government to protest strongly against his conduct. Mr. Gladstone, however, cannot refer to this as an instance in which Russia upheld the cause of arbitrary power against the liberty and independence of nations, because he was the most eloquent defender of the principles which Count Nesselrode invoked in his protest against the policy of Lord Palmerston, and with Mr. Gladstone went the majority in the House of Lords, and a considerable number of the most eminent Liberals in the House of Commons.

In 1849 Russia assisted Austria in suppressing the Magyar rebellion, with the approval of most English Conservatives.

In 1853 Russia attacked Turkey, and was attacked by England on account of the principle of an exclusive protectorate, which, by the Anglo-Turkish Convention, England has now adopted as her own.

In 1871 Russia, with the sanction of all Europe, repealed the Black Sea clause of the Treaty of Paris —a reform which had been proposed by Austria four years before.

---

[1] Both parties in your Parliament united in condemning this step, but it was strenuously defended by the Earl of Beaconsfield, then Mr. Disraeli, while his leader, Lord George Bentinck, warmly thanked the Emperor of Russia for his action in the matter.

In 1878 Russia, with the sanction of the English Government, restored Bessarabia, which had been taken away after the Crimean War.

Now, on the other hand, let me put down the instances in which our policy commended itself to views of Liberal England :—

At the beginning of this century, Russia, allied with England, rescued the liberties and independence of Europe from the ascendancy of Napoleon.

In 1826 Russia freed Servia, England standing neutral.

In 1829 Russia, assisted only at first by England, achieved the independence of Greece.

In 1831 Russia co-operated with England in establishing the Kingdom of Belgium.

In 1833 Russia co-operated with England to prevent the destruction of the Ottoman Empire by Mehemet Ali.

In 1840 Russia again united with England to save Turkey from disruption by France and Egypt.

In 1850 Russia, in concert with England, compelled Germany to evacuate Schleswig-Holstein.

In 1851 Russia saved Belgium from Napoleon III. with the hearty approval of the English Government.

In 1859 Russia, opposed by England, supported the French liberation of Italy.[1]

[1] Lord Beaconsfield, then Mr. Disraeli, strongly condemned Lord Palmerston for pursuing 'the phantom of an unlimited Italy.' Nine years before the same authority, who resisted Bulgarian liberation on account of British interests, applied the same doctrine to Italy. In his speech on Lord Palmerston's Foreign Policy in 1850, Mr. Disraeli declared 'it was a great English interest' that the north of Italy should belong to Austria, and that Sicily should belong to Naples.'

In 1860 Russia, supported by England, approved of the French occupation of the Lebanon.

In 1866 Russia supported Prussia in the Prusso-Italian war with Austria—England being neutral—which began German unity, completed the unity of Italy, and resulted in the freedom of Hungary.

In 1867 Russia, in concert with England, secured the evacuation by the Turks of the Servian fortresses.

In 1868, Russia, opposed by England, supported the Cretan insurrection (unfortunately, not perseveringly enough).[1]

In 1870, Russia—England being neutral—supported Germany by neutralising Austria, and thus secured the completion of German unity and the overthrow of the French Empire.

In 1875, Russia, in concert with England, prevented a German attack on France.

In 1877, Russia, opposed by England, secured the liberation of Bulgaria, the tutelage of Turkey, and the complete independence of Servia, Montenegro, and Roumania.

The concert between the two Governments is significant. Can you, then, wonder at our doubting the sanity of those who systematically speak as if the

[1] In Russia we greatly regret the misunderstandings existing between the Slavs and the Greeks. Amongst Russian Slavophils there are very few indeed who are not at the same time sympathisers with their Greek co-religionists. I well remember the moral support which the Candiotes found in Russia at the time of their rising. Amongst others, my brother, Nicholas Kiréeff, whose Slavonic sympathies have been sufficiently proved, then quite a young man, was enthusiastically supporting the Candiote cause, collecting money and organising all sorts of funds for the relief and assistance of the insurgents. Everything was done which could be done, so far as the Russian people was concerned.

effacement of Russia from the political map and the elimination of Russia from the balance of power ought to be the chief ends of English diplomacy? The State that took the leading share in freeing Europe from the yoke of Napoleon, and in the emancipation of the East from the yoke of the Turk, and that has successfully exerted her influence to secure the preservation of Belgium, the liberation of Italy, the unity of Germany, and the transformation of Austria, is not one whose presence can be spared from the Council table of Europe without loss to the cause of Liberty, Nationality, and Justice.

Letter from M. Emile de Laveleye.

On the appearance of the foregoing letter in the press, M. de Laveleye addressed to me the following letter:—

Chère Madame,—Permettez-moi deux mots à l'appui de votre thèse que la Russie a souvent défendu en Europe la cause de la liberté.

Vous admettez un tort qui n'existe pas, et vous oubliez un fait libéral que les Mémoires du Prince Metternich, récemment parus, mettent en pleine lumière.

La Russie n'a pas approuvé la Révolution de 1830, c'est vrai, mais elle a eu parfaitement raison. La réunion de la Belgique et de la Hollande était ce que le traité de Vienne avait fait de mieux. C'était le rétablissement des Pays Bas du XVIe siècle, formation historique reposant sur des convenances géographiques évidentes. La Hollande apportait le commerce et les colonies, la Belgique l'industrie et l'agriculture. Les Pays Bas unis étaient un élément de stabilité européenne, car c'était un trop gros morceau pour être avalé, soit par l'Allemagne, soit par la France. Depuis 1830 la

Belgique n'a cessé de trembler pour son existence. C'est là un fait certain. La Révolution de 1830 a été faite principalement par les prêtres contre un roi protestant, et les plus prévoyants parmi les Libéraux étaient *Orangistes* et regrettaient la séparation d'avec la Hollande. La Russie dans son opposition défendait donc la cause du libéralisme et du véritable équilibre européen. . N'est-il pas évident que notre situation serait autrement forte si nous étions restés unis à la Hollande, si nous avions son commerce et ses colonies ? Aussi on s'efforce de réparer la faute de 1830 par une union douannière. Donc le tort que vous admettez au passé libéral de la Russie en 1830 n'existe pas. Tout au contraire, la France a soutenu notre révolution parcequ'elle comptait bien nous annexer, et l'Angleterre parcequ'elle était jalouse du commerce en Hollande.

Voici l'oubli. Metternich raconte avec indignation qu'en 1814 l'Empereur Alexandre, au lieu de restaurer les Bourbons, voulait qu'on convoquât une Assemblée qui aurait librement choisi la forme de gouvernement qui convenait à la France. Il prévoyait que la restauration ne pouvait durer. Metternich ne le dit pas, mais il est connu que l'Empereur Alexandre eût admis même la République. Ne se montrait-il pas prévoyant, en même temps que dévoué à la cause du progrès et de la liberté ?

Et votre Empereur actuel n'a-t-il pas bien mérité de l'humanité en abolissant le servage, et en affranchissant les populations soumises au détestable régime turc ? Ce qu'il faut à la Russie actuellement, ce n'est pas le Parlement, mais un Souverain *qui s'inspire des traditions démocratiques du Slavisme.*

Ceci serait trop long à développer. Je m'arrête en me disant votre bien dévoué,

EMILE DE LAVELEYE.

Décembre 28, 1879.

Translation.

Dear Madam,—Allow me to add two words in support of

your thesis, that Russia has often in Europe defended the cause of liberty.

You admit a fault which does not exist, and you forget a liberal deed, which Prince Metternich's Memoirs, newly published, brings into full relief.

Russia, it is true, has not approved the Revolution of 1830, and in this she was perfectly right. The union of Belgium with Holland was the best thing done by the Treaty of Vienna. It was the re-establishment of the Netherlands of the 16th century, an historical formation, based upon palpable geographical conveniences. Holland contributed her commerce and her colonies; Belgium brought industry and agriculture.

The United Netherlands formed an element of European stability, because it was too large a morsel to be swallowed either by Germany or by France.

Since 1830 Belgium has never ceased trembling for her existence. That, at least, is certain. The Revolution of 1830 was principally got up by the priests against a Protestant king, and the most farseeing amongst the Liberals were all *Orangistes*, and regretted the separation from Holland.

Russia, in her opposition, defended therefore the cause of Liberalism, and that of the true equilibrium. Is it not evident that our position would be infinitely stronger had we remained united to Holland, and shared in her commerce and her colonies? We are now making strenuous endeavours to repair the mistake of 1830 by the establishment of a Customs Union.

Thus the fault you admit in the Liberal past of Russia does not exist. Just the opposite. France supported our revolution, hoping to annex us, and England being jealous of the commerce of Holland.

Here is your omission. Metternich relates with indignation that in 1814 the Emperor Alexander, instead of restoring the Bourbons, desired that there should be convoked an Assembly, empowered freely to choose the form of government most convenient for France.

He foresaw that the Restoration could not last. Metternich does not say what is well known, that the Emperor Alexander would even have accepted a Republic.

Did he not prove his foresight as well as his devotion to the cause of progress and liberty?

And your present Emperor, has he not deserved well of Humanity, in abolishing serfdom, and in liberating the populations subjected to the detestable Turkish rule?

What is needed for Russia now is not a Parliament, but a Sovereign, inspired by the democratic traditions of Slavism.

But this subject would lead me too far; I close it in remaining,

      Yours truly, EMILE DE LAVELEYE.

December 28, 1879, Liége.

CHAPTER V.

'RUSSIAN AGGRESSION.'

OF all the reproaches brought against Russia the most persistent and the most touching is that of her 'greed for territory.' 'Russian aggression' is the fashionable *mot d'ordre* now in England. Well, if we are aggressive, is it not another instance of the similarity between the two countries? Does it not only prove how closely we try to imitate the Imperial policy of England?

Permit me to quote here an English official testimony concerning what has been called 'comparative aggression.' Mr. T. H. Farrer, Permanent Under-Secretary of your Board of Trade, wrote an article in the *Fortnightly Review* of March, 1878, which contained many useful statistics on this point. He writes :—

We are apt to impute to Russia an aggressive policy, and this accusation may be just; but what is the case with ourselves? The conquests of England have been much larger than those of Russia in area, whilst they have been beyond all comparison greater in value and population. The conquests of England within the last hundred and thirty years amount to 2,650,000 square miles, and nearly 250,000,000 people. All these are conquests, and all these conquests, except Jamaica and one of the small West Indian Islands, have been made since the middle of the last century. Countries colonised and unconquered, such as Australia, are not included.[1] Russian conquests within the last one hundred and thirty years only amount to 1,642,000 square miles, with a population of 17,133,000. Add to this that, whilst Russia has extended her borders, England has sought her conquests beyond seas, and has established a garrison in every point of vantage in every corner of the globe. Under these circumstances it is not for England to complain of aggression and conquest. Whatever the motives and whatever the results, the broad fact remains that England has acquired by conquest an empire more extensive, more populous, more wealthy, than any nation of the modern world.

You say you annex unwillingly under 'imperious necessity,' and you alone among the nations are destitute of 'earth hunger.' Possibly. Judging, however, by results, it appears that although you have no appetite, no one contrives to make a larger meal.

Necessity is as imperious with Russia as with England, nor are our destinies less inexorable. Fortunately, yours always take you to rich and fertile land, good business, profitable customers, or commanding positions; although, to find them, 'imperious necessity' takes you thousands of miles from home.

Russia has never yet annexed a foot of land that is not conterminous with her frontier. Time after time she has tried to arrest the natural and inevitable advance of her frontiers, and she has always tried in vain. Her conquests are free from the sus-

[1] Among these unmentioned annexations are Australasia, 3,086,518 square miles, and 2,500,000 inhabitants, and the Transvaal, 114,360 square miles, and 300,000 inhabitants. Cyprus of course is not annexed —only occupied.

picion of profit.[1] Our annexations (I am sorry to say) are almost all what Afghanistan will probably be to you—a permanent source of ruinous expenditure.

Russia and England, of all nations, ought to be the readiest to excuse each other's failings, because alone among nations we have to grapple with the same difficulties.[2]

To us belongs the sceptre of Asia. Whether we like it or not, that continent has been given both to Russia and to England as a common heritage. Neither can exclude the other from its share in the arduous work of civilising and educating the Oriental world.

To Russia has been given the cold inhospitable North, and the barren burning steppe; while to you

---

[1] 'The Russians can hardly have been drawn into Turkestan by the expectation of making money there. . . . Russia's acquisitions in Turkestan have entailed upon it fresh and heavy burdens. The possession of Turkestan seems to me to be a burden laid on Russia rather than a boon granted to her. Were it otherwise, I should not grudge it her, for it seems to be the opinion of all rational observers that Providence has committed in that country a civilising mission to her care. . . . If Russia be formidable with Turkestan, she would be still more formidable without it. For her it is cost, it is care, it is liability to attack, it is responsibility.'—Mr. Gladstone: 'Russian Policy and Deeds in Turkestan,' *Contemporary Review*, Nov. 1876, pp. 879, 881, 882.

[2] 'A fussy and fretful jealousy of the territorial acquisitions of others, entertained in a country which exceeds all others in its multiplied annexations all over the globe, is not a little detrimental, as I think, to our dignity, and is peculiarly odious, and even not a little despicable, in the eyes of the nations.'—Mr. Gladstone: 'Russian Policy and Deeds in Turkestan,' *Contemporary Review*, Nov. 1876, p. 880. 'During the last hundred years England has, for every square league of territory annexed to Russia, by force, violence, or fraud, appropriated to herself three; nor are the means whereby Great Britain has augmented her possessions a whit less reprehensible than those which have been resorted to by the Northern Power for a similar purpose.'—Cobden's *Political Writings*, 'Russian and British Aggression,' p. 86.

belong the teeming myriads of the South, with all the fabled wealth of Hindostan.

You have antique civilisations in ruins at your feet; we have but to deal with the nomad of the desert, and the savage and the fanatical Tartars of Turkestan.

Is it reasonable to expect from our officers that strict execution of every engagement, under the stress and strain of the struggle to maintain their footing, whilst 'carrying the torch of civilisation amongst barrels of gunpowder,' which you never succeeded in exacting from your representatives amongst the mild Hindoos?

When the history of British India is described, even by Englishmen, as one long series of violated pledges and disobeyed instructions, why do you talk as if Russians were sinners beyond all other sinners, because in our advance across Central Asia you can detect discrepancies between intention and performance?

Granted, 'Russia is advancing towards India!' but no faster than you are advancing towards Russian Turkestan.[1] Within the last forty years each of us has taken a stride towards the Hindoo Koosh, and it is not Russia who is invading Afghanistan. Why do you quarrel with a law of nature? It was Sir Robert Peel who said, 'When civilisation and bar-

---

[1] 'We talk coolly of the gigantic strides—that is the stock phrase—made by Russia in her career of Asiatic conquest. But her gains have been as nothing to the gains of the British Empire during the same period in conquests and annexations.'—Duke of Argyll, *Eastern Question*, vol. ii. p. 223.

barism come into contact, the latter must inevitably give way,' and if that were true in 1844 of Scinde, is it not equally true of the Khanates of Turkestan?

Your advance, although as rapid as ours, excites no fear in Russia. Why do you feel so nervous? As for 'Russian Intrigue,' well, let me quote Sir Henry Rawlinson as to the comparative danger, on that score, of each Power in Asia. 'It must always be remembered,' he says—although I fear his imperative 'must' is frequently disregarded even by himself —' it must always be remembered that Russia is far more vulnerable than England in this respect, and that we could instigate a great anti-Russian Mohammedan movement, north of the Oxus, with much greater facility than Russia could stir up the Sikhs and Hindoos beyond the Indus.'[1]

Sir Henry Rawlinson is 'an old Russophobist,' but he thinks the extension of Russian power in the East is inevitable. 'In reality,' he said, writing in 1874, 'when Russia had once crossed the Steppe, there could be no substantial or permanent check to her expansion until she was arrested by the barrier of British Indian influence,' and, again, 'Russia cannot stop midway in the career in which she has now entered.'

Take, as a typical instance of the hollowness of the complaints of the so-called 'Russian perfidy,' the case of Khiva. That we had no alternative but to send an expedition against that robber Khanate,

---

[1] *England and Russia in the East*, p. 305.

is admitted even by our most uncompromising opponents.[1]

Having sent that expedition to Khiva and reduced it to obedience, would we have been justified in leaving the Khan as free as before to resume the malpractices which necessitated our costly intervention? Really, the abuse and misrepresentation to which we have been subjected about the matter are not the best specimens of 'English fair play.' We promised not to annex Khiva, and we have not annexed Khiva. There is not a Russian in Khiva at this hour. We have been repeatedly pressed to take Khiva; but we have hitherto resisted the pressure, chiefly in order to keep—what many amongst us thought—our most unreasonable promise to England. Promises! pledges! Can one ever sufficiently foresee the future to justify giving assurances which may involve either the sacrifice of one's word or one's country's interest? I can-

[1] Of many I will only quote one. Writing of our first expedition against Khiva under Perofski, Sir Henry Rawlinson says: 'The expedition had long been contemplated. As a measure of mere frontier police, and irrespective of all considerations of external policy, it was urgently needed. With the exception, indeed, of the claim of the prescriptive *suzeraineté* over Khiva, there was not a single weak point in the Russian bill of indictment against Khiva. The Uzbegs of Khiva either directly, or through the Turkomans and Khirghiz who obeyed them, had for years committed every conceivable atrocity against the Russian Government. To manstealing and raids upon the friendly Khirghiz were added the constantly recurring plunder of caravans; attacks upon the Russian outposts, burdens upon trade which weighed it to the ground; outrages upon Russian subjects who ventured into the country; indignities to the Government, and finally a systematic course of agitation in the Steppe, undertaken with a view of inciting the Khirghiz to rebellion. The provocation, indeed, offered by Khiva was not less complete as a *casus belli* than the invasion of India by the Sikhs, which terminated in our own annexation of the Punjaub.'—*England and Russia in the East*, p. 149.

not understand how anyone can help burning with indignant wrath, when any foreign Minister has the audacity to demand such engagements!

Russia, unquestionably, has 'rectified her frontier,' at the expense of the Khan, but she left him to reign in Khiva over the Khanate. I cannot see how Russia can be said to have annexed Khiva because of that rectification, any more than Germany can be said to have annexed France, or France to have annexed Italy, because Prince Bismarck took Alsace and Lorraine, and the Emperor Napoleon, Nice and Savoy.

Yes. Russia established her influence over Khiva; and, I suppose, in spite of all you say about its independence, you are trying to do the same in Afghanistan.

It is not wise on your part perpetually to accuse us of breaking our word, when we are all the time inconveniencing ourselves in order to keep it. I was glad to read Mr. Forster's words on this point when he warned our enemies, that 'by constantly asserting that Russia has seized upon Khiva, they may at last be taken at their word, and Russia may do what she is constantly told she is doing, and which she has not done yet.

That admirable paper, the *Statesman*, which speaks out the truth with such refreshing frankness, deals with this subject more trenchantly than any Russian would care to do. Permit me to quote this testimony of an experienced Anglo-Indian journalist.

After referring to what he describes as a monstrous falsehood, so persistently circulated by English papers, that the Emperor has annexed Khiva, he says :—

The course of events, honestly interpreted, showed the absolute good faith of the Russian monarch. He kept his word to the letter. The public are told, in every conceivable form of falsehood, that Russia has annexed Khiva. It would be as true to say that England has annexed the moon. The Expedition to Khiva was attended by severe treatment of the Turkoman hordes in its neighbourhood. Fearing their resentment upon the withdrawal of the Russian forces, the Khan of Khiva made an urgent request for the retention of a part of the Russian army in Khiva itself. The request was refused, but the danger being real, it was finally settled that a small Cossack force of some eight hundred men should be posted on the Khivan frontier, where the Amu Daria discharges itself into the Sea of Aral; and a strip of land was assigned as the territorial limits of the force. The step was a military necessity, as Mr. Schuyler shows, and as subsequent events have proved. Attack after attack upon Khiva has been made by the Turkoman hordes since the Russian army withdrew, and the presence of this small Cossack force is simply the nucleus of defence against their invasions. The State of Khiva is to-day as independent as it ever was, the only change being that its slave market is closed—let us hope for ever. Instead of 'annexing' Khiva, as *we* annex territories, substituting therein our own alien executive for that of the subdued people, there is not a Russian, so far as we have been able to ascertain, in the whole Khivan State. Russia *is* feared beyond doubt in Central Asia; but she is respected at the same time, for her name is a synonym for the suppression of kidnapping, plundering, and slavery; and we, as Englishmen, rejoice with our whole heart at her progress in those regions, and view with bitter shame and humiliation the efforts of our countrymen to decry what she is doing. We wish, with our whole heart, that she were at Merv, for it is the last slave market in Central Asia.[1]

Unfortunately, such honest voices are too rare in the English press; although, I gratefully admit, that they find a responsive echo in the hearts of many of the best Englishmen.

Let me say, also, how delighted I was with the letter in the *Times*[2] from that staunch friend of all

---

[1] *Statesman*, December 13 and 27, 1879.

[2] Sir Charles Trevelyan, wrote as follows in the *Times*, Nov. 18, 1878:—'Khiva was the centre of the Turkoman slave-hunting system which had desolated the neighbouring provinces of Persia. This place was the mart for the sale of the unhappy people who had been torn from their homes, and the Khan derived great part of his revenue from the dues upon the traffic. During the short period of our influence in Central Asia, before our military occupation of Afghanistan collapsed, a British officer was deputed to Khiva to obtain the release of the Russian slaves, of whom a large number were safely delivered at Orenburg; but a whole population of Persian captives remained, who were finally emancipated and sent back to their homes by General Kaufmann.

'The assurance given by Count Schouvaloff to our Government is described as follows, in Lord Granville's letter to Lord A. Loftus of January 8, 1873:—" The object of the expedition was to punish acts of brigandage, to recover fifty Russian prisoners, and to teach the Khan that such conduct on his part could not be continued with the impunity in which the moderation of Russia had led him to believe. Not only was it far from the intention of the Emperor to take possession of Khiva, but positive orders had been prepared to prevent it, and directions given that the conditions imposed should be such as could not in any way lead to a prolonged occupation of Khiva." The hazards of the expedition were under-estimated. Of the three columns which were to converge from Tashkend, Orenburg, and the Caspian, the last never reached its destination, and the other two with difficulty escaped the danger of the desert which had always formed the defence of Khiva.

'In all these circumstances, how were the Russians to act in order to accomplish the object of the expedition and at the same time to keep faith with us? Could they reasonably be expected, after recovering their prisoners, to retire again behind the desert, leaving the Khivans and their allies the Turkomans to resume their inhuman practices with more than their previous security after this experience of the weak and strong points of their position? Should we have praised them for doing so?

good causes, Sir Charles Trevelyan. There are at least some few who do us justice in this matter. How much better our relations would be if you were guided by their counsels, and ceased ' to obstruct Russia in her costly and difficult task by habitual misconstruction and depreciation!'

The words of the Duke of Argyll are as emphatic, and even more categorical, than those of Sir Charles Trevelyan. The Duke says :—' It is generally asserted, and widely believed, that in the conquest of Khiva Russia has been guilty towards us of flagrant breaches of engagement. The papers presented to Parliament disprove this assertion altogether. They do more than this, they convict those who make these accusations of that kind of reckless misquotation, which, although often the effect of mere passion, approaches very nearly to the bad faith which they charge on Russia.'[1]

'Let Russia and England,' wrote Lord Mayo, 'declare to the world that they have a common mission in Asia, namely, the establishment of good government and the civilisation of the mighty nations

Should we ourselves have done so in like circumstances? What was actually done was that a military station was established on the north bank of the Oxus, and Khiva was placed by treaty in subordinate political relation to Russia. The town of Khiva and the rich irrigated country to the south of the Oxus were left to the Khan, while the country on the northern bank was in part transferred to Bokhara and in part retained by Russia. This has always been our own method of dealing with Pindarries, Mahratta, and other predatory tribes, there being no other way of controlling them and reducing them to order. Upon this statement of fact, I ask whether the Russian Government can justly be accused of having broken faith with us?' (See also *Causes of the Afghan War*, p. 239.)

[1] *Eastern Question*, vol. ii. p. 301.

committed to their care,' and even although the policy of Lord Beaconsfield should lead to the extinction of the 'line of independent States between their respective frontiers,' which Lord Mayo desired to maintain as a 'pledge of good faith;' if we meet at Merv, or on the slopes of the Hindoo Koosh, we shall meet, not as foes, but as friends!

CHAPTER VI.

RUSSIA AND THE AFGHAN WAR.

WHEN, in 1878, I wrote upon the Afghan war, which was then commencing, I had to contend against a widespread prejudice that Russia had behaved very badly to England in Afghanistan. To-day, except in ill-informed quarters, that prejudice has greatly subsided. The leaders of both parties in the State have repeatedly and publicly declared that the conduct of the Russian Government in sending an envoy to Cabul, at Midsummer, 1878, was perfectly justifiable, from every point of view, under the then existing circumstances. Lord Beaconsfield himself took the opportunity, last year, to state in the House of Lords that the Stoletoff Mission was 'quite permissible.' Here are the exact words of your Premier:—

Now, my Lords, I may speak on that matter with frankness. It is, indeed, much easier to speak on that matter than it would have been a year ago, or eight months ago. Eight months ago war was more than probable between this country and Russia. An imprudent word might have precipitated that war. At present we know, by the gracious speech from the Throne, that Her Majesty's relations with all Powers are friendly, and they are not less friendly with

Russia than with any other Power. I will say of the expedition which Russia was preparing at the time when she thought war was inevitable between our country and herself—I will say at once that *I hold that those preparations were perfectly allowable.* They would be no cause of quarrel to England if war did not take place, and if war did take place of course they would have contributed to bringing about the ultimate result, whatever that may have been. Had we been in the position of Russia, I doubt not we might have undertaken some enterprises of a similar character. . . . If war had taken place between the two countries, all the preparations which either had made would have been perfectly justifiable. When it was found war was not to take place, and Her Majesty's Government made representations to the Court of St. Petersburg, it was impossible to act with more promptitude than Russia did. Russia said at once, 'It is quite true that we did intend to attack you and injure you there as much as we could, but war has not taken place, and war, I trust, will not take place between Russia and England. We have already given orders for our troops to retire to their stations beyond the Oxus; our Ambassador shall be considered really as a temporary Ambassador on a mission of courtesy, and as soon as possible disappear.' I think that that was sufficient and satisfactory conduct on the part of Russia as regards this matter.[1]

Lord Salisbury and Sir Stafford Northcote also spoke emphatically on this point. On the other side, the testimonies have been not less numerous and emphatic. The Duke of Argyll, after referring to the preparations of the Indian Government to attack the Russian dominions in Central Asia, through Afghanistan, says:—

The British Government was, of course, quite right to

[1] Speech by Lord Beaconsfield in the House of Lords on the Afghan War, Dec. 10, 1878.

take every measure in its power to defeat Russia if it contemplated the probability of a war with that Power. But if the Government of England had a perfect right to make such preparations and to devise such plans, it will hardly be denied that Russia had an equal right to take precautions against them. It is true she had an engagement with us not to interfere in Afghanistan. But it will hardly be contended that she was to continue to be bound by this engagement when the Viceroy of India was known, or believed, to be organising an attack upon her, of which Afghanistan was to be the base. We may take it as certain that the whole of the Russian proceedings, including the Mission, were taken in connection with a policy of self-defence, and that the Mission to Cabul was a direct and immediate consequence, not of any preconceived design on the part of Russia to invade India, or gratuitously to break her engagements with us in respect to Afghanistan, but of the threatening policy of the British Cabinet in Europe, and of its intention, in pursuance of that policy, to make India the base of hostile operations against Russia.[1]

Am I, therefore, presuming too much when I say that the chiefs, both of the Ministry and Opposition, have fully justified the Stoletoff Mission?

It is sufficient for me to say that we did not depart from our engagement to exercise no influence in Afghanistan hostile to British sovereignty in India until the English Government broke its treaty engagement by sending your fleet through the Dardanelles, and that the position taken up by England in Asia Minor is far less defensible, from an international point of view, than the greatest offence which Russia has committed, even in the imminent prospect of war in Afghanistan.

[1] *Eastern Question*, vol. ii. pp. 495, 497.

The Cabul Mission was, as the Duke of Argyll phrases it, 'simply a countermove in the game of war,' and in that game England, not Russia, took the lead. While we were fighting to free Bulgaria, Lord Lytton was making strenuous attempts to induce the Ameer to enter into an offensive alliance with England against Russia, in which case Afghanistan would have been made the base of 30,000 English troops operating against us in Turkestan.[1] As the Duke of Argyll points out, this is in itself sufficient to justify all that was done by Russia to ward off the threatened blow, which, however, frankly speaking, we never dreaded very much, and now hardly dread at all.

The Afghan War has, at least, done one thing, which is very valuable. It has demonstrated the impossibility either of a Russian invasion of India, or of a British invasion of Turkestan. We have always told you that we could not get at your precious India, and we may be pardoned if we tell you that you would find it just as difficult to invade Russian Turkestan. Russia said this. England has proved it. The breakdown of your transport, which is the staple topic of all telegrams from Cabul and Candahar, is a continual reminder of the absurdity of Russophobia. Russia could as soon invade England by sea, as India through the rugged defiles of Afghan hills.

The two words, Transport and Commissariat, are fatal to any scheme of invasion. In the wilderness of hills which intervenes between us, there exists no

[1] *Pioneer*, September 4, 1878.

food to supply the wants of a modern army, even if either in Turkestan or India there could be collected animals sufficient to carry the *impedimenta* of the invaders.[1]

The whole of your camels, mules, horses, and oxen in India are as inadequate to convey a large army to Merv as our navy is to convey a Russian expedition to Calcutta.

' Russia cannot invade India, unless you advance the Indian frontier to the Oxus. Then, no doubt, we shall really be formidable to you. At present we can only do you harm by tempting your nervous, or 'Mervous,' authorities, to embark upon ruinous expenditure, in order to lock the doors upon a nightmare.[2] The first Afghan war cost you twenty millions. How much the second will cost you, your Government, probably, will not hurry too much to state. Yet you are further off your object to-day than ever you were before. When our Mission

---

[1] See Colonel Osborne's paper on 'India and Afghanistan,' *Contemporary Review*, October, 1879:—'The want of food, far more than the physical difficulties of the country, is, and always will be, the insuperable obstacle to carrying on extensive military operations in Afghanistan.' P. 204.

[2] This phrase is not mine but Lord Salisbury's. Speaking at the Merchant Taylors' banquet, in London, on June 11, 1877, on this very subject, the present Secretary for Foreign Affairs said :—' It has generally been acknowledged to be an imprudent act to go to war for an idea, but if there is anything more unsatisfactory than that it is going to war against a nightmare.' It was in this speech that Lord Salisbury so effectively ridiculed the policy—subsequently adopted as his own—of allowing your 'enemy to choose his own ground, to follow him across deserts and impassable mountain chains into a field which he has chosen for himself, instead of waiting till he comes within your own range, where only your peculiar arms and peculiar strength will enable you to deal with him with invincible effect.'

visited Cabul in 1878, the Afghans declared that the year 1842, when the English had ruined nearly the whole of their country, remained fresh in the memory of all the inhabitants. These memories have not been effaced by your triumphs in 1879, and the more you are disliked, the warmer will be the welcome which the Afghans will extend to your enemies, be they who they may.

So far from creating a barrier to Russia's advance to your frontier, your recent operations have removed the only political difficulty from our path, which would now be easy enough, if the real obstacles had not always been natural, not political.[1]

Your Ministers protest they want nothing so much as a friendly Afghanistan, but to simple-minded Russians your method of courtship is somewhat puzzling, and reminds me a little of the following anecdote :—

[1] Addressing the House of Commons on April 22, 1873, Sir Charles Wingfield, M.P., in the course of a very judicious speech, foretold the exact consequences which have followed your intervention :—' Whatever European Power first entered Afghanistan would make the Afghans their enemies. Our re-appearance in that country would revive the memories of our former occupation in the minds of the people. Whatever dependence might be placed on the ruler of the country, no reliance could be placed on the subjects. A national party would be formed which would rouse the fanatical feeling of the people against the English alliance, and would prove as great a source of weakness to the present ruler as it had done to a former one.' The same lesson is stated even more bluntly by an Englishman, who writes after witnessing the evil results of your expedition to Cabul. 'England's true policy,' he says, 'is to leave the Afghans alone, strengthen our own frontier, and if Russia should ever become our enemy, to pray for no better luck than that she may try to march a large army through the wilderness of hills swarming with hostile freebooters, which is the best bulwark of our Indian Empire. The Afghans are the allies of the second comers, and the friends of the enemies of their invaders.'

As Frederick the Great's father — Frederick William I.—was once walking in a wood, he perceived a man who was evidently hiding himself. After watching him for some time, at last the King took hold of him. 'What is the matter?' said he; 'why do you hide yourself from me?' 'I am afraid of your Majesty!' confessed the poor prisoner, with a trembling voice. 'Afraid!' exclaimed His Majesty, 'you ought to love me, and not be afraid; yes, to love me, I tell you! *Lieben muss man mich, nicht fürchten!*' and upon this the King belaboured the peasant with repeated blows from his cudgel, honestly thinking that a stick was the best channel for creating affectionate feelings.

This involuntarily comes to my memory when I read of the system which you are employing with the Afghans in order to gain their friendship. Even barbarous and aggressive Russia seems to have less difficulty in winning the affections of the Asiatic races than civilised and pacific England. On this point let me, as usual, revert to English testimony. In an article by Professor Monier Williams on 'Afghanistan and the Punjaub,' in the 'Contemporary Review' (January, 1879), I find some really remarkable admissions, mingled, however, with some very uncomplimentary observations as to the character of the Russian advance in Central Asia. We are so familiar with accusations, I will only quote the admissions. Your learned professor writes:—

Russia is far better informed than we are on all political subjects, European and Oriental. Its system assimilates itself far more readily than ours to the present condition of the Asiatic mind. It brings with it the manifest advantages of organised government and security of property. Hence *Russia's advance is often welcomed in Asia as a boon, where ours is deprecated as a grievance, or barely tolerated as a necessary infliction.*

The troubles you are suffering were all foreseen, as well as others which may easily come. Russia will not interfere with your operations. If we are to be enemies, the deeper you get entangled in Afghan affairs the better. The nearer you approach our frontiers, the more vulnerable you become. Annex Cabul and Candahar, if you please; but Russia told you long since what would be the consequences of such a step. One of our officials reported to our Government, forty years ago, 'Russia feels no anxiety at the interference of England in Afghanistan. The reports of Vitkevitch have satisfied her that, owing to the disorganised condition, the turbulent character, and the conflicting interests of the Afghan tribes, Cabul and Candahar can never form a bulwark for India. They are more likely to shatter the fabric to which they are violently attached, and cause it to crumble permanently to ruin.'

You avoided following our advice, but had you done so—had your gallant Major Cavagnari profited by Colonel Stoletoff's experience, he might have been alive to-day. When our Embassy was at Cabul, although the Afghans have no reason to be hostile to us, as they are to you, all its members were kept almost like prisoners, within four walls, and were refused permission even to see the town. They were told there was nothing to see, and that if they went out they would excite the fanaticism of the populace. Cabul for Christians is either a prison or a grave. Colonel Stoletoff avoided the latter, only by accepting the former. Major Cavagnari preserved his liberty, but lost his life.[1]

Last year Russia was put on the defensive, even by friendly Englishmen, for her conduct in Afghanistan. Now that the facts are more clearly seen, the guilt is seen not to be at our door, but at that of your own Government.

The Duke of Argyll's views upon that matter have been expressed with the fearless frankness characteristic of that illustrious statesman. After describing how your Government made the war, the Duke says :—

[1] The following extract from a letter written by a member of the Stoletoff Mission, dated Cabul, October, 1878, may not be without interest for English readers. After mentioning that Colonel Stoletoff had personal access to the Ameer, he says :—' The other members of the Mission began to feel weary of the monotonous life they spent within four walls. Every one was extremely anxious to visit the town, to see its bazaar, or, at any rate, to take a drive or ride round Cabul, which lay temptingly at the foot of the palace occupied by our Mission. Vain desire! At the palace gates stands the Guard of Honour, which allows no one to pass without the permission of the Vizier. Watchmen are stationed at every wall. All this appeared too reverential to the members of the Embassy. They several times expressed to General Stoletoff their desire to visit the city or its environs, but always met with a decided refusal, which was explained on the ground that there was nothing worth seeing in the town. Another reason adduced was the fear of exciting the fanaticism of the populace.' The same writer mentions that the only escort accompanying the Russian mission on its way to Cabul was composed of twenty Cossacks and a few Uzbecks, and that there never was any question of an offensive and defensive alliance with Afghanistan, which 'is simply an invention of the English press, ever ready to magnify a fly into an elephant.'

I confess I cannot write these sentences without emotion. They seem to me to be the record of sayings and of doings which cast an indelible disgrace upon our country. The page of history is full of the Proclamations and Manifestoes of powerful Kings and Governments who have desired to cover, under plausible pretexts, acts of violence and injustice against weaker States. It may well be doubted whether in the whole of this melancholy list any one specimen could be found more unfair in its accusations, more reckless in its assertions, than this Ultimatum Letter addressed to the Ameer of Cabul by the Cabinet of the Queen.[1]

That the despatch of our Mission to Cabul was 'perfectly allowable,' under the circumstances, is now admitted by all; but some people still seem to be troubled by General Kaufmann's correspondence with the Ameer.

I will not deny that the terms of the Anglo-Russian understanding might be interpreted so as to forbid even an exchange of the compliments of the season with the Ameer. It is sufficient to point out that it is quite as capable of another interpretation, and that General Kaufmann, in sending messages of courtesy to Cabul was acting in good faith. Knowing him, as I do, I confess it even shocks me to discuss his good faith: it is so obvious; for his interpretation of the understanding was admitted by the Indian Government itself.

To write a letter of courtesy is not to exercise influence; nor is every Bokhariot postman a 'Russian agent.' Your Government advised the Ameer to cultivate friendly relations with General Kaufmann,

---

[1] *Eastern Question,* vol. ii. p. 514.

and how could he do so, if he were forbidden, even to receive a letter? But is it not curious that among the official papers upon which this latest charge against Russia is based, the Indian Government refers complacently to one of General Kaufmann's many letters to the Ameer as one of the incontrovertible proofs that Russia was loyally fulfilling her engagement with England? Surely, if General Kaufmann's letters to Cabul were so flagrant a breach of our promise, as even the *Daily News* said last year, your Indian Government would not refer to one of these letters as a clear proof that Russia was keeping her word. The correspondence was no secret. Your Viceroy, I believe, used to dictate the Ameer's replies.

General Kaufmann sent an English duplicate of his first letter to Shere Ali. 'Probably,' says the author of 'The Causes of the Afghan War,' 'with a view to its being made known to the Government of India, and there is nothing all through the correspondence to indicate any desire on the part of Kaufmann to keep it secret from the British authorities.'[1]

Lord Mayo, so far from officially resenting the correspondence, officially informed Shere Ali that General Kaufmann's letter should be a source of satisfaction and an additional ground of confidence to the Ameer, and that the assurances they contained had given him (Lord Mayo) unfeigned satisfaction, for he saw in them a further and additional security

---

[1] Page 254.

for the permanency of the Ameer's kingdom and the establishment of his power.[1]

Besides, to prove, still more, General Kaufmann's good faith, let me quote the remark, that 'Both General Kaufmann and Shere Ali had every reason to believe that a correspondence, sanctioned and encouraged by men like Lord Mayo, Lord Napier of Magdala, and Sir J. Fitzjames Stephen, could not be otherwise than agreeable to the British Government.'[2]

Lord Northbrook was of the same opinion. He officially informed Shere Ali that, so far from regarding these letters with apprehension, the Viceroy and Governor-General in Council saw in them an additional reason for believing that the Russian authorities desired to maintain no relations but those of amity with the Government of Afghanistan.[3]

Not until your Government began to pick a quarrel with the Ameer, and to prepare for war with Russia, was there any complaint of these letters. The change was on your side; not on ours. Nor could General Kaufmann be expected to understand that what was a useful and commendable expression of friendship before the rejection of the Berlin Memorandum became unscrupulous intrigue after that date.

After Lord Lytton broke off all communication with the Ameer, in May, 1877, and began to prepare for hostilities with Russia, I do not know what was done; but if after that date the relations between

[1] *Blue Book, Central Asia*, No. 1 (1878), p. 184.
[2] *Causes of the Afghan War*, p. 263.
[3] *Central Asia*, No. 1 (1878), p. 198.

General Kaufmann and the late Ameer became more intimate, it was your doing. To prepare to resist a meditated attack is 'perfectly allowable,' under such circumstances; and Russia's good faith cannot be affected by anything which took place between the Peshawur Conference of May, 1877, and the retirement of the Stoletoff Mission, at the close of 1878, a period during which Russia was daily expecting to be attacked by England.[1]

There is only one other objection which is taken to our conduct, and that is, that although we have acted within our right towards England, we acted cruelly and treacherously to Shere Ali. Having compelled him to receive our Mission, we are told, we should have supported him in his war with you.

I hardly think such a quixotic interpretation of duty would commend itself to the judgment of English statesmen. Under great pressure, Shere Ali received our Mission when war was believed to be imminent; but he did not commit himself to us in any way, and as soon as the crisis passed away, our Mission was withdrawn. I hardly think we were bound in honour to go to war with England, because your Ministers eagerly availed themselves of the pretext afforded by the appearance of our Mission to declare the war they had been preparing since 1876. We had not committed the Ameer in any way. We did not advise him to refuse to receive the British Mission. We had received nothing at his hands.

[1] This point is clearly and succinctly stated by that courageous and uncompromising assailant of popular misconceptions concerning Russia, the Rev. Malcolm MacColl, in the *Spectator*, Jan. 3, 1880.

Our advance to his capital was forced upon us by your threats of war. Why, then, should we have made your attack upon the Ameer a *casus belli*?

'Afghanistan was beyond the sphere of our interests.' Our intervention on the Ameer's behalf, diplomatically or otherwise, would have inflamed your animosity against us both, without soothing anything. Pardon me, but if your Ministers had been but reasonable, and had given the Ameer a little breathing time, he would have been able to clear himself of all suspicion of complicity with our advance; but the opportunity was denied him, and Lord Lytton, delighted with so plausible a pretext, hurried into war. This incident, I admit, is a painful one. But, perhaps, after all, it will not be without its uses, if it enables you to understand that a real *entente cordiale* between England and Russia might do more good than the present policy of systematic antagonism, and would better serve the interests of peace and the prosperity of both.

CHAPTER VII.

RUSSIANS IN CENTRAL ASIA.

'THE Russians have as much right to conquer Central Asia as the English to seize India,' observed a polite Englishman, the other day, evidently thinking that he had gone to the extreme of condescending kindness !

'May I be quite frank?' said I. 'Well, it seems to me that we have a great deal better right in Central Asia than you have in India!' So startling a remark led to a long explanation. Perhaps Russian views on that point might be of some little interest in England. I scarcely hope to convince many of my readers, but I think it really is a duty to speak out one's mind sometimes, even when you feel yourself nothing but a poor exponent of the cause of truth. I know my own shortcomings, but personal considerations must be put aside under certain circumstances.

Well, now, as to the question of Central Asia. Turkestan is at our door. Neither precipitous mountain range nor stormy sea divided the Russian plain from the Tartar steppe. Our merchants have always traded with the Khanates; caravans have wended their way wearily over the monotonous expanse of the Central Asian desert for centuries. Every disturbance in Turkestan affected business in Russia. It became a necessity, for the protection of the legitimate channels of commerce, to establish some authority in these regions more respectable than the nomadic tribes who levied black mail with a threat of death. Step by step, in the course of successive generations, the Russian civiliser encroached upon the Tartar savage. Evils tolerable at a distance are intolerable next door. Anarchy, objectionable everywhere, is unbearable when it infringes upon the frontiers of order. The extension of our sovereignty over the tribes of Tartary was the unavoidable consequence of our geographical position.[1] Now: Was it so with you in India? You had to pass the Cape of Good Hope, and sail half round the world, before you reached the land which you have subdued. The internal tranquillity of India had no bearing upon English interests. So you had, at first, no more right to conquer Hindostan than Russia has to annex Brazil.

Russia in Central Asia is without a rival, as she is without an ally. If she did not establish order, toleration, and peace among those rude tribes on her frontiers, the work would have remained undone to this day. In India, on the contrary, you have to

---

[1] Mr. Gladstone in his third Midlothian speech says:—'The position of Russia in Central Asia I believe to be one that has in the main been forced upon her against her will. She has been compelled—and this is the impartial opinion of the world—she has been compelled to extend her frontier southward in Central Asia by causes in some degree analogous to, but certainly more stringent and imperative than, the causes which have commonly led us to extend, in a far more important manner, our frontier in India.'

justify your conquest, not only against the reproaches of the conquered nations, but against the protests of the Dutch, the Portuguese, and the French, whom you ejected from the dominions which you had marked for your own. Russia in Central Asia does the police work of an enormous expanse of thinly-populated, poverty-stricken land. She taxes the peasants of Saratoff and Kieff to maintain order in Khokand and Tashkent. The Administration spends two roubles in collecting one. The English people, I think, pay nothing for the government of India. The Hindoos had to pay the expense of their conquest, and they defray at this moment the whole charges of the foreign administration which is maintained in India by English bayonets.

India is rich. Central Asia is poor. The whole of the revenue raised in Turkestan is not half a million in the year. In India you raise more than fifty millions.

There was little to plunder in Tashkent—much less than the English nabobs found in one of the great cities of Northern India.

There was more need for Russians in Central Asia than there was for Englishmen in Bengal. The Tartar of the Steppe needs a policeman much more than the timid Bengalee. India had a civilisation of her own, the splendour of which is attested to this day by those architectural remains to which Mr. Fergusson has devoted such patient genius and so many years of unremitting toil. The Khanates were hotbeds of savagery and fanaticism. The condition of these Tartar States was unspeakably bad. Arminius Vambéry is one of the greatest Russian-haters in the world, but he admits that our soldiers have made it possible for Europeans to live in Bokhara. Formerly, Vambéry himself could only visit the city disguised as a Mohammedan. Mr. Schuyler says:—'The rule of Russia is on the whole beneficial to the natives, and it would be manifestly unjust to them to withdraw her protection, and leave them to anarchy and to the unbridled rule of fanatical despots.'

We do not grudge England her Indian Empire, but when we are reproached with territorial greed for having annexed some deserts close to our frontiers, we have a right to ask England to look to herself. India is yours, and improved by your rule. May it remain yours for ever! But the happy possessors of that magnificent Empire should not reproach us for our poor Tartar steppes. To understand the difficulties of our position in Central Asia, look not to India, but to your West African Settlements. You hold territories there which do not pay their expenses; they involve occasional wars which you wisely undertake without humbly asking the benediction of Russia or any other Power. Nevertheless, you do not give them up; you even extend them from time to time without asking for our leave. Your keeping these provinces is perhaps more generous than giving them up; but there are Russians cruel enough to read with a little smile of your troubles with the King of Ashantee when they remember with what admirable fortitude you bore our difficulties with the Khan of Khiva.

In Central Asia Russians suppress the slave-trade as you do on the African coast, although at the first your views upon the subject were less philanthropic —if I remember well. Wherever the Russian flag flies freedom to the slave is guaranteed. If England had but joined us in our crusade against the Turk, the last stronghold of the slave-trade in Europe would have already ceased to exist. English people have no right to ignore this phase of the question when they can refer to such an unimpeachable 'Statement of Facts on Turkey and the Slave Trade' as that written by Mr. F. W. Chesson, whose name is familiar to everyone as the energetic and fearless defender of the oppressed. One of the numerous complaints against us Russians is that we do not open the markets of Central Asia to the manufactures of all the world. Were you free-traders when you first conquered India? The East India Company, I believe, held as strict a monopoly as ever existed in the world.

Promises to desist from further conquests, as English experience goes,[1] cannot always be kept. The

---

[1] Since the Afghan war there is no need to refer to so distant a date as 1783. Speaking of the negotiations which preceded the commencement of hostilities, the Duke of Argyll says:—'In a very humiliating way, the whole of these transactions carry us back to the days of Clive. We are reminded only too much of the unscrupulousness of his conduct. . . . I speak of what was bad or doubtful in his conduct, not of what was great. In this aspect of them the proceedings I have recorded have been worse than his. . . . The Government of India has paltered with the force of existing Treaties; it has repudiated solemn pledges; it has repeated over and over again insincere professions; and it has prepared new Treaties full of "tricky saving clauses."'—*Eastern Question*, vol. ii. pp. 516 to 518.

illustrious Burke, in the House of Commons in 1783, said that 'from Mount Imaus to Cape Comorin there is not a single Prince or State with which the English Government had come into contact which they had not sold. There was not a single treaty which they ever made with a native State or Prince which they had not broken.'

But we admit, in spite of Burke's severe blame, that, though probably only yielding to the necessity of her position, England, at all events, has given to India the blessings of a civilised and stable Government. Is Russia not entitled to the same amount of credit?

Even Lord Beaconsfield views with no mistrust the advance of Russia in Asia—that is, if you can believe what he said not so very long ago from his place in Parliament—where, I suppose, he speaks with more precision than after dinner at the Guildhall. The Premier used the following words—which I quote the more gladly because it is so seldom that I can appeal to his testimony:—'I think that Asia is large enough for the destinies of Russia and England. Far from looking forward with alarm to the development of Russia in Central Asia, I see no reason why they should not conquer Tartary any more than why England should not have conquered India.'[1]

Why should English Turkophiles out-Herod Herod?

[1] May 1876.

CHAPTER VIII.

THE TRADITIONAL POLICY OF RUSSIA.

WHAT is the Traditional Policy of Russia?

The Traditional Policy of Russia is an alliance with England!

Long before Russia bowed beneath the Tartar yoke, our reigning Prince, Vladimir Monomachus, married Gyda, daughter of your noble Harold, who fell on the fatal field of Senlac.

The Tartar invasion, lasting nearly three centuries, did not favour communications, much less an alliance, between Russia and England.

But after we got rid of the Tartars, Ivan the Fourth, graphically surnamed the Terrible, sent an Embassy to your Queen Elizabeth to negotiate a close alliance with England, and according to several historians, he was even anxious to marry her. Your Queen, however, preferring 'single blessedness' refused, and the death of Ivan IV. brought the negotiations to an end.

Since then matrimonial ties were not spoken of for nearly three hundred years, but many efforts have been made by us to establish a cordial understanding, by other means, between the two nations.[1]

[1] It is curious to find that almost in the first sentence of the first

Our efforts, however, have too often been paralysed by lying legends and calumnies invented by our enemies, to prejudice the ignorant against us. One of these—perhaps the most famous—the spurious Will of Peter the Great, written nearly a hundred years after Peter's death by the ingenious Frenchman, Lesur, is frequently appealed to, as the most convincing proof of Russia's wickedness: nevertheless, forgery though it is, it contains one point which was well adapted to Russian views, viz., the Seventh Article, which is as follows:

'Seek the alliance of England, on account of our commerce, as being the country most useful to us for the development of our navy and mercantile marine, and for the exchange of our produce against her gold.'

Russian Emperors have always been of the opinion that Russia and England are natural allies, even although circumstances have occasionally thrown them into temporary antagonism to a mistaken English policy.

Up to the very outbreak of the Crimean War, our Emperor Nicholas was most sincerely anxious to be 'upon terms of closest amity with England.' In his famous conversations with Sir Hamilton Seymour, that anxious desire was most manifest.[1]

Speech from the Throne after the accession of the present Government to office the Queen speaks as follows:—'My relations with all foreign Powers continue to be most friendly. . . . The marriage of my son, the Duke of Edinburgh, with the Grand Duchess Marie Alexandrowna of Russia is at once a source of happiness to myself, and a pledge of friendship between two great Empires.'

[1] 'You know my opinions with regard to England. Were we agreed,

Mr. Kinglake says:—

The Emperor Nicholas had laid down for himself a rule, which was always to guide his conduct on the Eastern Question, and it seems to be certain that at this time (the eve of the Turkish war of 1853), even in his most angry moments, he intended to cling to his resolve. What he had determined was that no temptation should draw him into hostile conflict with England.[1]

As to the attitude of Russia before the late war, even our most exacting critics admit that our Emperor could not possibly have done more than he did to secure the alliance and the co-operation of England. The Livadia despatch was but the culmination of a long series of similar overtures for English friendship—overtures which, I regret to say, met with but cool and scanty responses from your Government.

In making these advances, our Government was only carrying out the ancient, the traditional policy of Russia. The change has been with you; not with us.

At the beginning of the seventeenth century, Boris Godounoff sent an envoy to London to urge that England should unite with Russia and other Christian powers to subdue the Turks and free the Christians of the East.[2]

During the eighteenth century, the two Powers

I am quite without anxiety as to the West of Europe; it is immaterial what the others may think or do.' Again in January, 1853, alluding to the probable fall of Turkey, 'It is very important that England and Russia should come to a perfectly good understanding upon these affairs, and that neither should take any decisive step of which the other is not apprised.'

[1] *Invasion of the Crimea*, vol. i. p. 199.
[2] See *ante*, ' Russia's Foreign Policy,' p. 295.

were frequently in alliance both in peace and in war. On one occasion, Russian soldiers garrisoned the Channel Islands. On another, Russian fleets were re-fitted in English dockyards. English admirals often commanded Russian navies, while Russian and English soldiers, as faithful allies, fought side by side on many a hard-contested field.

The great statesmen of both countries recognised the importance of the Anglo-Russian alliance. Our Minister, M. Panin, in 1766, informed the envoy of your Earl of Chatham, that he entertained 'the strongest desire of entering into the strictest engagements, and the most intimate friendship with England, being convinced that my policy could neither be solid nor perfect unless Great Britain were a party to it.' It was the repeatedly declared conviction of Prince Potemkin that the union of Russia and England was absolutely essential to the peace of the East.

That conviction has been strengthened, rather than weakened, by the history of the last hundred years. Prince Worontzoff, our ambassador at the Court of St. James, was a devoted advocate of the Anglo-Russian Alliance, and his convictions are shared by the Imperial Chancellor, Prince Gortschakoff.

The most illustrious English statesmen concurred with Prince Potemkin and M. Panin, in the value they placed on the alliance between the two countries. Chatham was not ashamed to declare that 'he was altogether a Russian.' Fox, Burke, even Pitt, as well as Canning and others nearer our time, have either concluded treaties of friendship with Russia, or expressed themselves as most favourable to the Russian alliance.[1]

It is not a century since it was the custom to refer to Russia in Parliament as 'the natural, ancient, and traditional ally of England.'

In the great crisis of European history, England and Russia were the foremost opponents of the Emperor Napoleon, and it was to their joint endeavours that Europe owed the overthrow of the ascendancy of France.

You have now occupied Cyprus as 'a strong place of arms,' to menace Russia, but your previous Mediterranean occupation—that of the Ionian Islands—was undertaken at the suggestion of your Russian ally. Nor did you always dread Russia as a Mediterranean Power, for England has insisted upon our fleet entering that sea, and once negotiations were even begun to cede us a naval station at Minorca, then an English possession.

Is it not a remarkable proof of the utility of the Russian alliance that on two occasions, when the English Government so far forgot its true interests as to threaten to make war upon Russia, the war should have been prevented by the vigorous protests of the English people?[2]

[1] 'The Whigs of that day (after the Congress of Vienna) were not behind the Tories in their devotion to the Czar. It may perhaps be more correctly said that the alliance with Russia received especially the approval of that distinguished section of the Whigs who followed in the footsteps of Charles Fox.'—*Thirty Years of Foreign Policy*, pp. 61-2.

[2] 1791 and 1876.

The instinct of the nation was wiser than the statecraft of its rulers, and the English succeeded on both occasions in doing that all but impossible thing —even in Constitutional countries—of restraining a Prime Minister who was bent on going to war. We are not ungrateful for the generous sympathies and natural friendliness of the English people. We only regret that in two important crises of your history, your Constitutional Government so misrepresented your real feelings as to render it necessary, to prevent war, to overrule your Ministry by an almost revolutionary agitation.

When Empress Catherine II. heard of the services which Mr. Fox had rendered to the cause of humanity in restraining Mr. Pitt from making war upon Russia about Otchakoff, she placed his bust between those of Cicero and Demosthenes, exclaiming, 'Il a delivré par son éloquence la patrie et la Russie d'une guerre pour la quelle il n'y avait ni justice ni raisons.'

Mr. Fox, in his place in Parliament expressed himself highly gratified by the distinction conferred upon him by the Empress, and made the memorable declaration:—' With regard to Russia, it has ever been my opinion that she was the Power in Europe with whom the cultivation of reciprocal ties of friendship, both commercial and political, was most natural and of the greatest consequence to this country.'

Now, if Russians venture to express their gratitude to an English statesman, whose eloquence, like that of Mr. Fox, has indeed delivered both countries from a senseless war, he is decried as a 'Russian agent' and a traitor to his country. The change is not exactly an improvement, nor is it calculated to strengthen good feeling on either side.

Englishmen may yet discover that these prejudices against us are detrimental to their interests. Seventy years ago, an English author declared that Russia, the most powerful, the most natural, the most useful of our allies, has so intimate a connection of interests with us that the soundest policy must dictate to us a union of design and co-operation in action.[1] If that were true then, how much more so must it be now, for since then we have divided Asia between us?

Even Lord Palmerston, when the Crimean War was still an affair of yesterday, declared to our Ambassador, Count Chreptovitch, that 'Russia and England had great interests in common; and that as long as they did not come into collision about Turkey or Persia, there was no reason why they should not act in concert on many important matters.'[2]

To Russians, it seems that the danger of a collision about the affairs of these countries is the greatest of reasons why the two Powers should act in concert.

Russia has always particularly sought for concert with England in dealing with Turkey. Much as the Russian Government desired the English alliance which Lord Chatham pressed upon us, it was refused unless England would act in concert with us in Turkish affairs. That principle, rejected by Chatham, was accepted by Pitt in 1795. Only four years after

---

[1] Eton's *Survey of the Turkish Empire*, p. 404.
[2] Ashley's *Life of Lord Palmerston*, vol. ii. p. 116.

he had been threatening us with war, a treaty was concluded which conceded that principle of common action in the Levant, for which Russia had never ceased to contend.

Is not that fact a happy augury for the future? Four years after the War Vote of 1791, the two Powers entered into a close alliance. Who knows but the same thing may happen within four years of the War Vote of 1878?

Even during this century, Russia and England have oftener been friends than foes. In the Napoleonic wars, the English fleet menaced Constantinople because the Turks had declared war against Russia. It was not in Russia that the battle of Navarino was condemned as 'an untoward event,' and in 1877, in spite of the bitterness occasioned by the war, we celebrated its jubilee with enthusiasm.

As we fought together against the Turks, so we have also, I regret to say, been allied in support of the Sultan. When Mehemet Ali threatened to overturn the Ottoman Empire, Russian troops occupied Constantinople, while an English fleet cruised off the coast of Syria.

The Crimean war was, indeed, 'an untoward event,' but the despatches of Lord John Russell, before war broke out, bore repeated testimony to the earnestness and sincerity with which our Emperor laboured to establish a good understanding and concerted action with England in the affairs of Turkey.

Since the Peace of Paris, in 1856, Russia has never

been at war with England, while she has frequently energetically seconded English policy.

At the Conference of Constantinople, General Ignatieff abandoned his own scheme of reforms, in order to give a more effectual support to that of Lord Salisbury; and after the Conference failed, Russia exhausted every diplomatic expedient to preserve the concert with England, before she drew the sword.

Not until it was seen that the only concert with England was concert in inaction, with all wrongs unredressed, and all the Slavs left in slavery, did Russia act alone.

But even when compelled unassisted to do singlehanded the duty of all Europe, Russia displayed the most scrupulous regard for 'British Interests.' Ascertaining them from Lord Derby at the beginning of the war, Russia brought the contest to a triumphant close without threatening a single point specified by your Foreign Minister.

We sent you our terms of peace before we crossed the Danube, and we sent you the Treaty of San Stefano, as soon as it reached St. Petersburg.

At the Berlin Congress we gave way repeatedly to satisfy your demands, and surrendered all exclusive privileges in order to act in concert with Europe.

How England rewarded this, I need not say. But unless we surrendered the Christians of the East to the vengeance of the Turk, we could do no more. In fact, truly speaking, we even went too far. The aspirations, the ardent wishes of the Russian people have been sacrificed for your friendship. One step more would be almost treason to our brethren—a betrayal of our duty. Such a price could not be paid—no!—not even for the purchase of the English alliance.

If England, if the English people identify their interests with the maintenance of Turkish power over all the peoples south of the Balkans, then I reluctantly admit that any alliance between us is impossible. As has frequently been said, 'at any cost, without even counting the cost,' Russia must do her duty. For us, there is no choice possible between the Slavs and their oppressors. Some of our officials, estranged from their own nation by their false education, dislike the very name of Slavs; but as long as there is the slightest link between them and the Russian people, even they would not dare so far to forget their duty as to sanction an alliance on such terms.

Russians know well that nothing great can be obtained without sacrifices. If new sacrifices are needed, what does it prove? Only that we have not done enough. No power on earth can stop the natural development of events. The future of the Slavonic world is as clear to us as the path of honour which we have to follow.

But are we to believe that the English people, after all their protestations of sympathy with the Eastern Christians, will insist upon such a shameful price for their alliance, as a support of the Turkish power?

It is impossible!

I look forward confidently to the conclusion of a good understanding between Russia and England, based upon the peaceful but effective elimination of Turkish authority from Europe.

Only on that basis is real alliance possible.

And so with the farther East. Co-partners in the work of civilising Asia, our *entente cordiale* is the key to the peace of the Continent.

Destroy it, and from Constantinople to Japan there will be ceaseless intrigues, insurrections, and war.

Mr. J. Anthony Froude, whose courageous advocacy of an Anglo-Russian Alliance dates back to the dark times of the Crimean War, expressed this truth very clearly when he wrote in his admirable 'Short Studies on Great Subjects,' 'We may be sure that if it was understood in the East, that Russia and England, instead of enemies were cordial friends, that they recognised each other's position and would assist each other in difficulties, the imagination of resistance would be quenched in the certainty of its hopelessness.'

It is not sufficient that we should not be at open war, to secure peace in Asia. We must be staunch friends, and act in cordial concert within our respective spheres. The Oriental world is convulsed with war when Russia and England are in opposition. Cross purposes between St. Petersburg and London may be confined to despatches in Europe, but they result in crossed swords in Persia and Afghanistan.

The only hope of barbarism in Asia lies in discord between the two civilising Empires. If we are united, civilisation is safe; but a policy of antagonism, even although we do not draw the sword, may end in restoring Asia to the Asiatics.

Believe me, it is not Russia who will suffer most by persistence in this policy of hostility and suspicion. Our stake in Asia is trivial compared with yours. Turkestan entails a costly drain upon our exchequer, nor can we import Turkomans to make war in Europe. With you in India it is different. We do not want India. We could not take India if we did want it. But when the visit of a single Russian envoy to Cabul induces you to undertake a costly, useless war, what hope is there of peaceful progress, and the development of civilisation in the East, if the two Powers are to be permanently estranged?

Lord Napier and Ettrick, who, after he had left his ambassador's post at St. Petersburg, was considered in this country, as well as in Russia, as a decided Russophobist, referring, on December 9, 1878, in his speech in Parliament, to the Russian mission to Cabul, frankly said:—

Russia had moved forward in the direction of national sympathies and aspirations of the people, and with consummate prudence. With a country so constituted, it was necessary to employ judicious means for securing amity, if not absolutely alliance, and the best means the Government could employ was an absolute plainness and frankness, so that Russia should not be in any doubt as to the course we should pursue with reference to Afghanistan. He thought that, after the termination of the war, there should be a definite treaty between England and Russia, as it would be likely to have a tranquillising effect upon India.

Our interests are identical, our mission is the same; why then can we not revert to the traditional policy of Russia, and become once more firm allies and good friends?

It is not only in Asia that the two nations stand side by side. In Europe we occupy similar ground in resisting the authority of Papal Rome; each in our own way, we protest against the corruptions and abuses of the Vaticanate Church.

Thus presenting a common front, alike against the Mohammedan barbarism of Asia, and the spiritual despotism of Europe, is it not time that we should frankly recognise the similarity of our mission, and loyally support each other in the face of the common foe?

'The Russians,' says Mr. Froude, 'though our rivals in the East, had in Europe, till the outbreak of the Crimean War, been our surest allies.' Even since then, English Cabinets have had no reason to regret the existence of Russia in Europe. It is not so many years ago that Lord Beaconsfield's Government allied itself with the Russian Empire to prevent a renewal of the Franco-German War, and I believe it was Lord Beaconsfield who pointed, ten years ago, to an Anglo-Russian alliance as a means of preventing Napoleon's March '*à Berlin*,' which terminated so disastrously at Sedan.

We are also united in the great humanitarian crusade against slavery and the slave trade.

You look back with pride to the abolition of slavery in your colonies; we glory in the emancipation of our serfs—that measure which for ever secured our gratitude to Emperor Alexander, who understood and supported the best aspirations of his people.

It is your proud boast that slaves cannot breathe upon English soil. It is not less true of Russia, who for the last hundred years has waged unceasing war against the slave trade, both in Europe and in Asia. It was our conquest of the Crimea which suppressed the market in which Polish and Russian captives were sold like cattle by the Mussulman, and the first-fruits of our entry into Khiva was the release of all the slaves in the Khanate.

But why enter into details? Whether it is in the field of exploration, or in the domain of science, or in any other of the numberless departments of our complex civilisation, you will find that Russians are fellow-workers with you, neither unfriendly nor unworthy.

Why then should you persist in regarding us as worse than declared enemies?—A very intelligent friend of mine, who has enjoyed unusual opportunities of studying Russian and English policy writes to me :—

The popular clamour against Russia in England is not only unjust, but childish and contemptible, and defeats its own purpose. To tell you the truth, I sometimes blush for the half childish, half brutal national egotism of a great part of my countrymen. If we have to fight, let us do so and be done with it, respecting each other as honourable opponents, but (like yourself) I do not see the least necessity for fighting. It would be folly in England to go to war to put on his legs the incurably Sick Man, and it would be equally foolish of Russia to go to war in order to accelerate by a few years the inevitable death of the patient. How many difficulties might be removed by a genuine understanding between Russia and England!

Why should there not be such an understanding between us?

Surely it has been sufficiently proved that we could do each other a great deal of harm, although not without injuring many a noble cause, which we ought to serve, if we really care for Humanity and Civilization.

It is for you—not for us—now to decide whether we are to be Friends or Foes!

CHAPTER IX.

SOME LAST WORDS.

AND now my book is finished!

As I look over its pages and remember the friendly welcome which my poor attempts to promote a better understanding between England and Russia have received from some of the noblest men in both countries, I feel almost ashamed of the moments of despair and bitterness which I tried in vain to conceal. And let me say, also, in parting, how gladly I shall welcome the first proof that my bitterness was a little unjust. Whatever may be the difficulties of the present, they are, I hope, but temporary; and they have not been without some permanent compensation. Even the hostility manifested in certain quarters has not been without its uses, for it evoked a generous protest, which formed a new and precious link of sympathy and confidence between us. That sympathy and confidence may, I trust, be as an aurora, promising the advent of a new and brighter day, when 'the mist of distrust,' which has so long hung over us, will fade away and finally disappear.

The removal of national misunderstandings is a task which often baffles the wisdom of the greatest statesmen, and defies the effort of the most powerful monarchs. For a humble person like me to work in that direction, however feebly, is naturally regarded, even by myself, as somewhat ridiculous. My *rôle*, however, is that of a *pis aller*, whose abiding hope has been, that ere long so great a work may fall into more able and powerful hands.

The fear of ridicule has blighted many a noble aspiration, and the sacrifices demanded by loyalty to truth and justice are not confined to the battlefield alone. The struggle for the Ideal—by its very essence, unattainable—is always somewhat quixotic; but would life be worth living without it?

Coming back to the principal object of my book, I must repeat what I have already said several times: England and Russia, cordially united, can overcome many difficulties, otherwise insuperable, and serve many good causes worthy of the support of two great Christian Powers.

We must unite in order to atone for the sufferings already occasioned to others by our mutual hostility. It is a debt of honour, which has to be paid before the others, and no time should be lost before moving in that direction.

But unless there is a radical change for the better, there may be a change for the worse, the consequences of which, in many respects, would be fatal.

The issue now lies, not in the hands of the Cabinets, but in those of the peoples.

To bring about an *entente cordiale* between England and Russia is indispensable for the civilisation of the Orient, and is the only good standpoint from which can be approached the great problems of Europe and Asia.

I may be told, perhaps, that by expressing too frankly and unreservedly the feelings of Russians on England's policy, I injure more than I serve the cause I have at heart. But this would be an indirect accusation of England against which I protest.

In spite of all that has been done, written, and said, I firmly believe that many Englishmen will not lose sight of the motive which guided my pen, and pardon my want of skilful reserve and concealment.

To understand why we are displeased with each other is the first indispensable step for removing the misunderstanding. Had I minced my words too much, had I shrunk from stating facts with the utmost frankness, I should not have been a faithful and true exponent of Russian views.

Once more, then, I review in these 'last words' the question which I have pressed, I fear, perhaps almost *ad nauseam*, in every page: Why can we not be friends?

This inflamed animosity, so sedulously fostered by interested parties, is a reproach to our intelligence and our sense of duty.

We both have nothing to gain, and very much to lose, by substituting hatred for cordiality and suspicion for confidence; nor is it we alone who suffer. Every human being between the outposts of the two Empires is more or less affected by the relations existing between England and Russia.

The Russian people have been reluctantly driven into an attitude of antagonism to England. Gladly would we hail any prospect of escape from that involuntary position, and heartily would we welcome your co-operation in that task of developing the liberties of the Christian East, which is now proclaimed as the policy of Liberal England, but which has always been the Historical Mission of my country.

O. K.

APPENDIX.

THE following was Mr. Froude's Preface to the first series of the O. K. Letters, published in December, 1877, under the title, 'Is Russia Wrong?'

Very few words will suffice for an introduction of the following letters. The writer is a Russian lady well acquainted with England, who has seen with regret the misconceptions which she considers prevail among us as to the character of her countrymen; she has therefore employed such skill as she possesses in an honourable attempt to remove those misconceptions. Individuals, however great their opportunities, can but speak with certainty of what they personally know, and 'O. K.' may draw too wide inferences from the experiences of her own circle; but she writes in good faith, and any contribution to our knowledge, which is true as far as it goes, ought to be welcome to us—welcome to us especially at the present crisis, when the wise or unwise conduct of English statesmen may affect incalculably for good or evil the fortunes of many millions of mankind. To Russia and England has fallen the task of introducing European civilisation into Asia. It is a thankless labour at the best; but circumstances have forced an obligation upon both of us, which neither they nor we can relinquish; and our success depends for its character on the relations which we can establish between ourselves. If we can work harmoniously together as for a common object, the progress of the Asiatic people will be peaceful and rapid. If we are to be jealous rivals, watching each other's movements with suspicion, and on the look-out to thwart and defeat each other, every kingdom and tribe from the Bosphorus to the Wall of China will be a centre of intrigue; and establishment of the new order of things may be retarded for centuries, or disgraced by wars and revolutions from which we shall all alike be sufferers. On the broadest grounds, therefore, it is our interest to be on good terms with Russia, unless there is something in the Muscovite proceedings so unqualifiedly bad that we are positively obliged to separate ourselves from them. And before arriving at such a conclusion, we must take more pains than we have done hitherto to know what the Russians are. If we could 'crumple' them up as Mr. Cobden spoke of doing, we might prefer to reign in the East without a rival. But 'crumpling up' is a long process, in which nothing is certain but the expense of it. That enterprise we shall certainly not attempt. There remains, therefore, the alternative: either to settle into an attitude of fixed hostility to a Power which will always exist side by side by us, or to place on Russia's action towards the Asiatic races the same favourable construction which we allow to our own, and to ask ourselves whether in Russia's conduct there is anything materially different from what we too accept as necessary in similar circumstances.

The war of 1854 was a first step in what I considered then, and consider now, to have been the wrong course—a course leading direct, if persisted in, to most deplorable issues. That war had been made inevitable from the indignation of the Liberal party throughout Europe at Russia's interference in Hungary. Professedly a war in defence of Turkey, it was fought really for European liberty. European liberty is no longer in danger, nor has the behaviour of Turkey since the peace been of a kind to give her a claim on our interest for her own sake. The Ottoman Empire has for half a century existed upon sufferance. An independence accompanied with a right of interference by other nations with its internal administration has lost its real meaning, and the great Powers have been long agreed that the Porte cannot be left to govern its Christian subjects after its own pleasure. The question is merely in whom the right of supervision is to reside. Before the Crimean war they were under the sole protectorate of Russia. The Treaty of Paris abolished an exclusive privilege which was considered dangerous, and substituted for it, by implication, a general European protectorate. It seemed likely to many of us that, while other objects of the war might have been secured, the ostensible occasion of it would be forgotten; that the Christians, having no longer Russia to appeal to, would be worse treated than before; and that after a very few years the problem of how to compel the Turk to respect his engagements would certainly return. Such anticipations, in the enthusiasm of the moment, were ridiculed as absurd and unpatriotic. The Turk himself was to rise out of the war regenerate, and a 'new creature.' He was to be the advanced guard of enlightenment, the bulwark of Europe against barbarism. There was no measure to the hopes in which English people indulged in those days of delight and excitement. But facts have gone their natural way. The Turk has gone back, not forward. He remains what he has always been, a blight upon every province on which he has set his heel. His Christian subjects have appealed once more for help; and the great Powers, England included, have admitted the justice of their complaints, and the necessity of a remedy. Unhappily England could not agree with the other Powers on the nature of the remedy required. Russia, unable to trust further to promises so often made and so uniformly broken, has been obliged to take active measures, and at once the Crimean ashes have again been blown into a flame; there is a cry that Russia has sinister aims of her own, that English interests are in danger, and that we must rush to the support of our ancient friend and ally. How we are decently to do it, under what plea, and for what purpose, after the part which we took at the Conference, is not explained. The rest of Europe is not alarmed. The rest of Europe is satisfied that the Turk must be coerced, and looks on, if not pleased, yet at least indifferent. If we go into the struggle, we must go in without a single ally, and when we have succeeded in defeating Russia, and re-establishing Turkey (there is another possibility, that we may not succeed, but this I will not contemplate),—as soon as we have succeeded, what then? After the censures to which we stand committed on Turkey's misconduct we cannot in decency hand back Bulgaria to her without some check upon her tyranny. We shall be obliged to take the responsibility on ourselves. England will have to be sole protector of the Bulgarian Christians, and it is absolutely certain that they would then be wholly and entirely at the Turk's mercy. It is absolutely certain that we should be contracting obligations which we could not fulfil if we wished. We should demand a few fine promises from the Porte, which would be forgotten as soon as made. A British protectorate is too ridiculous to be thought of; and if the alternative be to place Bulgaria under a government of its own, that is precisely the thing which Russia is trying to do. To go to war with such a dilemma staring us in the face, and with no object which we can distinctly define, would be as absurd an enterprise as England was ever entangled in. Yet even after Lord Derby's seeming recognition of the character of the situation, there is still room for misgiving. In constitutional countries politicians will snatch at passing gusts of popular excitement to win a momentary victory for themselves or their party. Our Premier, unless he has been misrepresented, has dreamt of closing his political career with a transformation scene— Europe in flames behind him, and himself posing like harlequin before the footlights. Happily there is a power which is stronger than even Parliamentary majorities—in public opinion; and public opinion has, I trust, already decided that English bayonets shall not be stained again in defence of Turkish tyranny. It will be well if we can proceed, when the present war is over, to consider dispassionately the wider problems, of which the Turkish difficulty is only a part; and if the letters of 'O. K.' assist ever so little in making us acquainted with the Russian character, the writer will have reason to congratulate herself on so happy a result of her efforts.

The Jewish Question.

This hostility to Jews is not confined to Slavs. A distinguished Englishman, who is very familiar with the movements of German thought, writes as follows to the 'Nonconformist,' January 8, 1880:—

There is an Eastern Question, a Nihilist Question, a Social Democratic Question, and so forth; and there is also a Jewish Question, at any rate, so it is thought in Berlin, in Germany. But what is meant by the 'Jewish Question?' Not a question of the emancipation of the Jews from the yoke of the Christian, not a question of giving the Jews equal rights with Christians, but, so, with just a spice of paradox, one might put it, a question of *the emancipation of the Christians from the yoke of the Jews, and of the Christians keeping equal rights with the Jews.* That the paradox is not all my own, the title of a pamphlet, which has gone through eleven editions in, I believe, about as many months, will tell you, it runs, 'The Victory of Judaism over Germanism.' It is written by a well-known German Publicist, W. Marr, and what does he say? Let me quote a few passages:—

'The 1800 years' war with Judaism approaches its end. Let us confess it openly—Germanism has had its Sedan. We have lost our armies, and we are not allowed to Gambettize, we are not allowed to carry on a useless war with volunteers. We have been vanquished in an open struggle. . . . . We are no longer a match for this foreign race. *Even freedom has become a Jewish monopoly. It is compelled to regulate itself by the social political dogmas of the Jews.* . . . . My voice is that of one crying in the desert, and I have only laid down facts—irrefragable facts. Let us accommodate ourselves to the inevitable, if we cannot alter it. That inevitable is *Finis Germaniæ*!'

Let us hear another writer, a well-known Professor of History, Henrich von Freitschke. In the November number of the 'Preussische Jahrbücher' he wrote as follows. I summarise rather than quote literally:—

'A great movement is going on in the depths of our nation. Among its symptoms none strikes one as so strange as the irritation against the Jews. A few months ago the old *Hepp Hepp* cry might be said to be raised by the Jews against the Christians, instead of by the Christians against the Jews; criticism of national faults of the Germans, French, and all other peoples were freely admitted into the daily papers; but if any one ventured, in however mild a tongue, to point out the faults of the Jews, at once he was branded by almost the entire press as a barbarian and religious persecutor. The feeling referred to is the reason why the Breslau people rejected Lasker, having resolved to elect no Jew as their representative. Up into the very highest circles of culture, amongst men who are as far removed as possible from every thought of ecclesiastical intolerance or national pride, one hears it said with unparalleled unanimity, *The Jews are our misfortune*. There has always been a gulf between the Western and the Semitic character. There will always be Jews who are nothing but German-speaking Orientals. There will always be, too, a specifically Jewish culture, and it has undoubted rights of its own. But the antagonism between West and East will be bearable if the Jews, who talk so much about toleration, will only learn to be really tolerant, and to show some respect for the faith, the customs, and the feelings of the German people, which has given them the rights of men and citizens. But the complete lack of this respect in a part of the mercantile and literary Jewish community is the deepest reason for the passionate embitterment of which I have spoken.'

Let us hear yet another voice, that of the Court Chaplain, Stocker, a thoroughly honest, well-meaning, and fairly representative man, now a Prussian Deputy for one of the districts of Berlin, than whom scarcely anyone has been more bitterly and either maliciously or ignorantly assailed by so-called Liberals all over the world during the last two years. He says :—

'The Jewish question has long been a burning question : for the last few months the fire has burst into flames. It is not fed either by religious fanaticism or by political passion. Orthodox and Freethinkers, Conservatives and Liberals speak and write about it with the like passionateness; they all treat the Jews not as the apple of religious discord and intolerance, but as a matter of social anxiety. "The social question," writes Glagau, " is the Jew question." We do not think that Germany is as near its end as W. Marr prophesies (in the pamphlet from which I have already quoted); ' but symptoms of disease in our national body have unquestionably been laid bare, and social hostility is never absolutely groundless. . . . . *Modern Judaism is in very deed a great danger for the life of the German nation.* . . . . Modern Judaism is certainly an irreligious force— a force which everywhere bitterly attacks Christianity, uproots both the Christian faith and national sentiment, and in return offers nothing but the idolatrous reverence of itself." And as Auerbach says in his 'Waldfried,' "Educated Jews are not so much Jews as non-Christians!" Hence their enthusiasm for creedless schools and the like.'

INDEX.

ABERDEEN, Lord, and Emperor Nicholas, 146; on Russian foreign policy, 306

Afghanistan, 'outside sphere of Russian interests,' 79, 345; 'England's true policy in,' 337; Vitkevitch on, 339; Russian pledges kept in, 341; Duke of Argyll on English policy in, 341; on English bad faith to, 350

Afghan, the, Correspondence and General Kaufmann, 341

Afghan War, the, Russian neutrality in, 79; brings British frontier to Russian, 279; increases Russia's power of offence, 279, 337; Mr. Gladstone on Russia and the, 285; Russian Mission to Cabul justifiable, 332; Russia and the, 332; Lord Beaconsfield on, 333; Duke of Argyll on, 334; proved impossibility of invading India, 335; cost of first, 336; Colonel Osborne on difficulty of campaigning in, 336; not calculated to produce friendship, 337; Sir Charles Wingfield, 337; Cavagnari and Stoletoff, 339

Aggression, Russian, 321; Russian and English since 1750, 322; Cobden on, 323

Aksakoff, Mr., President of Moscow Slavonic Committee, 20; not a Russian Mazzini, 20; Mr. Wallace on, 24; 'exiled,' 106; bank director, 107
— speeches of, on the Servian war, 24; on Russian reverses in 1877, 52; on the Berlin Congress, 98
— on work of Slavonic committees, 25; Russian diplomacy, 25, 58, 103, 104; the roots of Russian power, 27; spread of Slavophilism, 27; General Tchernayeff, 28; death of Nicholas Kiréeff, 29; volunteers for Servia, 30; money raised, 32; how spent, 33; the Russian debt to the Servians, 34; the Russian soldier, 53; effect of reverses on the people, 54; historic mission of Russia, 54, 56, 57; to spread 'peace, liberty, and fraternal equality,' 57; complaints of higher classes, 55, 59; 'the sin of forsaking Russian nationality,' 55, 59; British interests, 58; Austria-Hungary and the Slavs, 58; the limitation of war, 59; the Berlin Congress, 98; Prince Tcherkassky, 98; Russia and the Western Powers, 99; Bulgaria 'sawn asunder alive,' 100–103; Turkish garrisons in Balkans, 102; Slavonic development, 103; diplomatic Nihilists, 104; the Constantinople Conference, 104; England and her sepoys, 105; Austria-Hungary, 'a heel of

ALE

Achilles,' 105; 'the Balkan States for Balkan peoples,' 149

Alexander I. and Turkey, 171; concludes treaty with England, 171; treats with Napoleon at Tilsit, 171; wishes to re-establish Poland at Congress of Vienna, 204; on Constitutional Government, 250; liberator of Europe, 302; Stein on, 303; esteemed by Napoleon, 303; reactionary in later years, 304; liberality towards France, 304; too liberal for Metternich, 318

Alexander II., Emperor, 'passionately desirous of peace,' 6; but, if necessary, will act alone, 6; Moscow speech, enthusiastic reception of, 11; on Constantinople, 174; on 'Russian designs on India,' 174; desires good understanding with England, 174; visited Siberia, 220; emancipator of serfs, liberator of southern Slavs, 230; Mr. Gladstone on, 230; confidence in, 243, 255; attempt on the life of, 252, and the Tzarewitch, 268; progress under, 275; M. de Laveleye on, 320

Alexander Nevsky, St., receives title of Grand-Duke from Tartars, 41

America, civil war in United States of, Russian and English sympathies, 307

Anarchy, in Poland, 200, 225; besetting sin of Slavs, 225; in Russia, 226; in Central Asia, banished by Russians, 349

Anglo-Russian Alliance, the, or *entente cordiale*, Lord Rochford on, in 1772, 82; desired by Emperor Alexander II. in 1876, 174; how sought by Russia, 263, 288; Russia's overtures rebuffed by England, 265; Russian noble on, 269; initiative must now be taken by England, 269; the traditional policy of England, 272, 358; for Asia and the East, the watchword of civilisation, 284; not indispensable to Russia, 288; prevents German at-

ANN

tack on France 1875, 291; Lord Beaconsfield urges it in 1870, 364; civilising mission in Asia, 323; the traditional policy of Russia, 352; matrimonial ties past and present, 352; Peter the Great, 353; Catherine II., 357; Alexander I., 171, 359; Alexander II., 174; Panin, 355; Potemkin, 355; Woronzoff, 355; Gortschakoff, 355; Lord Robert Cecil, 295; Chatham, 355; Burke, 355; Canning, 356; Fox, 356, 357; Pitt, 359; Palmerston, 358; Mr. Bright, 270; Sir Charles Trevelyan, 270; Mr. W. H. Smith, 292; Mr. Lowther, 293; Lord Mayo, 330; Lord Napier and Ettrick, 363; *Statesman*, 182; in the seventeenth century, 354; in the eighteenth, 355; in 1765, 359; 1812, 315, 359; 1827, 295, 315, 359; 1830, 300; 1833, 315, 359; 1840, 315, 359; 1850, 315; 1860, 315; 1867, 316; 1875, 291, 316, 364; and 1876, 281; English people twice prevent armed rupture of, 356; basis of, in East of Europe, 361; key to peace of Asia, 363; evils caused by want of, 363, 372; in the hands of the peoples, 368; need for, 368

Anglo-Turkish Convention, the, 134; Russian opinion on, 134; the *Nord* on, 135; violates Treaty of Paris 135, 137, 138, 139; a sham, 136; Turkish frontier undefended, 136; destroys European concert, 137; justifies Treaty of Kainardji, 137; gives Russia right to deal directly with Sultan, 140; and occupy Turkish territory, 140; justifies Russian principle in the Crimean war, 311, 314; worse than Russian Mission to Cabul, 334

Annand, James, on national misrepresentations, 189

Anne Ivanovna, Empress, 233, 246 accepts Oligarchic Constitution 233, 246; restores autocracy, 246

Index. 381

ANN

Annexations, Russian from Turkey, 51, 74, 107, 313; of Armenia, 50; Finland, 193; the Crimea, 365; Poland, 200; Circassia, 208; Turkestan, 333, 347; of Russia and England since 1750, 322; Cobden on, 200, 323; Duke of Argyll on, 324; Russian, benefit the annexed, 200

Argyll, the Duke of, speech translated into Russian, 39; supports cause of Christian East, 268; on secret societies, 19; the English entry of Dardanelles, 72; Berlin Congress, 106; Russia as liberator of the East, 236, 310; Treaty of Berlin, 310; Russian and English conquests in Asia, 324; Khiva, 330; Russian mission to Cabul, 334; English policy in Afghanistan, 341; English bad faith to Afghans, 350

Aristocracy, Polish, ruin of Poland, 225; character of, by Cobden, 199; by M. de Circourt, 205; denounced by Lord Beaconsfield, 202; Russian, attempt to destroy autocracy, 233, 246; present position of, in Russia, 232

Armenia, annexation of, discussed, 50

Armenian generals, 191, 235

Ashantee War parallel to Khiva Expedition, 349

Asia, sceptre of, given to England and Russia, 323, 362

Askold and Dir attack Byzantium, 168

Assassination, attempt on the Emperor, 252; no proof of 'ruthless despotism,' 254; political effect of, 256; consequences if successful, 259; English press on, 252. See Nihilism

Attempt, the, on the Emperor, 252

Austria-Hungary, and the Slavs, 59, 130, 132, 150, 152; Mr. Aksakoff on, 59, 105; influence of, on San Stefano Treaty, 76; at Berlin Congress, 97,

AUT

99, 103; Russia not hostile to, 129; Prince Gortschakoff on, 130; 'the sick woman of Europe,' 133; 'a carpet bagger,' Stillman, 151; occupies Bosnia at Russia's suggestion, 130, 174; Talleyrand proposes eastward extension of, 132; must not annex the Balkan, 132; nor Constantinople, 167; probable future of, 132, 150, 152; Kossuth on annexations by, 150; M. de Laveleye on, 151, 290; Sir William Harcourt on, 154; admired in West, hated in East, 152; why? Chrzanowski on cause of, 152; Mérimée, 297; as a Danubian power interested in Black Sea and Constantinople, 162; project for partition of Turkey, 170; partitions Poland, 197; partition of, attempted by Poland, 201; opposes national idea in Italy, 166; and in the Balkan, 166; compensated for nothing, but not content, 266; shares in Russia's evil deeds, 312; Mr. Gladstone on, 154; saved by Russia, 1849, 297; ingratitude of, 296; transformation of, 309; originally proposed repeal of Black Sea clause, 312; annexes Cracow, 312, 314

Austro-German Alliance, the, Lord Salisbury on, 123; a menace to France and Italy, 131; Sir W. Harcourt on, 123, 154; M. de Laveleye on, 290; alleged cause of, 291

Autocracy, the, in Russia, 223; greatness of Russia due to, 223; never stronger than to-day, 223; De Tocqueville on, 224, 232; preserves national existence and secures progress, 225; needed to defeat Tartars, 226; and eject Turks from Europe, 227; dictatorship *en permanence*, 227; civilising power, 228, 237; reforms of Peter the Great, 229; of Alexander II., 230; no desire to limit, 231; needs omniscience, 231, 245; democratic origin of, 232;

'the sword of democracy,' 235; destroyed by oligarchy, 233, 246; restored by people, 233, 246; popular belief in, 233, 255; secures *la carrière ouverte aux talens*, 232; exists for the people, 235; Mr. Carlyle on, 238; Lord Beaconsfield on, 238, 251; only alternative to bureaucracy, 255; only check on dishonest officials, 255; strengthened by attempted assassination, 256; not opposed to Constitutionalism abroad, 305; often more liberal in its foreign policy than Constitutional States, 305-317; M. de Laveleye on, 318

Azoff taken by Cossacks, 248; and refused by Zemskie Sobory, 249

BAKER, Ex-Colonel Valentine, fights against Russia, 75, 83
Bakunin, the Nihilist leader, manifesto of, 256
Balkan, the peninsula, for the Balkan peoples, Aksakoff, 149; takes the place of Italy, 117, 166
Balkans, the, to be garrisoned by Turks, Aksakoff on, 102; not garrisoned, 110; Sir W. Harcourt on, 110
Baltic provinces, local franchises in, 190
Bariatinsky, Prince, 68
Barbarism, 'must recede before civilisation,' Peel, 324; Anglo-Russian war against, 363
Barry Herbert, on Siberia, 213; on Russian loyalty, 233
Batoum, Russia's right to, 51; resented by English, 85; Lord Beaconsfield's delight at cession of, 141
Beaconsfield, the Earl of, on secret societies, 20, 25; his Guildhall speeches, 95, 266, 268; abandons his policy at Berlin, 96; 'an infallible Pope,' 96; sacrifices Bulgaria, 112, 203; is pleased at pacific surrender of Batoum, 141; follows Castlereagh's precedent, 203; accused by the *Golos* of stock-jobbing, 185; denounces the Poles, 201; eulogises the Circassians, 207; on absolute monarchy, 238, 250; on representative government, 251; on the press and monarchy, 251; on Jewish revolutionists, 253; results of his policy in England, 265; Mr. Gladstone on, 267; popular with Russian Anglophobes, 279; weakens England, 279; on annexation of Cracow, 201, 314; on Russian Mission to Cabul, 333; on Russia in Central Asia, 351; allied with Russia in 1875, 291, 364; recommends Russian alliance in 1870, 364; fears excited by, in England, in 1877, 374

Belgium, Russian policy in, 299; condemned by Mr. Gladstone, 299; vindicated by M. de Laveleye, 318; Russia supports independence of, 300; protects Belgium from Napoleon III., 301; M. de Laveleye on insurrection of 1830, 318

Bentinck, Lord George, approves annexation of Cracow, 314

Berlin Congress, the, On the Eve of, 88; After the, 95; Mr. Aksakoff on, 99; the Duke of Argyll on, 106; Mr. Gladstone on, 97; Bulgarians not heard at, 118

Berlin Treaty, the Russian Government on, 107; doomed like that of Villafranca, 117; three-quarters of, taken from Treaty of San Stefano, 283; 23rd Article not executed, 119

Bessarabia ceded to Russia, 49, 74, 314

Beust, Count, and the Concordat, 274; proposes tutelage of Turkey and repeal of Black Sea Treaty, 312

Bismarck, Prince, his visit to Vienna, 127, 291; M. de Laveleye's expla-

BLA

nation of, 291; on difficulty of learning Russian, 209; on Russia's non-entry into Constantinople, 242; on change of political opinions, 273; offers Constantinople to Russia, 291; approves Russia's intervention in Hungary, 298

Black Sea Treaty, the repeal of neutralisation clauses, 1871, 312; proposed by Count Beust, 1867, 312

Blunt, Consul, proclamation to Hellenic Insurgents, 85

Bosnia, occupation proposed by Russia, 130, 174; gave cool welcome to Austrians, 152

Boris Godounoff elected to throne by Zemskie Sobory, 232; reproves Queen Elizabeth for helping the Turks, 295; seeks alliance with other powers against Turks, 295, 354

Bourke, Hon. R., delusion of, about Mr. Gladstone's pamphlet, 39

Brackenbury, Colonel, on Russian soldiers, 47

Bright, Mr., gratefully remembered in Russia, 268, 311; pleads from friendship between Russia and England, 270

Bruce, a Scotch general of Peter's, 235

Bulgaria, effect of atrocities in, in Russia, 23, 29, 102; to be freed entirely, 48; will not be Russian, 76; threatened by the Salisbury Circular, 76; not badly treated at San Stefano, 73, 76; 'sawn asunder alive,' Mr. Aksakoff, 100; divided, 111; insurrection in southwestern, 113; how divided at Berlin, 114; one-third re-enslaved without guarantees, 101, 115; will yet be united, 117; its limits, 116; defined at San Stefano, 155; divided against Russia's will, 155, 267, 311; constitution of, not Russian, 155, 240; suggested ports for, 159; in tenth century menaced Byzan-

CAR

tium, 169; crushed by Sviatoslaf, 169; resurrection of, opposed by Lord Beaconsfield, 203; sacrificed by Lord Beaconsfield, 113, 267; union of, approved by English Liberals, 284; opposed by English Government, 311

Bulgarian delegates, MM. Zancoff and Balabanoff, 65

Bulgarians, and their Liberators, 61; abused by Mr. Forbes, 63; degraded by Turkish oppression, 65; prosperity of, 64; character of, MacGahan on, 64; Sir Henry Havelock, 66; Sir George Campbell, 156; General Tchernayeff, 156; protest against Berlin Treaty, 118; not heard at Congress, 118; demand execution of 23rd Article, 119; difference between north and south, 155; English observers on, 156; well treated by Russian soldiers, 188

Burke, Edmund, on Turkish alliance, 272; on English in India, 351

Byzantium, influence of, on Russia, 167. See Constantinople.

CABUL, Russian Mission to, justified, 332; by Lord Beaconsfield, 333; by Duke of Argyll, 334; a prison or grave to Europeans, 340; Colonel Stoletoff and Major Cavagnari at, 340; and Candahar as bulwarks to India, Vitkevitch, 339

Campbell, Sir George, on Russians and Bulgarians, 156; on Kiepert's map, note to, 120

Canning, George, on English neutrality, 77; coerced Turks, 78; on Russia's defeat of Napoleon, 303; opposed by George IV., 313; allied with Russia, 359

Capital punishment in England and Russia, 184

Carlyle, Thomas, on absolute govern-

CAS

ment, 238; on prestige, 264; Russians grateful to, 268; on Russia and Russophobia, 293

Castlereagh, Lord, opposes Polish independence at Vienna, 204

Cat, Army, the, 'pillar of British Constitution,' 184

Catherine I., 234

Catherine II., project about Constantinople, 170; Alexander II. on, 174; on mercy and justice, 213; 'sovereign exists for the people,' 235; summons representative assembly, 248; describes it to Voltaire, 249; on Fox, 357

Cavagnari, Major, murdered at Cabul, 340

Centralisation, democratic tendency towards, De Tocqueville, 232; M. Thiers on, 237; necessary to civilise Russia, 237

Chatham, Lord, 'altogether a Russian,' 355; refuses Russian alliance in East, 358

Chesson, F. W., on slave trade in Turkey, 350

Chinese less suspicious than English, 186; English opium trade with, 189; tactics imitated by Lord Beaconsfield, 91

Chreptovitch, Count, 358

Chrzanowski, General, on Austrian and Russian rule, 152

Circassians eulogised by Lord Beaconsfield, 207; true character of, 208; Russian conquest of, 208

Circourt, M. de, on Finland, 192; Poland, 193, 205; Polish mendacity, 207

Civilisation, the growth of cities, 228; in Russia, from above, 228; must conquer barbarism, 324; of Asia, the mission of Russia and England, 323, 362, 372

Clarendon, Lord, work of, at Paris undone by Lord Beaconsfield, 137; on French and Russian intervention in Italy, 308

CON

Cobden, Richard, on Poland, 199; Russian annexations, 200; British conquests, 323

Commune suppressed more cruelly than Nihilism, 257

Concert of Europe. See European Concert.

Concessions, Russian, to England, 73, 243, 264; denounced by Mr. Aksakoff, 105

Concordat, Count Beust and the, 274

Congress, On the Eve of the, 88; After the, 95. See Berlin.

Congresses, Berlin, 95, 99, 107; Paris, 137; Vienna, 204; Laybach, 313; Verona, 313

Conservatives, English, fear Russia, 181; formerly allied with Russia, 296; support Russia in reaction, 296, 313. See Beaconsfield, and England.

Conservatism, Russian, 229

Constantine, 'Constitution' mistaken for wife of, 250

Constantine, Grand-Duke, his Polish mission of reconciliation, 191, 202

Constantinople, in the Past, more important than to-day, 160; a great commercial emporium, 161; to Russia, as Rome is to France, 166; five times attacked by Russia, 167; seized by Crusaders, 168; Russian attacks on, 167; of Scandinavian origin, 168; by Askold and Dir, 168; Oleg, 169; Igor, 169; Sviatoslaf, 169; Yaroslaf, 169; designs of Catherine II., 170, 174; never to be under same sceptre as Moscow, 171; the Tilsit interview on, 171; not entered by Russia in 1829, 172, 174; occupied in 1833, 172; Crimean war not aimed at, 173

— and the War, Russians desire to make peace in, not to annex, 49, 241; never entered by Russia, 163; English scare about, 164; indignation at non-entry of army

CON

into, 73, 241; General Grant on, 241; Bismarck on, 242
— the Future of, 'last word of Eastern Question,' 3, 160; no longer a talisman of Empire, 160; commercial decay of, 161; importance of, to Euxine States, 162; political importance of, to Russia, 162; may be left to Turks 'with a cabbage garden,' 163; cannot pass to Austria, 165, 167; not desired by Russia, 174, 176; Alexander II. on, 174; Prince Gortschakoff on, 175; must belong to no Great Power, 165, 175; Mr. Gladstone on, 175; Fuad Pasha, 176; would be Achilles' heel of Russia, 176; Emperor Nicholas on, 176; Mr. Cowen, 176; future discussed, 177; free city or capital of Asia Minor, 177; said to be offered to Russia by Bismarck, 1875, 291

Constitution, the Bulgarian, 155, 240
— of England a plutocracy, 280

Constitutional States sometimes support despotism abroad, 305; France in Spain, 306; England in Turkey, 310

Constitutionalism in Russia, obstacles to, Lord Beaconsfield, 223; Polish anarchy, 233; Nihilism, 234; popular ignorance, 228, 255
— comparative failure of, in Italy, 244; Duke of Somerset on, 238; Lord Beaconsfield on, 257; English zealots of, inconsistent, 240; representative assemblies in Russia, 231, 244, 247, 248; Russian Constitutionalists, 250; Alexander I. on, 250. In Russia, see Zemskie Sobory.

Convict system, Russian, milder than English, 213

Corporal punishment in Russia and England, 184

Cossacks, enthusiasm for late war, 17; Sir H. Havelock on, 188; capture Azoff, 247; ravage Russia in seventeenth century, 227

DEM

Coup d'Etat, severity after, 258; Lord Palmerston condones, Nicholas condemns, 306

Courtney, Mr. Leonard, on English Liberals and the war, 113; on Liberal policy in the East, 283

Cowen, Mr. Joseph, ridicules the dread of Russian aggression, 176

Cox, Sir George, suggests English address to Emperor of Russia, 49

Cracow, annexation of, by Austria, Lord Beaconsfield on, 200, 314; Lord Georg Bentinck on, 314

Crete, insurrection in, supported by Russian people, 316; opposed by England, 316

Crimean war, Mr. Aksakoff on, 27; not designed against Constantinople, 173; Russia's principle in, justified by Anglo-Turkish Convention, 311, 314

Criminal convictions in Russia and England, 215

Cross and Crescent, 41

Crusades, Norseman element in, 168; Constantinople captured during, 168

Cyprus concession, the, 138; Mr. Gladstone on, 138; value as precedent to Russia, 140; possible cession to Greece, 159; seized without Parliamentary sanction, 248

*D*AILY NEWS, publishes letters from Moscow, 1876. 9, 186; accuses Russia of bad faith in Afghanistan, 342

Danube, Confederation of the, probable future for Austria, 132, 152; Austria's interest in the, 162; Bosphorus, real mouth of the, 162

Dardanelles forced by English fleet, 72, 334

Decembrists, the character of, 250

'*Dedans, nous sommes*,' 163

Democracy, supports autocracy in Russia, 232, 246; Prince Mestchersky on, 232; centralising instinct of, 232

DER

Derby, Earl of, and the Protocol, 14; on last word of the Eastern Question, 160; says peace is the greatest of British interests, 275
Despotism. See Autocracy.
Diebitch, General, 296
Diplomatists, Stockmar's opinion of, 12; Mr. Aksakoff on, 103, 104
Dir and Askold attack Constantinople, 168
Dolgorouky, Prince Jacob, and the salt tax, 195
Drenteln, General, intercedes for his would-be assassin, 259

EASTERN Question, last and first word of, 3, 160; future of, 123; difficulties of, not in Turkey, but in Europe, 108; not local, but Imperial, 156; suggested solutions of, 158, 159, 177
Education, classical, in Russia, 126
Egypt and English neutrality, 82; and Austro-German alliance, 131
Elizabeth, Queen, reign of, parallel to Russia of to-day, 48; reproved by Boris Godounoff for helping Turks, 295; Ivan IV., and marriage negotiations, 352
'Elizabethan Policy,' 48
Emperor of Russia. See Alexander II., and Autocracy.
England, Eastern policy of, in 1876, maintains *status quo*, 5; Mr. Aksakoff on, 58; in 1877 a sham neutrality, 77; in 1878 violates treaties, 74, 187, 189; conspires with Austria to re-enslave Bulgaria, 97, 101, 113, 115; prevents annexation to Greece, 76-7, 266; menaces Russia, 91; results of, in Russia, 264; in England, 265; Mr. Gladstone on, 267; opposed to freedom, 310
— Foreign policy of, less liberal than Russia's, 294; in the East, 310; in Italy, 307; in Austria, 309; in Germany, 308; in Greece, 266, 295, 311,

EUR

314, 315; in Bulgaria, 311; in Roumania, 311; in Belgium, M. de Laveleye on, 318
— and Russia. See Russia and England and Anglo-Russian alliance.
— Russian concessions to, condemned, 73; opposes cession of Batoum, 85; imports Sepoys to Malta, 91, 105; occupies Cyprus, 138; objects to Russian occupation of Constantinople, 243; meditates attack on Russia in Turkestan, 335
— Traditional Policy of, 227
English aggression, Mr. Farrer on, 322; Mr. Gladstone, 323; Cobden, 323; Duke of Argyll, 324
— Constitution, a plutocracy, 280; convict system, harsher than Russia's, 215; Historians on Russia's side, 293; ignorance of French language, 163; Kings, an English opinion of, 229; people twice prevent war with Russia, 356; reserves hardly exceed one Russian army corps, 91; selfishness, 279; volunteers in Turkey differ from Russian, 74; number of, 83
— Neutrality, 77; Canning on, 77; contrasted with Russian, 79; conditions of, 82; in American war, 83; fourteen English officers in Turkish gendarmerie, 83; in Greece, 85; in the Rhodope, 85; in Lazistan, 85
— parties, Russia and, 277. See Conservatives and Liberals.
— Prejudices, Some, 181; Father Coleridge on, 182; foreign origin of, 183; due to ignorance, 182; illustrations of, 183; the Knout, 184; Russian agents, 187; administration, 190; Poland, 191; Finland, 192
Europe, inimical to Slavs, 76
European concert broken by England, 140, 265; Wellington, Duke of, desired, 144; foreshadowed by Boris Godounoff, 295; Russia desires, 144, 359

EXE

Executions in England, private, 184; number of, 258

Exile, of Mr. Aksakoff, 106; number sent to, 215. See Siberia

FARRER, Mr. T. H., on English aggression, 321

Fenians on English prisons, 216

Finland, better governed by Russia than Sweden, 193; Home Rule in, 192; contrast to Poland, 193; loyalty of, 194

Flogging in English army, 184

Forbes, Mr., correspondence of, read in Russia, 54, 63; on War Correspondents, 61; Russians, Turks and Bulgarians, 61; Russian corruption, 65

Forster, Mr. on alliances, 129; his amendment withdrawn, 281; on Khiva, 327

Fox, Charles James, on Anglo-Russian Alliance, 357; Catherine II. on, 357

France, Russia has no hostility to, 129; Austro-German alliance a menace to, 131; and Rome, 166; centralisation in, 237; intervention of, in Spain, 305; and Alexander I., 304; protected by Russia and England, 1875, 291; allied with Russia in freeing Italy, 307; Revolution of 1830 in, and Russia, 306; supported Belgian revolution, 319

Frederick the Great and his cudgel, 338

Freeman, Mr. E. A., collects money for Slav refugees, 22; Russia grateful to, 268; protests against re-enslavement of Macedonia, 117

French language, English ignorance of, 163

Friends or Foes ? 263

Froude, Mr. J. A., on Ireland, 199; on Anglo-Russian alliance, 362, 364; preface to 'Is Russia Wrong,' 371

GLA

Fuad Pasha on Russia and Constantinople, 176

GALICIA, Polish population of, 205; Massacre in, 202

George IV. opposed Canning's policy in Spain, 313

Germany, at last discovered by Lord Salisbury, 127; unity of, promoted by Russia, 127, 309; effect of union of, on balance of power, 128, 275, 309; Russian alliance with, 129, 309; alleged cause of hostility of, to Russia, 291; Russian policy in, in 1819, 304; in 1870, telegram of Emperor William, 309. See Bismarck.

Girardin, M. Emile de, on Poland, 191; discussion on Constantinople at house of, 242

Gladstone, Mr., his pamphlet in Russia, 39; on the Southern Slavs, 43; on Berlin Congress, 97; has not denounced re-enslavement of S. W. Bulgaria, 101; on Anglo-Turkish Convention, 138, 139; Heirs of the Sick Man, 153; Russia and Constantinople, 175; Alexander II., 230; Historians, 255; results of English policy in East, 267; the Liberals and the East, 277; his resolutions apparently withdrawn, 281; appeared to advocate war with Russia about Afghanistan, 285; writes 'Friends or Foes of Russia?' 285; how regarded in Russia, 285; appears to repudiate Russia's friendship, 287; on Servian volunteers, 285; 'Friendship for every Country,' 287; on Russia's foreign policy, 296; replied to, 290; his indictment of Austria, 154; of Russia, 296; his speech on the Pacifico case, 314; on Russians in Central Asia, 323; on English jealousy of Russia, 323; accused of being a Russian agent, 358; resembles Fox, 357

GLA

Gladstone, Mr., 'A reply to, on Russia's Foreign Policy,' 290

Goethe on the best form of Government, 236

Gordon, a Scotch general of Peter's, 235

Gortschakoff, Prince, on Russian policy in Turkey, 1876, 4; alleged interview with *Soleil* Reporter, 128; saying of, about Austria, 130; protested in 1877 against division of Bulgaria, 155; on Constantinople, 175; in favour of Anglo-Russian alliance, 355

Grant, Gen., on Russian non-entry into Constantinople, 241

Granville, Earl, on benevolent neutrality, 86

Greece, proposed cessions to by Russia, 76; English intervention in, 85; suggested additions to, 159; cannot have Constantinople, 177; betrayed by England, 266; English Liberals would help, 283; freed more by Russia than England, 295; Russian and English policy in, 295, 311, 314, 315

Greek project, the, of 1787, 170

HARCOURT Sir W. on the Berlin treaty, 110; Heirs of Sick Man, 154; Downfall of Turkey, 146; on the Salisbury Evangel, 123

Harold's daughter Gyda marries Vladimir Monomachus, 352

Havelock, Sir Henry, on Bulgarians, 66; on Russian soldiers, 187

Herzegovina, rising in, not originated by Russia, 22

Herald Angel, Lord Salisbury as, 123

Historians, English on Russian side, 293

Holland, should not have been severed from Belgium, 318

Holland, Lord regrets Russia did not take Constantinople, 172

Hungary, Russian intervention in, 296; causes of, 297; approved of by English Conservatives, 297; Mr. Gladstone on, 297; humanity of Russian army in, 297; Lord Beaconsfield on, 297

JEW

IGOR attacks Constantinople, 169 Indemnity or war fine levied on Turks, 52

India, impairs England's strength, 92; not enthusiastically loyal, 92; impossibility of Russian invasion of asserted by Alexander II., 174; proved by Afghan war, 335; danger to from Russia imaginary, 181; splendour of Empire in, 161; Russian advance towards, 324; a conquered Afghanistan no bulwark to, 339; richer than Turkestan, 348; English promises broken in conquest of, 351

Infallibility, Decree of, leads to abolition of Concordat in Austria-Hungary, 274

Internationale, *l'*, supports Nihilists, 254

Ionian Islands occupied to oblige Russia, 356

Ireland, England's Poland, 197; Constitutional safeguards sometimes suspended in, 256; Mr. Froude on English in, 199

Italy, England sympathised with, 117; was as Bulgaria is, 117, 166; liberation partly due to Russia, 307; Austro-German alliance a menace to, 131; constitutional government not working well in, 244

Ivan III., broke power of Tartars, 41

Ivan IV., consulted Zemskie Sobory about Polish War, 231; marriage negotiations of, 352

JEWS support Nihilists, 253; hostile to Christians, 253; Lord Beaconsfield on, as revolutionists, 253; Dr. Sandwith on, 253

Jewish Question, the, 375

Johnstone, Mr. Butler, at Constantinople, 86; on Poland, 203; on Russian progress, 275

KAIRNARDJI, treaty of justified by Anglo-Turkish Convention, 137
Kars, taken thrice by Russia, 50; dominates Asia Minor, 136
Katkoff, Mr., and the *Moscow Gazette*, 125; and Poland, 125; and classical education, 126; and the Slavonic cause, 126; family of, 125
Kaufmann, Gen., in Turkestan, 68; acts with good faith in Afghanistan, 341; his correspondence with Shere Ali, 342; approved by Lord Mayo, only condemned by Lord Lytton, 343
Khiva, the truth about, 325; Sir H. Rawlinson on *casus belli* with, 926; Mr. Forster on, 327; the *Statesman*, 328; Sir Charles Trevelyan, 329; Duke of Argyll, 330; Count Schouvaloff's assurance about, 329
Kiepert, M., the Geographer, 120; Sir George Campbell on the Bulgaria of, note to map, 120
Kinglake, Mr. A. W., describes death of Nich. Kiréeff, 35-8; on Crimean war, 173; on the victims of the Coup d'État, 258; on Russia and the balance of power, 302; on Emperor Nicholas's friendship for England, 354
Kiréeff, Nicholas, first Russian volunteer killed in Servia, 29; effect of his death in Russia, Mr. Aksakoff on, 29; death at Zaitschar described, 36; character of, Dr. Overbeck on, 38; and the Cretan insurrection, 316
Klaczko, M., on Emperor Nicholas, 298; on the Black Sea Treaty, 312
Knout, the, introduced into Russia, 1474, 41; abolished 1862, 184
Kossuth, Louis, on benevolent neutrality, 86; on Austrian annexations, 150

Kotzebue, Count, 67
Koznakoff, Gen., Governor-General of Siberia, 213

LAST Words, Some, 367
Laveleye, M. Emile de, on Russian foreign policy, 317; on Austrians in the Balkan Peninsula, 151; explains cause of Bismarck's visit to Vienna, 291; on Belgium and Holland, 317; thinks Russia does not want a Parliament, 318, but a democratic Slavonic Emperor, 318; on the liberal policy of Alexander I., 318
Layard, Sir Austin, appointment of, 79; opposes treaty of San Stefano, 86
Laybach, Congress of, 313
Lefort, Admiral, 235
Legislative Commission, great, at Moscow, 248
Leontieff, Mr., 125
Leopold, King, on Russian protection of Belgium, 301
Liberals, English, Mr. Gladstone on Eastern policy of, 277; why distrusted in Russia, 284; will support Berlin Treaty, 282; Mr. Courtney on, 283; What will be their policy? 284; more in accord with Russian than English foreign policy, 294; standing motto of 'Friendship with every country,' Mr. Gladstone, 287
Liberals, Russian, accused of Nihilism, 233
Liddon, Canon, 268
Lithuania, Russo-Polish question in, 203
Loftus, Lord Augustus, on Russian enthusiasm in 1876, 16; reports interview with Emperor, 174, 268; with Russian nobleman, 269
Lomonossoff, a peasant, 235
Lowell, J. R., on English neutrality, 83
Lowther, Mr. James, on Anglo-Russian alliance, 293
Lytton, Lord, objects to the Kaufmann Correspondence, 343; and makes war on Afghanistan, 345

MAC

MACEDONIA, re-enslaved, 114; atrocities continuing in, 115, 119; insurrection in, 112; protest from, 119; Mr. Freeman on, 117
MacGahan, Mr., letters read in Russia, 54; on Bulgarians, 64-6; recommends Enos as port for Bulgaria, 159
Macchiavelli on Dictatorship, 227
MacColl, Rev. Malcolm, on Russia and Afghanistan, 344
Manchester Examiner, Correspondent of, on Poland, 198
Martens, Professor, on Afghan war, 278, 285
Martin, Mr. Theodore, 'Historian in Waiting' cited, 308
Marvin, Mr., ' The indiscreet copyist,' 88
Mayo, Lord, on the common mission of England and Russia in Asia, 330; on the Kaufmann Correspondence, 342
Mehemet Ali, England and Russia allied against, 315
Menshikoff began life as a pastrycook, 235
Mérimée, M., on Austrians and Russians in Hungary, 297
Merv, the last slave market in Asia, 328; England and Russia may meet as friends at, 331; England cannot send a large army to, 336
Mezentzoff, Gen., murder of, 257
Michael of Twer, St., martyred by Tartars, 42
Minine, the butcher, 247
Minorca, proposed cession to Russia of, 356
Minsk, the fabled outrage on nuns of, 207
Mirsky, the assassin, 259
Mohammedans in Russia, well treated, 190
Monarchy, Lord Beaconsfield on, 238, 251. See Autocracy.
Monomachus defeats Yaroslaf the Great, 169

NEU

Monomachus, Vladimir, marries Gyda, Harold's daughter, 352
Montenegro, Gen. Tchernayeff proposed to go to, 22, 28; money sent to, 33: not badly treated at San Stefano, 73, 76
Moscow, heart of Russia, 13; differs from St. Petersburg, 13; detests the Protocol, 13; burnt twice by Tartars, 41; attacked by Poles, 199 225, 227, 247; Zemskie Sobory meet at, 246, 247; Great Legislative Commission at, 248; burnt as a sacrifice to European freedom, 302
Moscow Gazette, best exponent of Russian views, 125
Moscow Slavophils in 1848, 297
Münich, Gen., 235
Murray, Mr., English Ambassador at Constantinople, 1772, 80

NAPIER, Lord, and Ettrick, on Anglo-Russian Alliance, 363
Napier, Lord, of Magdala, on England's dangers in India, 92; approves of the Kaufmann Correspondence, 343
Naples, Russia interferes against Carbonari of, 304, 313
Napoleon I. at Tilsit, 171; overthrown by Russia, 303; the invasion of England by, frustrated by Russia, 304
Napoleon III, severity after Coup d' État, 258; meditates annexation of Belgium, 301; frustrated by Russia, 301; Emperor Nicholas and, 306
Navarino, Battle of, 295; jubilee in Russia, 359
Nesselrode, Count, on Russian policy in Turkey, 146; Constantinople, 165; Pacifico case, 314
Neutrality, Earl Granville and Kossuth on benevolent, 86; English in Russo-Turkish war, 77; in 1772, Turkophil ambassador reproved for breach of, 81. See English Neutrality.

Newcastle Chronicle, article on Siberia and Captain Wiggins, 207

Newspapers read in every village in Russia, 54; correspondents of, in English and Russian wars, 61; on character of Russian soldiers, 188; English and '*nous sommes dedans*' 163; on attempt on the Emperor; 252; on Khiva, 328; Nihilist, how published, 254

Nicholas, Emperor, on the Sick Man, 144; Conversations with Sir H. Seymour, 143, 162, 176, 298; and Lord Aberdeen, 146; on the Turk as Gatekeeper of the Bosphorus, 162; on Constantinople, 176; character of, 298; Mr. Klaczko on, 298; horror of Revolution, 299; in Belgium, 299; in Hungary, 297; and the Coup d'Etat, 306; desired peace with England, 354

Nihilism, Russian Liberals accused of, 233

Nihilists attempt life of Emperor, 253; supported by Jews, the *International*, and some Foreign Embassies, 254; Anarchists and Communards, 257; not Constitutionalists or Panslavists, 257; their no-faith, 256; Bakumin's programme, 256; treated with leniency, 257; which they reward by murder, 259; danger of popular massacre of, 259

Nobility in Russia, privileges almost gone, 232

Nordenskjold's, Professor, Walrus Hunter in Siberia, 220

North, Lord, observes a more real neutrality than Lord Beaconsfield, 81

Northbrook, Lord, on the Kaufmann Correspondence with Shere Ali, 343

Northern Echo, Russian correspondence in, 7, 9

OLEG attacks Constantinople, 168
Opium Trade, the, Russian view of, 189

Osborne, Col. on campaigning in Afghanistan, 337

Ottoman Empire, and the Triple Alliance, 3; destroyed by Lord Beaconsfield's policy, 6; death-blow dealt by the Herzegovinese, 22; death-warrant signed by Timour the Tartar, 44: present condition of, 143; Austrian pretensions to succeed to, 150: the rightful heirs of, 159; altered position of, 275; exists, but does not answer the end of its being, 276; projects of partition of, Talleyrand, 132; Greek project, 170; Alexander I., 171; Napoleon I., 172

Overbeck, Dr. J. J., on Nicholas Kiréeff, 38

Oxenstierne and Bulstrode Whitelocke, 263

PACIFICO case, the, England, Russia and Greece, 314

Palmerston, Lord, on Turkey, 142; on Russian occupation of Constantinople, 173; on Pacifico case, 314; on England and Russia, 358

Panslavism, see Slavophils and Slavonic Societies

Panin, M., on Anglo-Russian Alliance, 355

Paris, Treaty of, torn up by Berlin Congress, 109; broken by Anglo-Turkish Convention, 138; Black Sea Clauses, repeal of proposed by Austria, 312

Parliament, English, 'a chatting club,' 244; 'Russia does not need a,' M. de Laveleye, 318. In Russia, see Zemskie Sobory and Constitutionalism.

Party Government, effect on foreign states, 294

Partitions. See Austria, Ottoman Empire, and Poland.

Peel, Sir Robert, and Emperor Nicholas, 146; on civilisation and barbarism in Asia, 324

PET

Peter the Great, builds St. Petersburg, 10, 161; and Prince Jacob Dolgourouki, 195; Cobden on, 229; Conservative objections to, 229; the Reforming Tzar, 230; his work, 230; Poushkin on, 230; spurious will of, 353

Petersburg, St., cosmopolitan, 10; opposed to the war, 11; enthusiasm for Servia at, 16; subscriptions to Slavonic cause at, 32

Pitt, William, proposes war vote against Russia, 1791, 359; concludes Russian alliance, 1795, 359

Plevna, Before the Fall of, 45; reverses before, how received in Russia, 54; Mr. Forbes' account of, circulated in Russia, 63; After, 70

Plutocracy, English Constitution a, 280

Pojarsky, Prince, 247

Poland and Circassia, 196
— anarchic and aristocratic, 199, 225; and Diplomacy, M. de Girardin on, 191; effect of intervention in, 125; at Congress of Vienna, Lord Castlereagh opposes resurrection of, 204; Cobden on, 199; Lord Beaconsfield on, 201; Mr. Butler Johnstone, 203; independence of, what it means, Cobden, 200; M. de Circourt, 206; insurrections in, caused by aristocracy, Lord Beaconsfield, 201; origin of insurrection of 1863, 190, 203, 205; question in dispute not Polish but Lithuanian, 191, 203, 206
— Partition of, the English Foreign Secretary on, 1772, 81; the English Parliament and, 200; Lord Beaconsfield on, 201; Austria's share in, 197; not without provocation, 199, 201, 206, 225, 227, 231, 247; Cobden on, 199; increases happiness of Poles, 198, 199, 202, 205, 206
— — proposed re-establishment of, 1814-5, 203; opposed by England,

RHO

204; under the Treaty of Vienna, 204; constitution granted, 249; Home Rule offered, 1863, 191, 202: refused, 203; demands Lithuania, 191, 203, 206; Russia anxious to do justice to, 206: prosperity of, under Russian rule, 198, 199, 202, 205, 206; religious liberty in, 193, 207, 211

Poles, the, contrasted with Finns, 193; 'the Irish of the Continent,' 197; Lord Beaconsfield denounces, 201; 'worst nation in Europe,' M. de Circourt, 206; numbers of, 205; demand religious supremacy, 193; insurrectionary classes of, 202, 205; millions said to be in Siberia, 209.; Germanised in Posen, 225; hold high commands in Russian army, 236

Poltava, Battle of, Peter the Great at, 235

Potemkin, Prince, on Anglo-Russian alliance, 355

Prejudices, Some English, 181; national, 189; origin of, 182. See Prejudices

Press, complete liberty of the, desired in Russia, 243; Lord Beaconsfield on, 251. See Newspapers

Prestige, Mr. Carlyle on, 264

Protocol, detested in Moscow, 13; rejection due to Lord Derby, 14

RAMBAUD'S History of Russia, 132, 249, 304

Rawlinson, Sir Henry, on Russia's advance in Central Asia, 325; on Russia's *casus belli* against Khiva, 326

Republics in Russia before Tartar conquest, 41

Representative Government. See Constitutionalism and Zemskie Sobory.

Rhodope, the, insurrection in, fomented by Englishmen, 85; fables of atrocities in, 187, 188

Index. 393

RIE

Rieger, Dr., Bohemian Panslavist, on Slavonic sympathy with Russia, 130
Rochford, Lord, English Foreign Minister in 1772, 81
Roman Catholics not persecuted in Poland, 193, 211
Romanoff, dynasty sprang from popular election, 247; Michel, and the Zemskie Sobory, 247
Rome, the old and the new, 167; church of, opposed by England and Russia, 364
Roumania not dissatisfied with Dobrudscha, 49, 74; cession of Bessarabia by, 74; liberated by Russia, 288, 295; union of, supported by Russia, 311
Roumelia, Eastern, not co-extensive with Southern Bulgaria, 101, 115; area and population, 114; a vexatious absurdity, 158; constitution of, might be adopted further south, 158
Rurik, and successors divide Russia, 226
Russia and Afghan War, 332. See Afghan War
Russia, and Austria, 130, 132, 150, 165, 167, 297, 309, 312; Belgium, 299, 301; Bulgaria, 76, 100, 112, 155, 267, 288, 295, 311; Circassia, 208; Constantinople, 160, 174, 241, 291; Finland, 192, 193; France, 129, 291, 304, 306; Germany, 127, 288, 291, 304, 313; Greece, 76, 288, 295, 311; Hungary, 296, 314; Italy, 288, 307; Khiva, 325; Montenegro, 73, 316; Naples, 304, 313; Poland, 192, 196, 199, 204, 249; Roumania, 49, 74, 288, 295, 311; Servia, 34, 288, 295; Spain, 304, 313; Sweden, 192; Tartars, 40, 226; Turkey, 40, 107, 144, 170, 296, 310, 314
Russia and England, parallels and contrasts between, in Azoff and Cyprus, 248; Circassia and Afghanistan, 208; Finland and Wales, 192;

RUS

Khiva and Ashantee, 349; Poland and Ireland, 197; Servia and the Netherlands, 18; Siberia and New South Wales, 210; Turkestan and India, 323, 348; Turkish protectorates of, 137, 311, 314; aggression, 322; annexations, 333; broken pledges, 324; capital punishment, 184; cat and knout, 184; censorship, 92; civilising mission, 362; conquest, 323; constitution, 236, 244; convict system, 215; corporal punishment, 184; war correspondents, 61; corruption and favouritism, 66; the coup d'état, 306; European concert, 138, 140; Imperial powers, 338; liberation of the oppressed, 266; neutrality, 77; Napoleonic wars, 302; religion, 364; slavery and the slave trade, 365; San Stefano and Cyprus, 138; General Tchernayeff and Sir Philip Sydney, 84; treaties annulled, 107, 137; foreign policy of, 290; in America, 307; Austria, 309, 315; Belgium, 296, 315; Bulgaria, 295, 311; Cracow, 312, 314; Crete, 316; France, 302; Germany, 304, 315–6; Greece, 255, 311, 314, 315; Hungary, 296; Lebanon, 315; Italy, 288, 307; Montenegro, 316; Naples, 304, 306, 316; Poland, 204; Roumania, 295, 311, 315; Schleswig Holstein, 315; Servia, 295, 315, 316; Spain, 304, 313; Turkey, 266, 296, 310, 314, 315, 316
Russia, anarchy, early, of, 226; autocracy, saved by, 228; and the Black Sea, 312; Mr. Carlyle on, 293
— Constitutionalism in, 239
— democracy of, 232; an empire of villages, 228
— and English Parties, 277
— Foreign Policy of, a Reply to Mr. Gladstone, 290
— Lord Aberdeen on, 306; Mr. Gladstone on, 296; 'Friends or Foes' of,

RUS

285; historic mission of, 56, 60, 293; inured to ingratitude, 291; as a liberating power, 267, 288, 310; prejudices against, 181; progress of, since 1854, Mr Butler Johnstone, 275

Russia, Traditional Policy of, 352
— saved Europe from Tartars, 43; Tartar conquest of, 43, 226; treaty of Kaïrnardji, 137; of Paris, 107, 137; of Berlin, 107, 283; vicissitudes of, 227

Russian 'agents,' 145; 'aggression an exploded illusion,' Mr. Cowen, 176
— Aggression, 321
— Autocracy, 223
— concessions during the war, 73, 264; at the Congress, 102; constitutionalism, 239; corruption, 65; democracy, 232; disasters during war, 52; generals, 68; intrigue, 325; language difficult to learn, 209; nationality, 'sin of forsaking,' 55; nobility, 232
— the, Government, opposed to war, 6, 11; pacific efforts paralysed by England, 6; policy of, in the East, 1876, 5, 174; blamed by Russians for being too pacific, 7, 58, 73, 103; true to all its obligations, 25; opposed to volunteering for Servia, 11, 84; withholds information about the war, 54; 'exiles' Mr. Aksakoff, for denouncing Berlin Treaty, 106; official view of Berlin Treaty, 107; proposes Austrian occupation of Bosnia and naval demonstration at Constantinople, 174
— the, People, enthusiasm for the war in 1876, 7, 13, 29, 31, 46, 47, 54, 100, 194, 246; attested by Lord Augustus Loftus, 16; by 'a retired Cossack,' 17; by Mr. Wallace, 17; and by Dr. Sandwith, 287; apathetic in 1875, 23; poor more enthusiastic than rich, 32; popular hatred of Turks, 29; its cause, 40;

RUS

volunteering for Servia, 29, 56; in opposition to the Government, 11, 84; 'Two Russias,' 11; difference not understood in Servia, 34; 'in debt to the Servians,' 34; speeches of Mr. Aksakoff, 24, 52, 98; shrink from no disaster, 46, 47, 54; women, enthusiasm of, 47; educated classes less enthusiastic, 55; fight for 'peace, liberty, and fraternal equality,' 57; suffering caused by war, 52, 75; condemned concessions to England, 73; not alarmed at English menaces, 92, 105; humiliated at Berlin, 104; popular view of the cause and objects of the war, 100; would rather fight than consent to divide Bulgaria, 105; ready to surrender everything to completely liberate the Christians, 194; disappointed that peace was not made in Constantinople, 241; estranged from England, 280; would welcome alliance with, 269, 370; sceptical about England's sympathies with the Christians, 282; support autocracy, 232; restore it, 233, 246
— Soldiers, character of, Colonel Brackenbury, 47; Mr. Aksakoff, 53; Mr. Forbes, 63; Sir Henry Havelock, 187; humanity of, in Hungary, 297

Russians, the, Sir George Campbell on, 156; are reluctant to notice libels, 129, 185, 224
— in Central Asia, 346; cause of their advance, 347; Mr. Gladstone on, 323, 347; Duke of Argyll, 324; Sir Henry Rawlinson, 325; Vambéry, 349; Mr. Schuyler, 349; Turkestan not profitable to, 323, 348; civilising mission of, 323; suppress slave trade, 350; Protectionists, 350; Lord Mayo on, 330; Professor Monier Williams, 339. See Afghanistan, Khiva, Turkestan.

Russias, the Two, Moscow and St. Petersburg, 8; difference between

RUS

national and official not understood in Servia, 34

Russophobia, origin of, ignorance, 182; foreign misrepresentations, 182; some absurdities and inconsistencies of, 88; a national delirium, 292; Mr. Carlyle on, 293

Russophobists, Sir Henry Layard, 79; Mr. Murray, 1772, 80; Mr. Cowen, 176; Louis Kossuth, 150; Mr. Butler Johnstone, 275; Sir Henry Rawlinson, 325; M. Vambéry, 349

Russo-Turkish War, the, national not imperial, humanitarian not predatory, 3, 6, 14, 21, 23, 29, 34, 38, 46, 55, 79, 100; Russian Government endeavoured to avert, 6, 58; efforts paralysed by English Government, 6; popular in Moscow not in St. Petersburg, 11, 55; 'the most heroic war in the world,' Mr. Aksakoff, 54; denounced by the educated classes, 55; made by the people through the Slavonic Societies, 20, 55; Mr. Aksakoff on the cause and objects of, 100; Mr. Kinglake on origin of, 35; Dr. Overbeck on, 38; not a gladiator's but a liberator's war, 46; ennobling effect of, 47; expected to be over by July, 1877, 51; sacrifices entailed by, 51, 57, 205, 268; no compensation possible for losses caused by, 52; necessary to Russia's development, 57; 'a high moral duty,' 57; reverses in, Mr. Aksakoff on, 52; its limitation denounced, 59

SAGHALIEN, only 400 convicts sent to, 258

Salisbury, Lord, on large maps, 18; 'Elizabethan policy,' 18; circular of, how regarded in Russia, 75; annuls it by secret agreement, 88; as Herald Angel, 123, 291; Manchester speech of, 123; *Journal de St. Petersbourg* on, 124; Russian opinion on, 125; defied by the Turks, 126; disco-

SER

vers Germany, 127; styled 'the veracious,' 127; pre-occupied in 1876 with 'creating pretexts' for Afghan war, 181; deceives those who confided in the Circular of, 266; supported by Russia at Constantinople, 281; ingratitude of, 291; on going to war against nightmare, 336; on a forward policy in Asia, 336

Salonica, probable free port, 159

Sandwich, Dr., on Jews in the East, 253; on Russian enthusiasm, 287

Schamyl and Shere Ali, 208

Schleswig-Holstein, Anglo-Russian action in, 315

Schouvaloff, Count, the secret agreement with, 88; his unlucky French phrase '*nous sommes dedans*,' 163; and Khiva, 329

Scotchmen in Russian service, 235

Schuyler, Mr., on Russians in Central Asia, 349

Secret societies, Duke of Argyll on, 19; Lord Beaconsfield on, 20, 25; Slavonic societies not secret, 20

Sepoys, effect of bringing to Malta, on Russia, 93, 105

Serfdom unknown before Tartar conquest, 41; Polish origin of, 206

Serfs, emancipation of, political consequences of, 27; freed by Alexander II., 230, 288; Mr. Gladstone on, 230

Servia, sufferings of, by war, 34; Russia indebted to, 34; railway to Salonica, 159; projected annexation by Austria, 1787, 170; liberated by Russia, 288, 295

Servian volunteers, Russian volunteering objected to at St. Petersburg, 11, 84; Lord Augustus Loftus on, 16; compared to English in Netherlands, 18; number 4,000, 23; Mr. Aksakoff on, 29, 56; Nicholas Kiréeff, first volunteer killed, 29, 38; movement not due to Mr. Gladstone's pamphlet, 39; Mr. Gladstone's tribute to, 285

SER

Servian war not made by secret societies, 20, 25
Seymour, Sir Hamilton, conversations with, 144, 162, 176, 298
Shere Ali, General Kaufmann's Correspondence with, 342; Russia not bound to defend, 345
Siberia, 209; misconceptions about, 211; and English convict settlements, 213; number exiled since 1800, 211; since 1860, 215; area of, 212, 219, 221; why convicts sent to, 212; mines of, comparatively few exiles in, 212; miners happy, 218; three-fourths not convicts, 220; defect of, too much freedom and leniency, 213, 215; ceasing to be a punishment, 220; Governor General Koznakoff on, 225; soil and climate, Herbert Barry on, 214, 258; Captain Wiggins, 217; the *Standard*, 219, 221; political offenders, 216; quicksilver mines substitute for death penalty, 216; Polish falsehoods concerning, 207, 216, 219; infinitely richer than Canada, 219; a vast market, 221; river system of, 221; Mr. Seebohm on, 221
Sick Man, Heirs of, 142; Emperor Nicholas on, 144; Lord Palmerston, 142
— Woman, the, of Europe, 133
Silistria, defeat of Russians at, in 972, 169
Slavery and the slave trade, England and Russia crusaders against, 328; in Turkey, 350
Slavism, democratic, 320
Slavonic societies not secret, 20; made the Russo-Turkish war, 20, 55; charitable, 21, 28; did not originate rising in the Herzegovina, 22; Mr. Aksakoff on, 24; not prepared for work thrust on them, 26; first steps in 1875, 28; operations of, 28; spontaneous and universal spread of, 30; supported chiefly by

STO

the poor, 32; money raised by, 32; how spent, 33; denounced by educated and official classes, 55
Slavophils, Moscow, in 1848, 297
Slavs, protect Europe from Asia, 43; Russia's mission to, 57; Austria-Hungary unjust to, 58; Russia, chief representative of, 103; Austrian sympathies with Russia, 130; form a majority of subjects of Francis Joseph, 130; 'Slav countries belong to Slavs,' 149; Kossuth on, 150; will dominate the future of Austria, 152, 309; must *fare da se*, 153; anarchy, the besetting sin of, 225; only Slav country free, independent and strong, 231; 'stand on the threshold of the morning,' 289; of Hungary protected but not recognised by Russia in 1848, 297
Smith, Mr. W. H., on friendship with Russia, 292
Somerset, Duke of, on representative government, 238
Spain, Russian policy in, 1822, 304; M. Thiers on French intervention in, 305
Speranski, 335
Standard, the, on Siberia, 219
Statesman, the, on origin of Russophobia, 182; on Khiva, 328
Status quo, in Turkey in 1876, internal and external incompatible, 5
Stefano, San, Treaty of, excites displeasure in Russia, 73; a humble half measure, 90; loyally submitted to Congress, 138; on the boundaries of Bulgaria, 158; three-fourths re-enacted at Berlin, 283; communicated to England, 360
Stein on Alexander I., 303
Stephen, Sir J. Fitzjames, approved of the Kaufmann Correspondence, 343
Stillman, Mr. W. J., *Times* correspondent in the Herzegovina, 22; on Austria-Hungary, 151
Stockmar, Baron, on diplomatists,

STO

12; on Russian policy in Belgium, 299
Stoletoff's Mission at Cabul, 339. See Afghan War.
Suez Canal, discrowns Constantinople, 161
Sviatoslaf crushes Bulgaria, and is defeated by Zimisces, 169
Swedes, bad rulers of Finland, 192; at Novgorod the Great, 228

TALLEYRAND proposes Austrian annexation of Northern Turkey, 132
Tartar conquest of Russia, 40, 226; its duration, 40; nature, 42; results, 43, 227
Tartars burn Moscow twice, 42, 227; St. Louis of France on, 42; Russia saved Europe from, 43; justify the autocracy, 227
Tcherkassky, Prince, Mr. Aksakoff on, 98
Tchernayeff, Gen., volunteers to go to Montenegro, 22, 28; goes to Servia, 28; assisted by Slavonic Society, 29, 33; not employed in Turkish war, 57, 69; resembles Sir Philip Sydney more than Hobart Pasha, 81; his opinion of Bulgarians, 157
Tennyson, Mr., and the knout, 182
Thiers, M., on Austria and Rome, 166; on centralisation in France, 237; on French intervention in Spain, 1822, 305
Tilsit, negotiations and treaty of, 172
Times, the, Mr. Stillman, correspondent of, in the Herzegovina, 22; Mr. Wallace at St. Petersburg, 8; a weathercock, 125; publishes letters from Moscow in 1876, 186; derides Russian suspicion of Nihilistic intrigue in Foreign Embassies, 254
Timour the Tartar signs death-warrant of Turkey, 44

TUR

Tocqueville, De, on the moral element in submission to despotism, 224; on centralising instinct of democracy, 232
Todleben, Gen., why not employed earlier in the war, 68
Traditional policy of England, 272; was Russian, 272, 354; needs revision, 276
Traditional policy of Russia, 352. See Anglo-Russian Alliance.
Treaties of Berlin, 95, 99, 107; Kairnardji, 137; Paris, 109, 138, 312; Vienna, 204, 318; Villafranca, 117
Treaty obligations, Russia and English Liberals on, 283
Trevelyan, Sir Charles, on England and Russia, 270; on Khiva, 329
Triple Alliance, the, and the East, 3; decease of, not lamented by Russia, 129
Turkish-Anglo Convention, 134. See Anglo-Turkish Convention.
Turkey, Russian policy in 1876, maintains *status quo* plus tributary states, 5; future policy in, 107; Russia desires no annexations, 145; seeks European concert, 148; and territorial integrity of, 149; regards Turkey as good gatekeeper of Bosphorus, 162; supported Turkey in 1833 and 1840, 164; liberating mission of Russia in, approved by English Liberals, 295, 310
Turkish alliance with England, Mr. Aksakoff on, 58; denounced by Burke, 272; Lord Holland, 272; Fox, 357; Boris Godounoff on, 295, 354; comparatively recent, 272
Turks insult Lord Salisbury, 126; defy Europe and civilisation, 275. See Russo-Turkish War.
Turkestan, a questionable paradise, 68; not profitable, 323, 348; Russia's civilising mission in, 323; Mr. Gladstone on, 323; more like African settlements than Indian Empire, 349. See Russians in Central Asia.

TZA

Tzar. See Autocracy and Alexander II.

Tzargrad, name of Constantinople, 167

VAMBÉRY, M., on Russian rule in Bokhara, 349

Variags, or Varangians, expeditions against Byzantium, 169; summoned by Russians, 226

Venice, possessions in East in 1787, 170

Verona, Congress of, 313

Vienna, Congress of, Poland at, 204; adds Belgium to Holland, 318

Vikings, early Russian monarchs, 168

Villafranca, Treaty of, destroyed by aspirations of nationality, 117

Villages, Russia an empire of, 228

Vitkevitch on Afghanistan, 339

Vladimir Monomachus married daughter of Harold, 352

Volunteers, Russian, in Servia. See Servian Volunteers.

Volunteers, English in Netherlands, 19; in Turkey, 75, 83

WALLACE, Mr. D. M., *Times* correspondent at St. Petersburg, 8; on Russian enthusiasm for war, 17; Mr. Aksakoff, 24; Russian autocracy, 223

War correspondents, advantages of, 54; in Russia and England, 61;

ZIM

their testimony concerning Russia, 187

War vote, the, of six millions, 75, 359

Wellington, Duke of, on European concert in Turkey, 147; regrets Constantinople was not entered by Russia, 172; on Poland, 204; anecdote of, 274

Whitelocke, Bulstrode, ambassador to Sweden, 263

Wiggins, Captain, on Siberia, 217

Williams, Professor Monier, on England and Russia in Asia, 338

Wingfield, Sir Charles, on England's Afghan policy, 337

Worontzoff, Prince, advocates Anglo-Russian alliance, 355

YAROSLAF the Great defeated by Monomachus, 169

ZEMSKIE Sobory, nature of, 231; consulted by Ivan IV., 231; offer crown to Boris Godounoff, 232; re-establishment desired, 243; meaning of, 244; objected to by some officials, 245, 247; suppress oligarchy and restore autocracy, 246; founded Romanoff dynasty, 247; consulted by Michel Romanoff, on Polish war, 247; on annexation of Azoff, 248

Zimisces, John, defeats Sviatoslaf, 169

39 Paternoster Row, E.C.
London, *April* 1881.

GENERAL LISTS OF WORKS

PUBLISHED BY

Messrs. Longmans, Green & Co.

HISTORY, POLITICS, HISTORICAL MEMOIRS, &c.

History of England from the Conclusion of the Great War in 1815. By Spencer Walpole. 8vo. Vols. I. & II. 1815-1832 (Second Edition, revised) price 36*s*. Vol. III. 1832-1841, price 18*s*.

History of England in the 18th Century. By W. E. H. Lecky, M.A. Vols. I. & II. 1700-1760. Second Edition. 2 vols. 8vo. 36*s*.

The History of England from the Accession of James II. By the Right Hon. Lord Macaulay.
Student's Edition, 2 vols. cr. 8vo. 12*s*.
People's Edition, 4 vols. cr. 8vo. 16*s*.
Cabinet Edition, 8 vols. post 8vo. 48*s*.
Library Edition, 5 vols. 8vo. £4.

Lord Macaulay's Works. Complete and uniform Library Edition. Edited by his Sister, Lady Trevelyan. 8 vols. 8vo. with Portrait, £5. 5*s*.

Critical and Historical Essays contributed to the Edinburgh Review. By the Right Hon. Lord Macaulay.
Cheap Edition, crown 8vo. 3*s*. 6*d*.
Student's Edition, crown 8vo. 6*s*.
People's Edition, 2 vols. crown 8vo. 8*s*.
Cabinet Edition, 4 vols. 24*s*.
Library Edition, 3 vols. 8vo. 36*s*.

The History of England from the Fall of Wolsey to the Defeat of the Spanish Armada. By J. A. Froude, M.A.
Popular Edition, 12 vols. crown, £2. 2*s*.
Cabinet Edition, 12 vols. crown, £3. 12*s*.

The English in Ireland in the Eighteenth Century. By J. A. Froude, M.A. 3 vols. crown 8vo. 18*s*.

Journal of the Reigns of King George IV. and King William IV. By the late C. C. F. Greville, Esq. Edited by H. Reeve, Esq. Fifth Edition. 3 vols. 8vo. price 36*s*.

The Life of Napoleon III. derived from State Records, Unpublished Family Correspondence, and Personal Testimony. By Blanchard Jerrold. In Four Volumes, 8vo. with numerous Portraits and Facsimiles. Vols. I. to III. price 18*s*. each.

Russia Before and After the War. By the Author of 'Society in St. Petersburg' &c. Translated from the German (with later Additions by the Author) by Edward Fairfax Taylor. Second Edition. 8vo. 14*s*.

Russia and England from 1876 to 1880; a Protest and an Appeal. By O. K. Author of 'Is Russia Wrong?' With a Preface by J. A. Froude, M.A. Portrait and Maps. 8vo. 14*s*.

A

The Early History of Charles James Fox. By GEORGE OTTO TREVELYAN, M.P. Third Edition. 8vo. 18s.

The Constitutional History of England since the Accession of George III. 1760-1870. By Sir THOMAS ERSKINE MAY, K.C.B. D.C.L. Sixth Edition. 3 vols. crown 8vo. 18s.

Democracy in Europe; a History. By Sir THOMAS ERSKINE MAY, K.C.B. D.C.L. 2 vols. 8vo. 32s.

Introductory Lectures on Modern History delivered in 1841 and 1842. By the late THOMAS ARNOLD, D.D. 8vo. 7s. 6d.

On Parliamentary Government in England. By ALPHEUS TODD. 2 vols. 8vo. 37s.

Parliamentary Government in the British Colonies. By ALPHEUS TODD. 8vo. 21s.

History of Civilisation in England and France, Spain and Scotland. By HENRY THOMAS BUCKLE. 3 vols. crown 8vo. 24s.

Lectures on the History of England from the Earliest Times to the Death of King Edward II. By W. LONGMAN, F.S.A. Maps and Illustrations. 8vo. 15s.

History of the Life & Times of Edward III. By W. LONGMAN, F.S.A. With 9 Maps, 8 Plates, and 16 Woodcuts. 2 vols. 8vo. 28s.

The Historical Geography of Europe. By EDWARD A. FREEMAN, D.C.L. LL.D. With 65 Maps. 2 vols. 8vo. 31s. 6d.

History of England under the Duke of Buckingham and Charles I. 1624-1628. By S. R. GARDINER. 2 vols. 8vo. Maps, 24s.

The Personal Government of Charles I. from the Death of Buckingham to the Declaration in favour of Ship Money, 1628-1637. By S. R. GARDINER. 2 vols. 8vo. 24s.

Memorials of the Civil War between King Charles I. and the Parliament of England as it affected Herefordshire and the Adjacent Counties. By the Rev. J. WEBB, M.A. Edited and completed by the Rev. T. W. WEBB, M.A. 2 vols. 8vo. Illustrations, 42s.

Popular History of France, from the Earliest Times to the Death of Louis XIV. By Miss SEWELL. Crown 8vo. Maps, 7s. 6d.

A Student's Manual of the History of India from the Earliest Period to the Present. By Col. MEADOWS TAYLOR, M.R.A.S. Third Thousand. Crown 8vo. Maps, 7s. 6d.

Lord Minto in India; Correspondence of the First Earl of Minto, while Governor-General of India, from 1807 to 1814. Edited by his Great-Niece, the COUNTESS of MINTO. Post 8vo. Maps, 12s.

Waterloo Lectures; a Study of the Campaign of 1815. By Col. C. C. CHESNEY, R.E. 8vo. 10s. 6d.

The Oxford Reformers— John Colet, Erasmus, and Thomas More; a History of their Fellow-Work. By F. SEEBOHM. 8vo. 14s.

History of the Romans under the Empire. By Dean MERIVALE, D.D. 8 vols. post 8vo. 48s.

General History of Rome from B.C. 753 to A.D. 476. By Dean MERIVALE, D.D. Crown 8vo. Maps, price 7s. 6d.

The Fall of the Roman Republic; a Short History of the Last Century of the Commonwealth. By Dean MERIVALE, D.D. 12mo. 7s. 6d.

The History of Rome. By WILHELM IHNE. VOLS. I. to III. 8vo. price 45s.

Carthage and the Carthaginians. By R. BOSWORTH SMITH, M.A. Second Edition. Maps, Plans, &c. Crown 8vo. 10s. 6d.

History of Ancient Egypt. By G. RAWLINSON, M.A. With Map and numerous Illustrations. 2 vols. 8vo. price 63s.

The Seventh Great Oriental Monarchy; or, a History of the Sassanians. By G. RAWLINSON, M.A. With Map and 95 Illustrations. 8vo. 28s.

The History of European Morals from Augustus to Charlemagne. By W. E. H. LECKY, M.A. 2 vols. crown 8vo. 16s.

History of the Rise and Influence of the Spirit of Rationalism in Europe. By W. E. H. LECKY, M.A. 2 vols. crown 8vo. 16s.

The History of Philosophy, from Thales to Comte. By GEORGE HENRY LEWES. Fifth Edition. 2 vols. 8vo. 32s.

A History of Classical Greek Literature. By the Rev. J. P. P. MAHAFFY, M.A. Crown 8vo. VOL. I. Poets, 7s. 6d. VOL. II. Prose Writers, 7s. 6d.

Zeller's Stoics, Epicureans, and Sceptics. Translated by the Rev. O. J. REICHEL, M.A. New Edition revised. Crown 8vo. 15s.

Zeller's Socrates & the Socratic Schools. Translated by the Rev. O. J. REICHEL, M.A. Second Edition. Crown 8vo. 10s. 6d.

Zeller's Plato & the Older Academy. Translated by S. FRANCES ALLEYNE and ALFRED GOODWIN, B.A. Crown 8vo. 18s.

Zeller's Pre-Socratic Schools; a History of Greek Philosophy from the Earliest Period to the time of Socrates. Translated by SARAH F. ALLEYNE. 2 vols. crown 8vo. 30s.

Zeller's Aristotle and the Elder Peripatetics. Translated by B. F. C. COSTELLOE, Balliol College, Oxford. Crown 8vo. [*In preparation.*

⁎⁎* The above volume will complete the Authorised English Translation of Dr. ZELLER'S Work on the Philosophy of the Greeks.

Epochs of Modern History. Edited by C. COLBECK, M.A.
Church's Beginning of the Middle Ages, 2s. 6d.
Cox's Crusades, 2s. 6d.
Creighton's Age of Elizabeth, 2s. 6d.
Gairdner's Houses of Lancaster and York, 2s. 6d.
Gardiner's Puritan Revolution, 2s. 6d.
———— Thirty Years' War, 2s. 6d.
Hale's Fall of the Stuarts, 2s. 6d.
Johnson's Normans in Europe, 2s. 6d.
Longman's Frederic the Great and the Seven Years' War, 2s. 6d.
Ludlow's War of American Independence, 2s. 6d.
Morris's Age of Anne, 2s. 6d.
Seebohm's Protestant Revolution, 2/6.
Stubbs's Early Plantagenets, 2s. 6d.
Warburton's Edward III. 2s. 6d.

Epochs of Ancient History. Edited by the Rev. Sir G. W. COX, Bart. M.A. & C. SANKEY, M.A.
Beesly's Gracchi, Marius & Sulla, 2s. 6d.
Capes's Age of the Antonines, 2s. 6d.
———— Early Roman Empire, 2s. 6d.
Cox's Athenian Empire, 2s. 6d.
———— Greeks & Persians, 2s. 6d.
Curteis's Macedonian Empire, 2s. 6d.
Ihne's Rome to its Capture by the Gauls, 2s. 6d.
Merivale's Roman Triumvirates, 2s. 6d.
Sankey's Spartan & Theban Supremacies, 2s. 6d.
Smith's Rome and Carthage, the Punic Wars, 2s. 6d.

Creighton's Shilling History of England, introductory to 'Epochs of English History.' Fcp. 1s.

Epochs of English History. Edited by the Rev. MANDELL CREIGHTON, M.A. Fcp. 8vo. 5s.
Browning's Modern England, 1820-1874, 9d.
Cordery's Struggle against Absolute Monarchy, 1603-1688, 9d.
Creighton's (Mrs.) England a Continental Power, 1066-1216, 9d.
Creighton's (Rev. M.) Tudors and the Reformation, 1485-1603, 9d.
Rowley's Rise of the People, 1215-1485, price 9d.
Rowley's Settlement of the Constitution, 1688-1778, 9d.
Tancock's England during the American & European Wars, 1778-1820, 9d.
York-Powell's Early England to the Conquest, 1s.

The Student's Manual of Ancient History; the Political History, Geography and Social State of the Principal Nations of Antiquity. By W. COOKE TAYLOR, LL.D. Cr. 8vo. 7s. 6d.

The Student's Manual of Modern History; the Rise and Progress of the Principal European Nations. By W. COOKE TAYLOR, LL.D. Crown 8vo. 7s. 6d.

BIOGRAPHICAL WORKS.

Reminiscences. By THOMAS CARLYLE. Edited by JAMES ANTHONY FROUDE, M.A. formerly Fellow of Exeter College, Oxford. 2 vols. crown 8vo. 18s.

Autobiography. By JOHN STUART MILL. 8vo. 7s. 6d.

Felix Mendelssohn's Letters, translated by Lady WALLACE. 2 vols. crown 8vo. 5s. each.

Memoirs of the Life of Anna Jameson, Author of 'Sacred and Legendary Art' &c. By her Niece, G. MACPHERSON. 8vo. Portrait, 12s. 6d.

The Life and Letters of Lord Macaulay. By his Nephew, G. OTTO TREVELYAN, M.P.
CABINET EDITION, 2 vols. crown 8vo. 12s.
LIBRARY EDITION, 2 vols. 8vo. 36s.

William Law, Nonjuror and Mystic, Author of 'A Serious Call to a Devout and Holy Life' &c. a Sketch of his Life, Character, and Opinions. By J. H. OVERTON, M.A. Vicar of Legbourne. 8vo. 15s.

The Missionary Secretariat of Henry Venn, B.D. Prebendary of St. Paul's, and Hon. Sec. of the Church Missionary Society. By the Rev. W. KNIGHT, M.A. With Additions by Mr. Venn's Two Sons, and a Portrait. 8vo. 18s.

A Dictionary of General Biography. By W. L. R. CATES. Third Edition, revised throughout and completed to the Present Time; with new matter equal to One Hundred pages, comprising nearly Four Hundred Memoirs and Notices of Persons recently deceased. 8vo. 28s.

Apologia pro Vitâ Suâ; Being a History of his Religious Opinions by JOHN HENRY NEWMAN, D.D. Crown 8vo. 6s.

Biographical Studies. By the late WALTER BAGEHOT, M.A. Fellow of University College, London. Uniform with 'Literary Studies' and 'Economic Studies' by the same Author. 8vo. 12s.

Leaders of Public Opinion in Ireland; Swift, Flood, Grattan, O'Connell. By W. E. H. LECKY, M.A. Crown 8vo. 7s. 6d.

Essays in Ecclesiastical Biography. By the Right Hon. Sir J. STEPHEN, LL.D. Crown 8vo. 7s. 6d.

Cæsar; a Sketch. By JAMES ANTHONY FROUDE, M.A. formerly Fellow of Exeter College, Oxford. With Portrait and Map. 8vo. 16s.

Life of the Duke of Wellington. By the Rev. G. R. GLEIG, M.A. Crown 8vo. Portrait, 6s.

Memoirs of Sir Henry Havelock, K.C.B. By JOHN CLARK MARSHMAN. Crown 8vo. 3s. 6d.

Vicissitudes of Families. By Sir BERNARD BURKE, C.B. Two vols. crown 8vo. 21s.

Maunder's Treasury of Biography, reconstructed and in great part re-written, with above 1,600 additional Memoirs by W. L. R. CATES. Fcp. 8vo. 6s.

MENTAL and POLITICAL PHILOSOPHY.

Comte's System of Positive Polity, or Treatise upon Sociology. By various Translators. 4 vols. 8vo. £4.

De Tocqueville's Democracy in America, translated by H. REEVE. 2 vols. crown 8vo. 16s.

Analysis of the Phenomena of the Human Mind. By JAMES MILL. With Notes, Illustrative and Critical. 2 vols. 8vo. 28s.

On Representative Government. By JOHN STUART MILL. Crown 8vo. 2s.

On Liberty. By JOHN STUART MILL. Post 8vo. 7s. 6d. crown 8vo. 1s. 4d.

Principles of Political Economy. By JOHN STUART MILL. 2 vols. 8vo. 30s. or 1 vol. crown 8vo. 5s.

Essays on some Unsettled Questions of Political Economy. By JOHN STUART MILL. 8vo. 6s. 6d.

Utilitarianism. By JOHN STUART MILL. 8vo. 5s.

The Subjection of Women. By JOHN STUART MILL. Fourth Edition. Crown 8vo. 6s.

Examination of Sir William Hamilton's Philosophy. By JOHN STUART MILL. 8vo. 16s.

A System of Logic, Ratiocinative and Inductive. By JOHN STUART MILL. 2 vols. 8vo. 25s.

Dissertations and Discussions. By JOHN STUART MILL. 4 vols. 8vo. £2. 7s.

The A B C of Philosophy; a Text-Book for Students. By the Rev. T. GRIFFITH, M.A. Prebendary of St. Paul's. Crown 8vo. 5s.

A Systematic View of the Science of Jurisprudence. By SHELDON AMOS, M.A. 8vo. 18s.

Path and Goal; a Discussion on the Elements of Civilisation and the Conditions of Happiness. By M. M. KALISCH, Ph.D. M.A. 8vo. price 12s. 6d.

The Law of Nations considered as Independent Political Communities. By Sir TRAVERS TWISS, D.C.L. 2 vols. 8vo. £1. 13s.

A Primer of the English Constitution and Government. By S. AMOS, M.A. Crown 8vo. 6s.

Fifty Years of the English Constitution, 1830-1880. By SHELDON AMOS, M.A. Crown 8vo. 10s. 6d.

Principles of Economical Philosophy. By H. D. MACLEOD, M.A. Second Edition, in 2 vols. VOL. I. 8vo. 15s. VOL. II. PART 1. 12s.

Lord Bacon's Works, collected & edited by R. L. ELLIS, M.A. J. SPEDDING, M.A. and D. D. HEATH. 7 vols. 8vo. £3. 13s. 6d.

Letters and Life of Francis Bacon, including all his Occasional Works. Collected and edited, with a Commentary, by J. SPEDDING. 7 vols. 8vo. £4. 4s.

The Institutes of Justinian; with English Introduction, Translation, and Notes. By T. C. SANDARS, M.A. 8vo. 18s.

The Nicomachean Ethics of Aristotle, translated into English by R. WILLIAMS, B.A. Crown 8vo. price 7s. 6d.

Aristotle's Politics, Books I. III. IV. (VII.) Greek Text, with an English Translation by W. E. BOLLAND, M.A. and Short Essays by A. LANG, M.A. Crown 8vo. 7s. 6d.

The Politics of Aristotle; Greek Text, with English Notes. By RICHARD CONGREVE, M.A. 8vo. 18s.

The Ethics of Aristotle; with Essays and Notes. By Sir A. GRANT, Bart. LL.D. 2 vols. 8vo. 32s.

Bacon's Essays, with Annotations. By R. WHATELY, D.D. 8vo. 10s. 6d.

An Introduction to Logic. By WILLIAM H. STANLEY MONCK, M.A. Professor of Moral Philosophy in the University of Dublin. Crown 8vo. price 5s.

Picture Logic; an Attempt to Popularise the Science of Reasoning. By A. SWINBOURNE, B.A. Post 8vo. 5s.

Elements of Logic. By R. WHATELY, D.D. 8vo. 10s. 6d. Crown 8vo. 4s. 6d.

Elements of Rhetoric. By R. WHATELY, D.D. 8vo. 10s. 6d. Crown 8vo. 4s. 6d.

The Senses and the Intellect. By A. BAIN, LL.D. 8vo. 15s.

The Veil of Isis, or Idealism. By THOMAS E. WEBB, LL.D. Q.C. Regius Professor of Laws, and Public Orator in the University of Dublin. [*Nearly ready.*

On the Influence of Authority in Matters of Opinion. By the late Sir. G. C. LEWIS, Bart. 8vo. 14s.

The Emotions and the Will. By A. BAIN, LL.D. 8vo. 15s.

Mental and Moral Science; a Compendium of Psychology and Ethics. By A. BAIN, LL.D. Crown 8vo. 10s. 6d.

An Outline of the Necessary Laws of Thought; a Treatise on Pure and Applied Logic. By W. THOMSON, D.D. Crown 8vo. 6s.

Essays in Political and Moral Philosophy. By T. E. CLIFFE LESLIE, Hon. LL.D. Dubl. of Lincoln's Inn, Barrister-at-Law. 8vo. 10s. 6d.

Hume's Philosophical Works: Edited, with Notes, &c. by T. H. GREEN, M.A. and the Rev. T. H. GROSE, M.A. 4 vols. 8vo. 56s. Or separately, Essays, 2 vols. 28s. Treatise on Human Nature, 2 vols. 28s.

Six Lectures on the History of German Thought, from the Seven Years' War to Goethe's Death, delivered in 1879 at the Royal Institution of Great Britain. By KARL HILLEBRAND. Crown 8vo. 7s. 6d.

MISCELLANEOUS & CRITICAL WORKS.

Faiths and Fashions; Short Essays republished. By Lady VIOLET GREVILE. Crown 8vo. 7s. 6d.

Selected Essays, chiefly from Contributions to the Edinburgh and Quarterly Reviews. By A. HAYWARD, Q.C. 2 vols. crown 8vo. 12s.

Miscellaneous Writings of J. Conington, M.A. Edited by J. A. SYMONDS, M.A. 2 vols. 8vo. 28s.

Short Studies on Great Subjects. By J. A. FROUDE, M.A. 3 vols. crown 8vo. 18s.

Literary Studies. By the late WALTER BAGEHOT, M.A. Fellow of University College, London. Edited, with a Prefatory Memoir, by R. H. HUTTON. Second Edition. 2 vols. 8vo. with Portrait, 28s.

Manual of English Literature, Historical and Critical. By T. ARNOLD, M.A. Crown 8vo. 7s. 6d.

English Authors; Specimens of English Poetry and Prose from the earliest times to the present day; with references throughout to the 'Manual of English Literature.' Edited by T. ARNOLD, M.A. Crown 8vo. [*In the press.*

The Wit and Wisdom of the Rev. Sydney Smith. Crown 8vo. 3s. 6d.

Lord Macaulay's Miscellaneous Writings:—
LIBRARY EDITION, 2 vols. 8vo. 21s.
PEOPLE'S EDITION, 1 vol. cr. 8vo. 4s. 6d.

Lord Macaulay's Miscellaneous Writings and Speeches.
Student's Edition. Crown 8vo. 6s.
Cabinet Edition, including Indian Penal Code, Lays of Ancient Rome, and other Poems. 4 vols. post 8vo. 24s.

Speeches of Lord Macaulay, corrected by Himself. Crown 8vo. 3s. 6d.

Selections from the Writings of Lord Macaulay. Edited, with Notes, by G. O. TREVELYAN, M.P. Crown. 8vo. 6s.

Miscellaneous Works of Thomas Arnold, D.D. late Head Master of Rugby School. 8vo. 7s. 6d.

A Thousand Thoughts from Various Authors. Selected and arranged by ARTHUR B. DAVISON. Crown 8vo. 7s. 6d.

A Cavalier's Note Book;
being Notes, Anecdotes, and Observations of W. BLUNDELL, of Crosby, Lancashire, Esq. Captain in the Royalist Army of 1642. Edited by the Rev. T. ELLISON GIBSON. Small 4to. with Facsimile, 14s.

German Home Life; a Series of Essays on the Domestic Life of Germany. Crown 8vo. 6s.

Realities of Irish Life.
By W. STEUART TRENCH. Crown 8vo. 2s. 6d. boards, or 3s. 6d. cloth.

Apparitions; a Narrative of Facts. By the Rev. B. W. SAVILE, M.A. Second Edition. Crown 8vo. price 5s.

Evenings with the Skeptics; or, Free Discussion on Free Thinkers. By JOHN OWEN, Rector of East Anstey, Devon. 2 vols. 8vo. 32s.

Selected Essays on Language, Mythology, and Religion.
By F. MAX MÜLLER, K.M. Foreign Member of the French Institute. 2 vols. crown 8vo. 16s.

Lectures on the Science of Language. By F. MAX MÜLLER, K.M. 2 vols. crown 8vo. 16s.

Chips from a German Workshop; Essays on the Science of Religion, and on Mythology, Traditions & Customs. By F. MAX MÜLLER, K.M. 4 vols. 8vo. £1. 16s.

Language & Languages.
A Revised Edition of Chapters on Language and Families of Speech. By F. W. FARRAR, D.D. F.R.S. Crown 8vo. 6s.

The Essays and Contributions of A. K. H. B. Uniform Cabinet Editions in crown 8vo.
Recreations of a Country Parson, Three Series, 3s. 6d. each.
Landscapes, Churches, and Moralities, price 3s. 6d.
Seaside Musings, 3s. 6d.
Changed Aspects of Unchanged Truths, 3s. 6d.
Counsel and Comfort from a City Pulpit, 3s. 6d.
Lessons of Middle Age, 3s. 6d.
Leisure Hours in Town, 3s. 6d.
Autumn Holidays of a Country Parson, price 3s. 6d.
Sunday Afternoons at the Parish Church of a University City, 3s. 6d.
The Commonplace Philosopher in Town and Country, 3s. 6d.
Present-Day Thoughts, 3s. 6d.
Critical Essays of a Country Parson, price 3s. 6d.
The Graver Thoughts of a Country Parson. Three Series, 3s. 6d. each.

DICTIONARIES and OTHER BOOKS of REFERENCE.

One-Volume Dictionary of the English Language. By R. G. LATHAM, M.A. M.D. Medium 8vo. 14s.

Larger Dictionary of the English Language. By R. G. LATHAM, M.A. M.D. Founded on Johnson's English Dictionary as edited by the Rev. H. J. TODD. 4 vols. 4to. £7.

Roget's Thesaurus of English Words and Phrases, classified and arranged so as to facilitate the expression of Ideas, and assist in Literary Composition. Revised and enlarged by the Author's Son, J. L. ROGET. Crown 8vo. 10s. 6d.

English Synonymes. By E. J. WHATELY. Edited by R. WHATELY, D.D. Fcp. 8vo. 3s.

Handbook of the English Language. By R. G. LATHAM, M.A. M.D. Crown 8vo. 6s.

Contanseau's Practical Dictionary of the French and English Languages. Post 8vo. price 7s. 6d.

Contanseau's Pocket Dictionary, French and English, abridged from the Practical Dictionary by the Author. Square 18mo. 3s. 6d.

A Practical Dictionary of the German and English Languages. By Rev. W. L. BLACKLEY, M.A. & Dr. C. M. FRIEDLÄNDER. Post 8vo. 7s. 6d.

A New Pocket Dictionary of the German and English Languages. By F. W. LONGMAN, Ball. Coll. Oxford. Square 18mo. 5s.

Becker's Gallus; Roman Scenes of the Time of Augustus. Translated by the Rev. F. METCALFE, M.A. Post 8vo. 7s. 6d.

Becker's Charicles; Illustrations of the Private Life of the Ancient Greeks. Translated by the Rev. F. METCALFE, M.A. Post 8vo. 7s. 6d.

A Dictionary of Roman and Greek Antiquities. With 2,000 Woodcuts illustrative of the Arts and Life of the Greeks and Romans. By A. RICH, B.A. Crown 8vo. 7s. 6d.

A Greek-English Lexicon. By H. G. LIDDELL, D.D. Dean of Christchurch, and R. SCOTT, D.D. Dean of Rochester. Crown 4to. 36s.

Liddell & Scott's Lexicon, Greek and English, abridged for Schools. Square 12mo. 7s. 6d.

An English-Greek Lexicon, containing all the Greek Words used by Writers of good authority. By C. D. YONGE, M.A. 4to. 21s. School Abridgment, square 12mo. 8s. 6d.

A Latin-English Dictionary. By JOHN T. WHITE, D.D. Oxon. and J. E. RIDDLE, M.A. Oxon. Sixth Edition, revised. Quarto 21s.

White's College Latin-English Dictionary, for the use of University Students. Royal 8vo. 12s.

M'Culloch's Dictionary of Commerce and Commercial Navigation. Re-edited, with a Supplement shewing the Progress of British Commercial Legislation to the Year 1880, by HUGH G. REID. With 11 Maps and 30 Charts. 8vo. 63s.

Keith Johnston's General Dictionary of Geography, Descriptive, Physical, Statistical, and Historical; a complete Gazetteer of the World. Medium 8vo. 42s.

The Public Schools Atlas of Ancient Geography, in 28 entirely new Coloured Maps. Edited by the Rev. G. BUTLER, M.A. Imperial 8vo. or imperial 4to. 7s. 6d.

The Public Schools Atlas of Modern Geography, in 31 entirely new Coloured Maps. Edited by the Rev. G. BUTLER, M.A. Uniform, 5s.

ASTRONOMY and METEOROLOGY.

Outlines of Astronomy.
By Sir J. F. W. HERSCHEL, Bart. M.A. Latest Edition, with Plates and Diagrams. Square crown 8vo. 12s.

Essays on Astronomy.
A Series of Papers on Planets and Meteors, the Sun and Sun-surrounding Space, Stars and Star Cloudlets. By R. A. PROCTOR, B.A. With 10 Plates and 24 Woodcuts. 8vo. 12s.

The Moon; her Motions, Aspects, Scenery, and Physical Condition. By R. A. PROCTOR, B.A. With Plates, Charts, Woodcuts, and Lunar Photographs. Crown 8vo. 10s. 6d.

The Sun; Ruler, Light, Fire, and Life of the Planetary System. By R. A. PROCTOR, B.A. With Plates & Woodcuts. Crown 8vo. 14s.

The Orbs Around Us;
a Series of Essays on the Moon & Planets, Meteors & Comets, the Sun & Coloured Pairs of Suns. By R. A. PROCTOR, B.A. With Chart and Diagrams. Crown 8vo. 7s. 6d.

The Universe of Stars;
Presenting Researches into and New Views respecting the Constitution of the Heavens. By R. A. PROCTOR, B.A. Second Edition, with 22 Charts (4 Coloured) and 22 Diagrams. 8vo. price 10s. 6d.

Other Worlds than Ours;
The Plurality of Worlds Studied under the Light of Recent Scientific Researches. By R. A. PROCTOR, B.A. With 14 Illustrations. Cr. 8vo. 10s. 6d.

Saturn and its System.
By R. A. PROCTOR, B.A. 8vo. with 14 Plates, 14s.

The Moon, and the Condition and Configurations of its Surface. By E. NEISON, F.R.A.S. With 26 Maps & 5 Plates. Medium 8vo. 31s. 6d.

Celestial Objects for Common Telescopes. By the Rev. T. W. WEBB, M.A. Fourth Edition, revised and adapted to the Present State of Sidereal Science; Map, Plate, Woodcuts. Crown 8vo. 9s.

A New Star Atlas, for the Library, the School, and the Observatory, in 12 Circular Maps (with 2 Index Plates). By R. A. PROCTOR, B.A. Crown 8vo. 5s.

Larger Star Atlas, for the Library, in Twelve Circular Maps, with Introduction and 2 Index Plates. By R. A. PROCTOR, B.A. Folio, 15s. or Maps only, 12s. 6d.

Air and Rain; the Beginnings of a Chemical Climatology. By R. A. SMITH, F.R.S. 8vo. 24s.

NATURAL HISTORY and PHYSICAL SCIENCE.

Elementary Treatise on Physics, Experimental and Applied, for the use of Colleges and Schools. Translated and edited from GANOT's *Traité Élémentaire de Physique* (with the Author's sanction) by EDMUND ATKINSON, Ph.D. F.C.S. Professor of Experimental Science, Staff College. Ninth Edition, revised and enlarged; with 4 Coloured Plates and 844 Woodcuts. Large crown 8vo. 15s.

Natural Philosophy for General Readers and Young Persons; a Course of Physics divested of Mathematical Formulæ and expressed in the language of daily life. Translated and edited from GANOT's *Cours de Physique* (with the Author's sanction) by EDMUND ATKINSON, Ph.D. F.C.S. Professor of Experimental Science, Staff College. Fourth Edition, revised; with 2 Plates and 471 Woodcuts. Crown 8vo. 7s. 6d.

Professor Helmholtz on the Sensations of Tone, as a Physiological Basis for the Theory of Music. Translated by A. J. ELLIS, F.R.S. 8vo. 36s.

Professor Helmholtz' Popular Lectures on Scientific Subjects. Translated and edited by EDMUND ATKINSON, Ph.D. F.C.S. Professor of Chemistry &c. Staff College, Sandhurst. FIRST SERIES, with a Preface by Professor TYNDALL, F.R.S. Second Edition, with 51 Woodcuts. Crown 8vo. 7s. 6d.

Professor Helmholtz' Popular Lectures on Scientific Subjects, SECOND SERIES, on the Origin and Signification of Geometrical Axioms, the relation of Form, Shade, Colour and Harmony of Colour to Painting, the Origin of the Planetary System, &c. Translated by EDMUND ATKINSON, Ph.D. F.C.S. Professor of Chemistry &c. Staff College, Sandhurst. With 17 Woodcuts. Crown 8vo. 7s. 6d.

Arnott's Elements of Physics or Natural Philosophy. Seventh Edition, edited by A. BAIN, LL.D. and A. S. TAYLOR, M.D. F.R.S. Crown 8vo. Woodcuts, 12s. 6d.

The Correlation of Physical Forces. By the Hon. Sir W. R. GROVE, F.R.S. &c. Sixth Edition, revised and augmented. 8vo. 15s.

A Treatise on Magnetism, General and Terrestrial. By H. LLOYD, D.D. D.C.L. &c. late Provost of Trinity College, Dublin. 8vo. 10s. 6d.

Elementary Treatise on the Wave-Theory of Light. By H. LLOYD, D.D. D.C.L. &c. late Provost of Trinity College, Dublin. 8vo. price 10s. 6d.

The Mathematical and other Tracts of the late James M'Cullagh, F.T.C.D. Professor of Natural Philosophy in the University of Dublin. Now first collected, and Edited by the Rev. J. H. JELLETT, B.D. and the Rev. S. HAUGHTON, M.D. Fellows of Trin. Coll. Dublin. 8vo. 15s.

A Text-Book of Systematic Mineralogy. By H. BAUERMAN, F.G.S. Associate of the Royal School of Mines. With numerous Woodcuts. Small 8vo. 6s.

A Text-Book of Descriptive Mineralogy. In the same Series of *Text-Books of Science*, and by the same Author. Small 8vo. Woodcuts. [*In preparation.*

Fragments of Science. By JOHN TYNDALL, F.R.S. Sixth Edition, revised and augmented. 2 vols. crown 8vo. 16s.

Heat a Mode of Motion. By JOHN TYNDALL, F.R.S. Sixth Edition (Thirteenth Thousand), thoroughly revised and enlarged. Crown 8vo. 12s.

Sound. By JOHN TYNDALL, F.R.S. Fourth Edition, including Recent Researches. [*Nearly ready.*

Contributions to Molecular Physics in the domain of Radiant Heat. By JOHN TYNDALL, F.R.S. Plates and Woodcuts. 8vo. 16s.

Professor Tyndall's Researches on Diamagnetism and Magne-Crystallic Action; including Diamagnetic Polarity. New Edition in preparation.

Professor Tyndall's Lectures on Light, delivered in America in 1872 and 1873. With Portrait, Plate & Diagrams. Crown 8vo. 7s. 6d.

Professor Tyndall's Lessons in Electricity at the Royal Institution, 1875-6. With 58 Woodcuts. Crown 8vo. 2s. 6d.

Professor Tyndall's Notes of a Course of Seven Lectures on Electrical Phenomena and Theories, delivered at the Royal Institution. Crown 8vo. 1s. sewed, 1s. 6d. cloth.

Professor Tyndall's Notes of a Course of Nine Lectures on Light, delivered at the Royal Institution. Crown 8vo. 1s. swd., 1s. 6d. cloth.

Text-Books of Science,
Mechanical and Physical, adapted for the use of Artisans and of Students in Public and Science Schools. Small 8vo. with Woodcuts, &c.

Abney's Photography, 3s. 6d.

Anderson's (Sir John) Strength of Materials, 3s. 6d.

Armstrong's Organic Chemistry, 3s. 6d.

Ball's Elements of Astronomy, 6s.

Barry's Railway Appliances, 3s. 6d.

Bauerman's Systematic Mineralogy, 6s.

Bloxam's Metals, 3s. 6d.

Goodeve's Mechanics, 3s. 6d.

Gore's Electro-Metallurgy, 6s.

Griffin's Algebra & Trigonometry, 3/6.

Jenkin's Electricity & Magnetism, 3/6.

Maxwell's Theory of Heat, 3s. 6d.

Merrifield's Technical Arithmetic, 3s. 6d.

Miller's Inorganic Chemistry, 3s. 6d.

Preece & Sivewright's Telegraphy, 3/6.

Rutley's Study of Rocks, 4s. 6d.

Shelley's Workshop Appliances, 3s. 6d.

Thomé's Structural and Physiological Botany, 6s.

Thorpe's Quantitative Analysis, 4s. 6d.

Thorpe & Muir's Qualitative Analysis, price 3s. 6d.

Tilden's Chemical Philosophy, 3s. 6d.

Unwin's Machine Design, 3s. 6d.

Watson's Plane & Solid Geometry, 3/6.

Six Lectures on Physical Geography,
delivered in 1876, with some Additions. By the Rev. SAMUEL HAUGHTON, F.R.S. M.D. D.C.L. With 23 Diagrams. 8vo. 15s.

An Introduction to the
Systematic Zoology and Morphology of Vertebrate Animals. By A. MACALISTER, M.D. With 28 Diagrams. 8vo. 10s. 6d.

The Comparative Anatomy
and Physiology of the Vertebrate Animals. By RICHARD OWEN, F.R.S. With 1,472 Woodcuts. 3 vols. 8vo. £3. 13s. 6d.

Homes without Hands;
a Description of the Habitations of Animals, classed according to their Principle of Construction. By the Rev. J. G. WOOD, M.A. With about 140 Vignettes on Wood. 8vo. 14s.

Wood's Strange Dwellings;
a Description of the Habitations of Animals, abridged from 'Homes without Hands.' With Frontispiece and 60 Woodcuts. Crown 8vo. 7s. 6d.

Wood's Insects at Home;
a Popular Account of British Insects, their Structure, Habits, and Transformations. 8vo. Woodcuts, 14s.

Wood's Insects Abroad;
a Popular Account of Foreign Insects, their Structure, Habits, and Transformations. 8vo. Woodcuts, 14s.

Wood's Out of Doors; a
Selection of Original Articles on Practical Natural History. With 6 Illustrations. Crown 8vo. 7s. 6d.

Wood's Bible Animals; a
description of every Living Creature mentioned in the Scriptures, from the Ape to the Coral. With 112 Vignettes. 8vo. 14s.

The Sea and its Living
Wonders. By Dr. G. HARTWIG. 8vo. with many Illustrations, 10s. 6d.

Hartwig's Tropical
World. With about 200 Illustrations. 8vo. 10s. 6d.

Hartwig's Polar World;
a Description of Man and Nature in the Arctic and Antarctic Regions of the Globe. Maps, Plates & Woodcuts. 8vo. 10s. 6d.

Hartwig's Subterranean
World. With Maps and Woodcuts. 8vo. 10s. 6d.

Hartwig's Aerial World;
a Popular Account of the Phenomena and Life of the Atmosphere. Map, Plates, Woodcuts. 8vo. 10s. 6d.

A Familiar History of
Birds. By E. STANLEY, D.D. New Edition, revised and enlarged, with 160 Woodcuts. Crown 8vo. 6s.

Rural Bird Life; Essays on Ornithology, with Instructions for Preserving Objects relating to that Science. By CHARLES DIXON. With Coloured Frontispiece and 44 Woodcuts by G. Pearson. Crown 8vo. 7s. 6d.

The Note-book of an Amateur Geologist. By JOHN EDWARD LEE, F.G.S. F.S.A. &c. With numerous Woodcuts and 200 Lithographic Plates of Sketches and Sections. 8vo. 21s.

Rocks Classified and Described. By BERNHARD VON COTTA. An English Translation, by P. H. LAWRENCE, with English, German, and French Synonymes. Post 8vo. 14s.

The Geology of England and Wales; a Concise Account of the Lithological Characters, Leading Fossils, and Economic Products of the Rocks. By H. B. WOODWARD, F.G.S. Crown 8vo. Map & Woodcuts, 14s.

Keller's Lake Dwellings of Switzerland, and other Parts of Europe. Translated by JOHN E. LEE, F.S.A. F.G.S. With 206 Illustrations. 2 vols. royal 8vo. 42s.

Heer's Primæval World of Switzerland. Edited by JAMES HEYWOOD, M.A. F.R.S. With Map, 19 Plates, & 372 Woodcuts. 2 vols. 8vo. 16s.

The Puzzle of Life and How it Has Been Put Together; a Short History of Praehistoric Vegetable and Animal Life on the Earth. By A. NICOLS, F.R.G.S. With 12 Illustrations. Crown 8vo. 3s. 6d.

The Origin of Civilisation, and the Primitive Condition of Man; Mental and Social Condition of Savages. By Sir J. LUBBOCK, Bart. M.P. F.R.S. 8vo. Woodcuts, 18s.

Light Science for Leisure Hours; Familiar Essays on Scientific Subjects, Natural Phenomena, &c. By R. A. PROCTOR, B.A. 2 vols. crown 8vo. 7s. 6d. each.

A Dictionary of Science, Literature, and Art. Re-edited by the Rev. Sir G. W. COX, Bart. M.A. 3 vols. medium 8vo. 63s.

Hullah's Course of Lectures on the History of Modern Music. 8vo. 8s. 6d.

Hullah's Second Course of Lectures on the Transition Period of Musical History. 8vo. 10s. 6d.

Loudon's Encyclopædia of Plants; the Specific Character, Description, Culture, History, &c. of all Plants found in Great Britain. With 12,000 Woodcuts. 8vo. 42s.

De Caisne & Le Maout's Descriptive and Analytical Botany. Translated by Mrs. HOOKER; edited and arranged by J. D. HOOKER, M.D. With 5,500 Woodcuts. Imperial 8vo. price 31s. 6d.

Rivers's Orchard-House; or, the Cultivation of Fruit Trees under Glass. Sixteenth Edition. Crown 8vo. with 25 Woodcuts, 5s.

The Rose Amateur's Guide. By THOMAS RIVERS. Latest Edition. Fcp. 8vo. 4s. 6d.

Town and Window Gardening, including the Structure, Habits and Uses of Plants. By Mrs. BUCKTON With 127 Woodcuts. Crown 8vo. 2s.

Loudon's Encyclopædia of Gardening; the Theory and Practice of Horticulture, Floriculture, Arboriculture & Landscape Gardening. With 1,000 Woodcuts. 8vo. 21s.

CHEMISTRY and PHYSIOLOGY.

Experimental Chemistry for Junior Students. By J. E. REYNOLDS, M.D. F.R.S. Professor of Chemistry, University of Dublin. Part I. Introductory. Fcp. 8vo. 1s. 6d.

Practical Chemistry; the Principles of Qualitative Analysis. By W. A. TILDEN, D.Sc. Lond. F.C.S. Professor of Chemistry in Mason's College, Birmingham. Fcp. 8vo. 1s. 6d.

WORKS published by LONGMANS & CO. 13

Miller's Elements of Chemistry, Theoretical and Practical. Re-edited, with Additions, by H. MACLEOD, F.C.S. 3 vols. 8vo.
PART I. CHEMICAL PHYSICS. 16s.
PART II. INORGANIC CHEMISTRY, 24s.
PART III. ORGANIC CHEMISTRY, in Two Sections. SECTION I. 31s. 6d.

Annals of Chemical Medicine; including the Application of Chemistry to Physiology, Pathology, Therapeutics, Pharmacy, Toxicology, and Hygiene. Edited by J. L. W. THUDICHUM, M.D. VOL. I. 8vo. 14s.

Health in the House: Twenty-five Lectures on Elementary Physiology in its Application to the Daily Wants of Man and Animals. By Mrs. BUCKTON. Crown 8vo. Woodcuts, 2s.

A Dictionary of Chemistry and the Allied Branches of other Sciences. Edited by HENRY WATTS, F.C.S. 8 vols. medium 8vo. £12.12s.6d.
Third Supplement, completing the Record of Chemical Discovery to the year 1877. PART II. completion, is now ready, price 50s.

Select Methods in Chemical Analysis, chiefly Inorganic. By W. CROOKES, F.R.S. With 22 Woodcuts. Crown 8vo. 12s. 6d.

The History, Products, and Processes of the Alkali Trade, including the most recent Improvements. By C. T. KINGZETT, F.C.S. With 32 Woodcuts. 8vo. 12s.

Animal Chemistry, or the Relations of Chemistry to Physiology and Pathology: a Manual for Medical Men and Scientific Chemists. By C. T. KINGZETT, F.C.S. 8vo. 18s.

The FINE ARTS and ILLUSTRATED EDITIONS.

Notes on Foreign Picture Galleries. By C. L. EASTLAKE, F.R.I.B.A. Keeper of the National Gallery, London. Crown 8vo. fully Illustrated. [*In preparation.*]
Vol. I. The Brera Gallery, Milan.
,, II. The Louvre, Paris.
,, III. The Pinacothek, Munich.

In Fairyland; Pictures from the Elf-World. By RICHARD DOYLE. With 16 coloured Plates, containing 36 Designs. Folio, 15s.

Lord Macaulay's Lays of Ancient Rome, with Ivry and the Armada. With 41 Wood Engravings by G. Pearson from Original Drawings by J. R. Weguelin. Crown 8vo. 6s.

Lord Macaulay's Lays of Ancient Rome. With Ninety Illustrations engraved on Wood from Drawings by G. Scharf. Fcp. 4to. 21s. or imperial 16mo. 10s. 6d.

The Three Cathedrals dedicated to St. Paul in London. By W. LONGMAN, F.S.A. With Illustrations. Square crown 8vo. 21s.

Moore's Lalla Rookh. TENNIEL'S Edition, with 68 Woodcut Illustrations. Crown 8vo. 10s. 6d.

Moore's Irish Melodies, MACLISE'S Edition, with 161 Steel Plates. Super-royal 8vo. 21s.

Lectures on Harmony, delivered at the Royal Institution. By G. A. MACFARREN. 8vo. 12s.

Sacred and Legendary Art. By Mrs. JAMESON. 6 vols. square crown 8vo. £5. 15s. 6d.

Jameson's Legends of the Saints and Martyrs. With 19 Etchings and 187 Woodcuts. 2 vols. 31s. 6d.

Jameson's Legends of the Monastic Orders. With 11 Etchings and 88 Woodcuts. 1 vol. 21s.

Jameson's Legends of the Madonna. With 27 Etchings and 165 Woodcuts. 1 vol. 21s.

Jameson's History of the Saviour, His Types and Precursors. Completed by Lady EASTLAKE. With 13 Etchings and 281 Woodcuts. 2 vols. 42s.

The USEFUL ARTS, MANUFACTURES, &c.

The Elements of Mechanism. By T. M. GOODEVE, M.A. Barrister-at-Law. New Edition, re-written and enlarged, with 342 Woodcuts. Crown 8vo. 6s.

The Amateur Mechanics' Practical Handbook; describing the different Tools required in the Workshop. By A. H. G. HOBSON. With 33 Woodcuts. Crown 8vo. 2s. 6d.

The Engineer's Valuing Assistant. By H. D. HOSKOLD, Civil and Mining Engineer. 8vo. price 31s. 6d.

Industrial Chemistry; a Manual for Manufacturers and for Colleges or Technical Schools; a Translation (by Dr. T. H. BARRY) of Stohmann and Engler's German Edition of PAYEN's 'Précis de Chimie Industrielle;' with Chapters on the Chemistry of the Metals, &c. by B. H. PAUL, Ph.D. With 698 Woodcuts. Medium 8vo. 42s.

Gwilt's Encyclopædia of Architecture, with above 1,600 Woodcuts. Revised and extended by W. PAPWORTH. 8vo. 52s. 6d.

Lathes and Turning, Simple, Mechanical, and Ornamental. By W. H. NORTHCOTT. Second Edition, with 338 Illustrations. 8vo. 18s.

The Theory of Strains in Girders and similar Structures, with Observations on the application of Theory to Practice, and Tables of the Strength and other Properties of Materials. By B. B. STONEY, M.A. M. Inst. C.E. Royal 8vo. with 5 Plates and 123 Woodcuts, 36s.

Recent Naval Administration; Shipbuilding for the Purposes of War. By T. BRASSEY, M.P. 6 vols. 8vo. with Illustrations by the Chevalier E. de Martino. [*In the press.*

A Treatise on Mills and Millwork. By the late Sir W. FAIRBAIRN, Bart. C.E. Fourth Edition, with 18 Plates and 333 Woodcuts. 1 vol. 8vo. 25s.

Useful Information for Engineers. By the late Sir W. FAIRBAIRN, Bart. C.E. With many Plates and Woodcuts. 3 vols. crown 8vo. 31s. 6d.

The Application of Cast and Wrought Iron to Building Purposes. By the late Sir W. FAIRBAIRN, Bart. C.E. With 6 Plates and 118 Woodcuts. 8vo. 16s.

Hints on Household Taste in Furniture, Upholstery, and other Details. By C. L. EASTLAKE. Fourth Edition, with 100 Illustrations. Square crown 8vo. 14s.

Handbook of Practical Telegraphy. By R. S. CULLEY, Memb. Inst. C.E. Seventh Edition. Plates & Woodcuts. 8vo. 16s.

A Treatise on the Steam Engine, in its various applications to Mines, Mills, Steam Navigation, Railways and Agriculture. By J. BOURNE, C.E. With Portrait, 37 Plates, and 546 Woodcuts. 4to. 42s.

Catechism of the Steam Engine, in its various Applications. By JOHN BOURNE, C.E. Fcp. 8vo. Woodcuts, 6s.

Handbook of the Steam Engine, a Key to the Author's Catechism of the Steam Engine. By J. BOURNE, C.E. Fcp. 8vo. Woodcuts, 9s.

Recent Improvements in the Steam Engine. By J. BOURNE, C.E. Fcp. 8vo. Woodcuts, 6s.

Examples of Steam and Gas Engines of the most recent Approved Types as employed in Mines, Factories, Steam Navigation, Railways and Agriculture, practically described. By JOHN BOURNE, C.E. With 54 Plates and 356 Woodcuts. 4to. 70s.

Ure's Dictionary of Arts, Manufactures, and Mines. Seventh Edition, re-written and enlarged by R. HUNT, F.R.S. assisted by numerous Contributors. With 2,604 Woodcuts. 4 vols. medium 8vo. £7. 7s.

Cresy's Encyclopædia of
Civil Engineering, Historical, Theoretical, and Practical. With above 3,000 Woodcuts. 8vo. 25s.

Kerl's Practical Treatise
on Metallurgy. Adapted from the last German Edition by W. CROOKES, F.R.S. &c. and E. RÖHRIG, Ph.D. 3 vols. 8vo. with 625 Woodcuts. £4 19s.

Ville on Artificial Manures,
their Chemical Selection and Scientific Application to Agriculture; a Series of Lectures given at the Experimental Farm at Vincennes. Translated and edited by W. CROOKES, F.R.S. With 31 Plates. 8vo. 21s.

Mitchell's Manual of
Practical Assaying. Fourth Edition, revised, with the Recent Discoveries incorporated, by W. CROOKES, F.R.S. Crown 8vo. Woodcuts, 31s. 6d.

The Art of Perfumery,
and the Methods of Obtaining the Odours of Plants; the Growth and general Flower Farm System of Raising Fragrant Herbs; with Instructions for the Manufacture of Perfumes for the Handkerchief, Scented Powders, Odorous Vinegars and Salts, Snuff, Dentifrices, Cosmetics, Perfumed Soap, &c. By G. W. S. PIESSE, Ph.D. F.C.S. Fourth Edition, with 96 Woodcuts. Square crown 8vo. 21s.

Loudon's Encyclopædia
of Gardening; the Theory and Practice of Horticulture, Floriculture, Arboriculture & Landscape Gardening. With 1,000 Woodcuts. 8vo. 21s.

Loudon's Encyclopædia
of Agriculture; the Laying-out, Improvement, and Management of Landed Property; the Cultivation and Economy of the Productions of Agriculture. With 1,100 Woodcuts. 8vo. 21s.

RELIGIOUS and MORAL WORKS.

A Handbook to the Bible,
or, Guide to the Study of the Holy Scriptures derived from Ancient Monuments and Modern Exploration. By F. R. CONDER, and Lieut. C. R. CONDER, R.E. Second Edit.; Maps, Plates of Coins, &c. Post 8vo. 7s. 6d.

A History of the Church
of England; Pre-Reformation Period. By the Rev. T. P. BOULTBEE, LL.D. 8vo. 15s.

Sketch of the History of
the Church of England to the Revolution of 1688. By T. V. SHORT, D.D. Crown 8vo. 7s. 6d.

The English Church in
the Eighteenth Century. By CHARLES J. ABBEY, late Fellow of University College, Oxford; and JOHN H. OVERTON, late Scholar of Lincoln College, Oxford. 2 vols. 8vo. 36s.

An Exposition of the 39
Articles, Historical and Doctrinal. By E. H. BROWNE, D.D. Bishop of Winchester. Eleventh Edition. 8vo. 16s.

A Commentary on the
39 Articles, forming an Introduction to the Theology of the Church of England. By the Rev. T. P. BOULTBEE, LL.D. New Edition. Crown 8vo. 6s.

Sermons preached mostly in the Chapel of Rugby School
by the late T. ARNOLD, D.D. Collective Edition, revised by the Author's Daughter, Mrs. W. E. FORSTER. 6 vols. crown 8vo. 30s. or separately, 5s. each.

Historical Lectures on
the Life of Our Lord Jesus Christ. By C. J. ELLICOTT, D.D. 8vo. 12s.

The Eclipse of Faith; or
a Visit to a Religious Sceptic. By HENRY ROGERS. Fcp. 8vo. 5s.

Defence of the Eclipse of
Faith. By H. ROGERS. Fcp. 8vo. 3s. 6d.

Nature, the Utility of
Religion, and Theism. Three Essays by JOHN STUART MILL. 8vo. 10s. 6d.

A Critical and Grammatical Commentary on St. Paul's Epistles. By C. J. ELLICOTT, D.D. 8vo. Galatians, 8s. 6d. Ephesians, 8s. 6d. Pastoral Epistles, 10s. 6d. Philippians, Colossians, & Philemon, 10s. 6d. Thessalonians, 7s. 6d.

Conybeare & Howson's Life and Epistles of St. Paul. Three Editions, copiously illustrated.

Library Edition, with all the Original Illustrations, Maps, Landscapes on Steel, Woodcuts, &c. 2 vols. 4to. 42s.

Intermediate Edition, with a Selection of Maps, Plates, and Woodcuts. 2 vols. square crown 8vo. 21s.

Student's Edition, revised and condensed, with 46 Illustrations and Maps. 1 vol. crown 8vo. 7s. 6d.

Smith's Voyage & Shipwreck of St. Paul; with Dissertations on the Life and Writings of St. Luke, and the Ships and Navigation of the Ancients. Fourth Edition, revised by the Author's Son; with a Memoir of the Author, a Preface by the BISHOP OF CARLISLE, and all the Original Illustrations. Crown 8vo. 7s. 6d.

The Angel-Messiah of Buddhists, Essenes, and Christians. By ERNEST DE BUNSEN. 8vo. 10s. 6d.

Bible Studies. By M. M. KALISCH, Ph.D. PART I. *The Prophecies of Balaam.* 8vo. 10s. 6d. PART II. *The Book of Jonah.* 8vo. price 10s. 6d.

Historical and Critical Commentary on the Old Testament; with a New Translation. By M. M. KALISCH, Ph.D. Vol. I. Genesis, 8vo. 18s. or adapted for the General Reader, 12s. Vol. II. Exodus, 15s. or adapted for the General Reader, 12s. Vol. III. Leviticus, Part I. 15s. or adapted for the General Reader, 8s. Vol. IV. Leviticus, Part II. 15s. or adapted for the General Reader, 8s.

The Four Gospels in Greek, with Greek-English Lexicon. By JOHN T. WHITE, D.D. Oxon. Square 32mo. 5s.

Ewald's History of Israel. Translated from the German by J. E. CARPENTER, M.A. with Preface by R. MARTINEAU, M.A. 5 vols. 8vo. 63s.

Ewald's Antiquities of Israel. Translated from the German by H. S. SOLLY, M.A. 8vo. 12s. 6d.

The Types of Genesis, briefly considered as revealing the Development of Human Nature. By A. JUKES. Crown 8vo. 7s. 6d.

The Second Death and the Restitution of all Things; with some Preliminary Remarks on the Nature and Inspiration of Holy Scripture. By A. JUKES. Crown 8vo. 3s. 6d.

The Gospel for the Nineteenth Century. Fourth Edition. 8vo. price 10s. 6d.

Supernatural Religion; an Inquiry into the Reality of Divine Revelation. Complete Edition, thoroughly revised. 3 vols. 8vo. 36s.

Lectures on the Origin and Growth of Religion, as illustrated by the Religions of India; being the Hibbert Lectures, delivered at the Chapter House, Westminster Abbey, in 1878, by F. MAX MÜLLER, K.M. 8vo. 10s. 6d.

Introduction to the Science of Religion, Four Lectures delivered at the Royal Institution; with Essays on False Analogies and the Philosophy of Mythology. By F. MAX MÜLLER, K.M. Crown 8vo. 10s. 6d.

Passing Thoughts on Religion. By Miss SEWELL. Fcp. 8vo. price 3s. 6d.

Thoughts for the Age. By Miss SEWELL. Fcp. 8vo. 3s. 6d.

Preparation for the Holy Communion; the Devotions chiefly from the works of Jeremy Taylor. By Miss SEWELL. 32mo. 3s.

Private Devotions for Young Persons. Compiled by ELIZABETH M. SEWELL, Author of 'Amy Herbert' &c. 18mo. 2s.

Bishop Jeremy Taylor's Entire Works; with Life by Bishop Heber. Revised and corrected by the Rev. C. P. EDEN. 10 vols. £5. 5s.

Hymns of Praise and Prayer. Corrected and edited by Rev. JOHN MARTINEAU, LL.D. Crown 8vo. 4s. 6d. 32mo. 1s. 6d.

Spiritual Songs for the Sundays and Holidays throughout the Year. By J. S. B. MONSELL, LL.D. Fcp. 8vo. 5s. 18mo. 2s.

Christ the Consoler; a Book of Comfort for the Sick. By ELLICE HOPKINS. Second Edition. Fcp. 8vo. 2s. 6d.

Lyra Germanica; Hymns translated from the German by Miss C. WINKWORTH. Fcp. 8vo. 5s.

Hours of Thought on Sacred Things; Two Volumes of Sermons. By JAMES MARTINEAU, D.D. LL.D. 2 vols. crown 8vo. 7s. 6d. each.

Endeavours after the Christian Life; Discourses. By JAMES MARTINEAU, D.D. LL.D. Fifth Edition. Crown 8vo. 7s. 6d.

The Pentateuch & Book of Joshua Critically Examined. By J. W. COLENSO, D.D. Bishop of Natal. Crown 8vo. 6s.

Lectures on the Pentateuch and the Moabite Stone; with Appendices. By J. W. COLENSO, D.D. Bishop of Natal. 8vo. 12s.

TRAVELS, VOYAGES, &c.

The Flight of the 'Lapwing'; a Naval Officer's Jottings in China, Formosa, and Japan. By the Hon. H. N. SHORE, R.N. With 2 Illustrations and 2 Maps. 8vo. 15s.

Turkish Armenia and Eastern Asia Minor. By the Rev. H. F. TOZER, M.A. F.R.G.S. With Map and 5 Illustrations. 8vo. 16s.

Sunshine and Storm in the East, or Cruises to Cyprus and Constantinople. By Mrs. BRASSEY. With 2 Maps and 114 Illustrations engraved on Wood by G. Pearson, chiefly from Drawings by the Hon. A. Y. Bingham; the Cover from an Original Design by Gustave Doré. 8vo. 21s.

A Voyage in the 'Sunbeam,' our Home on the Ocean for Eleven Months. By Mrs. BRASSEY. Cheaper Edition, with Map and 65 Wood Engravings. Crown 8vo. 7s. 6d.

Eight Years in Ceylon. By Sir SAMUEL W. BAKER, M.A. Crown 8vo. Woodcuts, 7s. 6d.

The Rifle and the Hound in Ceylon. By Sir SAMUEL W. BAKER, M.A. Crown 8vo. Woodcuts, 7s. 6d.

Sacred Palmlands; or, the Journal of a Spring Tour in Egypt and the Holy Land. By A. G. WELD. Crown 8vo. 7s. 6d.

One Thousand Miles up the Nile; a Journey through Egypt and Nubia to the Second Cataract. By Miss AMELIA B. EDWARDS. With Facsimiles, &c. and 80 Illustrations engraved on Wood from Drawings by the Author. Imperial 8vo. 42s.

Wintering in the Riviera; with Notes of Travel in Italy and France, and Practical Hints to Travellers. By WILLIAM MILLER, S.S.C. Edinburgh. With 12 Illustrations. Post 8vo. 7s. 6d.

San Remo and the Western Riviera, climatically and medically considered. By A. HILL HASSALL, M.D. Map and Woodcuts. Crown 8vo. 10s. 6d.

Himalayan and Sub-Himalayan Districts of British India, their Climate, Medical Topography, and Disease Distribution; with reasons for assigning a Malarious Origin to Goître and some other Diseases. By F. N. MACNAMARA, M.D. With Map and Fever Chart. 8vo. 21s.

The Alpine Club Map of
Switzerland, with parts of the Neighbouring Countries, on the scale of Four Miles to an Inch. Edited by R. C. NICHOLS, F.R.G.S. 4 Sheets in Portfolio, 42s. coloured, or 34s. uncoloured.

Dr. Rigby's Letters from
France, &c. in 1789. Edited by his Daughter, Lady EASTLAKE. Crown 8vo. 10s. 6d.

The Alpine Guide. By
JOHN BALL, M.R.I.A. Post 8vo. with Maps and other Illustrations :—

The Eastern Alps, 10s. 6d.

Central Alps, including all
the Oberland District, 7s. 6d.

Western Alps, including
Mont Blanc, Monte Rosa, Zermatt, &c. Price 6s. 6d.

On Alpine Travelling and
the Geology of the Alps. Price 1s. Either of the Three Volumes or Parts of the 'Alpine Guide' may be had with this Introduction prefixed, 1s. extra.

WORKS of FICTION.

Novels and Tales. By the
Right Hon. the EARL of BEACONSFIELD, K.G. The Cabinet Edition. Eleven Volumes, crown 8vo. 6s. each.

Endymion, 6s.

Lothair, 6s.	Venetia, 6s.
Coningsby, 6s.	Alroy, Ixion, &c. 6s.
Sybil, 6s.	Young Duke &c. 6s.
Tancred, 6s.	Vivian Grey, 6s.
	Henrietta Temple, 6s.
	Contarini Fleming, &c. 6s.

Blues and Buffs; a Contested Election and its Results. By ARTHUR MILLS. Crown 8vo. 6s.

Yellow Cap, and other
Fairy Stories for Children, viz. Rumpty-Dudget, Calladon, and Theeda. By JULIAN HAWTHORNE. Crown 8vo. 6s. cloth extra, gilt edges.

The Crookit Meg: a
Scottish Story of the Year One. By JOHN SKELTON, LL.D. Advocate, Author of 'Essays in Romance and Studies from Life' (by 'SHIRLEY'). Crown 8vo. 6s.

Buried Alive; or, Ten
Years of Penal Servitude in Siberia. By FEDOR DOSTOYEFFSKY. Translated from the German by MARIE VON THILO. Post 8vo. 10s. 6d.

'Apart from its interest as a picture of prison life, *Buried Alive* gives us several curious sketches of Russian life and character. Of course it is of the criminal side, but it seems to agree with what we learn from other sources of other classes.'
ST. JAMES'S GAZETTE.

Whispers from Fairyland. By the Right Hon. E. H. KNATCHBULL-HUGESSEN, M.P. With 9 Illustrations. Crown 8vo. 3s. 6d.

Higgledy-Piggledy; or,
Stories for Everybody and Everybody's Children. By the Right Hon. E. H. KNATCHBULL-HUGESSEN, M.P. With 9 Illustrations. Cr. 8vo. 3s. 6d.

Stories and Tales. By
ELIZABETH M. SEWELL. Cabinet Edition, in Ten Volumes, each containing a complete Tale or Story :—

Amy Herbert, 2s. 6d. Gertrude, 2s. 6d. The Earl's Daughter, 2s. 6d. The Experience of Life, 2s. 6d. Cleve Hall, 2s. 6d. Ivors, 2s. 6d. Katharine Ashton, 2s. 6d. Margaret Percival, 3s. 6d. Laneton Parsonage, 3s. 6d. Ursula, 3s. 6d.

The Modern Novelist's
Library. Each work complete in itself, price 2s. boards, or 2s. 6d. cloth :—

By Lord BEACONSFIELD.

Lothair.	Henrietta Temple.
Coningsby.	Contarini Fleming.
Sybil.	Alroy, Ixion, &c.
Tancred.	The Young Duke, &c.
Venetia.	Vivian Grey.

By ANTHONY TROLLOPE.
Barchester Towers.
The Warden.

THE MODERN NOVELIST'S LIBRARY—*continued.*

By Major WHYTE-MELVILLE.
Digby Grand. | Good for Nothing.
General Bounce. | Holmby House.
Kate Coventry. | The Interpreter.
The Gladiators. | Queen's Maries.

By the Author of 'The Rose Garden.'
Unawares.

By the Author of 'Mlle. Mori.'
The Atelier du Lys.
Mademoiselle Mori.

By Various Writers.
Atherstone Priory.
The Burgomaster's Family.
Elsa and her Vulture.
The Six Sisters of the Valleys.

Novels and Tales by the Right Honourable the Earl of Beaconsfield, K.G. Ten Volumes, crown 8vo. cloth extra, gilt edges, price 30s.

POETRY and THE DRAMA.

Poetical Works of Jean Ingelow. New Edition, reprinted, with Additional Matter, from the 23rd and 6th Editions of the two volumes respectively; with 2 Vignettes. 2 vols. fcp. 8vo. 12s.

Faust. From the German of GOETHE. By T. E. WEBB, LL.D. one of Her Majesty's Counsel in Ireland; sometime Fellow of Trinity College, now Regius Professor of Laws and Public Orator in the University of Dublin. 8vo. 12s. 6d.

Goethe's Faust. A New Translation, chiefly in Blank Verse; with a complete Introduction and copious Notes. By JAMES ADEY BIRDS, B.A. F.G.S. Large crown 8vo. 12s. 6d.

Goethe's Faust. The German Text, with an English Introduction and Notes for the use of Students. By ALBERT M. SELSS, M.A. Ph.D. &c. Professor of German in the University of Dublin. Crown 8vo. 5s.

Lays of Ancient Rome; with Ivry and the Armada. By LORD MACAULAY. 16mo. 3s. 6d.

The Poem of the Cid: a Translation from the Spanish, with Introduction and Notes. By JOHN ORMSBY. Crown 8vo. 5s.

Festus, a Poem. By PHILIP JAMES BAILEY. 10th Edition, enlarged & revised. Crown 8vo. 12s. 6d.

The Iliad of Homer, Homometrically translated by C. B. CAYLEY. 8vo. 12s. 6d.

The Æneid of Virgil. Translated into English Verse. By J. CONINGTON, M.A. Crown 8vo. 9s.

Bowdler's Family Shakspeare. Genuine Edition, in 1 vol. medium 8vo. large type, with 36 Woodcuts, 14s. or in 6 vols. fcp. 8vo. 21s.

Southey's Poetical Works, with the Author's last Corrections and Additions. Medium 8vo. with Portrait, 14s.

RURAL SPORTS, HORSE and CATTLE MANAGEMENT, &c.

Blaine's Encyclopædia of Rural Sports; Complete Accounts, Historical, Practical, and Descriptive, of Hunting, Shooting, Fishing, Racing, &c. With 600 Woodcuts. 8vo. 21s.

A Book on Angling; or, Treatise on the Art of Fishing in every branch; including full Illustrated Lists of Salmon Flies. By FRANCIS FRANCIS. Post 8vo. Portrait and Plates, 15s.

Wilcocks's Sea-Fisherman: comprising the Chief Methods of Hook and Line Fishing, a glance at Nets, and remarks on Boats and Boating. Post 8vo. Woodcuts, 12s. 6d.

The Fly-Fisher's Entomology. By ALFRED RONALDS. With 20 Coloured Plates. 8vo. 14s.

Horses and Roads; or, How to Keep a Horse Sound on his Legs. By FREE-LANCE. Second Edition. Crown 8vo. 6s.

Horses and Riding. By GEORGE NEVILE, M.A. With 31 Illustrations. Crown 8vo. 6s.

Youatt on the Horse. Revised and enlarged by W. WATSON, M.R.C.V.S. 8vo. Woodcuts, 7s. 6d.

Youatt's Work on the Dog. Revised and enlarged. 8vo. Woodcuts, 6s.

The Dog in Health and Disease. By STONEHENGE. Third Edition, with 78 Wood Engravings. Square crown 8vo. 7s. 6d.

The Greyhound. By STONEHENGE. Revised Edition, with 25 Portraits of Greyhounds, &c. Square crown 8vo. 15s.

Stables and Stable Fittings. By W. MILES. Imp. 8vo. with 13 Plates, 15s.

The Horse's Foot, and How to keep it Sound. By W. MILES. Imp. 8vo. Woodcuts, 12s. 6d.

A Plain Treatise on Horse-shoeing. By W. MILES. Post 8vo. Woodcuts, 2s. 6d.

Remarks on Horses' Teeth, addressed to Purchasers. By W. MILES. Post 8vo. 1s. 6d.

A Treatise on the Diseases of the Ox; being a Manual of Bovine Pathology specially adapted for the use of Veterinary Practitioners and Students. By J. H. STEEL, M.R.C.V.S. F.Z.S. With 2 Plates and 116 Woodcuts. 8vo. 15s.

WORKS of UTILITY and GENERAL INFORMATION.

Maunder's Biographical Treasury. Latest Edition, reconstructed and partly re-written, with above 1,600 additional Memoirs, by W. L. R. CATES. Fcp. 8vo. 6s.

Maunder's Treasury of Natural History; or, Popular Dictionary of Zoology. Revised and corrected Edition. Fcp. 8vo. with 900 Woodcuts, 6s.

Maunder's Treasury of Geography, Physical, Historical, Descriptive, and Political. Edited by W. HUGHES, F.R.G.S. With 7 Maps and 16 Plates. Fcp. 8vo. 6s.

Maunder's Historical Treasury; Introductory Outlines of Universal History, and Separate Histories of all Nations. Revised by the Rev. Sir G. W. COX, Bart. M.A. Fcp. 8vo. 6s.

Maunder's Treasury of Knowledge and Library of Reference; comprising an English Dictionary and Grammar, Universal Gazetteer, Classical Dictionary, Chronology, Law Dictionary, Synopsis of the Peerage, Useful Tables, &c. Fcp. 8vo. 6s.

Maunder's Scientific and Literary Treasury; a Popular Encyclopædia of Science, Literature, and Art. Latest Edition, partly re-written, with above 1,000 New Articles, by J. Y. JOHNSON. Fcp. 8vo. 6s.

The Treasury of Botany, or Popular Dictionary of the Vegetable Kingdom; with which is incorporated a Glossary of Botanical Terms. Edited by J. LINDLEY, F.R.S. and T. MOORE, F.L.S. With 274 Woodcuts and 20 Steel Plates. Two Parts, fcp. 8vo. 12s.

The Treasury of Bible Knowledge; being a Dictionary of the Books, Persons, Places, Events, and other Matters of which mention is made in Holy Scripture. By the Rev. J. AYRE, M.A. Maps, Plates & Woodcuts. Fcp. 8vo. 6s.

A Practical Treatise on Brewing; with Formulæ for Public Brewers & Instructions for Private Families. By W. BLACK. 8vo. 10s. 6d.

The Theory of the Modern Scientific Game of Whist. By W. POLE, F.R.S. Twelfth Edition. Fcp. 8vo. 2s. 6d.

The Correct Card; or, How to Play at Whist; a Whist Catechism. By Major A. CAMPBELL-WALKER, F.R.G.S. Latest Edition. Fcp. 8vo. 2s. 6d.

The Cabinet Lawyer; a Popular Digest of the Laws of England, Civil, Criminal, and Constitutional. Twenty-Fifth Edition, corrected and extended. Fcp. 8vo. 9s.

Chess Openings. By F.W. LONGMAN, Balliol College, Oxford. New Edition. Fcp. 8vo. 2s. 6d.

Pewtner's Comprehensive Specifier; a Guide to the Practical Specification of every kind of Building-Artificer's Work. Edited by W. YOUNG. Crown 8vo. 6s.

Modern Cookery for Private Families, reduced to a System of Easy Practice in a Series of carefully-tested Receipts. By ELIZA ACTON. With 8 Plates and 150 Woodcuts. Fcp. 8vo. 6s.

Food and Home Cookery. A Course of Instruction in Practical Cookery and Cleaning, for Children in Elementary Schools. By Mrs. BUCKTON. Woodcuts. Crown 8vo. 2s.

The Ventilation of Dwelling Houses and the Utilisation of Waste Heat from Open Fire-Places, &c. By F. EDWARDS, Jun. Second Edition. With numerous Lithographic Plates, comprising 106 Figures. Royal 8vo. 10s. 6d.

Hints to Mothers on the Management of their Health during the Period of Pregnancy and in the Lying-in Room. By THOMAS BULL, M.D. Fcp. 8vo. 2s. 6d.

The Maternal Management of Children in Health and Disease. By THOMAS BULL, M.D. Fcp. 8vo. 2s. 6d.

American Food and Farming. By FINLAY DUN, Special Correspondent for the 'Times.' 8vo. [*In the press*.

The Farm Valuer. By JOHN SCOTT, Land Valuer. Crown 8vo. 5s.

Rents and Purchases; or, the Valuation of Landed Property, Woods, Minerals, Buildings, &c. By JOHN SCOTT. Crown 8vo. 6s.

Economic Studies. By the late WALTER BAGEHOT, M.A. Fellow of University College, London. Edited by RICHARD HOLT HUTTON. 8vo. 10s. 6d.

Economics for Beginners By H. D. MACLEOD, M.A. Small crown 8vo. 2s. 6d.

The Elements of Banking. By H. D. MACLEOD, M.A. Fourth Edition. Crown 8vo. 5s.

The Theory and Practice of Banking. By H. D. MACLEOD, M.A. 2 vols. 8vo. 26s.

The Resources of Modern Countries; Essays towards an Estimate of the Economic Position of Nations and British Trade Prospects. By ALEX. WILSON. 2 vols. 8vo. 24s.

The Patentee's Manual; a Treatise on the Law and Practice of Letters Patent, for the use of Patentees and Inventors. By J. JOHNSON, Barrister-at-Law; and J. H. JOHNSON, Assoc. Inst. C.E. Solicitor and Patent Agent, Lincoln's Inn Fields and Glasgow. Fourth Edition, enlarged. 8vo. price 10s. 6d.

INDEX.

Abbey & Overton's English Church History ... 15
Abney's Photography ... 11
Acton's Modern Cookery ... 21
Alpine Club Map of Switzerland ... 18
—— Guide (The) ... 18
Amos's Jurisprudence ... 5
—— Primer of the Constitution ... 5
—— Fifty Years of the English Constitution ... 5
Anderson's Strength of Materials ... 11
Armstrong's Organic Chemistry ... 11
Arnold's (Dr.) Lectures on Modern History ... 2
—— Miscellaneous Works ... 7
—— Sermons ... 15
—— (T.) English Literature ... 6
—— Authors ... 6
Arnott's Elements of Physics ... 10
Atelier (The) du Lys ... 19
Atherstone Priory ... 19
Autumn Holidays of a Country Parson ... 7
Ayre's Treasury of Bible Knowledge ... 21
Bacon's Essays, by *Whately* ... 6
—— Life and Letters, by *Spedding* ... 5
—— Works ... 5
Bagehot's Biographical Studies ... 4
—— Economic Studies ... 21
—— Literary Studies ... 6
Bailey's Festus, a Poem ... 19
Bain's Mental and Moral Science ... 6
—— on the Senses and Intellect ... 6
—— Emotions and Will ... 6
Baker's Two Works on Ceylon ... 17
Ball's Alpine Guides ... 18
—— Elements of Astronomy ... 11
Barry on Railway Appliances ... 11
Bauerman's Mineralogy ... 10
Beaconsfield's (Lord) Novels and Tales 18 & 19
Becker's Charicles and Gallus ... 8
Beesly's Gracchi, Marius, and Sulla ... 3
Black's Treatise on Brewing ... 21
Blackley's German-English Dictionary ... 8
Blaine's Rural Sports ... 19
Bloxam's Metals ... 11
Bolland and *Lang's* Aristotle's Politics ... 5
Boultbee on 39 Articles ... 15
——'s History of the English Church ... 15
Bourne's Works on the Steam Engine ... 14
Bowdler's Family Shakespeare ... 19
Bramley-Moore's Six Sisters of the Valleys ... 19
Brande's Dictionary of Science, Literature, and Art ... 12
Brassey on Shipbuilding ... 14
Brassey's Sunshine and Storm in the East ... 17
—— Voyage of the 'Sunbeam' ... 17
Browne's Exposition of the 39 Articles ... 15
Browning's Modern England ... 3
Buckle's History of Civilisation ... 2
Buckton's Food and Home Cookery ... 21
—— Health in the House ... 13
—— Town and Window Gardening ... 12
Bull's Hints to Mothers ... 21
—— Maternal Management of Children ... 21
Bunsen's Angel-Messiah ... 16
Burgomaster's Family (The) ... 19
Buried Alive ... 18
Burke's Vicissitudes of Families ... 4
Cabinet Lawyer ... 21

Capes's Age of the Antonines ... 3
—— Early Roman Empire ... 3
Carlyle's Reminiscences ... 4
Cates's Biographical Dictionary ... 4
Cayley's Iliad of Homer ... 19
Changed Aspects of Unchanged Truths ... 7
Chesney's Waterloo Campaign ... 2
Church's Beginning of the Middle Ages ... 3
Colenso on Moabite Stone &c. ... 17
——'s Pentateuch and Book of Joshua ... 17
Commonplace Philosopher ... 7
Comte's Positive Polity ... 5
Conder's Handbook to the Bible ... 15
Congreve's Politics of Aristotle ... 5
Conington's Translation of Virgil's Æneid ... 19
—— Miscellaneous Writings ... 6
Contanseau's Two French Dictionaries ... 8
Conybeare and *Howson's* St. Paul ... 16
Cordery's Struggle against Absolute Monarchy ... 3
Cotta on Rocks, by *Lawrence* ... 12
Counsel and Comfort from a City Pulpit ... 7
Cox's (G. W.) Athenian Empire ... 3
—— Crusades ... 3
—— Greeks and Persians ... 3
Creighton's Age of Elizabeth ... 3
—— England a Continental Power ... 3
—— Shilling History of England ... 3
—— Tudors and the Reformation ... 3
Cresy's Encyclopædia of Civil Engineering ... 15
Critical Essays of a Country Parson ... 7
Crookes's Chemical Analysis ... 13
Culley's Handbook of Telegraphy ... 14
Curteis's Macedonian Empire ... 3
Davison's Thousand Thoughts ... 7
De Caisne and *Le Maout's* Botany ... 12
De Tocqueville's Democracy in America ... 5
Dixon's Rural Bird Life ... 12
Doyle's (R.) Fairyland ... 13
Dun's American Food and Farming ... 21
Eastlake's Foreign Picture Galleries ... 13
—— Hints on Household Taste ... 14
Edwards on Ventilation &c. ... 21
Edwards's Nile ... 17
Ellicott's Scripture Commentaries ... 16
—— Lectures on Life of Christ ... 15
Elsa and her Vulture ... 19
Epochs of Ancient History ... 3
—— English History ... 3
—— Modern History ... 3
Ewald's History of Israel ... 16
—— Antiquities of Israel ... 16
Fairbairn's Applications of Iron ... 14
—— Information for Engineers ... 14
—— Mills and Millwork ... 14
Farrar's Language and Languages ... 7
Francis's Fishing Book ... 19
Freeman's Historical Geography ... 2
Froude's Cæsar ... 4
—— English in Ireland ... 1
—— History of England ... 1
—— Short Studies ... 6
Gairdner's Houses of Lancaster and York ... 3
Ganot's Elementary Physics ... 9
—— Natural Philosophy ... 9
Gardiner's Buckingham and Charles I. ... 2
—— Personal Government of Charles I. ... 2

Gardiner's Puritan Resolution	3	Lessons of Middle Age	7
———— Thirty Years' War	3	Lewes's History of Philosophy	3
German Home Life	7	Lewis on Authority	6
Gibson's Cavalier's Note Book	7	Liddell and Scott's Greek-English Lexicons	8
Goethe's Faust, by Birds	19	Lindley and Moore's Treasury of Botany	20
———— by Selss	19	Lloyd's Magnetism	10
———— by Webb	19	———— Wave-Theory of Light	10
Goodeve's Mechanics	11	Longman's (F. W.) Chess Openings	21
———— Mechanism	14	———— Frederic the Great and the Seven Years' War	3
Gore's Electro-Metallurgy	11	———— German Dictionary	8
Gospel (The) for the Nineteenth Century	16	———— (W.) Edward the Third	2
Grant's Ethics of Aristotle	6	———— Lectures on History of England	2
Graver Thoughts of a Country Parson	7	———— Old and New St. Paul's	13
Greville's Faiths and Fancies	6	Loudon's Encyclopædia of Agriculture	15
———— Journal	1	———— Gardening	12
Griffin's Algebra and Trigonometry	11	———— Plants	12
Griffith's A B C of Philosophy	5	Lubbock's Origin of Civilisation	12
Grove on Correlation of Physical Forces	10	Ludlow's American War of Independence	3
Gwilt's Encyclopædia of Architecture	14	Lyra Germanica	17
Hale's Fall of the Stuarts	3	Macalister's Vertebrate Animals	11
Hartwig's Works on Natural History and Popular Science	11	Macaulay's (Lord) Essays	1
Hassall's Climate of San Remo	17	———— History of England	1
Haughton's Physical Geography	11	———— Lays, Illustrated Edits.	13
Hawthorne's Fairy Stories	18	———— Cheap Edition	19
Hayward's Selected Essays	6	———— Life and Letters	4
Heer's Primeval World of Switzerland	12	———— Miscellaneous Writings	7
Helmholtz on Tone	10	———— Speeches	7
Helmholtz's Scientific Lectures	10	———— Works	1
Herschel's Outlines of Astronomy	9	———— Writings, Selections from	7
Hillebrand's Lectures on German Thought	6	MacCullagh's Tracts	10
Hobson's Amateur Mechanic	14	McCulloch's Dictionary of Commerce	8
Hopkins's Christ the Consoler	17	Macfarren on Musical Harmony	13
Horses and Roads	20	Macleod's Economical Philosophy	5
Hoskold's Engineer's Valuing Assistant	14	———— Economics for Beginners	21
Hullah's History of Modern Music	12	———— Theory and Practice of Banking	21
———— Transition Period	12	———— Elements of Banking	21
Hume's Essays	6	Macnamara's Himalayan Districts of British India	17
———— Treatise on Human Nature	6	Mademoiselle Mori	19
Ihne's Rome to its Capture by the Gauls	3	Mahaffy's Classical Greek Literature	3
———— History of Rome	2	Marshman's Life of Havelock	4
Ingelow's Poems	19	Martineau's Christian Life	17
Jameson's Sacred and Legendary Art	13	———— Hours of Thought	17
———— Memoirs by Macpherson	4	———— Hymns	17
Jenkin's Electricity and Magnetism	11	Maunder's Popular Treasuries	20
Jerrold's Life of Napoleon	1	Maxwell's Theory of Heat	11
Johnson's Normans in Europe	3	May's History of Democracy	2
———— Patentee's Manual	21	———— History of England	2
Johnston's Geographical Dictionary	8	Melville's (Whyte) Novels and Tales	19
Jukes's Types of Genesis	16	Mendelssohn's Letters	4
Jukes on Second Death	16	Merivale's Fall of the Roman Republic	2
Kalisch's Bible Studies	16	———— General History of Rome	2
———— Commentary on the Bible	16	———— Roman Triumvirates	2
———— Path and Goal	5	———— Romans under the Empire	3
Keller's Lake Dwellings of Switzerland	12	Merrifield's Arithmetic and Mensuration	11
Kerl's Metallurgy, by Crookes and Röhrig	15	Miles on Horse's Foot and Horse Shoeing	20
Kingzett's Alkali Trade	13	———— on Horse's Teeth and Stables	20
———— Animal Chemistry	13	Mill (J.) on the Mind	5
Knatchbull-Hugessen's Fairy-Land	18	Mill's (J. S.) Autobiography	4
———— Higgledy-Piggledy	18	———— Dissertations & Discussions	5
Landscapes, Churches, &c.	7	———— Essays on Religion	15
Latham's English Dictionaries	8	———— Hamilton's Philosophy	5
———— Handbook of English Language	8	———— Liberty	5
Lecky's History of England	1	———— Political Economy	5
———— European Morals	3	———— Representative Government	5
———— Rationalism	3	———— Subjection of Women	5
———— Leaders of Public Opinion	4	———— System of Logic	5
Lee's Geologist's Note Book	12	———— Unsettled Questions	5
Leisure Hours in Town	7	———— Utilitarianism	5
Leslie's Essays in Political and Moral Philosophy	6	Miller's Elements of Chemistry	13

WORKS published by LONGMANS & CO.

Miller's Inorganic Chemistry	11
——— Wintering in the Riviera	17
Mills's Blues and Buffs	18
Minto (Lord) in India	2
Mitchell's Manual of Assaying	15
Modern Novelist's Library	18 & 19
Monck's Logic	6
Monsell's Spiritual Songs	17
Moore's Irish Melodies, Illustrated Edition	13
——— Lalla Rookh, Illustrated Edition	13
Morris's Age of Anne	3
Müller's Chips from a German Workshop	7
——— Hibbert Lectures on Religion	16
——— Science of Language	7
——— Science of Religion	16
——— Selected Essays	7
Neison on the Moon	9
Nevile's Horses and Riding	20
Newman's Apologia pro Vitâ Suâ	4
Nicols's Puzzle of Life	12
Northcott's Lathes & Turning	14
Ormsby's Poem of the Cid	19
Overton's Life, &c. of Law	4
Owen's Comparative Anatomy and Physiology of Vertebrate Animals	11
Owen's Evenings with the Skeptics	7
Payen's Industrial Chemistry	14
Pewtner's Comprehensive Specifier	21
Piesse's Art of Perfumery	15
Pole's Game of Whist	21
Powell's Early England	3
Preece & Sivewright's Telegraphy	11
Present-Day Thoughts	7
Proctor's Astronomical Works	9
——— Scientific Essays (Two Series)	12
Public Schools Atlases	8
Rawlinson's Ancient Egypt	3
——— Sassanians	3
Recreations of a Country Parson	7
Reynolds's Experimental Chemistry	12
Rich's Dictionary of Antiquities	8
Rigby's Letters from France, &c. in 1789	18
Rivers's Orchard House	12
——— Rose Amateur's Guide	12
Rogers's Eclipse of Faith	15
——— Defence of Eclipse of Faith	15
Roget's English Thesaurus	8
Ronalds' Fly-Fisher's Entomology	20
Rowley's Rise of the People	3
——— Settlement of the Constitution	3
Russia and England	1
——— Before and After the War	1
Rutley's Study of Rocks	11
Sandars's Justinian's Institutes	5
Sankey's Sparta and Thebes	3
Savile on Apparitions	7
Seaside Musings	7
Scott's Farm Valuer	21
——— Rents and Purchases	21
Seebohm's Oxford Reformers of 1498	2
——— Protestant Revolution	3
Sewell's History of France	2
——— Passing Thoughts on Religion	16
——— Preparation for Communion	16
——— Private Devotions	16
——— Stories and Tales	18
——— Thoughts for the Age	16
Shelley's Workshop Appliances	11
Shore's Flight of the 'Lapwing'	17
Short's Church History	15
Skelton's Crookit Meg	18
Smith's (Sydney) Wit and Wisdom	7
——— (Dr. R. A.) Air and Rain	9
——— (R. B.) Carthage & the Carthaginians	2
——— Rome and Carthage	3
——— (J.) Voyage and Shipwreck of St. Paul	16
Southey's Poetical Works	19
Stanley's Familiar History of Birds	11
Steel on Diseases of the Ox	29
Stephen's Ecclesiastical Biography	4
Stonehenge, Dog and Greyhound	20
Stoney on Strains	14
Stubbs's Early Plantagenets	3
Sunday Afternoons, by A. K. H. B.	7
Supernatural Religion	16
Swinbourne's Picture Logic	6
Tancock's England during the Wars, 1778–1820	3
Taylor's History of India	2
——— Ancient and Modern History	4
——— (Jeremy) Works, edited by Eden	17
Text-Books of Science	11
Thomé's Botany	11
Thomson's Laws of Thought	6
Thorpe's Quantitative Analysis	11
Thorpe and Muir's Qualitative Analysis	11
Thudichum's Annals of Chemical Medicine	13
Tilden's Chemical Philosophy	11
——— Practical Chemistry	12
Todd on Parliamentary Government	2
Tozer's Armenia and Asia Minor	17
Trench's Realities of Irish Life	17
Trevelyan's Life of Fox	2
Trollope's Warden and Barchester Towers	18
Twiss's Law of Nations	5
Tyndall's (Professor) Scientific Works	10
Unawares	19
Unwin's Machine Design	11
Ure's Arts, Manufactures, and Mines	14
Venn's Life, by Knight	4
Ville on Artificial Manures	15
Walker on Whist	21
Walpole's History of England	1
Warburton's Edward the Third	3
Watson's Geometry	11
Watts's Dictionary of Chemistry	13
Webb's Celestial Objects	9
——— Civil War in Herefordshire	2
——— Veil of Isis	6
Weld's Sacred Palmlands	17
Wellington's Life, by Gleig	4
Whately's English Synonymes	8
——— Logic	6
——— Rhetoric	6
White's Four Gospels in Greek	16
——— and Riddle's Latin Dictionaries	8
Wilcocks's Sea-Fisherman	20
Williams's Aristotle's Ethics	5
Wilson's Resources of Modern Countries	21
Wood's (J. G.) Popular Works on Natural History	11
Woodward's Geology	12
Yonge's English-Greek Lexicons	8
Youatt on the Dog and Horse	20
Zeller's Greek Philosophy	3

Spottiswoode & Co. Printers, New-street Square, London.

www.ingramcontent.com/pod-product-compliance
Lightning Source LLC
Chambersburg PA
CBHW022138300426
44115CB00006B/246